# The Nine Lives of Arnold

# The Nine Lives of Arnold

The Story of my Life
From Hamburg, Germany 1917, to leaving Jamaica,
B.W.I. 1953

## Arnold Paul Von der Porten

ISBN: 1-58721-597-7

This book is printed on acid free paper.

1stBooks – rev. 5/31/01

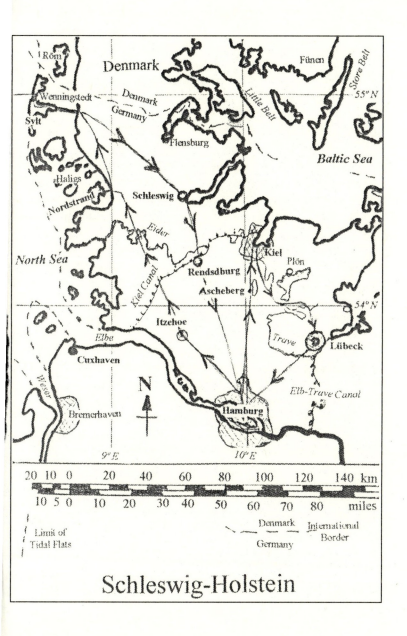

# Schleswig-Holstein

# FOREWORD

Who would want to read: *The Nine Lives of Arnold?*

Serious people who have wondered how it was possible for an intelligent and cultured people like the Germans to vote for a maniac like Hitler, history buffs and students who are interested in an entertaining and often humorous report on the time between the two World Wars, World War II, and its aftermath.

Born in 1917, Arnold von der Porten was raised in a family whose religion was democracy, he describes how the ominous threat of Nazism was fed by the fear of a Communist Revolution and by the foreign politics of the victorious Allies of the first World War.

As he left home, Arnold, a boy of 15, brought up in the genteel German middle class, was suddenly tossed into extreme poverty in the British Crown Colony of Jamaica. He describes all aspects of Jamaican life before World War II as he works himself up and eventually starts his own neon shop.

This narration and Arnold's 26 drawings are sure to be of great interest to people of all backgrounds and nationalities who wish to understand the time between the two World Wars with the rise of Hitler. Certainly it will be of great interest to British and Jamaican people as well as others who ever lived in, or read about a colony.

War comes. He is interned with Nazis, Fascists, and Jews alike. Life in a British internment camp. Released, he describes his experience in the Kingston business world. Arnold becomes well known. He marries Amy Barry of a prominent family.

Arnold illuminates a lot of historical events causing Hitler's rise, leading to World War II, the changing fortunes of that War, the Cold War. He was there when the British Empire was breaking up. The independence movement became hostile to foreigners. Amy and Arnold decided to migrate to America in 1953.

To my beloved children, grandchildren, their spouses, and their descendants. To all refugees, those who made it and those who perished, past, present, and future.

# **ACKNOWLEDGMENTS**

While writing this book, I was greatly encouraged by my wife and my far flung family. I was also cheered on by Professor Hilda Ross Ph.D. who teaches classes in *Writing Your Family History*. My daughter, Arlene E. Jacobs, deserves a lot of credit for editing the galley proof. I hereby want to thank them all.

x

# **PREFACE**

Many people, family, and friends, have told me, to write the story of my life. I have put it off long enough. Already some of the names of people have vanished from my memory, so I should not delay any longer. I chose the title as I had several close calls where my life could have ended very abruptly.

The world changed drastically during my lifetime. There were the inventions from the gramophone to space flight. There was revolution, inflation, depression, the rise of Hitler, emigration, poverty, War, internment, freedom, peace, marriage, and success all described between these covers.

Where the mist is cool,
In the fog, crows caw,
Where traditions rule,
But the weather's raw,
When men were at war and women forlorn,
Just then and there fate had me born.

Arnold P. Von der Porten.
December 21, 1992

# TABLE OF CONTENTS

xv

# ILLUSTRATIONS
## BY THE AUTHOR

*Feiger Gedanken,*
*Bängliches Schwanken,*
*Weibisches Zagen,*
*Ängsliches Klagen*
*Wendet kein Unglück,*
*Macht dich nicht frei.*

*Allen Gewalten*
*Zum Trutz sich erhalten,*
*Nimmer sich beugen,*
*Kräftig sich zeigen*
*Rufet die Arme*
*Der Götter herbei.*

Wolfgang v. Goethe

Cowardly thinking,
Apprehensive wavering,
Effeminate hesitation,
Fearful lamentation
Won't diminish your plight.
They can't set things right.

Show yourself strong
When the world does you wrong.
Never say: "Die."
Hold your head high!
Then gods lend their might
Till you'll triumph in fight!

Goethe
*Translated by:*
Arnold P. Von der Porten

# MY CHILDHOOD YEARS

My mother, Martha Dora (Rübner) von der Porten (everybody called her Dora), was born in Leipzig, Germany, on March 11, 1883. On her 34th birthday my father, Dr. Paul Maximilian von der Porten, born May 26, 1879, came home on a furlough. He was a medical doctor with the rank of Major in the German Army in World War I. I was born nine months later on November 30, 1917 at our home at the Eppendorfer Landstr. 15, Hamburg, Germany. My 9½ year older sister, Toni, maintained to the end of her days that I was the ugliest baby she had ever seen.

It was the beginning of "starvation winter". The Allied Forces, especially the British Navy, blockaded all German ports, and during her pregnancy my mother had fainted twice from hunger while she was standing in line to get her food rations. She also lost 11 lbs (5 kg) while she was carrying me.

Earlier, the same month that I was born, the democratic, but inept, Karenski Government was overthrown in Russia by Lenin and Trotsky. In 1918 most of the sailors of the German Navy and many civilian workers followed the example of their Russian "brothers" and started a revolution at the German naval base in Kiel. The revolution quickly spread to Berlin (the German capital), and Kaiser Wilhelm II fled to the Netherlands where the kindly Queen Wilhelmina gave him asylum.

Due to the War, blockade, and revolution, there were terrible shortages. Especially the babies suffered, and many died. Others, including myself, were very weak and suffered many sicknesses. I had just about every childhood disease imaginable, including: measles, mumps, and scarlet fever before I was five years old.

The Slavic and Hungarian soldiers at the Greek Front joined the Communists, revolted against the German speaking leadership of the Central Powers and killed their German speaking officers. The French General Geoffrey had helped organize that revolt. He now broke through in the Balkans and with the revolution spreading throughout the Central Powers, peace was forced on Turkey, Bulgaria, Austria-Hungary, and eventually Germany.

Unfortunately, tranquillity did not arrive with it. The returning soldiers found freezing cold apartments, starving families, a deteriorating currency, and dangerous streets due to the spreading unrest. The Western Allies kept the German and Austrian prisoners of war for a long time after the armistice until the Treaty of Versailles was signed. Due to the revolution and civil war, there was no authority to release the Central Powers' prisoners of war in Russia and their return was spread over many years. They were usually in a terrible condition when they came home.

Herbert Hoover, an American Quaker (ten years later he became the American President), organized relief with the Quakers and broke the British blockade. That is how my mother got enough milk to save me.

My father moved the family, Mama, Herbert (13), Antoinette (Toni, 10), Gerhard (9) and me (1) to the safer neighborhood from Eppendorf to Harvestehude in 1918. That house became home to me. Here the fathers of the neighborhood organized armed patrols to assist the police. The police station at the corner of the Alte Raabenstr. (Rabenstr. today's spelling.), and Mittelweg was surrounded by barbed wire. One of my earliest memories is that I was afraid for the poor policemen when the barbed wire was removed some years later.

Our house on Böttgerstr. 5 had a full basement. Facing the front from left to right, there was the wine cellar, where Papa actually aged wines, but its main use was the potato storage bin. Every autumn a man would empty a 100-kg (220-lb) bag of potatoes into it. That would last us till the next harvest. Next to it was the coal storage room. A two-ton truck would deliver coal and fill up the room once a year. Adjoining was the coal furnace room. A passage way with the fuse board and where the bicycles were stored led to the staircase to the entrance on the right, the marble floor kitchen to the left. Between the kitchen and the wine cellar was the pantry. It had a dumbwaiter in which the food was hoisted upstairs into the dining room, and the dirty dishes went back down into the kitchen. Against the wall in the kitchen was a wood burning hearth with an oven. On top of it was a gas range. There were two windows to the back garden. Towards the back of the staircase in the passage way was a toilet, then two adjoining store rooms, and an outside concrete staircase leading up to the back garden. There were two apple and two pear trees, a row of red currants and a row of gooseberries. Six rhubarb plants sprung up every spring.

On the main floor in front of and above the furnace room was Mama's covered verandah where she grew all types of indoor plants. Behind the verandah, above the furnace room, was Papa's smoking room adjoining Mama's salon. It was above the coal and the wine cellars and a section of the passage way. Next to the salon was the dining room above the pantry and the kitchen. Adjacent to it was the children's playroom above the toilet and storage rooms. Outside the children's room was a concrete deck with a cast iron stairway into the back garden. All the rooms on the main floor had a door to a corridor with a wardrobe to hang one's coats, and staircases down to the entrance of the house and up to the bedrooms. Above the smoking room was Toni's bedroom. Next to that, above the salon, was Gerhard's and my bedroom. I had inherited Herbert's bed, when he went to England. Before that event, I had Irma's room, while she still slept in a crib in my parents' room. Between the boys' and our parents' room was the bathroom with a geyser for hot water, with a door to the passage way with the staircase, and a door to our parents' bedroom above the dining room. Then came Irma's bedroom, a toilet and a balcony toward the back garden, above the children's playroom. On the top floor were the servants' quarters and three storage rooms.

HOME IN HAMBURG

N

FRONT GARDEN

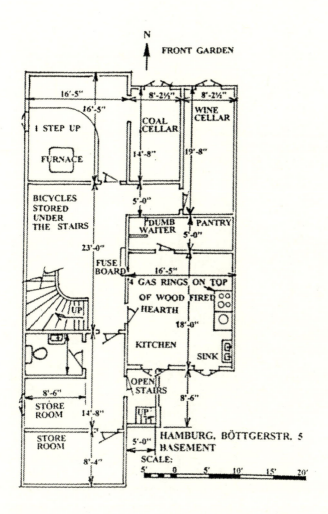

16'-5"

16'-5"

1 STEP UP

FURNACE

COAL
CELLAR

WINE
CELLAR

8'-2½"          8'-2½"

14'-8"          19'-8"

BICYCLES
STORED
UNDER
THE STAIRS

5'-0"

DUMB
WAITER        PANTRY

5'-0"

23'-0"

FUSE
BOARD

16'-5"

4 GAS RINGS ON TOP

OF WOOD FIRED

HEARTH

18'-0"

KITCHEN                    SINK

OPEN
STAIRS

8'-6"

8'-6"

STORE
ROOM

14'-8"

UP

STORE
ROOM

5'-0"

8'-4"

HAMBURG, BÖTTGERSTR. 5
BASEMENT

SCALE:

5'       0       5'      10'        15'       20'

5

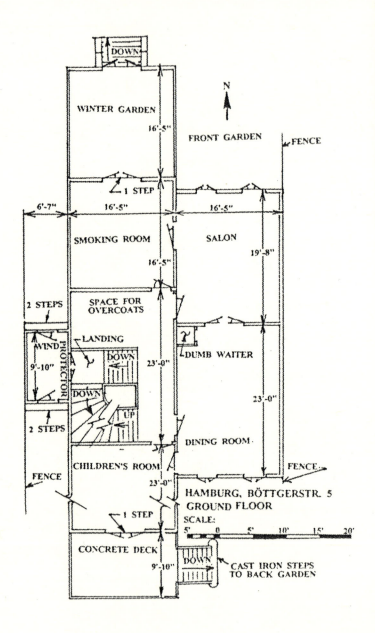

DOWN

WINTER GARDEN

16'-5"

FRONT GARDEN

N

FENCE

1 STEP

6'-7"    16'-5"    16'-5"

SMOKING ROOM    SALON

16'-5"

19'-8"

2 STEPS

SPACE FOR
OVERCOATS

LANDING

WIND PROTECTOR

9'-10"

DUMB WAITER

DOWN

23'-0"

DOWN

UP

23'-0"

2 STEPS

DINING ROOM

CHILDREN'S ROOM

FENCE

23'-0"

FENCE

1 STEP

HAMBURG, BÖTTGERSTR. 5
GROUND FLOOR
SCALE:
5'   0   5'   10'   15'   20'

CONCRETE DECK

9'-10"

DOWN

CAST IRON STEPS
TO BACK GARDEN

6

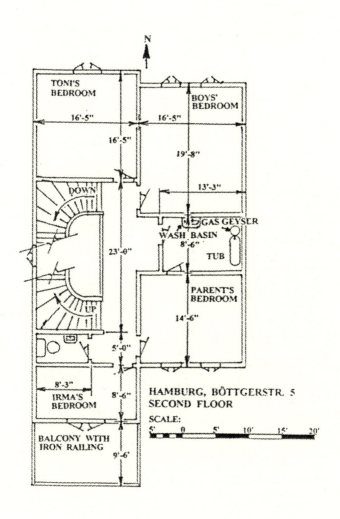

N

TONI'S BEDROOM

16'-5"

16'-5"

DOWN

23'-0"

UP

5'-0"

8'-3"

IRMA'S BEDROOM

8'-6"

BALCONY WITH IRON RAILING

9'-6"

BOYS' BEDROOM

16'-5"

19'-8"

13'-3"

GAS GEYSER

WASH BASIN

8'-6"

TUB

PARENT'S BEDROOM

14'-6"

HAMBURG, BÖTTGERSTR. 5
SECOND FLOOR

SCALE:

5'    0    5'    10'    15'    20'

7

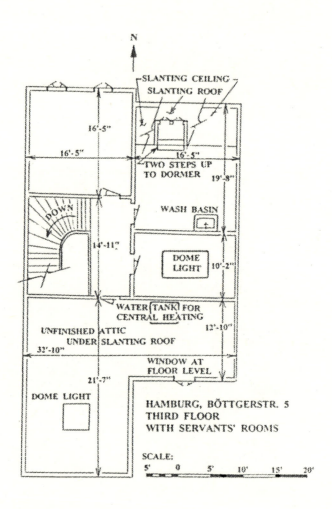

N

SLANTING CEILING
SLANTING ROOF

16'-5"

16'-5"

16'-5"

TWO STEPS UP
TO DORMER

19'-8"

DOWN

WASH BASIN

14'-11"

DOME
LIGHT

10'-2"

WATER TANK FOR
CENTRAL HEATING

12'-10"

UNFINISHED ATTIC
UNDER SLANTING ROOF

32'-10"

WINDOW AT
FLOOR LEVEL

21'-7"

DOME LIGHT

HAMBURG, BÖTTGERSTR. 5
THIRD FLOOR
WITH SERVANTS' ROOMS

SCALE:

5'  0  5'  10'  15'  20'

8

During the time of the revolution, when my parents had a few friends over, I witnessed a burglary engineered by one of the servants. She and two men removed all overcoats, including my parents' fur coats and those of their guests. One of the men saw me watching them. He wanted to take me along but the servant told him to leave me alone when she saw that he put his hands around my throat. She made me promise that I would not tell my parents. That I did! The servant quit at the end of the month and I told. Prosecution was impossible during those revolutionary times. Police were busy staying alive.

Another very early memory was an operation. I was only about three years old. I had a large abscess on the left side of my jaw. My Opa (my grandfather), Papa's younger brother, Uncle Ernst, and Papa came to my bed in my parents' bedroom. My grandfather wanted to cut directly through the skin into the abscess. Fortunately, Papa told him to cut in the middle of my chin and draw the pus from under my skin, so that the scar would not be so disfiguring.

Uncle Ernst administered the ether narcosis. Anesthesia was his specialty. My Opa did the cutting. It left a deep scar for the rest of my life. It looks very much like a deep dimple in the middle of my chin. I have Papa to thank that I do not have a disfiguring scar on the left side of my jaw.

I remember that I told Mama, who sat besides me with tears in her eyes, after the three doctors von der Porten had gone: "Don't bring him back, he hurt me." I meant Uncle Ernst, as he was the last one I saw, before the narcotic took effect.

# GERHARD LOOKS AFTER HIS LITTLE BROTHER

Papa was of the opinion that children should be seen but not heard. Fortunately, my brother Gerhard took a great interest in me. He was 8½ years older than I was. He showed me how to tie my shoelaces, play with tiny tin toy soldiers, and many other useful things. There was a boy in Gerhard's class whose father had a bicycle factory. Gerhard had him build me a tiny red bicycle, probably the smallest bicycle in all of Germany. I was three at the time. Gerhard taught me how to ride it. I would hold on to his saddle and he would tow me all around the neighborhood.

One day he heard that there was a strike and that the police would break it up. He towed me there. Workers on a four story unfinished housing development had taken positions on the roofs. A truck with police men drove by. The workers threw bricks at the police and the police shot at the men who tried to storm the truck. We threw down our bicycles and lay as flat and still as we could against the curb. When the truck had passed, we took off for home at breakneck speed.

When I was six, Gerhard gave me my first swimming lesson at the Alsterlust near the Lombards Bridge. Cabanas were built at the shore of the Alster, and a section of that lake was fenced off for swimmers. That place was eventually closed because the water was too polluted. Later I went to the Kellinghusenstr. indoor pool every chance I got.

Gerhard, after he left school and went to work, bought a canoe. He called it HAGAI, an acronym for the first letters of us five children: Herbert, Antoinette (Toni), Gerhard, Arnold, and Irma. He taught me how to paddle. It was easy if two paddled, one on each side, but it was much more difficult to keep a straight course if one alone paddled. A canoe tips over very easily. I had to be careful as at that time I could not yet swim and besides, the Alster water is terribly cold. I never tipped over.

# INFLATION, CURRENCY REFORM, AND RECOVERY

The Treaty of Versailles was signed in 1919. One of the results was that the German currency became worthless. Papa would treat patients for a potato or a pat of butter, but not for money.

One day, just before noon, Toni made me run with her to catch a trolley car. "Hurry-up! We must catch the trolley before noon as then the fares will go up, and I won't have enough money!"

Herbert was employed at a bank and could convert his pay to foreign currency. He was the rich man in our family. He bought some foreign currency and gave Gerhard a Czechoslovakian crown. Gerhard appreciated this coin very much. He treasured it, and it made him feel rich. He asked Herbert daily how much the crown was worth.

On my parents' anniversary, shortly before Herbert emigrated to England, my three elder siblings concocted a play. Gerhard played Papa; Toni, Mama; Herbert, himself; and I was supposed to be Gerhard. Irma was just a toddler at that time. I remember that tears ran down my parents' cheeks. They laughed so much.

The only line I had, was to ask Herbert: "What is the Czech crown worth today?"

Thereupon Herbert yelled at me at the top of his voice: "Don't keep pestering me with that same stupid question every day!"

I did not understand that play acting could involve such fierce yelling at me, and that he was not really mad at me, so I cried and Mama, who was laughing heartily, rushed over and took me in her arms. That was my acting debut.

In 1923, a very astute and intelligent coalition government of the centrist parties, and Hjalmar Schacht as minister of Finance, instituted a currency reform, and suddenly ended the runaway inflation. The Hamburg harbor boomed again. It did so literally. One could hear the riveting hammers from miles away before one could actually see the harbor. The shipyards were busy building a brand new merchant fleet. The old one had been given to Great Britain as war reparations payment.

Welding the plates of the ship hulls together had not yet been invented. The overlapping plates of the hulls were drilled through. Large rivets were heated in a forge. The red hot rivet would be picked up by a man with a scoop with a long handle and tossed to a catcher, who would catch the rivet in a cup with a long handle. With the help of a pair of tongs he would insert the rivet into the drilled hole. Another man then held the rivet in place with a pneumatic hammer, and a riveter inside the hull would hammer it tight with an air driven jackhammer. Many such hammers would be going at the same time on several different ship yards and the noise could be heard for miles.

Under the Treaty of Versailles, Hamburg had to turn over a part of the port to the Czechoslovakian Republic. That country had the use of that section of the port duty and tax free, and used it to transship its imports and exports to and from barges, which would sail up and down the Elbe. As the Czechs needed manpower this arrangement employed many Hamburgians.

The free trade zone was a great source of employment, too. Goods would be shipped from all over the world to Hamburg. German workers would improve the imports and ship them to the four corners of the earth. There would be no duty collected on those goods unless they were sold in Germany, but there were a lot of factories kept busy in the free trade zone. For instance, crude oil would arrive from Trinidad, be refined, and then be shipped out as gasoline, lubricating oil, heating oil, petroleum jelly, and many other products. Sewing needles would be imported from Birmingham, the eyes would be ground in by Hamburgian craftsmen and then shipped right back to Great Britain to have the eyes gold plated. That plating was essential to prevent rust. Stainless steel had not yet been invented. The Portuguese found that the damp, cool climate of North Germany was ideal for aging port wine. So, they stored and bottled it in the free trade zone. From there it was shipped all over the world. The free trade zone was originally implemented by the great and far sighted statesman, Otto v.*Bismarck shortly after the unification of Germany in 1871.

---

* When the "von" before a name is abreviated with "v.", it is a sign of German nobility.

12

It created a boom then, and it created a boom again in the nineteen twenties.

It was a good time. People had work and food. Mama took Irma and me shopping downtown. It was long before credit cards. Plastic was not yet invented. Mama needed neither cash nor a check book. She had a bank number. After the purchase, she just gave that number to the sales clerk who sometimes asked her for identification. At the end of the month, the bank would send a statement of all the deductions from her bank account for all of her purchases and of Papa's deposit to replenish the account.

At times Mama would treat us. We would go into a luxurious restaurant and have a pastry loaded with whipped cream, chocolate, cherries, and butter cream and a cup of cocoa. In one corner of the restaurant a trio would play classical music by Brahms, Haydn or Mozart. That would be one of the rare occasions when we heard any music. There was no music at home except Mama's little clock work driven music box. Often Mama took us home in a horse-drawn taxi. In the mid twenties, however, those disappeared, and we took the trolley. Mama preferred that to motorcar taxis.

# SCHOOL STARTS

When I was six, right after Easter in 1924, Mr. Bertram himself, the Principal of a very expensive private elementary school for boys, gave me an oral entrance exam. He checked how well I could calculate:

"Suppose there are seven apples, and you and I are to have half of them each, how would you divide them?"

"I would give you three and I would take three."

"Would that be all?"

"No." I noticed, how anxiously my father was looking at me, so I said, "I'll let Papa have one, too."

There was a roar of laughter and I was accepted. The school year started right after the Easter Holidays in Germany. The school was located at the street called Alster Ufer, translated, the Shore of the Alster. The large park surrounded a lake in the middle of the city which makes that metropolis unique.

On my third day at school, Papa wanted to take me to a photographer to have the customary studio picture taken with a brand new backpack and a huge bag of sweets in my hand. Unfortunately, my classmate, Heinrich Kleier, bet me that he lived farther from school than I did. I needed proof. I promptly forgot about the photographer and accompanied Heinrich to his home. He was right. On my way home from his house I lost my way and I did not make it home till after dark. Papa got on the phone at once and called off the police search for me. Mama could not hug me enough.

# MY BEST FRIEND

I noticed that a boy in the same grade in a parallel class lived at the corner of Mittelweg and Böttgerstr., just a few doors from us. He was accompanied to and from school by a nanny. After all, the school was a good kilometer away on the Alster Ufer near the Lombards Bridge. I followed them at a distance. I most certainly would not be seen with a nanny! We soon became good friends, however, and we were practically inseparable until I left Germany, though we never belonged to the same class in more ways than one.

Eckart v.Puttkamer was in the class of gifted children. I was in the class for remedial students. I never did any more homework than was absolutely necessary, whereas Eckart's *Mutti* (Mommy) saw to it that he really knew his poetry, arithmetic and could read fluently. My parents did not care.

Eckart was related to Prince Otto v.Bismarck's wife. She was born Johanna v.Puttkamer. My friend came from a long line of nobles on both his father's and his mother's sides. One of his ancestors had been a general under Frederick the Great.

His father had been a major in World War I, commanding a heavy machine gun battalion. At the time, in 1924, when I met him, he was Assistant Manager of Siemens & Halske for Hamburg, a very high position. That company was a large manufacturing conglomerate somewhat like General Electric in the United States. Siemens is also a huge company in the U.S. today.

My parents had no use for nobility. Papa proudly stated that Hamburg was the oldest continuous republic in the world. Our parents never got together socially but we were the very best of friends.

My Mother had been a suffragette before she got married. The story goes that she once dragged my old man to a women's rights demonstration. The speaker spotted him, the spy for the enemy, the only man in the huge crowd and demanded that he should also say his piece. My poor Papa was not much over 5 ft (1.22 m) tall. He certainly was no match for all those agitated Amazons. He got up on the speaker's platform and yelled: "I am for the equal rights of men!" The crowd applauded wildly and laughed happily, and Papa was off the hook.

Grandpa Rübner had been friends with leading socialists. He once told my mother: "War is good for generals, whores, and big industrialists." That sentiment was just about standard among the adults in my family.

Papa had a very thorough knowledge of history and the German classics. Many Sundays he would read German poetry to me, or tell me about Persian, Greek, Roman, and German mythology and history. I loved that. It was the only time I remember that I felt close to Papa.

# MY BIG EARS

From the Goldschmidt (my grandmother's) family I had been blessed with excessively large ears. Unfortunately, people did not consider this fact as a mark of beauty, but rather a good enough reason to tease me.

One January, when the Alster was frozen over, I told my parents that I was going to go ice skating on that huge expanse of ice.

Papa said: "As long as you have the wind behind you, you can use your ears as sails and you will make good speed."

I answered: "My ears and your brains together make a good jackass."

I could see a thunderstorm rising by looking at my old man's face. He sat straight up, but before he could open his mouth, Mama said to him:

"He has been teased enough about his ears. How would you like if somebody kept nagging you about anything at all?"

I was amazed. Mama never dared to bring my father's wrath upon herself by criticizing him. Papa's posture shrunk. He sat quite still for a few seconds. Then he asked me in his normal tone of voice:

"Who told you to say that?"

"Gerhard," I answered. "He told me to say that to the next person, whoever teased me about my ears."

Papa was not one to admit that he could possibly be wrong. He just sat there and smiled. He never again mentioned the size of my ears. After all, I inherited them from his side of the family.

# A VISIT TO MY MOTHER'S FAMILY

In the summer of 1927, Mama visited her parents and sisters and their families in Leipzig, the third largest city in Germany. She took me along. The train ride south took all day. My grandparents, Martha (née Koch) and Bernhard Rübner, owned the apartment building at Rabet 48. Among others, it also housed the entire extended family. My grandfather had no use for newfangled ideas, so the house had neither electricity nor running water. There was a pump and a well in the courtyard and kerosene lamps were used throughout the house.

Grandpa was a master cabinet maker. My much elder cousin, Rudi Lampe, was his partner. The workshop was on the ground floor. There was a hand driven lathe, turned by the brawn of the apprentice. The floor was covered inches deep with wood chips. In the middle of the shop hung a great big kerosene lamp. In modern days every fire inspector would have condemned that shop.

My cousin Rudi had a son, Herbert, a year younger than I was. Mama took us to the old town hall which was a museum. I was most impressed with the exhibit of the "Battle of the Peoples," or *"Völkerschlacht"*. It utilized the same tiny tin soldiers that Gerhard and I had at home. At Leipzig, Napoleon was decisively defeated by the Allied Forces of mainly Austria, Prussia, and Russia on October 18, 1813. We also went to the huge memorial which commemorates that battle. There is little else which I remember of that visit, except that all the family was very nice to Mama and me. I liked the train rides to there and home again.

# MY VON DER PORTEN GRANDPARENTS

The house of my grandparents, Adele (née Goldschmidt) and Maximilian von der Porten was as different from that of the Rübner's house as possible. It was an old, one-family, two-story-plus-basement house, inherited from my great-grandfather. It was crammed full of valuable art works, cast bronzes, paintings, and embroidery done by my Grandma. One could see the Hamburg Dammtor rail road station from its front porch across the wide meadow, called the *Moorweide* which was surrounded by tall horse chestnut trees.

My grandfather's medical office occupied the front room. Obviously, it had originally been furnished before it was known that bacteria could be harmful and prior to the discovery of anesthetics. The heavy oak desk was deeply carved as were a strong oak couch and a heavy oak chair. The latter two pieces of furniture were equipped with thick, wide leather belts to tie down the body, arms, legs, and head of the patients during operations performed without any anesthesia by my great-grandfather and later my grandfather. In one corner of the room were blood-stained sheets and an apron. All doors, walls and the ceiling were covered with fine brown leather, stuffed thickly with cotton to dampen the screams of the unfortunate patients.

During my lifetime Opa did all his operations with anesthetics, especially since his son, Ernst, specialized in anesthesia.

# HIGH SCHOOL

In 1928 I was accepted at the Heinrich Hertz Rëalgymnasium high school. I studied English as my first foreign language. I hated school and never did enough homework. Consequently I was a very poor student in the subjects which required the most homework such as English and German. I was just about average in mathematics, though I liked geometry very much. I excelled in history, drawing, biology, and music. I was better than average in physics, chemistry, and religion. Being weak and small, I squeaked by in gymnastics. My father was very much against sports. He considered them too dangerous.

He would not let me join the scouts, either. They were too dominated by political movements. Unlike in America where schools or religious groups sponsor scout troops, political organizations sponsored scout troops in Germany.

In Europe, boys and girls attended separate schools in those days. When my teacher put on a class play, I usually played the leading lady because I was so small.

Eckart, on the other hand, was accepted into the top high school in Hamburg, the Johannëum. There he took Latin as his first foreign language. He excelled in all subjects except gym, since he was even smaller and weaker than I was. He joined the posh Uhlenhorst Field Hockey Club. I would have loved to join, too, but Papa would not let me. Eckart's father bought him an air rifle and we practiced shooting in his basement. He became an excellent shot. I did fairly well, too, but he easily surpassed me.

# SUPER INVENTIONS: TALKIES, GRAMOPHONES, RADIO

Just around that time a great new invention appeared. It was called the "Talkies". Up to that time a piano player sat in front of the screen in the movies. He played more or less appropriate music for the events happening above him.

In Germany Ufa was the name of the top motion picture company. The *Ufa-Palast* (Palace), the poshest of all their theaters in Hamburg, at the corner of Dammtor Str. and Gänsemarkt (Goose Market), was always the place for first-run films. The scenes of action alternated with written texts of the words spoken by the actors. Dolly Haas, Greta Garbo, Jean Harlow, and Annie Ondra were favorite actresses. Charley Chaplain, Buster Keaton, and Harold Lloyd provided humorous films. At the Goose Market heavy traffic had replaced the geese for about a century.

For the occasion of the *Jazz Singer* with Al Jolson, the theater had to be wired for sound. All the little girls on our street, including my sister, Irma, led by me, the eldest and only boy, trooped to the theater. The words were sung and spoken in English and dubbed in, in German, at the bottom of the picture. It was a first. Though I could not read fast enough to get all the words, I understood sufficiently to dissolve in tears. I cried most of the two kilometer walk home. The show had a most profound effect on me. This first talkies main song, which became exceedingly popular, was "Sonny Boy".

The Ufa Palace was not the only place where they had reproduced sound. Toni had been given a gramophone. After winding it up with a crank handle, it would spin a record made from hard rubber, an extremely fragile material. A sharp needle followed grooves in the record and abracadabra, it made music! We no longer had to hire a piano player when Toni had a few friends over to have tea and to dance. The only slight shortcoming of the gramophone was that its drive spring was not strong enough to last through the whole record. In the middle of each dance someone, who happened to be close to the gramophone when it gave out had to jump over and rewind its spring. Technology was really making strides!

Another new and most extraordinary invention was talked about everywhere. Sound waves could be transformed into electric waves. Those electric waves could then be sent through the air and be reconverted to sound waves. Amazing! The word "electronic" had not yet been invented. What was more, Hamburg, the second largest city in Germany, was to have a broadcasting station!

Gerhard took one of my father's old cigar boxes. He made a roll out of cardboard, wrapped a lot of cotton-insulated bell wire around it and pronounced it a "coil." He mounted it on the cigar box along with a capacitor and lots of little things. He ran a wire three stories up through the roof and that was an antenna. He bought a crystal and fitted an adjustable needle over it and called it a "detector." The invention of vacuum radio tubes had to wait several years yet, and that of transistors for at least another 15 years to about the end of the second World War. He bought some resistors, batteries, and an earphone and called the whole thing a "radio receiver."

Papa had to be coaxed for a while before he put on the ear phones. Once he took the dare and put them on, he would not relinquish them, though we all wanted to hear what he heard. He just beat the tempo of some musical piece, which he alone heard, smiled and exclaimed: "Yes, yes, I can clearly hear music!"

Gerhard was a hero! Finally, I, too, was allowed to put on the earphones. At first I heard nothing but scratching sounds, Gerhard called them "static," a new word. At last, listening carefully as Gerhard adjusted the screw over the detector, I, too, could actually hear music despite the "static." That was really quite amazing.

# GERHARD'S WORK

When Gerhard left school in 1927 he was employed as a commercial apprentice at Hauer & Co., manufacturers and exporters of perfumes. One day Mr. Tai Ten-Quee, a very wealthy Chinese, who was Hauer & Co's agent in Kingston, Jamaica, British West Indies, visited the factory. Accompanying him to Hamburg were his wife, his daughter, and a young lady who was his daughter's friend. Gerhard, who already spoke English fairly well, showed the agent from Jamaica all around the factory and invited his family to our house for dinner. Both families got on very well with each other. Gerhard explained to Mr. Tai that it is customary for young men in commerce to work abroad with an agent of their company in order to get acquainted with a foreign country before servicing agents from their home office in Hamburg. Would Mr. Tai give Gerhard such an opportunity? Mr. Tai readily agreed to do so.

In October of 1929 the stock market crash brought on the big depression. Hauer & Co. went under and Gerhard was unemployed. He wrote to Mr. Tai Ten-Quee who employed him in his firm in Kingston. The only direct connection between Hamburg and Kingston was the Horn Line with its tiny 8,000, or so, ton steamers. They took four weeks to get there.

Mama, Papa, Toni, Irma, and I went to the pier to see Gerhard off. No-one noticed me very much. I decided to climb to the top of the foremast. I had a great view of the harbor. When the steam whistle blasted: "All visitors ashore!" I suddenly noticed how terrifyingly far the deck was below me. It was too scary to come down. Finally someone found me. After much shouting up and down, Gerhard climbed up and made me follow him step by step. I did not know then that one day I would service neon signs, where I would have to do a lot of climbing.

# CHRISTMAS TIME

I missed Gerhard, especially at Christmas. That great holiday was preceded by St. Nicholas Day on December, 6th. On the fifth, before going to bed we would place soup plates under our beds and St. Nicholas would mysteriously fill them with all sorts of cookies, marzipan, walnuts, dates, figs, hazelnuts, almonds, a tangerine, an apple, and an orange. Those were all delicacies that were expensive in Germany and were considered rare treats.

The week before Christmas the children's playroom was locked and the keyholes stuffed shut. On Christmas Eve, after dark, Papa, all smiles, would open the door ringing a bell. On the far end would stand a magnificent Christmas tree with lots of wax candles and all sorts of ornaments. There were long tables with presents for everyone. My soldiers were fighting battles.

Before we were allowed into the room, however, Mama would lead us in carols. Papa could not carry a tune. He did write plays and poetry very well, though. Then the two servants would come in, mumble a thank you, pick up their own little Christmas tree, their presents and go back to serve a huge dinner.

Papa's sister, Aunt Anna, and Uncle Leo Lippmann would join us. After the soup, there would be carp and white wine, followed by a roasted goose and red wine. We children were not allowed any alcoholic beverages until we were fifteen. The climax of the evening was plum pudding sprinkled with sugar, doused with rum and set ablaze. All lights were turned off for effect. Each person had two forks to stir the plum pudding so that most of the alcohol would burn away. When all the portions of pudding had burned out, the lights were turned on again. After dinner we were allowed to play until we could no longer keep our eyes open.

Christmas morning we would find a soup plate full of delicacies under our beds just as on St. Nicholas Day. Of course, I almost forgot, we, too, gave presents. They had to be handmade by us. Bought gifts were not accepted. One Christmas, Eckart got a beautiful Ping-Pong table and we became quite proficient at that game.

# THE RHINELAND IS OCCUPIED

Two teachers took us to a youth hostel in the Taunus mountains, not far north of Frankfurt on the Main River, in 1928. I was in sixth grade then. We made excursions from there, including one which was to the castle of Wilhelmshöhe with its colossal Hercules Statue and its beautiful artificial waterfall. It is one of the most beautiful castles in Germany. In 1870 during the Franco-Prussian War, King Wilhelm III of Prussia, a few months before he became Wilhelm I, Kaiser of the Germans, ordered the French Emperor, Napoleon III, to be restricted to that castle after he had surrendered with his army. Louis Napoleon escaped, but it did not do him any good. The French people toppled the monarchy and established the Second Republic. The dethroned emperor spent the rest of his life in London.

Another excursion was to Wiesbaden. In accordance with the Treaty of Versailles the British and French occupied the Rhineland, Germany's most fertile and arguably most beautiful area. The teacher told us that we should not say anything that might offend the British, as any of their soldiers had the power to arrest anyone, and German officials could not help anyone who was arrested. There had been no incidents in the British zone, so we were not too worried. The city of Wiesbaden had been a spa. Its mineral waters were renowned throughout the elite of the world. Before World War I many rich and famous, including the Kaiser, frequented the posh hotels in Wiesbaden.

In the afternoon we crossed the Rhine into Mainz, the birthplace of my grandmother Adele von der Porten. We saw Germany's oldest cathedral. Its sanctuary had been constructed in the ninth century. The first emperors of Germany built a palace in the city after Charlemagne's empire was divided among his three grandsons. The palace was kept as a museum. We saw its 900-year-old furniture. There were Senegal black soldiers lounging in the museum with their German whores.

One of the attendants told us, after he looked around, assured that no strange adult was within earshot: "One of the Senegalese defecated in the middle of the emperor's bed. We attendants stood by helpless, boiling with rage inside!"

Germans are especially incensed when they see Black soldiers in hostile uniforms, as no German State ever allowed Black slavery. Naturally, Germans feel that Blacks should be friendly to Germans instead of serving their former slavemasters.

There had been many incidents of sabotage against the French occupation forces and also of arrests of Germans by the French. We were very careful not to say anything while we were in Mainz. We were glad when we passed the British sentry in the middle of the bridge going back to Wiesbaden. We were even happier still when we were back at the youth hostel, which was a converted medieval castle with very massive columns and walls. It had an aura of security and permanence.

Back in Hamburg, a little while later, we heard that the German Government refused to pay any more reparations. French and Belgian troops invaded the Ruhr Land, Germany's most industrial zone, confiscated all steel and coal and shipped those goods to France and Belgium. The entire Country was in an uproar! There were stories of sabotage, murder, arrests, and executions.

Eventually the occupation of the Ruhr Land ended when the German Government promised to resume the reparation payments. These payments made the German people exceedingly bitter against the British and even more so against the French. Eventually all foreign forces were removed from German soil.

# A BICYCLE TRIP THROUGH HOLSTEIN

In the spring of 1929, I was eleven years old, Helmut Jürgens and I, he was a year older than I, decided to go on a bicycle trip on the long Whitsuntide (in America mostly called Pentecost) weekend. I had always wanted to see a real warship, so I wanted to ride to Kiel, Germany's only naval base. I also wanted to see the Holsten Tor, Lübeck's sixteenth century gate. Its replica is used as the trademark of all marzipan from Lübeck. I just loved marzipan from Lübeck! That city did not seem too far from Kiel on the map.

Helmut had one mark (25¢), and I had two marks. We loaded up our bicycles with dried food, canteens full of water, and an aluminum cooking pot and took off on Saturday right after school. I left the house very quietly. I told the servant, who had noticed my preparations, that I would be gone for a while. We never told our parents as we were sure that they would not have given us permission.

Trucks, in those days, did not move very fast. We were hardly out of Hamburg, when we spotted a truck which we could hold on to. We were aware of the fact that such hanging on was strictly against the law but most kids did it anyway. We made very good time that first day. The sun sets late in May in Germany and its afterglow lingers long on the horizon.

We stopped at a prosperous looking farm. We asked politely if we could sleep in the straw in the barn. After we assured the farmer that we would leave our matches with our bicycles, he let us sleep in the straw. We carried our battery-powered bicycle lamps, buried ourselves in the straw, and slept like logs.

At daybreak, about 4:00 a.m., a maid came to wake us. She brought us a liter of milk, a freshly baked black bread, and a delicious piece of properly smoked ham. We sat by the lake and watched the sun rise over the hills beyond, reflecting in the water. We were near Ascheberg and enjoying a most sumptuous breakfast.

We rode northward. We saw no trucks on the lonely gravel road. By noon we were hot and hungry. We stopped by a little pond. There was a little wooden pier, probably built for women to fetch water or for anglers to catch carp. We started a fire on the

27

meadow. Helmut was a scout and knew all about camping. We got out the dried soup powder, fetched water from the pond, and after we saw that the fire was burning properly, we stripped and jumped naked from the little pier. We were hot from the long ride that morning. We were in for the greatest surprise of our lives! That water could not have been much over 0°C and it was deep. It burnt like a hot wire against the back of my neck. I had never in my life swum so fast. We had no towels with us, so we ran up and down the meadow until we were dry and warm. The hot soup was delicious. We had also carried bread, butter and salami.

In the afternoon we were lucky. We found a little truck which carried a bull calf. Helmut hung on to the left, and I to the right. When the pavement became too rough to hold on, the young driver stopped and invited us into the cab. Helmut and I played our harmonicas and the driver sang the old folk tunes. The truck eventually turned off from where we were going. We were still a long way from Kiel, one third of the distance of our planned trip! We found a farm house. Here the hayloft was above the cattle stable. We did not care about the smell. We just slept.

We reached Kiel not long before noon. It drizzled. There were Germany's only cruiser and two destroyers in the harbor. The warships looked much less romantic than I had imagined. We were tired but stopped only for a very few minutes to look at the gray ships. We were a bit worried as we had been away from home for two of our planned three-day journey, and we had gone less than half the distance.

We rode on toward Lübeck. It was Monday afternoon and on Tuesday morning at 8:00 we had to be back in school! We reached Lübeck, the Queen of the Hansa League of yore. When we passed the world famous Holsten Tor it was already evening. We were dead tired. The muscles in my legs begged me to give up, and we were still a good 65 km (39 miles) from home.

The Lübeck-Hamburg highway was well paved and well traveled. The trucks moved too fast to hold on to. A few kilometers out of Lübeck we saw a big truck with a tarpaulin over it, which was held up by iron bars. Ideal! The driver was changing the left front tire, and we asked if he would give us a ride. He just cursed and told us to get lost.

We trudged on for a few more kilometers and the same truck passed us. His brakes squealed to a stop. As we rode past him, the driver told us to load our bikes on the back. We found it in our hearts to forgive him for having cursed us earlier and accepted his invitation very quickly. There was a whole gang of cyclists already on the truck. There were lots of harmonicas and even one concertina. All of us were in the best of spirits. We all knew more or less the same folk songs, and best of all, we were in Hamburg in an hour.

Mama shook her head, made sure that I took a hot bath and dumped my clothes into the hamper before going to sleep. The really dirty clothes presented no problem to Mama as a commercial laundry picked up, washed, and returned our clothes once a week.

# HOLIDAY IN AUMÜHLE

For the summer of 1929 the v.Puttkamers rented a beautiful house with a huge garden in the little town of Aumühle in the Saxon Forest. Close to that little town is Friedrichsruh, the estate to which Germany's greatest statesman, Otto v.Bismarck, retired and where there still stands his and his wife, Johanna (née v.Puttkamer) v.Bismarck's mausoleum. Aumühle is not too far east of Hamburg. The v.Puttkamers invited me to spend the summer with them. Eckart and I rode our bicycles, hiked, picked lots of strawberries, and had a genuinely tranquil time.

Eckart's father, a major in World War I, was convinced that there would be another war, and worried that our generation would fight it. He certainly proved to be right! He wanted Eckart to be as prepared as possible. He had bought Eckart a Tesching, a small six shooter revolver. Mrs. v.Puttkamer carried it and the gun license in her purse. We set out early one morning and went to a lonely part in the Saxon Forest, set up a target and Eckart practiced shooting six rounds.

Just as it was my turn, a ranger arrived. He gave Mrs. v.Puttkamer a very stern lecture on prohibition of discharging fire arms. I could see that she was very much hurt. She remained absolutely silent. It was the end of target practice. I never saw the Tesching again.

We had not done anything unsafe. The range of that gun was very limited and we had made sure that the target disk was on the ground, and that Eckart shot downward.

Except for this unpleasant incident, it was a truly happy time for all of us. The summer vacation was over far too soon.

# POLITICS AROUND US

Ever since the 1914/18 War, the radical parties, the Communists on the left, and the new upstart Nazis on the right, kept on denouncing the Weimar Constitution the very document that guaranteed them the right to do so. At first the Nazis hardly even existed. However, they grew frighteningly fast after the tariff war had been started by the American Congress passing the Hawley-Smoot Bill in 1930

The German national flag, black-red-gold which originally symbolized the colors of the revolution of 1848, was very unpopular throughout the entire Country. The reason for that was that these colors had officially represented Germany only since the hated Treaty of Versailles, and the Nation had experienced hard times ever since. The black German Eagle with its red beak and talons in a golden field in the middle of the national flag, was derisively referred to as the „*Pleite-Geier*" (Bankruptcy Vulture).

The parties to the right still flew the imperial colors, black-white-red, at their functions and at election time. It was not so much for love of the imperial family, but during the short time from 1871, after v.Bismarck had united all of Germany, except Austria, to World War I when those colors symbolized the *Reich,* Germany experienced an unparalleled rise in prosperity, principally thanks to the enlightened policies of v.Bismarck.

The parties to the left of center rallied to the red flag, the color of the successful Marxist revolutions of 1917 in Russia and then Germany in 1918. The Communists, who had splintered away from the Social Democrats, added the golden hammer and sickle in the top corner near the mast. The Social Democratic Party, by far the largest of the approximately 50 German parties, but never an absolute majority, at first flew the plain red flag. Later they added three parallel white arrows, pointing upward at a slight slant at the top corner near the mast.

Only the Catholic *Zentrum* and the *Staats-Partei,* the most central parties, honored the flag of the realm. Even the merchant fleet flew the old imperial colors, but with a black-red-gold insert at the top, near the mast. Most people just flew the inoffensive flags

31

of their home state on festive occasions, thus avoiding all political connotations. The flag of Hamburg is a white three-towered castle in a red field.

In the fall, on Constitution Day, 1929, a day not usually celebrated by many Germans, the government decided to bolster this very liberal and beneficial foundation of laws by organizing an enormous sporting event for all schools. I swam in a relay for my age group for my high school. We came in fourth. It was bitterly cold, and all of us were shivering at the open air pool at Lattenkamp. It was the first swimming competition I ever took part in. It was by no means my last.

# BISMARCK GYMNASIUM

After completing sixth grade at Easter, 1930, I asked my father to have me transferred from the Heinrich Hertz Rëalgymnasium, where my classmates were very snobbish, to the Oberrëalschule an der Bogenstr., later called the Bismarck Gymnasium. At that school, swimming, a compulsory subject, was given one year later, so I had swimming again. I became the best swimmer in my class. I liked my language and math teachers, Mr. Unbehaun and Mr. Blum, respectively, and above all my old Art teacher, Mr. Busse.

I liked my biology teacher, Dr. Meyer. He was a medical doctor. We studied the human body. The mention of reproductive organs and certainly of sex was strictly omitted. He taught us:

"Three types of food were required for our survival: Proteins, carbohydrates, and fat. If one of these three should be absent from our diet we would die. Besides that there is a mysterious need for some substance we know about but have not really discovered yet. We call that unknown: Vitamin. It is essential to sustain life.

"If that vitamin is missing from the diet, people get scurvy or beriberi. We know that the vitamin is in abundance in the citrus fruits, as lime juice very quickly cures the otherwise deadly scurvy. We also know that this substance is in the chaff of rice, as those Chinese who eat only polished rice get beriberi. If they go back to eating unpolished rice they return to health.

"One day, I am sure, researchers will be able to describe the substance and possibly even make it chemically just as Dr. Bayer was able to make artificial salicylic acid, Aspirin."

I was fascinated. Imagine that! There are still substances in this modern day and age which have yet to be discovered! I wanted to become a medical doctor more than ever. I got straight "A"s in biology.

I never did well in languages. Though I wrote essays fairly well, I wrote too slowly to complete one in a class period. Also, I made lots of spelling errors for which I was docked points. I did not learn poetry by heart easily, so I was usually given a "D" in German.

Because I never studied English vocabulary sufficiently, I was about to flunk out of school by the summer of 1930. My parents did not help me. Mama knew no English and Papa just fumed, but "had no time." Toni, at that time, was engaged to Henry Fitton, an Englishman. She was to go to England that summer to meet her future family-in-law. I was to accompany her to learn English. That was great!

# MY FIRST TRIP TO ENGLAND

Toni, now 22, was a good looking young lady. We boarded a small Grimsby Line steamer, which took two nights and a day to reach its little home port in Yorkshire. We each had a cabin to ourselves. On board was a Russian circus troupe who practiced the most stunning gymnastics on top of the bulkhead of the hold. I had never seen anything like that before.

Mama never believed in checking luggage and that is how we came to have seven pieces among the two of us. We had no trouble getting on the train in Grimsby. In London, a cabby helped us carry the baggage to the tube station. We gave him a few German coins. He was amazingly thankful and polite despite the paltry tip. I had never seen such an underground rail station as Charing Cross. There were many parallel platforms and several levels of them. Toni had on a natural colored raw silk suit with a matching tight fitting hat and long beads around her neck. The skirt ended just above the knees. She had on silk stockings (nylon was not yet invented) and tan high heel shoes. A young man was obviously staring at her. I was too young to understand why.

Suddenly a train pulled in just in front of us. We lost time arguing as to who should go in first. Toni did. I handed her three pieces of our belongings, and the train pulled out with its door wide open. I saw a few men restraining Toni from jumping out of the moving train.

There I stood in that huge station in a strange land with four pieces of luggage. I turned to the man who had been watching us. I wanted to know if the next train off this platform, we were on, would go to the same destination as the one that Toni was on. That required a lot more English vocabulary than I commanded. I regretted now that I had not followed *Studienrat* Unbehaun's advice and studied my vocabulary more thoroughly. Then this man in front of me said something. It did not sound like anything my teacher had ever taught me, so I asked him: "Do you speak English?"

He roared with laughter, lifted me up into the train which had just pulled in, pushed the four pieces of luggage after me and waved good-bye. That was Esperanto. Everybody could understand that.

The next stop was a small station with only one platform. A train pulled in, going the opposite direction from mine. I saw Toni boarding it. I yelled at her. She heard me and came running toward me. I yelled: "Pick up the luggage!"

The station master heard me and held both trains until Toni ran back for our baggage and raced to join me. We received some devastating stares from some of our fellow passengers. It was too soon after the first World War. Germans were still very unpopular in dear old England. Toni sat down besides me and burst into tears.

I asked her: "Why cry now? It is all over, and everything came out all right."

At last the tears subsided sufficiently for her to ask me: "Do you at least know where you are going, where the Fittons live?"

"No, I can't remember."

She got out a big manila shipping tag and wrote on it: "This boy does not speak English. If he is lost, please put him in a taxi and send him to this address:" Then followed the address in Forest Hill which I still do not remember. She hung the shipping tag around my neck on a strong brown string. That was my introduction to London.

We spent three delightful weeks with the Fitton family in London. Toni took me to the changing of the guards at the Buckingham Palace and many other places of interest. We were fortunate with the weather. One day I marveled that the pavement was bone dry. That never happened in Hamburg. There it always was dry inside and never quite dry outside.

One day just outside the Fittons' home, a much bemedaled veteran sold ice cream from a cart to a bunch of children. I went up to him, to buy some, too. When he heard my German accent, he ignored me completely and would not sell me anything.

I had three more weeks of summer holidays. Toni and I took a train to Ashton near Sheffield, to stay with the family of Henry's uncle. There I was on a working farm. Toni went home, but I stayed. In London I had learnt some Cockney, besides the proper

English. The woman in the little candy store at the corner loved to chat with me, and she spoke nothing but proper cockney.

Here in Yorkshire I had to learn or at least to understand, the very unique Yorkshire dialect. The three weeks went fast. Fortunately I had picked up quite a bit of this second dialect. I had no idea then how useful that knowledge was to become in the not too distant future.

Two cousins named Edith and Evelyn, both twenty-one years old, had never left the rural community of Ashton near Sheffield. They were to accompany me home to Hamburg. After all, I was only twelve. Papa had bought tickets for us for a steamer that left from Hull, a port not too far north of us, at 7:00 p.m. on Friday night. It was to reach Hamburg on Sunday at high tide.

To start the journey we were to board a train to Hull. We were told to enter the last car of the train, but I had heard somewhere that if a train had an accident the passengers in the last car are the ones who get hurt the worst, so I insisted that we travel in the first car.

The train was held up a long time in Rotheram, and the car we were in was pushed back and forth several times. We were not long under way when I noticed that the sun was setting on the wrong side of the train. It did not disturb me too much, as I thought, that the train was just making a loop around the city. After a while, though, I became quite nervous and told the girls, who just stared at me helplessly. It was almost 7:00 p.m., the time the ship was supposed to sail, and just moors as far as one could see, no water nor city in sight anywhere.

I went to look for a conductor. He asked: " 'ull?! This troyn goes to 'arrich!" He dropped his "H's". He spoke Cockney. We were not far from London but very far south from Hull! I had no idea where Harwich was, so I brought him to the girls. They could not understand his cockney and he could not understand their Yorkshire dialect. I had to interpret. We found out that Harwich was a seaport in the South-East, and that the train would reach it at about 11:00 p.m. When the girls eventually understood that, they grabbed their two suitcases each and wanted to jump off the train as it halted. The conductor and I stopped them physically.

I had a plan: "We take a trans-Channel steamer to the Continent and rail from there to Hamburg." I heard no opposition.

Harwich turned out to be a bleak place. It drizzled. The railway station did not even have a platform. A few street lights glimmered at a distance. At one spot, not too far away, the rain had a glow of reflected light. That was where we were headed. We arrived at a pier where a British ship was docked. A sailor stood guard at the top of the gang plank. He gruffly told us to go away.

The next ship was Dutch. Its entire top and masts were floodlit. There were buntings from stem to stern and the Blue Peter flew from the foremast. Having been raised in a seaport town, I knew that to be the flag signaling that the ship was getting ready to pull out to sea.

The sailor at the gang plank called an officer. He spoke very good English. He suggested that we rent two cabins in the first class for the night, and sail second class in the morning on the afterdeck of the ship. We slept soundly, the breakfast was good, the weather was perfect, the North Sea and the Channel were uncharacteristically smooth, glistening in the sunshine.

The Channel ferry berthed in Flushing *(Vlissingen)*, the Netherlands, around 4:00 p.m. on Saturday afternoon. The many trains were stationary in a huge glass covered hall. Their steam raised the temperature to above 40°C (104°F). It was practically unbearable!

I found a train where all cars were marked: *Deutsche Reichsbahn*. The cars had the unmistakable shape of the German express trains. Each car was labeled with the name of a German city. I looked in vain for the much longed for: Hamburg. The nearest to a North German city was Berlin. We entered that car. I reasoned that it would have to pass through Celle, and that we could wait there for a train to Hamburg. An English woman with a German passport, who was married to a German begged me to carry her two suitcases, as she recently had an operation and could not lift anything. She too was going to Hamburg. This extra load was almost too much!

I asked Edith and Evelyn (I never found out which was which), if we had enough money to travel second class, as third class had wooden seats and we would be traveling all night. I had no money and they would not tell how much they had, but they bought third class tickets.

As soon as the train got in motion, I looked for the conductor. He wore a Dutch Railroad uniform. I tried to speak English to him, then my little bit of French which was my second foreign language at school for the last half year. Finally I tried German. He understood and spoke it fluently. He gave me a map showing each stop of the train. He marked Hertogenbosch, west of the German border.

"That's where you get off. Wait exactly one hour till midnight for the express train to Hamburg." That was easy. I checked the name of each station as we arrived against the name on the map. They corresponded perfectly. I noticed that the train never stopped very long, so when the next stop was supposed to be Hertogenbosch, we moved our six suitcases next to the exit door, and as the train stopped, I jumped out, and the girls threw the suitcases after me. I stood on ballast stones. There was neither a platform nor a station.

A tall conductor came to me. I spoke English to him first, then German. He finally understood that I wanted to go to Hamburg. The train started to move. The conductor pushed the girls back through the door, lifted me up and pushed me in, closed the door, and threw the suitcases into the open windows at the startled passengers in the succeeding train compartments. It dawned on me that the train had stopped at a red block light not too far from the station. I just had time to collect our luggage and the most astonished stares and arrange our belongings at the exit door when the train halted at Hertogenbosch just long enough to get out.

The station was unbelievably clean despite of all the coal-fired locomotives passing through. One could have eaten off the pavement of the platform. The buildings were painted spotlessly white. There were geraniums and other flowers in boxes attached to each window. It was not easy for a little boy of twelve to stay awake after such an eventful day, but I managed.

The train, which pulled in at midnight, had many empty compartments. The seats were long enough to lie down on. I gave the girls the option to do so, taking one bench each. I would sit on a suitcase in the middle. They would not hear of it. As they told me that they would not go to sleep, I asked them to wake me when we passed through Harburg, since the next stop would be Hamburg Main Station.

I took off my jacket, used it as a pillow and stretched out on one bench. The girls wore suits with skirts, most certainly not with slacks! However, they seemed too shy to take off their jackets in front of me though they had on perfectly good blouses. After they made absolutely sure that I was soundly asleep, which, of course, I was not, the bolder one took off her jacket, used it as a pillow and lay down on the opposite bench. The other young lady sat in the corner next to her head.

When I woke up, it was bright daylight. The girls were looking out of the window. We were just pulling out of the Hamburg Main Railroad Station! I only hoped that this express train would halt at the next, a minor stop, the Dammtor Railroad Station! We quickly gathered our belongings as the train crossed the Lombards Bridge over the Alster. To my great relief it stopped a minute later at the Dammtor Station. It was about 5:00 a.m.

We lugged our suit cases to the trolley stop at the beginning of the Mittelweg, but no trolley came. It was too early in the morning. I walked back to the railroad station and got a taxi. As it was a one-way street, the cab took off in a direction away from the girls. When I finally arrived in front of them, they were dissolved in tears. They had obviously gotten the impression that I had abandoned them in the middle of this strange city in this strange country where they did not even speak the language! Oh, ye of little faith!

We arrived at home many hours earlier than we were expected. Papa was furious as the boat tickets from Hull to Hamburg were not refundable. Mama hugged me, but insisted that I take the time to take off my clothes before I went to sleep. The girls slept all day and night their first day in Germany. All that just because the Railway of Great Britain split the train in Rotheram, the front of which we took going south to Harwich, and the rear of which we were told to take (of course, I knew better), to go the north to Hull.

I took great pleasure taking our visitors swimming a couple of times, but school had started the day after we arrived. I had homework to do. I had to leave the entertaining to my big sister and Henry, their cousin.

# SYLT

During the dark days of hunger, revolution, and inflation in the wake of World War I, our school had instituted a program to send each class to Wenningstedt on Sylt (the North Sea Island nearest to the Danish border) for three weeks, so that the boys could get a lung full of fresh sea air away from the grimy city. They would have a chance to eat fresh sea food and substantial meals. This unique program was still functioning very well during my childhood days.

The school hostel was a wonderful place. Four boys slept in one room. We had to keep our dorms clean, and all of us had to make our beds in a uniform way. We also took turns cleaning the common rooms.

We had school in the mornings. In the afternoons we went swimming, weather and surf permitting. The teacher insisted that we get out of the water when our skin turned blue. That North Sea water was cold! We also went on hikes through the dunes or across the heather further inland. Each boy had to bring a sewing kit. Mr. Unbehaun, our form master, examined our clothes regularly, and we had to sew on buttons, stitch up triangles that we had torn into our shirts, and darn our socks, if needed. For the first time in my life I did not have a maid to do those things for me. It felt good that I could rely on myself and manage very well.

# THE GREAT DEPRESSION

Things were not improving in Germany in the 1930's. The Hawley-Smoot Bill forced through the American Congress by the Isolationists had started a terrible tariff war. It aggravated the misery caused by the 1929 crash and aggravated the severe unemployment, not only in Europe, but also, most certainly, in the United States, which was supposed to benefit from the high import duties.

It was only natural that countries which suddenly could no longer export to the United States, protected themselves against foreign imports. Up to that time, America had probably exported more than any other country in the world. With the new high customs duties those exports were suddenly stopped, and most factories that had produced goods for export had to shut down permanently. There was no unemployment insurance in those days in the U.S., and the suffering among the poor was exceedingly tragic.

There was also a prohibitive tax on goods if they were shipped from a foreign port to another foreign port in German ships. In Hamburg the newly built merchant fleet was anchored on the Elbe, ship tied to ship, rusting away. The unemployed and hungry sailors stood on the shore, staring at the dying harbor. There was a severe food shortage throughout Germany. It had lost all of her colonies from which she could have obtained food and raw materials, and to which she could have sold her manufactured goods. Germany's neighbors to the West had at least that opportunity.

Smelting of aluminum was new, and a debate raged as to whether or not the recently invented aluminum cookware was safe to use. Germany's coal mines, the principal source of energy, were deep underground, which made mining very expensive. Artificial fibers, such as nylon, polyester, dacron, orlon, and the many other plastics had not yet been invented.

To purchase food and just about every raw material she had to import: (cotton, wool, crude oil, copper, tin, aluminum, rubber, wheat, rice, edible oils, meat, and many other items), Germany had to spend foreign currency. One manufacturing concern after the other, many shipping lines and trading companies were forced to shut down permanently. They had always been the sources of foreign currency.

This was an ideal climate for the Comintern, the international branch of the Russian Communist Party. More and more often one heard the Communist greeting among the workers and the unemployed: "Hail Moscow." The Communist Party of Germany was to a large extent financed by Russia. Their main objective was to merge Germany with the Soviet Union.

Stresemann, the head of the tiny, slightly right of center *Deutsche Volkspartei* (German People's Party) was the idealistic pro League of Nations compromise *Reichskanzler* (Prime Minister). He was demoted to Foreign Minister when his party lost votes in the election.

To make matters worse, prices rose and many Communist labor unions called strikes. The hard pressed industrialists paid off Hitler, who ordered his Storm Trooper bully boys to beat up the strikers. One would have thought that the farms would be booming, but the high taxes bankrupted them at a time when food production was most urgently needed, and the fields lay fallow.

Stresemann remonstrated with the United States, France and Britain to cancel the horrendously high "reparation" levies, which Germany had been forced to agree to pay as a main clause of the Treaty of Versailles of 1919. After all, he argued, the Germans had gotten rid of their weapons, reduced their army and navy to virtual impotence, had neither war planes nor artillery, nor even one machine gun, and had chased all the princes, the warrior caste, beyond their borders. Why punish the people of a liberal democracy?

All over this wide world, Germans were then, and are still today, very unpopular. No-one abroad felt sorry if a few thousand of them died of malnutrition. At that time, Hitler was hardly more than a butt of jokes in Germany as well as abroad, though some circles started to think of him seriously. Stresemann, the farseeing Pan-European idealist, died of stress.

# SMOKING

One of the boys of the neighborhood was Hans Gerald Straff. He bet me that I could not smoke as much as he could. Up to that time it had never even occurred to me to smoke, but to this day I have always been a sucker for a challenge. We went to his apartment. His parents and his pretty little sister, Giesela, were out. His father was obviously an importer of cigarettes. He led me into a walk-in-closet. On all its walls from the floor to the ceiling were little cubbyholes about 10cm x 10cm x 10cm (4"x4"x4") deep. Each of these dozens of little shelves contained a different brand of cigarettes. Some were German, others English, Egyptian, Turkish, American, you name it. Some had black tobacco, some bright yellow, and every shade in between. The cigarette paper varied too: white, pink, blue, and various other shades. The cigarettes were straw tipped, filter tipped, cork tipped, gold tipped, not tipped at all. Some were tightly packed and round, others loosely packed and flat. The containers varied, too, from round metal tins to flat hinged cardboard boxes.

We took about 25 different ones each. We each had exactly the same ones. We sat down in his bedroom and lit one after the other. Some had blue smoke, others white. I felt sick almost right away but I would certainly not let on. The room was filled with so much smoke that one could hardly see from one end to the other. Hans Gerald was a year older than I was, and he obviously enjoyed himself.

As I wobbled out of the bedroom into the living room, there was his father's pipe on a little table next to a comfortable arm chair. I could not blame his father for preferring a pipe to that vile stuff which I had just tasted.

"I bet you, you can't smoke that pipe," piped up my "friend".

"I bet you, I can, too," I said, without too much conviction.

Hans Gerald stuffed that thing, and I clamped it between my teeth with resolve. He lit it, I sucked, coughed and gave up.

He accompanied me into the street.

"I bet you, you can't play soccer now."

"I bet you I can."

I went home and looked out of my bedroom window. There was Hans Gerald and all the boys of the neighborhood staring at my window. I knew that I was the only boy around who had a soccer ball with a good bladder.

In those days soccer balls were made of leather and had a replaceable rubber bladder inside. The bladder had to be pumped up. The tube to the pump had to be tied off, and stuffed into the leather skin, which then had to be laced shut with leather thongs using a special awl.

So, now, I had the precious ball, and I had promised to play. My heart - more accurately my stomach - was not in it, but a promise is a promise. We walked a kilometer or so to the soccer field. Our sweaters marked the goal length. I sat down behind the goal. Hans Gerald, a veteran smoker and also an accurate kicker, sent the ball flying at me. "Stop this one!" he shouted.

I quickly bent over, to avoid it. That did it! Liquid exploded out of every opening of my body, except, maybe, my ears and nostrils. I stank! I could not get up. They carried me home. One boy each carried a leg, one each an arm, one my head and the smallest one carried my valuable soccer ball. Only half an hour earlier I did not want to be separated from it, which is why I went along. Now I could not care less if I lost all of my worldly possessions.

That is how they delivered me to my horrified Mama. "Oh, it's nothing, Mrs. von der Porten, he only got a kick in his stomach."

Mama dumped me into the bath tub, clothes and all. She alarmed Papa, who came home right away. Mama cleaned me up and carried me to bed. I thought I was going to die. "Don't worry, Arnold, Papa will soon be home and give you something to make you feel better."

Papa did come. He took one look at me. "Acute nicotine poisoning. He deserves a good spanking, but he is suffering enough. Just let him alone. Don't give him anything to eat or drink till morning. Then give him some thin oat porridge, no sugar or milk."

He turned around and went back to his practice, giving me nothing to alleviate my suffering. I swore that I would never smoke again!  How could such a despicable boy as Hans Gerald have such a gorgeous sister as Giesela?

# EARLY TEENAGE YEARS

Once in a while I liked to take long bicycle rides to the harbor. The big ships fascinated me. Though I had a dynamo for my bicycle lamp, I often did not use it because it slowed down the cycle.

One evening while riding home, a policeman stopped me. He said that he was going to give me a ticket. I told him in my best English that I did not understand him because I spoke no German.

He said with a perfectly straight face: "Great, I have not been on the harbor beat for nothing for the last five years. I speak English fluently. I am going to give you a ticket for riding a bicycle without a light. Your being a foreigner does not give you the right to violate the law. What do you say young man?"

His English was much better than mine was at that time. I turned red as a beet. He, of course, knew the truth. He saw my profound embarrassment and had a good laugh. He let me go. I quickly turned on my dynamo and took off as fast as I could. I never tried such a trick again.

At just about that time Mickey Mouse became popular. All the girls wore and swapped Mickey Mouse pins. Short Mickey Mouse films were usually run before the main features. We kids never heard of Walt Disney, the creator of Mickey. It was amazing to me then, how a veritable cult could develop from such a silly cartoon figure.

The only other popular cartoon figure was a Swedish comic strip called Adamson, which showed excellent humor. For instance, Adamson, a small, insignificant looking man, eats in a swanky restaurant. The meal is served on a beautifully embroidered table cloth, with crystal glasses, and expensive china. As the waiter lays down the bill.

Adamson asks: "Is this for everything?"
"Yes, Sir."
Next frame: "Is this bill all inclusive?"
"Yes!"
Next frame: "the whole lot?"
**"YES!"**

47

Next frame: Adamson picks up the table cloth by its four corners with everything on it, and walks out. The waiter faints.

I never was an avid reader, but there were some books which had great influence on me. One was *The Seawolf* by Count Luckner. It was a World War I story of a German raider. It was a normal looking square rigger, but it had a powerful diesel engine and a naval gun, camouflaged under a deck load of lumber. The crew of this raider never killed anyone, but played havoc with enemy shipping.

Another book was the *S.M.S. Emden*. This light cruiser was stationed in Tsing Tao, the German colony in North China, at the outbreak of the War in 1914. It captured a lot of British shipping, but the crew never killed anyone. It was eventually sunk by the heavy Australian cruiser *H.M.S. Sidney.* Those books gave me great enthusiasm for the German Navy. Half of the crew of the Emden was ashore during the final battle. They destroyed a British cable station. They confiscated a British ship and made it to the Turkish Empire. They took part in the battle for the Dardanelles.

I also enjoyed *Haia Safari* by General Lettow Forbeck, who wrote about his guerilla war he fought against the British and Portuguese in formerly German Colony of East Africa, Kenya and Mozambique.

But the book which influenced me the most was *The Microbe Hunters* by Paul de Kruif, a Dutch author. It was about the men who made the great medical discoveries, men such as Louis Pasteur, Semmelweiss, Robert Koch, Paul Ehrlich, Behrends, and many more. I was so enthusiastic that I decided to become a doctor, just like my father. My grades in Biology were straight "A"s. Unfortunately, politics form our lives to a much greater extent than we can anticipate, and we lose control.

# POLITICS IN THE SCHOOLS

World events were very much debated in school among us boys, but the teachers were not allowed to mention them. In compliance with the Treaty of Versailles, it was illegal to teach modern history or politics in German schools. The radical parties, especially the Communists and the Nazis, were always happy to challenge that treaty and they twisted all international stories to show that the neighboring countries had done all they could to destroy Germany. The French had an army of a million men, and Great Britain had the world's strongest navy. Their governments claimed that they were needed to enforce the League of Nations' rulings to maintain peace in the world.

Stresemann, the German Foreign Minister, had defended the French-British stance and supported their policies in the vain hope that those countries would reduce the heavy burden of "reparation payments" by Germany to them. Papa was an admirer of Stresemann and felt sad when he died.

The Nazis claimed that, since the Charter of the League of Nations called for all members to disarm, Great Britain and France should disarm, too. The Nazis also claimed that the only reason why those countries were so heavily armed was to keep Germany down, and to invade Germany again if it should stop once more to pay "reparations". The Western Allies as well as the German Coalition Government of the central parties denied these allegations.

Suddenly, the thunderbolt struck! Japan, quit the League of Nations and invaded China's Manchuria in 1931. Chiang Kai-shek's China was a member of the League of Nations. The well documented ferocity and cruelty of the Japanese forces in Manchuria were a disgrace to the human race, and most certainly to Japan.

Hitler screamed on the radio and published in his press: "Did I not tell you, the French and British are armed only to suppress the Germans. They won't move a finger to help Chiang Kai-shek, a fellow member of the League of Nations! Germans, you have been fed lies! Germany awake!"

His party gained enormously the next election, at the expense of all the parties which had gone out of their way to accommodate the Western Allies. The new red flag with its white circle and black swastika in the middle was being displayed prominently all over Germany now.

The swastika proved to be a very catchy design. Many girls replaced their Mickey Mouse pins with fancy, "cute" they called them, swastika pins. Some of those girls were even of Jewish descent. They knew, but ignored, that Hitler had made lots of anti-Semitic remarks. They lived to regret this infatuation bitterly!

# CHANGES IN OUR HOME

Gradually the family living in our house had shrunk. Herbert, Gerhard, and Toni, after she had married Henry Fitton, left the household.

My frail, widowed grandmother, Adele von der Porten, née Goldschmidt, moved into our house. The old family house at Testorpfstr. 5 was sold. A bathroom was built into part of the children's playroom. The main part of that room became her bedroom. The entire ground floor became her apartment. She also occupied the kitchen, though actually, her maid did that.

My dear Grandmother had a remarkable charity program. By the time of her death, on May 18, 1941, she had typed some six hundred books in Braille so that blind people could go to universities. Her type writer had only six keys and a space bar. When I last saw it in 1933, the hardwood topped keys were deeply worn by her fingers using them every day. Each Braille letter has six positions and each key corresponds to one of those positions. That means that on the average she had to hit four keys and the space bar for each letter.

On the floor above my grandmother's apartment, Irma's room was made into a kitchen. Our parents retained their bedroom. My room became the living room. Toni's former room became the dining room. Irma and I each got a room on the top floor. I loved that room with its dormer window and the slanting ceiling over the bed. It had running water. I chose a yellow and gold wall paper. Mama could get along with one servant. The maid had the room next to mine. All had doors only to the stairwell.

On December 3, 1932 Toni had a son, Harald. Toni often brought the baby. He really loved me. I would rather play with the baby-boy than do my homework. I built towers with our building blocks, and he laughed as he knocked them down.

Papa had bought a tiny second hand Opel. It was a shabby looking car. He only took it back and forth to work. When his brother, Ernst, bought an Adler (Eagle), Papa traded in his Opel for the identical model Uncle Ernst drove. What, let his younger brother show off in a much nicer car than his own?! Never!

I loved to play catch in the street, mostly with girls. I found girls most attractive but I was too shy to let them know. The only girl I did not find attractive was my little sister, Irma. We quarreled all the time. I always had to share everything with her, be it candies, a tangerine, or an apple. I shared, and she had the first choice. I learnt to cut an apple through the flower, through the middle, cutting the stem in half. I made sure that Irma could not possibly have a bigger piece than mine. She often took a frustratingly long time to choose. She, too, wanted to make sure, that I would not get the better of her.

# VISIT TO MARIA AND HERBERT IN NEW YORK

I had never been particularly close to my eldest brother, Herbert. In 1924, when he was 19, he migrated to England, from there to the Netherlands in 1925 and on May 1, 1927 he landed in New York. During the disastrous stock market crash in October, 1929, he was able to hold on to his job as a foreign loan advisor in the Chase National Bank, now the Chase Manhattan Bank, because he was fluent in quite a few European languages. His first foreign language in school was Latin, he was of course fluent in German, then English, Dutch, French, Spanish, and Italian. That made him most useful in the field he was in.

He met a charming girl from Stuttgart in Amsterdam. She followed him to New York on his urging. They got married there on October 5, 1929. I felt that I should meet my sister-in-law. It was 1932 now, I was 14, about 5ft (1.22m) tall and tipped the scale at 110 lbs (50 kg). I kept pestering Papa to send me to New York for my summer vacation. *"Quatsch!* (Rubbish!), that is far too expensive!"

Then one night, I had already gone to sleep, Papa roused me and asked: "Do you still want to go to America?"

"Yes, of course!"

"Do you want it badly enough, that you are willing to work your way over as a mess room boy?"

"Sure!" I was too green and too sleepy to comprehend, what I was letting myself in for.

"Well," Papa went on, "I know a doctor, who is employed by the Hamburg-America Line, who will certify that you are 17 years old (the minimum age for employment as a sailor), and you will be hired as a mess room boy."

"Great!"

We went to the Hamburg-American Line hiring hall. An elder sailor walked up to Papa. He pleaded emotionally: "Don't let that boy go to sea!" As I found out eventually, he knew what he was talking about.

In Germany boys wear shorts until they are confirmed in the

53

Church at fifteen. My first long pants were bought for me. I got three white waiter's jackets. Papa vaccinated me again. All sorts of preparations were made. Nothing was left out. Almost nothing, as it turned out.

As soon as school was out for the summer, I had to work eight hours on board the 23,000 ton: *D.S.* (*Dampf-Schiff,* steamship) *Hamburg.* I was assigned to the engineers' mess. There were thirteen engineers on board. Cases of dishes and tons of other supplies were loaded on board. Many were replenishing those in our pantry.

After working on board for about a week, the great day came. All the relatives, friends, and sweethearts of the crew were ordered ashore. The band struck up: *"Muss i' denn, muss i' denn zum Städele hinaus,...."* ("Now that I must leave my home town,...") the old folk song that was always played when German ships leave their home ports. The hawsers were winched in. The tugboat gradually inched the big liner clear from the pier.

Suddenly I remembered and shouted as loudly as I could: "What is Herbert's address?!" Papa put his hand to his ear. He did not understand.

The entire crew in unison: "What is Herbert's address?!"

Papa shouted back, but no-one could understand. Then all the relatives, friends, and sweethearts of the crew shouted in unison, and I got the all important address.

The steward, my immediate superior, told me: "The passengers will come on board in Cuxhaven," a tiny port town at the mouth of the Elbe, about 50 miles (80km) down river. "You must polish all the portholes in the thirteen state rooms of the engineers, the three in the mess room and the one in the pantry above the sink."

The inside and outside frames were made of brass. I polished and polished and when I was finally finished, the engineer in charge of the mess rooms said: "Not good enough, polish them again. They must shine like gold!"

I polished till my index fingers hurt something terribly. After I had made the portholes shine to the engineer's satisfaction, the steward told me that the dishes from the evening meal of the thirteen engineers had yet to be washed by me. I was ready to go to sleep, but first I had to cope with the pile of greasy dishes. While I

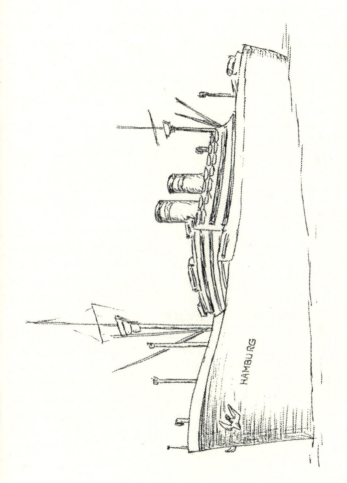

*STEAM SHIP IN HAMBURG*

was working, the steward and the other mess room boy, who was 20, sat in the steward's cabin, smoking.

Four of us mess room boys slept in a tiny cabin. I had an upper bunk. They all knew that I was green. First of all, my hands were very soft, and secondly, I was so much smaller than the others.

Next morning we were sailing on the North Sea. I had to fetch the breakfast from the second class kitchen one deck below, hurry up and wash the dishes. As we were approaching Southampton in England, I polish those green portholes again until they "shone like gold." We anchored in the stream. A tender came along side and delivered passengers and took some off. I wondered if anyone ever noticed that the portholes "shone like gold".

While the ship sailed across the Channel, I had to polish those miserable portholes again! By this time I hated, not only the portholes but all brass in general, especially the brass on the sleeve of the engineer in charge of the mess rooms. I worked at least 18 hours a day, and the sea was rough. Most of the time, while we were crossing the Channel, I felt like vomiting, but I had no time for that. We were about to reach Cherbourg, France.

The dishes and plates had to be preheated in a deep steam-heated oven with only one tiny door. I regularly burnt my lower arms on the sides of the door frame when I took out the dishes or plates. As I tried to get three dishes out of the oven at one time, they slipped and broke on the tile floor. I felt bad because of my clumsiness.

"Don't worry," said Seppel, the other mess room boy, "no one checks those, only the table silver, as that can't break." I soon broke more and acquired the nickname, *Schmeiss weg* (dash it away).

I said to the steward that we should take turns washing the dishes, and that he and Seppel should take a share of polishing the portholes, but the steward told me that it was my job. I did practically all the work, except serve at table. To make matters worse, they all dirtied plates, dishes, cups, and saucers unnecessarily.

Fortunately, the ship's architect had anticipated me. In his design, he had wisely put the sink directly underneath the porthole. That made it very easy for me to toss dishes right through the open porthole when they were too greasy. Cups with too much glued on sugar suffered the same fate. I did not see why a mess room for thirteen engineers should have more than thirteen plates, saucers, and cups, and nine dishes were quite enough, in my estimation. I worked toward making that a reality.

One of my duties was to get fruit from the refrigerated stores a deck below. The provisions master sat in the first store room which was for fruit and vegetables. There were two more colder store rooms, one for meat, and a very cold one for fish. It was hot in that coal fired ship. Besides, it was also an exceptionally hot summer.

The provisions master was a lonely, elder man. He asked me to sit down on his comfortable furniture of crates full of oranges. He said that I did not look well. He asked me a lot of questions concerning my job.

"If they cannot find you, they will have to work for a change. When I was your age..." and he spun one yarn after the other.

I was far too polite to cut him short or get up. From then on I visited the poor, lonely man often, helped myself to grapes or peaches, and listened to his long well-told stories.

Unfortunately, the shower rooms did not look too inviting, so I did not bathe. The lack of cleanliness, combined with a heat wave as we approached New York, caused me to have a most abominably itching, red rash over my entire body.

Finally, after six days, we docked in New York. Maria was on the pier waiting. We recognized each other from photos right away.

Several sailors came to me: "How can such a snazzy looking dame be waiting for a miserable runt like you? I'll give you 10 Marks, if you introduce me to her."

"No deal."

Boy, were they insistent! They ate their hearts out, when we took off together, Maria being a good 8cm (3") taller than I was then.

Maria and Herbert had a tiny apartment in Manhattan. I took a bath right away and then sat down to a very good meal. They showed me New York with its sky scrapers. They also took me to a "speak easy", where they sold a horrible tasting liquid which they called wine. Alcoholic beverages were illegal in 1932 during the Hoover administration.

Herbert played the piano. No one objected. My first

impression of the city was: What a dirty place! We took a trolley. It was marked: No Smoking. Herbert lit up anyhow. I was flabbergasted. I had never seen an adult disobeying a law or even a rule in Germany or in England, but here Herbert said: "Rules are there to be broken." Amazing! Incomprehensible!

I had to work eight hours each day on the ship. Most of the five nights I was in New York, Maria and Herbert showed me the town. They also took me to see Papa's cousin Hans von der Porten, his Norwegian wife, Julia, and their son Kenneth, 13. Hans was a dentist. He had his home and practice in a brownstone building on 94th St. I hardly had any sleep.

The fifth night in New York, Maria, Herbert, Julia, and Hans came on board, to have a lot of first class German wines and liqueurs and, incidentally to say good-bye to me. Of course, the bars on board had all been closed as soon as we entered American territorial waters three miles (5km) out. Many sailors, stewards, and mess room boys had bought lots of wines, beer and liqueurs before the closing. Now, the steward and Seppel sold their hoard to Herbert and Hans for an enormous profit.

Finally the loud speaker announced: "All visitors ashore!" We all said good-bye, and I headed for my bunk. I asked my room mates to wake me when we passed the Statue of Liberty, as I absolutely wanted to see that famous edifice.

The next thing I knew, it was bright day light. I lay soaking wet in my bunk. My head was where my feet were supposed to be.

I asked Seppel: "Why didn't you wake me when we passed the Statue of Liberty?"

"Wake you?! We shook you, shouted at you, hauled you out of your bunk, laid you on the table, even poured a bucket of water on you. The coal trimmers from next door came to our cabin, threatening to beat us up if we did not stop the racket. Finally, we dumped you back into your bunk, and you did not wake up till now. What did you drink?"

"I don't drink. I never drank anything at all last night."

He just smiled. I could have boxed him!

I made friends with an extremely important person. He was the pastry cook of the first class kitchen. He made huge trays of *petit fours* with chocolate cream, nougat, peach filling, almond paste, whipped cream, butter cream, you name it. They had all kinds of fancy toppings. After cutting these enormous trayfuls into tiny squares, he dumped the fringes into the garbage. All that good stuff! Just because it did not have the proper symmetrical shape, did not mean that it did not taste just as delicious as the rest of the cakes. I loaded several dishes full of those rejects and carried them into our cabin. Suddenly I was popular.

For the first time we got into friendly conversations. They even showed me large posters of naked girls, tacked to the inside of their lockers. I had never seen anything like that! "That's American Culture," they informed me.

They also boasted how they took part during their last Communist demonstration. One claimed proudly that he had carried the red flag on the *Moorweide,* (a meadow not far from our house) at a rally, where some Communist member of the *Reichstag* (Parliament) spoke. The pastry proved an excellent means to get the steward and Seppel to lighten my load a little, but just before we reached Cherbourg, I still had to polish all those green portholes.

We also had life boat drills, one on our way out, and one on our voyage home. My part in it demanded that I pick up my life jacket, lock specified portholes and lock the steel storm covers over them, run to a watertight compartment door (the ship was divided into many watertight compartments), shut it properly, and report to life boat No. 5. All on board were assigned specific life boats. We, the crew, were to help the passengers to get into the boats. That last part was left out of the drill, though all of the passengers showed up with their life jackets. We practiced swinging the life boats overboard on their davits. We actually lowered them a few feet. Fun was had by all.

My parents had bought me three sparkling white steward's jackets. I only wore them when I carried the garbage to the stern of the ship to dump it overboard. Those garbage pails were very heavy. I had to haul them past the second class passengers who occupied the stern third of the ship. The first class occupied the center above the crew's activities. The third class was in the bow third of the ocean liner. The classes were effectively separated by the bulkheads of the holds.

One nice day I saw a young gentleman and two young ladies

playing Ping-Pong. They were doing very poorly. I put down the putrid garbage cans, and showed them how to hold the rackets. We played together for about an hour. The engineer in charge of the mess rooms materialized. He kept walking around us in large circles. I ignored him completely. I assumed that he would tell me in no uncertain terms that ratings were not to socialize with the passengers as soon as he had me in the "No passengers allowed" area of the liner. My assumption proved to be correct. The reprimand was surprisingly mild.

Cherbourg was to become a memorable port. There was the exact twin of the New York Statue of Liberty. Her pedestal was not as imposing as the one in New York Harbor, but that made her look all the more gigantic. I was told that the two statues were facing each other. After all, the one in New York was a gift from the people of France to the people of the United States of America. The *D.S. Hamburg* never docked in Cherbourg. Tenders brought and removed passengers as we anchored in midstream.

Coffee played a big role with the engineers. I often had to carry cups of coffee deep down into the engine room. That was a huge, hot and fantastic area with its huge boilers and trimmers shoveling coal into the furnaces. There were two propeller shafts of one meter diameter leading to the stern of the ship. Each shaft had its own tunnel. The shafts glistened with oil. At the end of the tunnels was the rudder machine. Above it was a large diameter air duct, bringing fresh air directly from the stern deck of the ship.

We weighed anchor for Southampton, across the English Channel. In the bay of Cherbourg the water was as smooth as glass. I found out that I could stack and balance all of the thirteen cups, we still had left, in one hand. I showed that trick to Seppel. Where the smooth waters of the bay suddenly meet the rough waters of the Channel, the ship started to roll and twelve, of our thirteen cups, hit the tiles of our pantry. That left only one solitary cup for thirteen engineers! That was sure to be trouble.

I grabbed a book, a large tin comprising of all the pickled herring which were delicacies specially sent to us to be consumed exclusively by the engineers, but which I cherished more than any other food, a loaf of black bread, a knife and a large pot of coffee. I carried it all down to the rudder machine under the air shaft. I hid there for most of the rest of the journey. I did polish the portholes though, and my index fingers are still bent inward from that voyage.

A large tray full of pastry scraps paid the mess room boy from the officers' mess for some desperately needed cups. Now I had two places to hide, the rudder machine room and the fruit storage room. I made good use of both of them for the rest of the trip. The provision master was always glad to see me, and I found his stories most interesting.

It was certainly wonderful to see the North Sea again between Southampton and Cuxhaven. I was in the process of pulling three of our last nine dishes out of the steam oven in the pantry when I burnt my fore arms, which was not unusual.

I cried out: "Ouch!"

The hated steward, serving a meal next door in the mess room, laughingly called out: "Dash it away!"

Now, that was a direct order. No good man, deserving to be called a German, would disobey a direct order from his immediate superior. I picked up the three dishes as high over my head as I could and dashed them on the stone tile floor with all my might, so that there was not a splinter larger than a square centimeter to be found anywhere.

All the engineers from the mess hall and their near by state-rooms, the steward, and Seppel raced into the small pantry.

"What happened?"

"What happened?"

"They slipped," I said.

The engineer in charge of the mess rooms would have loved to knock me down. I could read that in his eyes, but those days were over thanks to the Marxist revolution in 1919. The most he could do, is say through clenched teeth: "You'll get the sack as soon as we reach Hamburg!" I told him, that I did not mind, as my summer vacations were over soon, and that I had to go back to school anyhow.

No one found me in my hiding places. In Cuxhaven the passengers went ashore, and we sailed up the river with the rising tide. Boy, was I glad to see Mama and Papa waiting for me on the pier! I was dead tired. I had lost more than 5 kg (11 lbs), but otherwise I was quite healthy and richer for the experience. The next day I went to the Hamburg-America Line office and received the first money I ever earned. No one mentioned dishes. I certainly did not.

# THE LAST DAYS OF THE WEIMAR REPUBLIC

1933 became a most eventful year, not only for me, but for all the world. I continued to do poorly at school. That was not exactly news. My friendship with Eckart was as solid as ever. Politics in Germany were absolutely chaotic. The two radical parties, though furiously working against each other, the Communists and the Nazis, blocked every budget proposal and bill submitted by the Government. The Cabinet played musical chairs, it was constantly being reshuffled. Finally Prime Minister Brüning had to suspend the parliament. He could do that for a limited time only under the Weimar (Federal) Constitution. (Weimar is the city where the constitutional committee had met and formulated the German Constitution.)

Brüning was the leader of the Catholic *Zentrum* Party. He had risen to that post as the leader of the Catholic Trade Union. The *Zentrum* Party, dominant mostly in the Catholic areas, had been the second largest party. It had to govern sometimes in conjunction with the right of center parties and at other times with the more Marxist oriented Social Democrats, the largest party. The Nazis were about to overtake each party in numbers.

Most unfortunately, not only for Germany, but for the whole world, Brüning was a very poor economist. His tight money policy, combined with the heavy burden of the war reparation payments, especially to France, shut down many industrial plants, and worse still, many farms, at a time of severe food shortages.

The world currencies, including Germany's, were still on the gold standard, and Germany had shipped all its gold to France as war reparations. As a result, the only backing for the German mark was foreign currency. All international transactions were quoted in British pounds. As Germany had a negative trade balance since the start of the tariff war, there was neither money nor credit for any imports. The Governments, one after the other, lost "no confidence" votes in the *Reichstag* (parliament), and elections followed elections.

President Herbert Hoover of the United States saw the plight and the mounting danger to world peace if, as a consequence of desperation, the Germans should lose their democratic form of government. In his 1932 election campaign he promised to initiate a conference to create an international monetary fund, so that poor countries, like Germany and Austria, could buy surplus food on credit. Thus, President Hoover hoped to alleviate hunger and frustration which caused political instability and endangered the peace with the well-to-do countries. The conferees were to meet in London, England.

Hitler prophesied loudly, so that no one could fail to hear: "This promised conference is only another stalling tactic by the Allies so that you will not vote for the 'New Order'. Don't believe that they will ever help us Germans! The Americans can poison their potatoes, slaughter their pigs and bury them to keep their farm prices out of the reach of the Germans. The Canadians can burn their wheat. In Brazil they feed the fire in their rail road engines with coffee, but we cannot eat the machinery we would like to export! They will never allow us to export! Germany awake!"

Hitler had obviously drawn the correct conclusion that the American election was not about the suffering in Germany and Austria. Clearly beer and whiskey, the repeal of the prohibition, and unemployment were the focal points of the 1932 American presidential election!

When Franklin Delano Roosevelt defeated President Hoover in the November election, he was asked what instructions he would give his negotiators at the London monetary conference. Roosevelt answered that he would never back an international monetary fund with American dollars. With that statement by the new American president-elect, Hitler's predictions came true.

Hitler screamed over the radio and printed in his press: "Didn't I tell you? Didn't I tell you?! They only played for time, so that you would not vote for me in the last election! Germany awake!"

In those days the greeting: "*Heil* Hitler" among the Nazis was not as prevalent as: "Germany awake."

The government fell again, and in the ensuing election Hitler's *National-Sozialistische Deutsche Arbeiter-Partei, (NSDAP)*, Nazis, as their opponents called them derisively for short, won an absolute majority in the legislature of the State of Oldenburg. It was the only state where the Nazis ever had an absolute majority up to then. That legislature then proceeded to make Hitler a Citizen of Oldenburg. Thereby he became a Citizen of Germany and could vote in Germany for the first time in his life. More importantly, he became eligible to hold a government office. Up to that time, Hitler had been a Citizen of Austria. Though he was the leader of the largest party in Germany, he had never been entitled to vote in any German election.

# THE THIRD REICH HITS LIKE A HURRICANE !

President Paul v.Hindenburg, in a desperate effort to appease Hitler, appointed v.Paapen *Reichskanzler* (Prime Minister). He hoped that Hitler would accept a minor role in a v.Paapen right of center cabinet. Hitler refused. After only two months the v.Paapen cabinet was forced to resign.

Franklin Delano Roosevelt took office as President of the United States on January 20, 1933. The aging German President, v.Hindenburg (85), with a heavy heart, asked Adolf Hitler to form a coalition government with the *Deutsch Nationale Volkspartei*, Hindenburg's party. It was small, but it was the party of all the industrialist and mercantile leaders. Thus, on President Roosevelt's 51st birthday, January 30, 1933, Adolf Hitler, at 43, became the Prime Minister of Germany. Roosevelt had assumed office only ten days earlier. He was to become tremendously instrumental in eventually destroying Hitler, yet the latter was to survive him by 18 days.

Monday morning, January 30th, 1933, I walked to school as usual. It was a slushy, dark, and drizzly morning in Hamburg. My mood was even gloomier than the weather. Hitler *Reichskanzler!* and another week of hated school. Along came Karl-Heinz Dannmeyer where we usually met on our way to school. He wore a boy scout uniform of a right of center affiliation.

"Karl-Heinz, it is against the law to wear a uniform to school!"

"Do you know what happened yesterday?"

"Certainly, Hitler was appointed *Reichskanzler* as of today. So what! He hasn't got an absolute majority. He'll be out at the next election, just like Stresemann, Brüning, v.Paapen and all the rest of them!"

"No, he won't! We are in now. We'll never let go. We'll free ourselves from the Versailles yoke! 'Not another word of negotiations. Death alone can defeat us! We are the storm columns of the Hitler dictatorship!' "

He enthusiastically quoted the words of a popular Nazi song.

It turned out that I was 100% wrong, and he 100% right. Death did defeat him, just as it did defeat about half of my other classmates. They were all killed in Word War II six to twelve years later.

We were marched into the Aula, the assembly hall, which was usual on Monday mornings. Each class had two rows of benches, and the form-master stood at the end by the window so that he could oversee his class. We always started the week with a religious service. A teacher would read a text from the Bible, the organ would play, and we would sing some hymns. This morning it turned out to be different. Dr. Züge, the headmaster, made a short announcement. He introduced Dr. Payn, a German teacher, as the new "Assistant Headmaster for Political Affairs."

Dr. Payn immediately launched into a vicious harangue against the Communists, the Jews, and the Reds who had not yet understood the meaning of the "New Order". They would soon feel Hitler's wrath, and as for those teachers who spoke against the Party, they would soon be eliminated!

He also reiterated how unfairly the Germans were treated by the former Allies who, according to him, had started the World War in 1914 and then had the temerity to accuse the Germans of having done so. He pointed out why so many Germans had turned to Hitler and had abandoned the democratic parties:

"We Germans did everything the Allies asked us to do. We disarmed. We got rid of the Kaiser and his Yunkers. Stresemann had asked: 'Why do you want to punish the poor people of a liberal, unarmed republic?' Did the Allies accommodate us even a little bit? No! They lied to us! Where are Wilson's sacrosanct 14 points? What became of their holy doctrine of self determination?! They took vast territories away from us! Where were the promised plebiscites?!

"They hit us with high tariffs! They starve this Nation! They rather destroy food than sell it to us on credit! We cannot eat our machinery! They never reduced the reparation payments by a single mark! They did not return one colony to us!

"The Charter of the League of Nations demands that all members disarm. We Germans did. Did France and Great Britain disarm?! No! They are armed to the teeth! They claim that they need the arms to maintain peace in the world.

"That is a laugh! When the Japanese invaded Manchuria a year and a half ago, did they stop them? Did they supply Chiang Kai-shek with even a single gun? No! China is a member of the League of Nations. France and Great Britain proved their own lie! They have their huge armed forces only to keep us Germans down, just as Hitler has always predicted! Germany awake!

"Doing their bidding has brought us nothing but misery! For fourteen years they have humiliated us. They call **us** the disgrace of the human race. It is **they** who are treating **us** disgracefully!

"Now we must try the opposite tack: We must defy them! We must defy all our enemies, foreign and domestic! Germany awake! Our flag has changed! Now we will all sing our national anthem while giving the salute of our new Third Reich!"

With that he unfurled the Nazi flag down the lectern. We all stood up to sing our beloved: *Deutschland, Deutschland über alles.... (Germany, Germany above all else....)* The hall reverberated, but I did not raise my right hand to the divisive salute. All my classmates did. After the last notes had faded, Dr. Payn yelled: "And now the [Nazi] anthem of Germany's future, the *Horst Wessel Lied!"* I sat down. All the other boys, as far as I could see, remained standing and sang the catchy tune, which had done so much to glamorize the Nazi movement.

Over the years I have come to the firm belief that no political nor religious movement can succeed without a rousing song which is simple to learn, plus a symbol which is easy to draw. The Hitler movement surely had both.

Dr. Payn had certainly reiterated all the reasons why so many decent German citizens had switched from the parties which had promised that Germany would regain its prosperity and international acceptance as an equal among other European nations by supporting the League of Nations. The radical nationalist movement appealed to German pride. It promised to defy the former enemies of World War I who had failed to cooperate with all German Governments. The Nazis promised to stop the Communists who wanted Germany to unite with the Soviet Union. Very, very few took the threat of terror against anti-Nazis, and especially against the Jews, seriously.

Immediately after we got into our classroom, our form-master

68

called on me: "von der Porten, why did you not salute when we sang our national anthem, and why did you sit down when we sang the *Horst Wessel Lied?*"

"Because party politics have no business in German Schools!" I felt my anger rise. My heart beat in my throat. And my ear tips burned. "It is divisive, and also against the Hamburg State Constitution as well as against the Federal Constitution!"

Some of my classmates started to boo me, but Mr. Unbehaun said: "von der Porten now has the floor. Anyone who wants to rebut him, can do so, after he sits down. Free speech has been guaranteed in Hamburg State for many centuries."

I took advantage of my right. I spoke of the proud history of Hamburg. I said: "Our greatest national hero, Otto v.Bismarck, after the Kaiser had sacked him, resided on Hamburgian Soil, as here he was guaranteed uncensored writing which was not the case in neighboring, his native Prussia." I also said: "The threats by Dr. Payn against all those who did not agree with him and his restrictive movement, were against the spirit of our traditions."

No one got up to rebut me as I sat down overwhelmed, in tears, sobbing uncontrollably. After the class, when the classroom had emptied, and I alone sat there to collect myself, three of my classmates came in to shake my hand. With that gesture, I, the second smallest boy in my class of 26, became the spokesman for the Anti-Nazis.

# THE LUTHERAN CHURCH

By this time I was taking Catechism every Saturday after school. It was taught by Pastor Reinhardt at the *Kleine Johanniskirche* (Little St. Johns Church) on the Mittelweg, about a kilometer (.6 miles) from our house.

In her youth Mama had been active in the Lutheran Young Women's League. The church, my mother used to go to in Leipzig, was the very church where Johann Sebastian Bach had been the organist some 80 years before my mother's time.

I was confirmed a member of the Lutheran Church at the Little St. Johns Church on Palm Sunday 1933. I was glad when the ceremony was over. Pastor Reinhardt came to our house and had dinner with us. He presented me with a beautiful hymn book with gold edging. I was not interested. To my amazement Papa, the dyed in the wool atheist, made a very gracious speech, praising the Church's laudable influence on civilization.

I was glad that this day meant, that from now on, I could wear long pants like a grown-up, though I did not feel any more grown-up than the day before. I was also very much relieved that I no longer had to go to church every Saturday and Sunday. At that time it did not dawn on me that, in about six months, I had to **be** a grown-up!

# TO SYLT AND BACK BY BICYCLE

That same eventful year, 1933, our class was to be among the earliest to go to our school hostel in Wenningstedt, Sylt. We had very good class spirit. Political differences had not destroyed it. We had chosen our class leader, Peter Kohrs, whom we all agreed to obey. We asked to be allowed to ride our bicycles to Sylt, some 240km (150 miles) to the NNW of Hamburg. We anticipated it to be a three day tour. Thirteen of us got permission from our parents and our school. It was the long Whitsuntide (Pentecost) weekend. We were to leave Saturday early in the morning, and were to meet the train with the rest of our class and two other classes at Nibüll, the last train stop east of the Hindenburg Dam. This marvel of engineering was the 10km (6 mile) rail road link from the mainland to Sylt across the tidal flat. Only trains were allowed to cross that dam.

Peter Kohrs directed every boy what to bring. I had to supply sausages for all the boys and a tent cloth. Three tent cloths fitted together to make a tent, one was the ground sheet, wide enough for three boys to lie on, and two made the roof. We had enough for three tents in a row plus one sheet to cover the end. Clothes had to cover the other end. In one tent four boys had to sleep. A Nazi flag was purchased from the class money, to fly at our little camp. Thus were the plans.

When we assembled, Peter checked all of our bicycles. He found that mine was in a deplorable state. It had never been oiled. The chain was rusty and slack. The cones of both wheels needed tightening, and so did some of the spokes. I had never done any kind of mechanical work and knew nothing about maintenance. Peter and two other boys did their best to get my bike into a reasonable shape. He was unhappy that it delayed our departure but he was very nice about it.

Already the very first afternoon it showed that I was not only the smallest, but also the weakest of the group. On top of that, I had the bicycle with the poorest bearings. I could not keep up with the rest of the boys. At the first rest stop that afternoon, Peter took all luggage off my bike and distributed it among my classmates. That showed a real team spirit as no one objected.

We reached our first night's stop as planned, just north of Itzehoe. Each boy had a job to do. The experienced Scouts and Hitler-Youths among us pitched the tents. They cut dried ferns as insulation under the ground cloths. We started a fire and boiled a much appreciated soup. I had to look for fire wood. That was easy. We were in a clearing in a forest. We had hot soup and sausage sandwiches on nourishing, delicious black bread. We sang folk songs and then turned in. At midnight we woke up due to the bitter cold. We huddled one against the other but we still felt miserably cold.

After some fitful sleep, Peter got us all up. The ground was covered with hoarfrost. The beauty of the white ice crystals covering everything as the red sun rose was lost on us. We just shivered. Peter ordered a boy to start a fire to make some hot cocoa. He told the rest of us to strip down to only shorts, socks, and shoes. Then he led us on a fairly fast jog through the forest until we were really hot. We dressed quickly as warmly as we could, had sandwiches and cocoa, doused the fire and resumed our cycling.

Even though the other boys carried my luggage, I had the worst time keeping up with my class mates. We had chosen the most westerly and most direct route through Ditmarschen. The land was below sea level. On both sides of the clay road were deep, full to the brim, drainage ditches. Beyond them, cattle grazed on the meadows where the grass reached the cows' bellies. Storks accompanied the bovines as frogs jumped from the muddy soil as the cows walked.

Slowing progress, our troubles were twofold: Farm wagons had knifed deep furrows into the surface of the road when it had rained. Now, after a fairly long dry spell, the clay was hard like clay flowerpots. We all had some falls. The other hindrance was a very sharp north-west wind. It was miserably tough going.

In the evening we were looking for a possible camp site. There was nothing but swampy meadows all around us. We had passed a few farms. There were fruit trees growing on their east sides where they were sheltered from the prevailing west winds. The tops of the trees near the houses were as high as the houses and their line

72

RIDING THROUGH SCHLESWIG-HOLSTEIN

sloped down at a ten degree angle right to the ground. There was nowhere to shelter from this fierce wind.

"We should find shelter behind the dike." We rode west, till we reached the North Sea. There was a high earthen dike, but also a very broad drainage canal behind it. The wind made a cooking fire impossible. There was no soil dry enough on which to rest any ground cloth.

We knew we were near Nordstrand, a *Halig*. Those small dike protected islands in the mud flats off the west coast of Schleswig-Holstein were called: *Haligs*. We also knew that it was inhabited. It was high tide. A dam constructed of piled up stones without cement led out to the island over a mile (2km) away. It had become too foggy to see the island. The dam was crowned with two 12 inch (30cm) boards laid side by side. It was too narrow to ride. We pushed the bikes on this narrow path. At times the waves washed over the boards and got our feet wet.

When we arrived on the island, a foot bridge led from the dike over a broad drainage ditch. Peter, who proved to be a superb class president, called on me, the most bedraggled looking of the lot, to go with him. We stopped at a farm house on a *Wurft*, a mound, high enough to prevent inundation of the house in case of a dike break. It was getting dark by now. A big German shepherd dog made us dismount and stand still. The farmer took his pipe out of his mouth long enough to whistle for his dog. The dog quickly ran back to its owner and sat by his side.

Peter asked the farmer: "Can we sleep in your hayloft?"

"Got any matches?"

"We'll leave them with our bikes. We have battery lamps."

"Yes, go ahead."

Peter turned to me: "Go, get the others." I did.

If the farmer was surprised or annoyed when he saw thirteen of us, I shall never know, as his face never showed any emotion. We made our cooking fire, had hot soup and sandwiches, doused the fire and climbed into the hayloft. We slept soundly, and above all, we were warm.

When we woke up the sun was already high in the sky. We skipped breakfast. We had to hurry up. The day before we had traveled a shorter distance than we had planned. The detour to the

74

*Halig* was the main reason. As we reached the dam going to the mainland, it was low ebb tide. There is a difference of 33ft (10m) between high and ebb tides off the German coasts. We now realized how high the dam was. Varying from 10 to 25ft (3 to 8m) below the crown of the dam, the wet gray clay of the mud flat glistened.

Walter Burnett suggested that we should ride on the narrow boards to the mainland. Peter said that those who dared could do so but he would not advise it. Walter challenged that those who would not follow him were sissies or were incompetent cyclists. With that Walter and two other boys mounted. For once, somewhat uncharacteristically, I resisted a dare.

We, the other ten, walked pushing our bicycles. Soon the superior cyclists were just three little dots far away. All of a sudden there were only two dots. We strained our eyes. We all agreed. There were only two dots. After a while there were three again. Eventually we came to a spot, at the right side of the dam some fifteen feet below us, where there was a perfect imprint of a boy from feet to the top of his head in the oozy gray mud flat. The imprint of a bicycle was right next to that of the boy's. So, we had an explanation why we saw only two dots for a time.

When we finally reached the mainland, there was Walter Burnett. He was solid gray, but laughing with just his eyes showing. His Hitler Youth uniform was completely obscured. Peter told us to find some sticks. We did. There was a fresh water pump. Its water was just above freezing. Narjes pumped, and we others had fun keeping Burnett under the pump with the help of our sticks. It was an effective, if noisy way to get most of the mud off the boy. His bicycle was washed next.

There being not a single towel among the thirteen of us, he had to strip, except for his shoes and socks, and jog about a kilometer to get dry and warm. He was also by far the tallest of us. We checked his luggage it was soaked, too. He had taken off all his clothes and had to wear the spare set of the second tallest. With his sleeves and pant legs too short, he looked very funny, as if he were ready to perform a clown act in a circus.

We knew that the train would not wait for us in Nibüll. We made very short rest stops. At the first one, we had a cold breakfast, as we had no time to make a fire. At lunch time, we did the same. That afternoon we made a real end spurt. We were exhausted when we arrived at the train station just minutes before the train pulled in.

We checked our bikes in the luggage car. We were received by our classmates with loud jubilation. Mr. Unbehaun greeted us with a smile from ear to ear. Thanks to the joy and pride we felt, all fatigue was forgotten. The train ride across the Hindenburg Dam was very short. We had to get back on our bicycles at Morsum, the first stop on Sylt.

The train continued to Keitum. The rest of the class got off at the next and final stop on the island, Westerland. They took the antiquated and very slow narrow gauge train to Wenningstedt. One boy made a sign: "The plucking of flowers, while the train is in motion, is strictly prohibited."

We thirteen cycled on, where heather grew on both sides of the narrow road. This short distance seemed to take forever. Our legs kept telling us: Enough is enough! That first night felt truly wonderful. The joy to sleep in a real bed again!

In the mornings we had to make our beds and clean our rooms. There were four boys to a room. Some of us were assigned to clean the staircase, the corridors and the class rooms. It did not take very long. The rest of the morning we had school, mainly the subjects Mr. Unbehaun always taught us: German, English, and French. Dr. Springer taught us Singing. He did not like the blood curdling songs of the Nazi movement, but the many Hitler Youths in our and the two other classes insisted on getting together and singing them anyway in their free time.

In the afternoons we bathed in the heavy, ice cold breakers pounding the white beach. As in the years before Mr. Unbehaun insisted that we get out and dry off, when our lips and bodies turned blue. Some afternoons we went on hikes in the dunes. That was rough going, as the sand was very soft. We also made a day's hike to the east coast of the island across the heather to the mud flats. We gathered lots of black mussels which grew in abundance on the pilings. At the hostel we had them steamed open. They were delicious.

The three weeks on Sylt went far too fast. We got out our bicycles and headed across the heather to the train station. Mr.

Unbehaun had most of our belongings mailed to our homes. We took only what we needed for the ride home. Just the thirteen of us took the train across the Hindenburg Dam, as the rest of the class stayed two days longer in Wenningstedt.

At Nibüll, we decided to ride east towards the town of Schleswig. We had no intention of riding again on the below sea level, shelterless marshlands with its roads of hardened clay furrows. We were aware of the fact that the land east of Ditmarschen was anything but flat, but it offered shelter and made us independent from the goodwill of the farmers. The ride home was a lot more relaxed. We did not have a train to meet.

The most outstanding memory of that ride was the bridge over the Kiel Canal at Rendsburg. Its approach started from almost sea level, rising to a height that even the tallest ships could pass under it. Of course, on our way to Sylt, we had crossed a similar bridge further south-west. It was not far north-west on Itzehoe, but at that time we had not had time to stop and dwell on the subject. The canal was built shortly after Kaiser Wilhelm II ascended to the throne in the last quarter of the last century. Its purpose was to enable shipping to travel between the Baltic Sea and the North Sea without going around Jutland. This was especially important for the brand new German Navy. At the time we crossed the two bridges, coming and going, there was not a ship in sight.

We were again lucky with farmers. They let us sleep in their barns. We reached Hamburg in good time, despite some steep hills to ride up, but then there were just as many declines that allowed us to speed. Multispeed bicycles had not yet been invented.

Now that the trip was over and all of the excited talk about it had subsided, the question arose as to what to do with the Nazi flag which was purchased for the trip with class money. Of course, officially the black-red-gold flag was still the German national flag, though I had not seen one since January 30th. We were all given raffle tickets, and I won the flag.

"What are you going to do with it?" asked Mr. Unbehaun.

"I'm going to cut it into little frazzles and flush it down the toilet!"

"You can't do that! We are going to raffle it again."

This time I was not given a ticket.

# THE MASTER RACE

At school we were taught a new subject: *Rassenkunde*. (Race Science.) The new teacher was a very mediocre looking specimen of the "master race" wearing a storm trooper uniform to school on his first day. He picked me out, explaining to the class that he could see by the shape of my skull, my facial angle, and the height of my cheek bones that I was of truly Arian descent of various Germanic tribes which he then proceeded to name.

How could he go wrong, demonstrating his great knowledge on a boy whose name started with: von? After a while I could not stand it any more, and I told him that I come from a Jewish family on my father's side. He immediately let go of me and picked a blond boy. I thought to myself, but did not say, that he proved the exact opposite of what he had set out to prove. He demonstrated clearly for the entire class to see, that he could NOT tell my ancestry by my features.

I told this ludicrous story to Mr. Unbehaun. He did not think it funny. Knowing where his bread was buttered, he had joined the Nazi Party and the storm troopers. At any rate, this was the first and the last lesson in Race Science for our class.

I told Papa about this incident. He was upset. It was just another example of the Nazi poisons of the youth, as he saw it. He told me: "All this talk of an Arian, Jewish, or any other pure race, is absolute rubbish! In Ethiopia the Jews are black, in China they are yellow, in Egypt they are brown, and here in Germany they are white.

"When the temple in Jerusalem was destroyed and the Jews were dispersed throughout the Roman Empire, they became the traders. Many followed the Roman armies. That is how they came to Germany, to the towns which were founded by the Romans: Vienna, Frankfurt, Trier, Mainz, Wiesbaden, and many others. Armies of soldiers of every description, crisscrossed Germany. There were Celts from the West, Mongols from Asia, just to name some. The Romans used many Arab soldiers from Syria at a time when the general population was illiterate. As recently as 1812 Hamburg was occupied by 1,500 Spanish troops, brought here by

Napoleon. Spain had been ruled by Moors from North Africa for 700 years and Spaniards are therefore certainly not of a pure race.

"The Jews, away from Israel, had to read and write in at least two languages by the time they were thirteen, Hebrew, and the tongue of the population around them. If they dealt with the Roman Army they had to know Latin as a third language. That skill was needed to supply the armies and to be general merchants. They often became the go-betweens between the hated conquerors and the local population. That is why the Jews were sought after.

"As many Jews followed armies, they were separated from their families and fathered and raised children from gentile women. Many women, among them, of course, also Jewish women, were raped by the conquering soldiers. Thus many women raised children from gentile fathers in the Hebrew Faith.

"Right after the twelfth century crusades, Germans started to annex Slavic territory in the name of Christianity, teaching entire Slavic tribes German, such as the Wenden, Prussians, and Poles who then became Germans. Despite of all the violent times, the absorption of foreigners was more often than not quite peaceful. Migrants of many races and religions came from all over Europe, especially from the East. So talk of pure Germans, pure Arians, or pure Semites is utter nonsense!

"During the time that Iberia (Spain and Portugal) was a Roman Colony, Jews settled in their cities. They had a written language and a religion with a very high code of ethics. The Romans, too, had a written language, but they were the conquerors, often enslaving people, levying taxes, and were generally hated by the Iberians. Many ambitious parents who wanted to improve the lot of their children had their sons tutored and later employed by Jews. Of course, they mingled freely and often converted to Judaism. That is the reason why so many Sephardic Jews look so much like Spaniards and Portuguese today.

"Due to the horrors of the inquisition around 1500 AD, quite a few Jews in Portugal had themselves baptized rather than let themselves be tortured and murdered. They fled their homeland to settle in many northern European cities, including Hamburg over the objection of the Lutheran clergy. They brought with them important trade connections and gave the city a powerful boost in commerce with the lucrative Mediterranean trade. They also reverted to Judaism.

"About a century later, German Jews from South and Central Germany, settled just west of Hamburg in Altona. Altona, Hamburg's immediate neighbor in Schleswig-Holstein, was then ruled by the much more tolerant Count of Schauenburg and later by the equally tolerant Danish Kings. Those nobles needed cash. They charged the Jews protection money annually.

"Eventually they settled in Hamburg, even though the Lutheran clergy and the legislature often harassed them. For many years the Jews of Portuguese and those of German descent had separate congregations, but with time they integrated. Refugees from pogroms in Slavic countries swelled their numbers until they were about one percent of the city's population. The freedom the Jews enjoyed here in Hamburg and also in neighboring Prussia for the last two centuries, erased cultural differences more and more. Intermarriage between Lutheran and Jewish partners has become increasingly commonplace."

# *D.S. HAMBURG* REVISITED

It was almost exactly a year since I had sailed on the *D.S. Hamburg* to New York. The beautiful passenger liner was in port. I went on board and to the cabin where I had slept. The bunks were still in the same place but everything else was different. It was so clean, it sparkled. When I called it home, none of us had ever thought of cleaning the tiny cabin, except just sweeping it a little bit. Now a picture of Hitler hung on the wall and on the polished table stood a little Nazi flag. There was a conspicuous absence of any pin up girls. One of my former ship mates, a mess room boy from the officers' mess, had accompanied me.

I pointed to the picture of the *Führer* and to the little swastika flag and asked:

"What is this? Didn't you tell me how you carried the red flag on the *'Moorweide'* during the Communist demonstration?"

"You crazy or something? Me?! Never, never! Carry a what?"

He was highly agitated. He looked about him to see, who might have heard this terrible accusation. He was happy to see me go. I was highly amused.

Many years later, in retrospect, my being amused showed how stupidly I failed to comprehend what enormous changes had taken place all around me. I had been so trusting that nothing could happen to him but a little teasing.

I failed to realize that his, as well as my own life, was at stake for talking against the Nazis. In those days I was still so naïve that I thought that nothing bad could happen to us by talking as we pleased. It had not yet sunk in that Hitler had created a Germany of fear. Half the people were afraid of losing their freedom, yes, even their lives. They were scared that someone might reveal that in their past, when there was freedom of expression, they had said something which was now forbidden.

The fear certainly permeated the Nazi Leadership, even Hitler himself. All photos showed him wearing an army type cap in public. After his fall, the American press revealed that this "cap" was really a helmet made of hardened steel in the shape of a cap. It was covered with cloth to look like a cap. That "cap" would indicate that he probably wore bullet proof armor under his clothing at all times when he appeared in public. He was scared!

# AGAIN TO ENGLAND AND BACK

I was still doing terrible badly at all three languages, German, English, and French at school, due to the fact that I never did sufficient home work. Papa hired a university student to tutor me. It helped for a short time, but Papa soon dismissed him when he found out that Mr. Cappel had joined the S.S., Himmler's feared elite. Papa tried to impress upon me how much more urgent it was becoming every day to learn English. He, himself, and Mama were taking English lessons. Their dictionary, which I still use quite frequently, was "the new revised edition of 1929 of *Langenscheidt.*" Mama, who had never studied any foreign languages, did not take the lessons too seriously and did very poorly. Papa who had learned Latin, Classical Greek and spoke French, did a lot better.

In those days I did not yet have the necessary self-discipline to study seriously on my own. I also was too naïve to be aware that I was flirting with death by keeping up my anti-Nazi remarks. At fifteen I lived in the shelter of my parents' comfortable home where all of my needs were always taken care of. The thought, that all that could change due to one remark, simply did not occur to me. My ignorance kept me from living in fear.

My father analyzed current events objectively and more clearly than anybody else I knew, and therefore, predicted the future correctly. He decided to send Toni and me to England again. As boys my age did not wear shorts in England, Mama bought me a suit with "Plusfours." They were very fashionable then. They were wide, baggy pants, buckled just below the knees and worn with knee socks.

Toni and I again took a boat to Grimsby. The British Grimsby Liners were under 10,000 tons and carried about 20 passengers. We traveled to London by train and to the Fitton residence by subway without incident. Henry's parents were very nice to me. Henry also had a brother my age, and several sisters. I noticed that blond Margret, a year or so younger than I, was particularly attractive. I was too shy to tell her so. Kathryn, a few years older than I, took me to museums, the National Gallery, and showed me much of London.

One day, in Oxford St., we were boarding one of the famous double-decker busses. As a well brought up German boy, I let all the ladies board first. When the conductor decided that the bus was full, he shut the door, rang a bell and the bus took off. I had no money on me. I had no idea how to get to Forest Hills, and from there to the street, the name of which I never could remember, where the Fittons lived. I ran after the bus right through the crowded streets, stepping on toes and pushing people aside. I finally caught up to the bus two blocks away. Fortunately for me, it was stuck in traffic.

I saw wonderful world famous attractions of London, including the National Gallery. I always loved paintings. The stay there was calm and relaxing. What did surprise me, however, was the strong pacifistic sentiment, and the lack of interest shown by the people as to what was happening in Germany. People, generally ignored the hostile attitude by Hitler towards Great Britain and her former allies.

Kathryn took me by train to Grimsby. The train stopped right on the wharf. Kathryn barely had time to say good-bye and go right back into the train. It took off almost right away.

The water level in the port is that of the North Sea at high tide and is kept that way by means of two locks as the tide runs out. Our voyage was to take two nights and a day. I was the first passenger on board the ship. After a short while two young men came. I called them Latsch and Bommel (Mutt and Jeff) in my mind, as one was tall and slim, the other short and fat.

Jeff asked the captain: "When shall we sail?"

"As soon as the other passengers arrive."

"We have time to go ashore and have a quick drink, right?"

"I suppose so."

They left their suitcases on board and took off.

At 7:00 p.m. all the other passengers arrived, and the steamer cast off punctually and moved between the two locks. Our deck was towering high over the town and the sides of the lock were far below us. It happened to be low ebb tide. As the water was drained from the lock at its sea end, the walls of the locks blocked our view. The roof of the bridge was about level with the top of the walls.

Suddenly Mutt and Jeff appeared on the top of the wall. They yelled vehemently that they wanted to come on board. After some shouting back and forth, a crew man threw a line to them. They tied the top rung of a ladder, which they had found on the wall, to the rope. The top of the ladder was hauled to the bridge, so that the ladder spanned the distance from the wall to the ship. It was just long enough.

Mutt started to crawl on all fours across the ladder. It started to bend ominously. After all, a ladder is not built to be used horizontally. And then, it did not look exactly new either. It had seen better days. As he neared the middle, it started to swing rhythmically. He had to stop several times to wait till the ladder stopped swinging. Everybody cheered loudly when he at last made it to the bridge.

Now it was Jeff's turn. He looked even more awkward than his partner. The yelling and predictions of doom grew correspondingly louder. One man offered bets that Jeff would fall. The poor "rolly polly" fellow must have sweated a pint of whiskey but he eventually made it.

I loved to stand right by the bow of the ship and watch it slice though the North Sea. I did that immediately after dinner. On my way to the bow I passed a group of Black men sitting on the bulkhead of the forward hold. They were apparently quartered at the very front of the ship. As I stood at the bow there were lots of jellyfish, but I did not see any other marine life. The gulls flew around the ship as usual, waiting for the mess room boys to dump the garbage overboard. One must remember that in those days plastics were not yet invented. Whatever was not consumed by the gulls or the fish, was very much biodegradable, or, if made of metal, or occasionally of ceramics, it quickly sank to the bottom.

Shortly after dark I decided to go to sleep. I planned to get up early in the morning and enjoy the wide expanse of the sea all around me. The cabin assigned to me had four bunks. I picked the upper one directly below the porthole. I washed myself, climbed into my bunk, and drew the curtain shut. I had hardly dozed off, when the door was flung open violently, and Mutt and Jeff appeared. Jeff immediately asked me if I wanted whiskey, gin, or beer. They both smelled as if they had seriously depleted the stock of the ship's bar. I had a difficult time convincing them that I did not want anything to drink. The pair told me that they needed a night cap, and they trouped off. Half an hour, or so, later the pair was back. Jeff, who always did all the talking, complained bitterly that they were "expelled" from the bar, as it was closing, and it was only 11:00 o'clock (23:00)!

They undressed. Mutt decided that he had to do some calisthenics right here in the tiny cabin. He did deep knee bends, swung his arms about and finally he took the other upper berth. Jeff was not one to be outdone! He decided to do pull ups, using the curtain rods as a high bar. At the very first pull up, the curtain rods of all four bunks, plus Jeff, landed on the floor, making quite a racket. Jeff gave me his expert opinion that the ship was built from inferior material. The rods should have supported his weight. He noted that the screws had pulled out of the wall. He got a large hair brush and proceeded to hammer the screws back into the holes from which they had been pulled. The effect was an enormous amount of noise which must have reverberated throughout the vessel but the curtain rods kept falling down.

Jeff wanted to find out a little about me: "Do you attend a public school?" (That is what the schools for the upper class are called in England)

"No," I said. "I am German and attend school in Hamburg."

*"Du Idiot!"* he scolded me, switching to German. "Here I go wracking my brain speaking English to you, and I could simply have spoken German with you all this time! This calls for a drink."

Mutt reminded him that the bar was closed.

At that moment the door opened and a tall pitch-black man walked in.

"What do you want?" Jeff demanded.

"This is my cabin," he answered.

He immediately started to undress and put on a long white night gown which made him look a little ridiculous. Jeff made all kinds of humorous remarks in German, of course, which, fortunately, the African did not understand, so he laughed along with us. He explained to us, in immaculate English, that he was leading a group of Africans from former German East Africa (Tanzania), to visit

Germany. The rest of the group slept at the bow near the crew's quarters, but he, as their leader, was assigned this cabin.

He praised, and demonstrated to us, how well one could shine one's shoes with spittle and newspaper. We thought that very amusing and the four of us had a good laugh. Suddenly Jeff remembered that he had not yet completed his exercises. So, he started to "bicycle", kicking the springs of Mutt's berth making the poor victim bob up and down under loud protests. The African, below me, must have enjoyed watching this, but he thought it much more fun, to emulate and outdo little Jeff. Subsequently he bounced me practically against the ceiling and almost out of my bunk to the floor. Naturally, I protested loudly and prolonged, but the man below me proved to have terrific strength and endurance. Fortunately, he did eventually quit before sunrise, and we all went to sleep.

In the morning, as I stood by the railing looking at the glistening sea, I got into a conversation with a lady. She told me that she and her husband had the cabin next to ours. She said that she had been contemplating to complaining about the noise we were making. But when she realized that we spoke German, she decided that she would not complain about a fellow countryman to a British officer. She implored me to use my influence to reduce the noise level for the coming night, and to go to sleep before 2:30 a.m. I knew that whiskey and beer had more power than I had, but I promised nonetheless.

Mutt and Jeff took advantage of the fact that the bar was open all day, so that they fell asleep as soon as they hit the sack. My friend from Africa came in shortly after they had gone to sleep. He told me that life was much better in the colony when he was a child, when it was under German rule. That was why his group wanted to see Germany. I was amazed. Did he not hear about all the nasty threats Hitler had made against all the, what he called, "inferior" races? For once I kept my mouth shut.

The summer holidays were over, and it was back to school for me. During break time, there in the school yard was Mutt. He was in the top class of the extension school (roughly second year of college in the U.S.). We laughed, recollecting the experiences of our trip back from England.

To my great surprise, I also met little Jeff one day on a street down town. He told me that he worked in an import and export firm. He also told me that he had written a letter of complaint to the Grimsby Line because they assigned a Negro to his cabin. That, I call nerve! He of all people. First he wrecked the cabin, then he kept most of the passengers and officers awake with his hammering against the steel wall of our quarters, and now he had the gall to complain!

# NAZIS HURT THE FAMILY

In our family the jokes about the "semi-literate Nazis" and their ideology sounded more and more contrived and hollow. In March of 1933 Hitler dismissed all the elected state governments and appointed *"Gauleiter"* (Governors) to reorganize the civil service under the watchful eyes of the *"Gestapo" (Geheime Staatspolizei* = Secret State Police). The husband of my father's sister, Uncle Leo Lippmann, lost his position of *"Staatsrat für Finanz"*, the ranking civil servant in the Finance Department of the *"Freie und Hansastadt Hamburg"* ("Free and Hansa City of Hamburg,") reporting only to the elected Senator for Finance. From the dawn of German history the "Free Cities of Germany" had been republics with very loose ties to any central government. The imposition of *"Gauleiter"* over those cities removed the word: "Free" in fact, even if not on paper, from those German cities for the time the Nazis constituted the federal government.

The Hansa League was formed in the 12th century for the mutual protection of the free cities of northern Germany. It expanded around the entire Baltic Sea and as far east as Novgorod in Russia. For a time, the Hansa was also very active in the North Sea trade and the over-land trade in northern Germany and what is now northern Poland. The power and influence of the Hansa steadily declined after the start of the 30 Years' War, 1618/48.

At the time of my childhood there were only three Hansa Cities left: Lübeck, which was once the "Queen of the Hansa," Hamburg, and Bremen. All flags of the Hansa Cities were red with white escutcheons.

While Aunt Anna and Uncle Leo were on vacation in northern Italy, the Nazi Government had my uncle indicted on bribery charges. The prosecutor advised the "Jew, Lippmann" not to return to German soil, as he would be arrested, sent to prison for the rest of his life and, at any rate, it would be too late to defend himself, since the trial had already begun.

Upon the receipt of this notification, Uncle Leo who valued his reputation and that of the government of which he had only recently been a respected member, more than his own life, rented a plane and had himself flown home to Hamburg to defend himself. Renting a plane was most unusual in 1933. Judges in those days still upheld the laws as they were on the books. Uncle Leo was acquitted, but it proved to be a Pyrrhic victory.

He concentrated his very considerable talents on writing the family history with exceedingly careful research. He also took over the financial management of the Jewish Congregation of Hamburg. It became his depressing task to bail out, or buy Jews out of concentration camps. Up to that time Uncle Leo, just like the rest of my father's family, had never been an active member of the Jewish Congregation. They were all "Free Thinkers" and great admirers of Charles Darwin, Ernst Heckel, and many other great biologists and humanists. The gradually increasing intolerance by the Nazi Government forced the Jews to try to help each other. A trickle of emigration by Jews and other anti-Nazis started.

One day Uncle Leo came to our house. He insisted that I be present. Usually Papa would send me out of the room when grown up visitors came.

"Paul, when Hindenburg [the venerated but aging (85) President of Germany] dies, Hitler will most certainly ignore the Treaty of Versailles and re-introduce conscription. Then they won't allow any German male out of the Country until he has served his stint in the armed forces. The French and the British will not stand still for that. The French have a million men under arms. There is no German force that could prevent the British Navy from sailing up the Elbe at this time, if the British want to. You don't want Arnold to fight for the Nazis, do you?"

"Certainly not! I'll write Herbert and Gerhard and ask if they will take Arnold. Leo, when are we going to leave?"

"We? Leave?! Never!"

"But Leo, did you read *Mein Kampf (My Fight)*?"

It was Germany's best seller. Hitler wrote that lengthy book while serving a prison term after his unsuccessful *Putsch* (uprising) in 1923.

Papa went on: "He states quite clearly that 'those who are not for me, are against me. And those who are against me must die!' He also states that all Jews and Communists must die! Die! Do you hear me? Die!"

"Nonsense, Paul, electioneering rhetoric. Once elected, even the most radical government will become conservative. Besides, we have laws and a state and a federal constitution which protect minorities. Furthermore, Hitler will never get an absolute majority. The next election he will be thrown out. What will happen then, if all the politicians of the opposition have left the Country? Who will be there to run the government? No, Paul. This is not Russia."

He looked calm and very confident. His opinion was by no means unique. Aunt Anna, Uncle Leo and many millions others who shared those views, paid with their lives for assuming that the Nazis were decent humans.

# CAPTIVATING THE YOUTH

Not long after summer recess in this eventful year of 1933, one day at school Mr. Unbehaun announced that a young recruiter from the Hitler Youth would come to talk to us in the next period. Unconstitutional! I was furious but I had to listen. The young man came into the class room in Hitler Youth uniform and spoke very enticingly about hiking, singing around camp fires, and camaraderie. He never mentioned politics.

Karl-Heinz Dannmeyer, who sat next to me, whispered: "He spoke well, didn't he?"

"I'll never join! Recruiting for a political movement in a school is against the law. I would never join a group which deliberately breaks the law."

"It's not for Reds and Commies anyway!"

I was enraged! Calling me a Red or a Commy! I did not know at that time that I was not even eligible to join, as all of my father's ancestors had been Jewish. It did not matter that my father had never joined any congregation, as he and his parents were atheistic humanists to the end of their lives.

Be that as it may, I was neither a Red nor a Commy. I gave Karl-Heinz a good jab with my elbow, so that he fell into the aisle. Mr. Unbehaun immediately gave me a "black mark". Three such marks and one has flunked out of high school! I was boiling inside. The break came just then.

We all went into the school yard. I challenged Karl-Heinz to a fight. He gave me a thorough beating but I unintentionally hit him on the Adams apple and he collapsed. Several boys grabbed him and me and made us stoop down among the milling crowd. That effectively hid us from the teacher who was looking for us to punish us for fighting.

We got back into the class room, sitting side by side somewhat disheveled. Mr. Unbehaun gave us one look. He could not help smiling.

"Shake hands," he said.

We did, and were friends again as we had been for a long time before.

Unfortunately, the rumor spread around school that I was a Red and a Commy, and therefore would not join the Hitler Youth. Mr. Unbehaun called in my father and advised him that he should not send me back to school after the end of the semester "for my own safety."

"Besides," he said, "Arnold will not be able to graduate, because he has not attained the necessary political maturity."

So, I would be out of high school half a year before I could graduate.

The last day before the fall recess arrived, I knew, it would be the last of my school days. It was my last English class.

Studienrat Unbehaun called on me: "von der Porten,"

"Yes, Sir."

"I have done you a lot of favors while you were in my class."

"Yes, Sir."

"You know that I shaved your 'D' in English to a 'C' last Easter so that you could be promoted to this class."

"Yes, Sir."

"I also shaved your grades in German to a 'C' and in French to a 'D' when you really deserved an 'F' for the same reason."

"Yes, Sir."

"Now I understand that you are leaving this Country to live in an English speaking country."

"Yes, Sir."

"Will you do me a great favor when you arrive there?"

"Yes, Sir!" I was happy at the thought that I would have the chance to repay my wonderful teacher in a small measure for all the favors he had done me.

"Will you please never tell anybody, ever, who taught you English."

# EMIGRATION

Papa sent me to a night school to learn typing and accounting. It felt strange, seeing all the other children going to school during the day, while I stayed home having nothing to do. Papa had written the letters to Herbert and Gerhard, just as he had told Uncle Leo that he would. Herbert had answered from New York that he could not take care of me, as Maria was expecting her first baby. Gerhard, on the other hand, promised that he would do all he could to help me. Toni and Henry had become the proud parents of Harald, December 3rd, 1931. Those three Fittons were getting ready to move to England.

My German passport, which I had used to travel to England, was still valid. There were no legal immigration restrictions against Germans in Jamaica. We went out to buy me six nice white suits, a sun helmet, new light underwear, white shoes, white socks, six long sleeve white shirts, and a tuxedo. I had all the trimmings for a rich plantation owner, except money. The maximum amount which anyone was allowed to take out of Germany was $M$ 100.oo ($25.oo). I had saved more than that out of my allowance. All money I had over the $M$ 100.oo I gave to Papa. It was not very much.

Not long after that, it was announced on the radio, that Hitler would make an important proclamation early Saturday morning, on the 14th of October. We listened. Hitler screamed at the world that the "Dictates of Versailles" were not worth the paper they were written on. In defiance of them, German troops were reoccupying the demilitarized zone of the Rhineland at that very moment. Germany was resigning from the League of Nations, which failed to fulfill its promises to treat all nations equally, effective immediately. Germany would not pay another Pfennig in reparations!

Papa was shaken. He tuned in Radio Paris. I had studied French for three and a half years as my second foreign language. I could understand most of what the announcer had to say. Papa's French was quite good and he understood every word:

"Here at the *Place de Concord* the people stand shoulder to shoulder. As far as one can see down the boulevards there are people. There is no room for vehicles anywhere. Now I'll hold the microphone out of the window of the studio. Listen to the crowd!"

"*Au Berlin, au Berlin!* (To Berlin, to Berlin!)"

Papa said: "That means war! You are not going to fight for those Nazi swine. You will leave for Jamaica today!"

In those days Germany did not yet have an air force, artillery, nor even a machine gun in compliance with the Treaty of Versailles. Hitler had timed his bluff very shrewdly. The French Forces outnumbered the German Army 10 : 1 and they were much better equipped than any other military in the world. The French Government, however, was in a struggle for its survival, and could not afford to offend the large block of pacifist voters. A preemptive strike could possibly precipitate the fall of the Government and let the opposition win.

The British Fleet was the largest and the most modern in the world. It could easily have sailed up the German rivers. Their powerful naval guns could certainly have silenced any German opposition. England had, however, a very pacifistic Tory Government at that time. The visionary right wing of the Tories, led by Winston Churchill, was vocal, but lacked numbers. On the other hand, if the Labor Party could woo some of the conservative voting pacifists over to their side, Mr. Baldwin's Tory Government would fall.

The state censored newspapers and radio reports were too unreliable, so that Papa could not have evaluated any of this. Tearfully Mama started packing my new things into a large steamer trunk. Papa and I walked to the corner of Böttgerstr. and Mittelweg. We could not get across the Mittelweg, where his car was garaged. Thousands of S.A. (Storm Troupers), Hitler Youths, women's and girls' auxiliaries, bugle corps, drum and fife bands were marching and singing their blood thirsty songs. They promised to kill all Jews, beat the French, punish England, and eliminate the Communists in Russia all at once. Lots of banners waved and flags fluttered. They walked twelve abreast. They seemed to come from the Dammtor railroad station marching to the City Park. The only weapons they had, were little replicas of bayonets with swastikas on their hilts and "Blood and Honor" engraved on the blades. They all seemed in great spirits but they certainly were no match for regular soldiers.

Papa said: "Those fools! They are like cattle which does not realize, when it marches to its own slaughter, and they are singing happily, too!"

We turned around, and walked from the Böttgerstr. to the Magdalenenstr., Alte Raabenstr., the beautifully landscaped Alster Ufer (Bank of the Alster) across the Lombards Bridge to the Hotel Atlantic. There was the branch of the British Cooks Travel Bureau. We bought a one way ticket by rail to Holland, by ferry across the Channel, and by train to London. Papa telegraphed his Uncle Ernst Goldschmidt in London, to meet me at the train.

We walked home and had our last meal together in Hamburg. Papa drove us to the Dammtor Station. There were Mama, Papa, Irma and I. The two Lachmann girls who lived across the street from us, Ricarda 13 and Edna 11, had come by bicycle. I had a crush on Ricarda but I was too shy to tell her. Somehow she must have known.

At 2:00 p.m. (14:00) the train pulled in. Papa admonished me to talk to no one, until I had crossed the Dutch border at 10:00 p.m. (22:00) that evening. The train pulled out. Papa all smiles, Mama all tears, all waved, and I sat back.

There were a very pleasant looking elderly couple sitting across from me. We were the only ones in the compartment. No one said a word. At the Netherlands border, first German, then Dutch officials checked my passport. The German official asked me how much money I had. He did not search me, nor did he check my trunk, which was in the baggage car. When the train pulled out, I exchanged some pleasantries with my fellow passengers.

I was dead tired when the train finally arrived at Flushing *(Vlissingen)*. I boarded the Channel ferry. I had a small cabin all to myself near the stern. The passage was very stormy. The steel storm cover was locked tightly over the port hole. The bow and the stern of the vessel were being submerged alternately. Every time the bow dipped deep down into the waves, most of the propeller at the stern came out of the water and shook the ship most violently. It would have been impossible for an ordinary person to go to sleep, but my day had been a long and eventful experience. I eventually went to sleep.

When I woke up it was bright daylight. I was in England. The train was waiting alongside the ship. Before I knew it, I was in London. A liveried chauffeur spotted me. He told me that Uncle Ernst had sent him to pick me up.

# I HAVE TO BE AN ADULT

In Hamburg I had been quite used to luxury but I had never seen as elaborate a house as my Granduncle Ernst Goldschmidt's. The house was in Kensington, near the center of the city. In the evenings my tuxedo was laid out on my bed and the cuff links were in the cuffs of my dress shirt. I had to dress for dinner. My father's cousins, Nelly and Dorothy wore beautiful long evening dresses, William, Cecyl, and Granduncle Ernst wore tuxedos. A servant stood behind each chair, and pushed it in as one sat down, and pulled it out as one got up. The dishes, table silver and glasses were of the finest quality, and the dinner itself was of a great variety. After dinner my Granduncle took the elevator upstairs where I was taught how to play bridge. I liked that very much. In the days the chauffeur took me sight-seeing.

Despite all the luxury surrounding me and being treated as an adult, I was very anxious to continue on my journey to Jamaica. After about two weeks in London, an Elders & Fyffs banana boat was found that had space to take me to Kingston.

On October 31, 1933, a boat train took me to Swansea, Wales. It was obviously a coal mining town and coal port. Coal from the mines made high conical hills very near the houses and the port facilities. The fresh snow made a stark contrast to the black hillsides and dark houses.

The first snow storm of the season howled through the riggings at a very high pitch whine. Though the small empty banana boat was tied firmly to the pier, it rubbed with ominous noisy groans against the stout wooden pilings. I was assigned a single cabin. The captain had obviously waited for the boat train to arrive, as the ship cast off almost immediately after I had come on board. My big steamer trunk fitted perfectly under my bunk.

Just as we were getting under way the dinner bell rang. The dining room was half empty. Only the officers and engineers came for dinner. I was the only passenger who showed up. I was seated at a table for two. Opposite me sat a young officer. The anti-slide boards were up at the edges of each table. They were certainly needed. They prevented the dishes, glasses, and table silver from sliding to the floor.

The young officer talked of nothing but storms he had been through and about sea sickness. We were still in the bay between Cornwall and Wales, but the steamer rolled from side to side making everything that was not nailed down slide all across the table. The meal tasted as if everything had been made of raw, dry flour. I forced myself to eat every last crumb. I did not want that English officer to know that I was feeling rotten. I had to show him that I was as good a seaman as he was.

After an eternity the dinner was over and I ordered coffee. No one had told me that coffee was the worst thing to take when one felt nauseated. I did not suspect that it was the coffee which made me feel even worse, so I ordered another one. I had to get up, go upstairs on deck and get some fresh air! By this time the boat had passed Lands End and the waves banged fiercely against the hull.

The captain got up and walked toward me, shook my hand and said: "Young man you deserve the Iron Cross." (A German war decoration.) There I was, trying to be as un-German as I could possibly be, speaking my very best English on a British ship, sailing from a British port to a British Colony, trying to be more British than the British, and he tells me that Germany should be proud of me! I had no time to answer. I had to go up to get some fresh air!

As I opened the door of the mess room to the stair case and the passage to the state rooms of the passengers, the most horrible stench of sea sickness hit me. It was contagious. I raced up the stairs, opened the door to the lee side and made for the railing. I had eaten my dinner to feed the fish. I felt much better now in the ice cold fresh air and an empty stomach, but it was impossible to face that reeking passageway again.

The ship was standing straight into the howling west wind. After walking up and down on the lee side amidships holding on to the rail, I decided to venture to the bow. Ropes had been fastened from the midships' superstructure to the forecastle. I reached my destination safely as the stern dipped deep under water and consequently, the bow was lifted high.

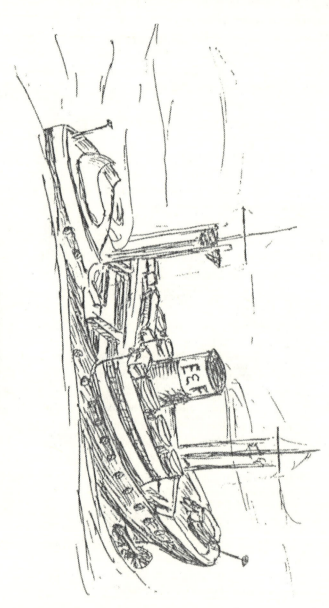

BANANA BOAT TO JAMAICA

Due to the storm, our vessel was off its prescribed course and headed straight for Ireland. That required a bow look out. The poor man was frightened when I suddenly appeared behind him. He yelled: "Duck!" There was a strong slanting iron protection in front of the anchor winches. He grabbed me, and we ducked under it, as a big wave washed over it. He had on an oil coat, high rubber boots and a Sou'wester on his head. That kept him dry, but I was pretty wet. I waited till the bow started to rise again and I made my way back to midships without any further incident.

At the stern there is a little shed. It houses paints and all sorts of maintenance gear. As the stern started to rise, I rushed down to the after bulkhead holding on to the ropes, and quickly climbed on top of the monkey isle, as the roof of the little shed was called. As the storm made the ship into a see-saw, the little shed was truly an island with me on top for a little while. A wave washed all around it. I felt good now, no more seasickness. It was about 2:00 a.m. and I was ready to brave the passage to my stateroom.

I slept till almost noon the next morning. It was too late for breakfast. At lunch I was again the only passenger to show up. The captain gave me a big smile, and the young officer opposite me talked about India. From then on, I had every meal, but I never saw another passenger until we passed the Azores six days out of Swansea. Though it was a bright warm day, one could hardly make out the islands, they were so far away.

The Azores marked the midpoint of our voyage. There were about ten passengers. I only talked to four. There were two English ladies who lived in Jamaica. They were dressed completely in white. They were fully occupied protecting their wide brimmed straw hats against the breeze. They had pleasant smiles and they looked very nice. We chatted a little bit about unimportant matters. There was a black Jamaican who told me that he was on his last leg home from Africa. He had some unpleasant experiences in Africa and was looking forward to going home.

The friendliest was an elderly Cockney mechanic. He told me that he had been hired by Masterton Ltd. in Kingston to repair motor cars. He, like myself, had never been to Jamaica. He claimed that the climate in London was detrimental to his health.

He hoped that he would feel better in Kingston. One glance at his furrowed face confirmed his story. He was skinny and seemed worn out. He told me to look him up, once he had settled in Kingston. All the passengers looked, as we would have said in Germany: "Like green cheese and spittle." They all showed that they had lain in their bunks for six days, surrendering to seasickness.

Our first port of call was Santa Marta in Colombia. I had never before seen such poverty. We were driven through slum in a taxi convoy to a little museum in this dusty little town to see a golden container enclosing the heart of Símon Bólivar. I had never even heard of him. A guide explained to me that Bólivar was the revolutionary hero who liberated South America from the Spanish at the time, when Spain needed all its soldiers in the Napoleonic wars, and when its once powerful navy had been destroyed off Cape Trafalgar by the British under Admiral Nelson.

The capsule containing the heart was quite ornate, and represented a striking contrast to all the barefoot, practically naked, little children playing happily in the streets in front of dilapidated huts. Many European sailors had obviously left souvenirs, as some of those reddish-brown children were blond, had blue eyes, and had a somewhat lighter skin color. The heat was most oppressive. Air conditioning did not exist yet in those days.

Bananas had been loaded, while we went sight seeing. All steel parts on the outside of the ship were too hot to touch. I was glad when we got under way again. The sea breeze felt refreshing as we headed north across the blue Caribbean Sea with flying fishes shooting out of the water. What a wonderful life!

# JAMAICA, A STRANGE ARRIVAL

I awoke about 4:00 o'clock. The ship's engines were silent. I looked out of the port hole. We were alongside a pier. It would have been pitch dark outside if it had not been for the flood lights from the ship. There was an open shed with tons of bananas. A powerful barefoot Black man, dressed in dirty pants and a dirty sleeveless undershirt, lifted stem after stem on top of the heads of women walking by him at a very fast pace. They never slowed down as they received their loads. They never even lifted their hands to adjust or hold the stems, nor even missed a swing of their arms. The banana blossoms stuck out in front on a long thin stem and the thick stem, from which the bunch once hung, stuck out in the back.

After the women had carried the bananas a few steps they passed another powerful man. He had a glistening, two foot long machete in his right hand. As the women approached, they held their arms straight down at their sides, while the man chopped off the blossoms in the front and the stem in the back with two quick and mighty blows. The women never slowed down. They had such perfect balance, they had no need to adjust their loads. None wore shoes. Their dresses ended below their knees and clung to their bodies. They wore a ring of sack cloth on their heads. Sweat glistened on their faces, arms and legs. They walked briskly past a little container, pulled a chain which rang a little bell and released a little coin into the women's hands. They quickly put the coins into their pockets and walked past a gang plank. There each woman would pick up the front of the stem and a man would grab its back. They never disturbed the burlap on her head, nor did it slow her down as she walked back to the shed. The man passed the stem from hand to hand up the gang plank as men stood in a row all the way to the gaping hold. An officer of the ship, dressed very neatly in a white uniform, stood above the entire scene. He took a tally of the stems as they disappeared into the bowels of the vessel.

I put on my house coat and walked into the mess hall. A lone steward was cleaning it.

"Where are we?"

"We are in Bowden, Sir."

"I thought, we were going to Kingston, Jamaica."

"Kingston is 30 miles west of here, Sir. You can go back to sleep, Sir."

I went back to watch the loading for a while and soon fell asleep again.

It was Wednesday morning, November 15, 1933. I had breakfast on board and went ashore on the railway pier in Kingston. My trunk was placed next to me. I waited anxiously for Gerhard. The sun was hot. At last he arrived in a bread van.

Gerhard helped me load the trunk into the van. The meeting was quite unemotional as if we had been together all along. He told me that he had some work to do after he took me home.

We drove through, what was in those days, quite a nice part of the town: Port Royal St., Princess St., Harbour St., King St., South Parade. There was a well kept park and a statue of Queen Victoria, East Parade, East Queen St., Victoria Ave. There the asphalt pavement ended. We drove north on Elleston Rd. The gravel surface was washed out here and there. We turned east on Vineyard Rd. At its end we turned a short distance south on Deanery Rd. then east again. Gerhard told me that it had rained for three weeks without let up, as a hurricane had passed the Island. We came to a poverty stricken neighborhood. Sewer water from washing laundry, showers, and kitchen utensils, was running in the gutters of Cumberland Lane in Franklin Pen. Later I found out that many neighborhoods were called, "Pen."

We stopped at a corner with a "Chinaman Shop." Just about all groceries in Jamaica were run by Chinese owners. Gerhard tooted the horn and two gates, made of eight foot (2.50 m) high corrugated iron sheets, opened to the left of the grocery. We drove into a yard.

Under a shed were five more Durant vans just like the one we had arrived in. They were all marked: "Meyer's Vienna Bakery." On the opposite side from the gate there was a little hut. It was made of "wattle and daub," strong vertical sticks with flexible sticks woven between them and plastered in and outsides with cement. The roof was thatched with coconut palm fronds. The entire edifice stood on several concrete supports, about two feet (60 cm) above the ground. There were two sets of two concrete steps, the flooring

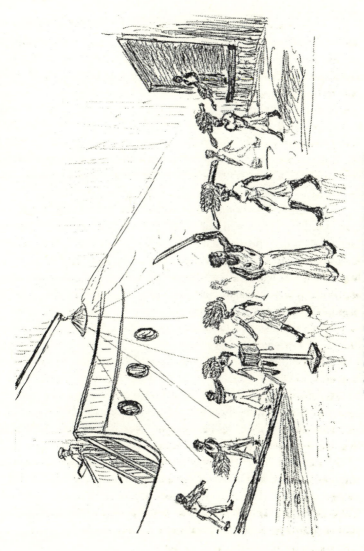

LOADING BANANAS AT PORT MORANT

was another step higher, and two doors led to the two rooms. This was home.

There was a door between the two rooms. My room was about seven by five feet (2.20 m x 1.50 m). Gerhard's was seven by seven feet. There was an iron bed with a coir (the fluffed up fibers of a coconut husk) mattress in each room. In Gerhard's was a wardrobe. My trunk fitted under my bed. That prevented the spring from sagging too much. There was a rack with coat hangers and a chair. I could touch the opposite wall while I lay in my bed.

A French hung window was next to the door in Gerhard's room. Along the longest side of the hut, where the steps were, there was a little yard the length of, and slightly wider than the house. In the south east corner was an outhouse, and next to it was a shower consisting of a bent half inch iron pipe with a globe valve. The enclosures and the doors were all made of corrugated iron.

We were hardly home, when it started to rain. I had never seen rain like that. One could not see 30 ft (10 m), it poured so heavily. Our yard, toilet and shower area were quickly inundated under at least six inches (15 cm) of water. Gerhard told me that it had rained like that for at least the last three weeks now and that many roads and bridges were washed out. The song "Stormy Weather" was the rage of the time as I soon found out.

Meals were served on a large verandah on the opposite side of the yard of where the vans were parked, in front of Mr. and Mrs. Meyer's room. Heinrich Meyer, a Swiss, was the main partner of Meyer's Vienna Bakery and Restaurant. Besides this fairly large bakery, Meyer's house, another house and Gerhard's and my compound, there were three restaurants and bread delivery routes.

The first evening neither Gerhard nor Mr. Meyer were there. We were thirteen people of twelve different nationalities at the table, needing four different languages to converse: German, English, French, and Spanish. Only the Swiss were represented by more than one. The only woman at the table was Mrs. Meyer, a Colombian. A Black servant in a crisp blue dress and a white, starched cap served a very good dinner. I turned in early.

GERHARD'S AND MY RESIDENCE IN JAMAICA

I was worried. Gerhard had quit his very well paying job as first clerk (office manager) at Tai Ten-Quee, and had gone into business with Heinrich Meyer and Gustav Muth, another Swiss. It seemed obvious that there was not much money around.

# MAILING LETTERS HOME

The first time I went to London I was twelve. I decided to go to the post office alone and buy a stamp to send a letter home to Hamburg. I asked for a one and a half penny stamp (3 cents). The post mistress at the window gave me two stamps, one for a penny and one for a half penny. I should have been satisfied and should have just taken the two stamps and stuck them on the envelope, but I wanted a single stamp worth one and a half pennies. The conversation became very frustrating, as I could not get through to her. Finally, she spread out a lot of different stamps, and let me choose. I picked out a 1½ penny stamp.

She said: "Ow, a three 'ai p'nce!"

That is what I was supposed to have asked for.

Now I was in Kingston, and I certainly remembered how to buy stamps. I went to the post office.

I told the post mistress at the window: "I would like a three 'ai p'nce stamp."

"Sar?" she asked me.

"I would like a three 'ai p'nce stamp."

I do not remember the details of the lengthy conversation which ensued. For one, I spoke my very best Oxford English, and as she got more and more excited, she lapsed into broad Jamaican dialect which was unfamiliar to me at that time. The upshot was that the poor frustrated lady laid out a lot of different stamps, just like her counterpart had done in London three and a half years earlier. I picked a 1½ penny stamp.

She said: "Oh, quatty!"

That is what I was supposed to have asked for. It is sometimes difficult to realize, that what people speak in dear old England and what they speak in Jamaica is supposed to be the same language.

The quatty is a tiny silver coin, marked 1½d (pence.) It is about one quarter the size and weight of a six pence or a U.S. dime. It is a museum piece, as it has not been minted for at least one century. One and a half pence was still called a quatty. Half a quatty, 3 farthings, was still called a gill until independence, when the Island adopted the decimal system with the Jamaican dollar.

# LIFE AT THE BAKERY

All the Swiss, including Mr. Meyer, had learned French as their second language at school. They had left home because they did not want to serve in the Swiss Army. All of them had lived in South America for a while and spoke fluent Spanish. Residing in Jamaica they had to learn English. All four Swiss spoke German, French, Spanish and English very well. The lone Swede could not talk to any one as he spoke nothing but Swedish, which no one could understand, so he was made the bookkeeper. Figures are the same in all languages. He had missed his ship in a drunken stupor. That was the way most had found shelter and work at the bakery.

There was also a Texan whose drawl I could not understand. He was marooned here as he had been a "bootlegger". That was the accepted name for those who smuggled alcoholic beverages into the United States before the recent repeal of prohibition. Unfortunately for him, the police still wanted him in his country. He was one of the van drivers.

The Russian, a former cadet under the Czar and later a follower of the Karenski Revolution, spoke good French and could converse with the Swiss. Arkadi Kusnietsoff had fled with some smugglers across the frozen Baltic Sea from Kronstadt, (the port of St. Petersburg), to Finland when Lenin overthrew Karenski. He had fled from there to Germany as the Finns sent Russians back to Russia if they were caught. The Communist Government under Lenin had forced that condition on the weak Finns. In Germany, too, a revolution raged at that time. Some Russians helped him to get a job on a ship. Many years later, he wound up in Jamaica and at the bakery. He played very good chess and after delivering his bread and cakes, he usually beat me at that game.

It rained for three weeks straight, practically uninterrupted. I was very homesick. I actually cried sometimes when I was alone. All my clothes grew mildew. The thatch of the roof which was also my ceiling was wet and dripped here and there.

One day, after it had stopped raining, I decided to take the tram car (trolley in American) to King Street all by myself. It was my first outing in Kingston. I put on my white shirt, white suit, white socks and white shoes. I put on a blue tie and donned my brand new sun helmet. I must have really looked like a throw-back from one of Rudyard Kipling's stories. I felt very superior to the rest of the passengers on the tram car. They did not wear such elegant clothing.

At the bottom of King Street, the end of the line, was Victoria Market. The tram had eight rows of seats. On the first four rows market women with baskets were not allowed. They climbed in, to sit on any of the last four rows, leaving the first four empty. I sat at the end of the seventh row. I had no idea why all those women with those huge baskets did not occupy the first few rows but insisted on crowding around me. There was hardly any space left when one of the fattest, sweat dripping women shoved her big basket against my legs and said with the sweetest possible voice:

"Move over na me love."

The impertinence! an outrage! calling me her love! She then proceeded to climb up the three steps and with her fat sit-upon, shoved me over to the next market woman, squeezing me between the two of them. The conductor, collecting my two pence fare, suggested that I move to one of the nearly empty benches in front. That I did, though I felt that the market women should not have defeated me!

On my 16th birthday, only 15 days after my arrival in Jamaica, Rudolf Hess, the chief pastry cook, baked me a beautiful birthday cake. He decorated it with a coconut palm and a boy climbing it. The next morning I had a job. I tallied the breads and cakes at 3:30 a.m. as they were loaded into the vans. They started to leave at 4:00 a.m. All baking was done at night.

Gerhard worked far too hard. I had to wake him at 6:30 a.m. He would put a Royal Blend cigarette between his fingers and go back to sleep. The cigarette would burn down, hurt his nicotine stained fingers, and he would jump out of bed, light another, take a shower and get dressed. After a quick breakfast he would go to work. He seemed to do most of the work. His partners, "Henry" Meyer and "Gushti" Muth, especially the latter, seemed to spend more time drinking and chasing girls.

Fridays were pay days. I got four shillings ($ 1.oo). I do not know what the others got. They all went drinking and spent their

111

money on girls in the bars. Gerhard warned me to stay away from girls. "They are all diseased, and if you do not know how to protect yourself, you will get horribly ill." I was terribly scared and followed Gerhard's orders. I was wondering how all those men could work so hard all week, then go out one night and throw away all their hard earned cash so stupidly and then feel sick with a hang over the next morning to boot!

I often went swimming. Sirgani's beach was only about two miles (3 km) away from the bakery. It cost six pence (12½ ¢) to swim there. There were cabins for men on the right and for women on the left. There was a shark fence enclosing about 150 x 150 ft (50 x 50 m). The shark fence consisted of coconut trunks rammed into the bottom of the harbor about two feet (60 cm) apart. The trunks of the coconut palm rot very slowly in sea water and last a very long time. A wide plank was nailed to join all the tops. It provided a wide enough space to walk on or fish. Six pence was a lot of money for me then but swimming was the only luxury I could afford. The two mile walk from Sirgani's was all up hill, and when I arrived home I was all sweaty again. A bicycle would have been a great help. I missed mine in Hamburg.

I wrote my parents and after several letters back and forth, Papa sent me my old bicycle and a letter bitterly complaining about all the inconvenience I had caused him. He had to have it packed for ocean transport and have it sent to the Horn Line to ship it to Jamaica. At that time he had already decided that he would emigrate. He knew that he would not be allowed to take money out of Germany. It would have been very easy for him to have ordered a new bicycle from a store and have it delivered to me in Kingston. It would have cost him nothing as he would not be allowed to take any cash out of Germany.

My legs, especially my ankles, were badly bitten by mosquitoes. Unfortunately, I scratched them open and both ankles became very badly infected. I eventually learned not to scratch and let them itch. So the infections eventually healed but they left scars for the rest of my life.

# THE CONTINENTAL CLUB

Gerhard imported two couples of musicians from Hamburg. The three partners started a beautiful night club and restaurant on the south east corner of King and Harbour Streets. The opening night was packed. Alcohol and money flowed in rivers. Unfortunately, the three owners got hopelessly drunk, and the proceeds were stolen by the waiters. Gerhard hardly ever drank alcohol. The few times where he should have remained absolutely sober, however, he followed the crowd and got drunk.

The Continental Club became very popular and should have soon paid for itself but it had bad flaws. The bar, the engine driving such an establishment, was located directly over the kitchen. It was poorly ventilated and consequently extremely hot. It was also too small. The saxophone player from Hamburg, his wife, the pianist, and the violinist, especially the latter, were very good. People came specially just to hear him. Unfortunately, his wife who played the drums, was a dud.

The management was very poor. Gerhard, then 24, ran the day operations of the bakery and did the accounting. He worked many long hours. Mr. Meyer and Gushti Muth were supposed to run the night club. Both were very heavy drinkers and Gushti had a habit of getting fresh with the ladies. That foolish behavior lost many of the more affluent customers. Credit was readily extended, even to dead beats. All three owners bought themselves second-hand cars. Gerhard purchased a Plymouth Roadster. That was a two-seater with a dickey seat which could fold away.

At first I had the job of giving out leaflets at the tourist boats. Arkadi became the bar tender. He was very good looking and consequently very popular with the ladies. The bar was too much for one person, especially when that person would rather flirt with the women than serve the waiters and keep a record of the cash. I was made cashier of the bar. As Arkadi took off with the sister of Mr. Meyer's mistress more and more often, I was in fact the bartender. Meyer ignored his legal Colombian wife in a shameful way.

There was one customer who seemed very friendly. He went

by the name of Berlini. Gerhard warned me that this fellow from Odessa was wanted by the police all over Europe. "Never leave the cash register out of sight when he was around." Gerhard also hired a German-Jewish refugee by the name of Loewenstein as the night cashier for the restaurant section downstairs on the ground floor. I often saw Loewenstein talking to Berlini late at nights, so I warned Loewenstein to be careful and not to trust Berlini.

A few days later at 4 a.m., just after closing time, when I was alone in the bar counting the cash receipts, Berlini rushed into the bar. He brandished a revolver, cursed me, and threatened to blow my brains out if I should ever dare to say anything against him again. He was so furious and was shaking so much that I was afraid that his gun would go off due to his being so agitated. I was scared stiff, and was trembling all over. For once I kept my mouth shut.

Soon afterwards Loewenstein quit. A few months later Badetscher, the very personable Swiss and second pastry cook who spoke Spanish perfectly, showed me a Havana newspaper with a photo of Berlini and Loewenstein. They had been arrested for uttering counterfeit U.S. dollars. It then dawned on me that Berlini had a key to the cash register and could turn its counter back. He and Loewenstein skimmed off the profits of the restaurant sales for all the time that Loewenstein worked there. I heard that every Havana prison was a living hell. Still, I could not bring myself to feel sorry for the two.

Henry Meyer and Gushti Muth collected a bunch of cronies about themselves and went drinking a lot, away from the Club. Meyer also took money out of the registers, and set them back so that Gerhard would not know. Gerhard never had enough money to pay the bills though the restaurant downstairs, and the nightclub upstairs were very popular.

Gerhard introduced me to a very vivacious, petite and cheerful young brunette lady. Her name was Dorrie Eisenmenger. She was from Offenbach on Main. I liked her right away. Gerhard said that he wanted to marry her. He did propose. He told me that she was homesick and wanted to go back to Germany. She would not want to live in Jamaica permanently, so she would not marry him.

Gerhard was not one to show his feelings. I could see, however, that he was hurt when she went home to the Reich. Of course, she remembered Germany before the Nazis ruled. She could not have imagined that the attitudes of the people of Offenbach had changed so dramatically. When she left years ago, her hometown was part of the British occupation zone. When she returned hate was preached effectively by all the media against everybody except the Nazis.

People who have left home for a while, remember it as much more desirable than it actually is. Persons who left their country for a long period will have changed drastically and will find their former home a strange place. What the homecoming traveler is subconsciously really looking for, is his or her innocent youth. The matured traveler will not find it and will be disillusioned. Gerhard told me this many years later from his own experience. I have found it to be absolutely true. I have known many people who have spent all their savings traveling back and forth trying to find the feeling of "being at home".

Each night, when the Continental Club closed at 4 a.m., I stayed on as watchman and opened the door for three cleaning women who came at 5 a.m. At 7 a. m. when the staff arrived to prepare to serve the breakfast customers, I rode my bicycle the two miles (3km) home in the broiling sun.

Christmas, 1933, at the time when the Club was packed, and the owners should have made a lot of money, the three of them got hopelessly drunk. I stayed at the cash register for 54 hours. The four hours that the place was closed, I slumped over the counter and slept. It was a disgrace that none of the owners, including Gerhard, could discipline himself enough to remain sober, schedule relief for the cashier and watch the money.

There were two very important customers, Mr. Kelly, the American Consul, and his cronies and Mr. Deters, the unofficial German Consul, and his cronies. They were good buddies. They came into the bar almost every night and drank.

They insisted that I should drink with them. I had a Gordons Gin bottle half full of water and a White Horse Whiskey bottle half full of tea under the counter for just such occasions. After all, I had just turned sixteen and was very skinny. Unfortunately, they soon caught on and insisted that I pour for myself from the same bottle as the one I used to pour their drinks. That was how it came about that

I consumed much more alcohol than was safe for my skinny little body. Nevertheless, I was always careful not to get drunk. I could always write down my receipts, close the cash register at 4 a.m. and supervise the cleaning crew till 7 a.m. I never fell asleep at work.

One morning, riding my bicycle home, I collapsed on Cumberland Lane. Some women dragged me home. I was delirious for a week. The doctor told Gerhard that it was acute alcohol poisoning. I took over the cash register downstairs for the kitchen. I never took another drink for many years.

I told Gerhard that Meyer kept on taking money out of the cash register without accounting for it. There was a confrontation and I had to leave the bakery. Gerhard rented a room for me in a house owned by two spinsters by the name of de Casseries on Connoley Ave. Breakfast was included, and I was to go to the restaurant for lunch but I never got any money or supper. Consequently I was always very hungry. I did not know how to get myself a job. I was too despondent even to go swimming. I hoped that Gerhard would have some time even to come to see me. He never did.

The four German musicians went back to Germany. Meyer's Vienna Bakery, Restaurant, and Continental Club went broke. Meyer, his wife, and Rudolf Hess, the chief pastry cook, went to Costa Rica.

Gushti, who seemed to have some money of his own, had a very pretty Cuban girlfriend, Luci Cantero. She worked in the American Consulate as a secretary.

Gerhard was saddled with all the debt. It was very unfair. He had been the only one who had really worked very hard. Meyer and Muth had done all the carousing with the money they had skimmed off the cash registers behind Gerhard's back. They were the ones who caused the collapse of the potentially lucrative business. Gerhard trusted them and was too inexperienced in life to recognize the danger in time to, either get out, take over the restaurant part of the business and let them keep the bakery, or vice versa, or kick them out if that had been possible.

# LIFE WITHOUT DIRECTION

I found a job with Mr. Abner, an American. He had opened an American style soda fountain in King Street. I became a "soda jerk" at 10 shillings (U.S. $2.50) per week. That was the same amount as I had been getting at the Continental Club for three times as many working hours. It was a terrible job. I kept telling myself that any money earned honestly was decent. My fellow workers were very low class, and the toilet facilities were abominable. I stuck it out for a while. What else could I do?

Gerhard was hired by the Jamaica Public Service Co., Ltd. as a salesman on salary plus commission. He was to sell appliances and anything else that would use electricity. It turned out to become a very good job. We moved to the lower floor in a house on Elleston Rd.

Gerhard was able to get me a job as a salesman's apprentice at the DaCordova Agency. Mr. Levy used me as a watchman of his office when he traveled around the country. He did that most of the week. I learned next to nothing. It was most boring. The pay was no better than before. The money I earned went for clothing. A pair of shoes cost 25% more than my week's pay. I was required to look presentable. I did not have enough money to buy any lunch, so I was hungry most of the days.

From the bakery days Gerhard employed an old servant by the name of Eva. Christmas, 1934, was approaching. Gerhard was invited to the country for the holidays by some friends. He left me with enough very good food. Eva took off and stole the food for the holidays and disappeared for the Christmas. I had nothing to eat for three days. I could not get out of bed. Every time I sat up I became so dizzy that I fell back. That is how Gerhard found me on December 27th, 1934. When one is broke, a foreigner, and especially a German, one has no friends.

# GOALS APPEAR IN THE FAR DISTANCE

Early in 1935, Gerhard found me a job as a refrigeration apprentice at the Jamaica Public Service Co., Ltd. I had to work 54 hours per week, plus all the overtime the service manager felt like giving me, for six shillings (U.S. $1.50) per week. It certainly was not much pay, but at least I worked for a reputable firm for the first time and learned something useful. The job seemed to have a future. Gerhard sold a lot of Kelvinator refrigerators. I saw to it that they went out in the best possible condition.

The most common defect on the Kelvinators was the seal leak. In those days the sealed unit, where the motor and the compressor were in the same sealed enclosure, was not yet invented. The compressor was belt driven by a 1/6 or a 1/4 horse power repulsion start motor. The crankcase of the compressor was under vacuum when the unit was running. A bronze seal, working against a shoulder on the shaft, was supposed to prevent air from seeping into the compressor. The seal also prevented the refrigerant, sulfur dioxide, from leaking into the house, when the unit was turned off. I spent many days hand grinding and polishing the shoulders of compressor shafts. Another common failure of the refrigerator was oil on the commutator of the motor, mostly due to over oiling by a serviceman.

Sulfur dioxide was a horrible refrigerant. With moisture it formed sulfurous acid ($H_2SO_3$) which corroded all parts very rapidly, turning them black. It, of course, also combined with the sweat on your hands, ate into your skin, and turned your hands black. Washing them did not help.

Frigidaire, owned by General Motors at that time, was the only refrigerator which was permitted to use Freon as a refrigerant. This fluorocarbon was made and patented by DuPont. In those days DuPont held the controlling shares of GM. Freon had many advantages. It did not smell. It was not corrosive. Its boiling point was higher than that of sulfur dioxide, so that the crank case of the compressor was never under vacuum. Therefore, the compressor did not suck in any air and moisture. Because Freon did not combine with moisture, it did not make you cough or eat into your skin. It was a pleasure to work on Frigidaires, but they seldom broke down.

# GERHARD GETS MARRIED

Gerhard proved to be a persistent suitor. He convinced Dorothea Eisenmenger that she should come back to Jamaica and marry him. She gave in, they got engaged, and she returned to Kingston. The date and time of the marriage was set for 2:00 p.m. March 30, 1935. Gerhard was to pick Dorrie up with his car at 1:15 at her friends' house where she was staying, so that the wedding could take place, as planned, at the Public Registrar's office by 2:00 p.m.

Gerhard did not want anyone at the Public Service to know that he got married. So, he went to work that morning. It so happened that the 30th of March was the last day of the fiscal year for the Kingston Public Hospital. Any unspent money of the 1934-35 budget would lapse that midnight.

The head nurse went into the Public Service store that day and bought lots and lots of appliances of every description from Gerhard. Unfortunately, she took her own sweet time about it. It was pushing three o'clock by the time Gerhard finally managed to tear himself loose and rush to pick up Dorrie. Her friends, with whom she was staying, already expressed their sincere sympathy for her for being stood up, left in a foreign country by a rogue of a man on what was supposed to be her glorious wedding day!

Dorrie and Gerhard made it just in time before the registrar was about to close his office. Gushti Muth had faith in Gerhard. He was the best man and waited patiently at the registrar's office. The registrar was a bit indignant and told them to hurry up, as he wanted to be on time for the start of a cricket match. Gerhard and Dorrie did not ask me to their wedding. Gerhard did not want me to ask for time off from work, as the whole Company would then have known that he got married. I never found out why he wanted it to be a secret.

He brought Dorrie home to Elleston Rd. He had bought a brand new Kelvinator as a wedding present. She went over to it at once and opened the motor compartment! I had installed many Kelvinators in recent times but I never saw any man, let alone a woman, open the motor compartment. We all had a good laugh.

120

In those days most households still had iceboxes. The iceman came and brought 25 lbs (11 kg) of ice from the ice factory on Harbour St. The iceboxes were usually infested with cockroaches. I know because I exchanged many for brand new Kelvinators. So the electric refrigerator was a most wonderful improvement to our way of life.

There was neither time nor money for them to take a honeymoon. For the first time since I left Hamburg, I felt that I was in a properly regulated household. I also felt that three was a crowd, and that I was superfluous.

Since Muth had been a partner in Meyer's Vienna Bakery, the creditors naturally haunted him. He married Luci and took off with her to Costa Rica. The last I heard of them, Luci had convinced him to drink some water instead of alcohol. He followed her advice, drank water, got typhoid fever, and died.

# MY JOB 1935-37

The refrigerant which Kelvinators used was sulfur dioxide which has a very strong acrid smell which makes the eyes tear and causes a painful cough. Kelvinators sometimes developed seal leaks. Seal leaks caused the compressors to suck in air. The air becomes compressed. It in turn drives out the sulfur dioxide, which in turn drives people out of their homes. The Jamaica Public Service gave me a bicycle and the instructions to check the refrigerator of every customer for seal leaks by checking the high and low pressures. I was also to oil the motors and clean their commutators.

In the two years since I had arrived in Jamaica, most of the streets in Kingston and other major towns had been paved. Even most of the roads which connected the towns were paved.

It was very hard work to pedal the bicycle laden with tools in the broiling sun up to St. Andrew several hundred feet above sea level where most of the customers lived. I always dressed in a nice white suit with shirt and tie and a sun helmet on my head. Fortunately, I still had them from Hamburg. The sleeves and pant cuffs had to be let out to their maximum, as I had grown a bit in the intervening two years.

I serviced about eight houses per day. Most of the visits were uneventful. I usually went to the back of the house, explained the reason for my coming there, went into the kitchen or pantry, put the gauges on the refrigerator, cleaned the commutator of the motor, oiled the motor, took off the gauges, packed up my tools, had the lady of the house sign my card, and took off for the next house. If I found something wrong I made a note, and told my superior and the customer. Only the better off people had electric refrigerators in those days.

One day, a little after 11 a.m., my last call before lunch time, I came to a house where the back door was wide open. No one answered my knock. There was no refrigerator in either the kitchen or the pantry. That was surprising. I checked my card and address. I was in the correct house all right. I went to the front verandah. From there the door to the living room was unlocked. I entered, and there was the Kelvinator. I opened it to turn it off. It contained no food, but it was full with mostly beer and all sorts of other beverages, both strong and weak. There were all kinds of clothes around the room, both male and female, on the chairs and on the floor. I had never seen a living room looking like this.

I attached my gauges to the compressor when two Cuban women came into the room. "Ola! Vot a cute young vite boy!" one exclaimed. As they came to me their house coats opened. They had no clothes on underneath. I had never seen a nude woman before. My heart beat in my mouth! They stooped down besides me, and put their arms on my shoulder. I never had such an experience.

I blushed. My ears burned. I had to get out of there! I quickly took my gauges off the refrigerator, thus releasing a small amount of sulfur dioxide. They coughed, sneezed, fled and cried: "He is keeleeng mee! He has poisoned mee!" I packed up my tools real fast, dispensed with the required signature and was out of there in a flash!

Another time I noticed oil on the compressor shaft, the first sign of a seal leak. I told the customer and the service manager. The customer accused the Company of trying to get money out of him for unnecessary repairs. A few days later a chauffeur of the Company fetched me from my home around midnight. He drove me to the shop first, so that I could pick up my tools, and then to the same customer. The entire family awaited us in the garden in their house coats. The seal had given way, and the acrid stench had driven everyone out of the house.

But each cloud has a silver lining. At least they would not have any insects in the house, surely not live ones. I removed the compressor and took it to our work shop, and then the driver took me home. Incidentally, I was not paid for this nor any other overtime. The customer accused me of having done something to his unit to cause this disaster.

At another time the Company received a complaint that their new Kelvinator did not get cold. I was dispatched there on my bicycle armed with a 24 hour recording clock. From the circular chart one could read what the temperature was in the unit at any given time, how often and at what time the door was opened,

SERVICING REFRIGERATORS

how long it remained open, how often the motor started, how long it would run, and how long it would remain off.

I found three or four servants working in the kitchen. I installed the recorder and came back for the results promptly after 24 hours. The lady of the house asked me very politely what I had found out. I showed her and explained to her what the chart revealed. That way she could see for herself that there was nothing wrong with her beautiful large refrigerator. It convinced her that it had been opened every few minutes from early morning to late at night. Yes, she had proof that it was even opened at four o'clock in the morning. It never got a chance to really cool down properly.

When I got back to the shop the service manager was furious!

"Why did you tell Mrs. Evans that her husband came home at four o'clock in the morning?! Her husband and Mr. Nichols are the best of friends. They go out drinking together! Don't you know anything?!" Mr. Nichols, of course, was the vice president of the huge American-Canadian concern, Stone and Webster, and the manager of the Jamaica Public Service, the all powerful man we worked for.

Mrs. Evans had naturally phoned Mrs. Nichols. Mrs. Nichols naturally gave her husband hell. He in turn gave the chief engineer hell. The latter blew up the service manager. And I, of course, got it in fortissimo. I, alas, had no one to let my fury out on as I was the end of the line.

"In future do not give out any technical information to anybody! That's an order!" And all the time I had thought that I had done a wonderful thing explaining the facts to the customer. I had convinced a dissatisfied customer so that she did not have a shadow of a doubt that the Company was blameless for the problems with her refrigerator. That had been the stated object of my service call. Sometimes I felt like a born loser.

In the future I reported all troubles to the service manager who in turn reported it to the chief engineer who then in turn had his secretary type a letter on beautiful blue and gold embossed stationery:

Dear Mr. Customer,

After careful and thorough examination, our highly qualified technical staff have determined that your Kelvinator......

The Jamaica Public Service Company, Ltd.

John B. Young, M.Sc.,M.E.E.
Chief Engineer.

JBY/srh

The "highly qualified staff," used in the plural form, was of course I, the six shilling per week apprentice.

# MEET OTHER SWIMMERS

My only relaxation at the time was swimming at Sirgani's Beach. I met a distinguished looking man and his girlfriend there. They swam laps very slowly. He introduced himself. He was Alexander Bustamante and his friend Miss Longbridge. He had started the very first labor union, the longshoremen's union, in Jamaica. I could not have imagined then that he would eventually rise to become the first Prime Minister, for 15 years, of independent Jamaica, and that he would one day be proclaimed the National Hero of Jamaica. We had friendly chats every time we met.

One evening, while I was swimming my usual laps in the about 50 m (150 ft) wide shark enclosure, using my usual breast stroke, a young fellow of about my age started to swim besides me. He paddled, seemingly effortless, on his back. That he could do that, obviously without the slightest bit of exertion, annoyed me a bit. What a show-off! It was still early. The sun would not set for quite a while yet. I quickened my pace a bit. He kept right besides me. I swam and swam until it was dark. I had to come out.

He came over to me and said: "You swim quite a good breast stroke."

"You are making fun of me. You just lay on your back and had no trouble keeping up with me."

"Yes, but I am V.G. Crawford."

"My name is Arnold Von der Porten."

He looked very surprised that his name was not known to me.

He said: "I am the short distance free style and back stroke swimming champion of Jamaica. You must come over to the Bournemouth Club."

"I have no money."

"Don't worry about that. Tell them that V.G. asked you to come."

That was the beginning of a long friendship with some of the best swimmers of the Island. V.G. and I remained friends till I left the Island.

127

# MY FELLOW WORKERS

We were four workers in the refrigeration service department. Besides me, there were Norris Spencer, the senior serviceman; Henry Hudson, the other serviceman, and Jack Harris the very gifted apprentice.

One afternoon we, four of us, decided to go swimming at Barned's Beach. It was similar and very near Sirgani's Beach, but it cost only three pence (7 cents). It was mostly used by Black, poor people and Sirgani's mostly by lighter and more affluent ones.

I told Spencer that I had never wrestled since I left school where I did poorly because I was so weak and small, but now I was almost fully grown and weighed 120 lbs (55 kg).

"Come, let's wrestle," said Spencer.

I took an upright stance, and Spencer crouched low to the ground.

Harris, the referee, said: "Go!"

Spencer made a dash, ramming his head into my stomach, pulled my legs from under me and pinned me on my back.

Harris said: "Out!"

I said: "Foul! You are not supposed to touch me anywhere below my waist!"

"Since when?"

They had never heard of "Roman-Greek" and I had never heard of "Catch as Catch Can" wrestling. I felt cheated. That was the end of all social contact with my fellow workers, except once more. This time it involved a world famous boxing match.

The big news was that Max Schmeling of Hamburg, the European heavyweight boxing champion, was to fight the "Brown Bomber," Joe Louis. No one in our household had a radio. Harris' family had a radio. The room was packed with people. I bet one shilling and six pence (37 cents), a quarter of my weekly pay, on Schmeling who had married my favorite film star, Dollie Haas. That alone made me admire him. I was the only White man in the room, and all were predicting that the Black man would beat the white man " 'cause black man better more no (than) white man."

There was a most embarrassing silence in the room when

Schmeling decked his opponent with three straight rights to the jaw and became the world heavyweight champion. I never collected the one shilling and six pence. That rankled me for some time. It taught me the lesson never to bet again.

# THE JAMAICA MACARONI FACTORY IS BORN

In the middle of 1935, the Jamaica Biscuit Factory burnt to the ground. It was a subsidiary of La Selles, De Mercado, Ltd., a very wealthy import and export firm. It had its own wharf. Its entry into manufacturing was a new, financially insignificant venture.

The power supply in Kingston was 40 Hertz at that time. That fact made all electrical equipment unique. For one, the standard motor speed for 40 Hz is 1,140 RPM. Machines built in the U.S. are built for 60 Hz or 1,780 RPM motors. The Europeans sell machinery to use 50 Hz motors or 1,460 RPM. All controls had to be made especially for 40 Hz. Gerhard was very well qualified to sell customers everything they needed. Gerhard went to see the young, unhappy manager of the ruined factory.

Mr. Magnus told him that they were trying to start a totally new line of business making macaroni, but they always became mildewed when they tried to dry them. Up to the time the factory burnt down their experiments were still unsuccessful. Now they were interested in getting the factory going again, but just with their well established lines of biscuits (cookies in American).

"What are you doing with the macaroni machinery?" asked Gerhard.

"Its bearings were made of babbitt and they had melted away. We had not yet perfected the process, and we won't have time to devote to any new product. We are not going to repair the machines. We are selling them to Germany for scrap for £ 25.-.-." ($125.oo).

Gerhard was indignant. "The Germans will make guns out of your machines and shoot a lot of good people with your scrap iron."

They came to an agreement. Gerhard paid £ 5.-.- down, and promised to pay £1.-.- per month, and the machinery would be his.

Handsome and blond Mr. Magnus was about Gerhard's height and age. He could have sold the machinery to the Germans for spot cash. He could most likely have made a little profit on the shipping and handling. But he probably saw merit in Gerhard's argument that the hated Nazis would make guns out of his machines. After all, he was a descendent of the old Portuguese Jewish families who had settled in Jamaica long before the British conquered the Island in the terrible war of attrition between 1655 and 1660. Without the help of the Portuguese Jews, the British would probably not have succeeded to kill out the Spanish in Jamaica.

At that time Dorrie, Gerhard, and I lived in a nice little house on Grafton Rd. in Vineyard Pen. It had a fairly large, ramshackle garage. The machinery; the press, the kneader, the mixer, the line shaft, babbitt bearing housings, gears and pulleys were delivered there.

Mr. Badetscher, the No.2 pastry cook from the Meyer's Vienna Bakery days, moved in with us. He knew how to make macaroni. He also wanted to make cheese. There was a dairy which sold fresh milk. All unsold milk was delivered to us instead of throwing it away. Badetscher experimented with the cheese making, but it was a flop. We would have to have refrigerated equipment. That needed money. That was one thing we did not have.

Dorrie, Gerhard, and I started to repair the machinery. It was pitch black from soot. I soon gave up. I was never going to be a partner. I felt that my effort was not appreciated. Besides, it deprived me of my time to go swimming. Dorrie, on the other hand, worked practically day and night cleaning the many parts. Badetscher experimented with different flours and methods of drying pasta.

Finally the machinery was ready for assembly and the pouring of the babbitt bearings. Gerhard rented a large building at 4 Arlington Ave. We installed the machinery on the ground floor. The three of us lived upstairs. For the machinery and drying rooms we had to remove some walls inside the building. That would make it difficult to restore it to its original condition. The landlord, Mr. Aguilar, practically forced Gerhard to buy the building on very easy terms. It proved to be an excellent financial move for Gerhard.

The mechanic who usually pours the bearings for the tram cars (trolley cars in American) in the Jamaica Public Service repair shop poured all the bearings of the macaroni machinery. The bearing housing had to be heated red hot with a blow torch before the molten babbitt could be poured into the housing, otherwise the housing might have cracked. The hotter the housing, the more it would expand, thereby allowing more babbitt to enter. As it cooled, the housing would shrink tightly against the babbitt. The shaft, on the other hand, had to be oiled and dusted with chalk so that the babbitt would not stick to it.

Gerhard bought a 3 HP 3 phase induction motor from the Public Service. We drove the line shaft with gears. That drive was terribly noisy! Various pulleys and clutches transmitted power to the three machines. As predicted, the drying was the most difficult part of the process. Dorrie worked practically day and night moving the goods from room to room, as the macaroni would crack lengthwise if they dried too quickly, or mildew, if they dried too slowly.

Badetscher tried to save Dorrie steps and motions with the knowledge he had acquired from methods engineers in his native Switzerland, but Dorrie felt that he was only criticizing her. She did not understand that he was trying to help her. He was working normally hard, but compared to Dorrie he was lazy.

They called the product "Star" brand. The boxes were printed locally by the Gleaner Printers. They looked like very poor and unattractive copies of the popular Alpha Macaroni boxes. The shelf life of the macaroni was very short, as weevils got into the boxes. The customers returned the spoilt goods for their money back, and never bought Star Brand again. Badetscher gave up and went to Costa Rica, but Dorrie was determined to make the factory pay.

Gerhard had a large plywood box built. It could hold ten 100 lbs (45 kg) flour bags at a time. All flour was put into it before it was used. A small container of water was placed on top of the flour. A teaspoon of cyanide was dumped into the water. The box had to be sealed tightly before the worker could inhale her next breath. Thus all weevil eggs were killed overnight.

Gerhard also imported good looking milk cartons from Canada. The brand name was changed to Dora Macaroni. The cartons were sealed practically hermetically. After they were filled, they were gassed over night. The next morning they were shipped to Eustace Chen who had a grocery wholesale import business. At that time, with few exceptions, there was a tremendous prejudice against any product made in Jamaica. It certainly did not hurt that all Dora

Macaroni, Dora Spaghetti, and Dora Vermicelli boxes were marked: "Printed in Canada".

The name Dora was chosen as our mother, Gerhard's and mine, as well as Dorrie's mother, were called Dora. It is, therefore, quite logical that this particular name had to spell success. Very gradually the factory started to break even. It was very labor intensive. Gerhard made a hinged contraption to break the macaroni and spaghetti to length. Between Badetscher and himself, they had devised a way to fold vermicelli quickly in an attractive pattern which also facilitated good air flow for drying. In two of the rooms Gerhard installed three removable air tunnels to dry vermicelli. Air was blown through them by fans mounted on 1/4 HP Delco motors.

Gerhard had accepted the responsibility to pay back all the debt which Meyer's Vienna Bakery and the Continental Club had incurred. The new Jamaica Macaroni Factory proved to be no help as it barely broke even, despite Dorrie working harder than I have ever seen anyone work. She developed tremendous physical strength in her arms. To prevent mildew, she would carry three foot long sticks head high, full of macaroni from one drying area to another for hours at a time, after the help had gone home or on weekends. Yet the little woman could not have weighed 100 lbs (45 kg). I did it some weekends when Dorrie and Gerhard went out. Even for me, who was by that time quite an athlete due to swimming, the work was very tiring.

# MORE REFRIGERATION WORK

When I became a second year apprentice I got a big raise. I now earned 10 shillings a week ($ 2.oo). Gerhard had sold one newly-rich Syrian lady a super deluxe model Kelvinator, the very best they made. It had a baked porcelain-enamel finish inside and outside. It had three doors. The one on the left opened to a refrigerator, the one on the right to a large freezer, and the one in the middle to vertical rows of ice trays. She phoned Gerhard the day after I had installed the unit. She was very irate.

"Take this thing back, and bring me back my old icebox!"

I was dispatched to see what was wrong. The lady glared at me angrily as she received me in the pantry where the offending refrigerator stood.

She yelled: "It took me all day yesterday to make ice cubes and to distribute them all over the refrigerator and freezer, and I still did not get 25 lbs (11 kg). That is too much work!"

It was not at all easy to convince her that the refrigerator and the freezer would keep cold, even if she never emptied any ice cube tray and distributed the ice all over. When I left her, we were both happy. I felt that I had earned all of my week's pay that one afternoon.

We had tiny English made Ford cars to drive us from the shop to and from work. Hudson was in the driver's seat. I sat besides him. Harris and our new, very gifted, apprentice, Henriques, sat behind us. It was already after 5:00 p.m., and as we did not get overtime pay, Hudson drove like a mad man down Slipe Rd. There was a truck in front of us blocking our view. Next to it was a tram (trolley) car.

Hudson opted to pass the tram on the wrong side of the road. We were beside the tram and were faced by another one coming the opposite direction. I pressed against the floor board with all my might and clutched the dashboard. Hudson swerved all the way over into the oncoming traffic, squeezed between the back of the trolley and a sharply braking oncoming car and got in front of the truck which had blocked our view.

He must have gotten us at least ten seconds earlier to the shop than he would have if he had followed the law and the truck. Ten seconds may have been worth it to him but we others felt pretty sick and wished that he had stayed behind the truck.

"That's nothing," Hudson informed us. "The other day I was in the same position, only instead of an oncoming car, there was a big oncoming truck. It did not slow down, so I just lifted up the steering wheel, and the car jumped right over the truck."

A deathly silence.

Then: "And when you wake up, Sah. Wha' happen'?" asked Henriques.

We all laughed. That brought our stomachs back into the proper positions and removed our hearts from our mouths back into our chests. I did my best not to be in a car which Hudson drove from then on.

One day I answered a service call that a Frigidaire was using too much current. Frigidaire used Freon, the new Du Pont refrigerant. It was the most trouble-free refrigerator on the market. I put on my gauges. It checked out perfect. The frustrated owner kept on calling.

I drove there when I was not expected. There was the servant, an iron in her hand, her back turned to the open refrigerator door, an ironing board in front of her, lots of clean laundry, some ironed, and some to be ironed, and a coal basin heating four irons. The woman's back was nice and cool, and I could understand why the unit used so much current. In those days air conditioners were not yet known in Jamaica.

I would have liked to read the letter which the chief engineer sent to the customer. Even more, I would have liked to see the face of the customer when she received that letter.

# WATER POLO

One day the German Cruiser *Emden* was in port. It was a training ship for cadets. I met one of Eckart's former classmates walking up King Street. He looked very smart in his white cadet uniform. We greeted each other politely. The swastika on his uniform annoyed me so that I did not stop to start any conversation with him.

The Nazis used the opportunity to show off. They had top athletes on board. Their soccer team easily defeated the Jamaican all-star team. They beat the top Jamaicans in sailing, boxing, wrestling, tennis and now they came to the swimming club to play the Jamaican water polo team.

I went to the Bournemouth Club to see the game. It looked very unfair. There were those German giants, all at least six feet (almost 2 m) tall, weighing at least 200 lbs (90 kg). On the opposite side were the seven, Jamaicans average weight of 130 lbs (60 kg) at the most, with their coach, Walter Lowe, a Jewish refugee, formerly an all-star player on the Viennese team.

The pool is deep enough that no player can stand. At each end is 3m x 1m (10 ft. x 3 ft) goal. According to the international rules of those days there was no substitution. If a man dropped out for any reason, his team had to continue with a man short and would almost certainly lose. The ball was the size of a volley ball. It was made of leather which soaked up water. It was shot like a cannon ball at the goal. I had watched the game twice before when I visited England a few years ago. Those teams had looked pretty evenly matched but this game looked like boys against giants!

As the teams lined up, the Germans shouted three loud: *"Sieg heil!"* (Hail victory). They had their right arms stretched out stiffly in their Nazi salute. There was an embarrassed silence. Before the start of the game the five best swimmers of each team swam a relay. The little Jamaicans won. I was astonished!

The water polo game started. All seven of each team were waiting at their own goal line. The whistle blew, the ball was thrown into the center of the pool, and the teams raced for it. The Jamaican center forward beat the German to the ball. He passed it back to one of the two fullbacks, and swam toward the opponents' goal but stayed clear of the two meter (6 ft) line. The fullback threw the ball over the head of one of the forwards, directly between his arms. The forward shot at the goal. "Goal!" The crowd screamed and clapped wildly! 1 : 0 Jamaica.

According to the new international rules, the team which suffered the point loss, gets the ball in the middle of the pool, similar to soccer but complying with the rules which were in force then, after every goal each team started from its own goal line to swim for the ball in the middle of the pool. The Jamaicans got the ball again, and scored almost immediately. 2 : 0.

I heard the German captain say to his men: *"Ruppen."* (Foul them.).

In no time at all the Jamaicans had bloody noses but they out maneuvered the Germans all the same and quickly scored a third goal.

As they swam back to their own goal line I heard the Jamaican captain say:

"Let's drown them."

As the whistle blew the Jamaicans again got the ball. They passed it from side to side of the pool always close to the Germans but usually not close enough for them to get it. Once in a while the Germans got the ball but they could never pass it close enough to the Jamaican goal to take an effective shot. The Jamaicans swam every day, something one could not do on a warship on a world cruise. It soon showed. The visitors could hardly stay afloat, they were so exhausted. The game lasts 15 minutes each half time.

After the three minutes' half-time the Jamaicans resumed their tactic. The visitors probably wished that they had never even thought of using their powerful arms to hurt a single opponent. They had a difficult time keeping their heads above water. Just a few minutes before the game was over the Jamaicans decided to score again and shot two goals in short order. The score was 5 : 0. It seemed that the Germans could hardly swim out of the pool. They looked so finished. They shook hands, stretched out their arms and shouted their *"Sieg heil,"* which, to me, seemed to make no sense at all since they lost. Then all players disappeared in the direction of the cabanas.

The Jamaicans invited the Germans to play the "A" teams of the Kingston Swimming Club and the Jamaica Amateurs Swimming Club. They accepted and were defeated by each club, but at least they scored some goals.

After those games I just had to play water polo. A new team, Kingston "C," was formed, and I was their goalie. It was like target practice. The other teams swam all over mine and kept on shooting at my goal. I stopped many a shot with my nose, which was bleeding sooner or later in every game we played. Though the score was usually in the vicinity of 10 : 0 or worse, I became a very good goalkeeper. In one game, I remember, one of the opponents had to rescue one of my teammates as the latter just could not swim any more and was drowning. After all one has to swim about two miles (3 km) each game with your opponent impeding you all the time. It is justifiably called the world's most exhausting team sport.

Early in 1936, I was promoted to be the goalkeeper of the Kingston "B" team. It was the third best team in the league. Towards the end of 1936, Malcolm Finleyson, the captain of the Jamaica Amateurs "A" team, asked me to be their goalkeeper. I accepted and changed clubs. We were the second best team in a league of six teams.

One day, while I was still the goalie for the Kingston Swimming Club's "B" team, a game was scheduled at 5:00 p.m. in the middle of the week. I could not possibly make it, as I worked up to that hour. I phoned Douglas Campbell. I knew he had the use of a car.

"Don't worry, Arnold, we'll pick you up. The games never start on time anyhow."

The Campbells arrived with six in the tiny four seater Opel. Douggy's brother, Bully, drove. We raced east on North St. as fast as the little thing would go with the seven of us squeezed in tightly. At Duke St. a car was about to cross North St. from the south and one from the north. They had the right of way but Bully never slowed down. To avoid us, one car slammed into a wall after crossing the sidewalk and the other skidded sideways right behind us.

"I have no brakes, you know," Bully said calmly.

"And then you race like that through one of the busiest intersections in all of Kingston?"

"Of course, I have to get there fast before an accident happens."

We all laughed and I hoped that my stomach would return to its normal position before the game got under way.

# ELECTRIC DAIRY FOR OSKAR LORD

Gerhard was a most successful salesman. He sold more than the three other salesmen and the sales manager put together. The sales manager, Mr. Caithness, and especially the second best salesman, Mr. MacDonald, were very jealous. Gerhard sold three electric dairies to three brothers: Oskar, Eric and George Lord. A fourth Lord brother managed the United Dairy Company on Old Hope Road in Kingston which was owned by all four brothers.

The dairy farms were in Old Harbour, 25 miles (40 km) west of Kingston. There was no electric power there. Company employees were not insured if they ventured beyond the power net. Gerhard obtained permission that I could install the machinery under the condition that I would do it on my own time after work and on weekends, and that I would not charge the customer any money. It was Company policy not to allow any employee to earn any money outside of his regular job. The commission meant a lot to Gerhard, and I readily agreed to do the work.

After work the milk truck drove me to Old Harbour. Oskar Lord had a very prosperous looking plantation. There were irrigated banana and sugar cane fields, but surprisingly, I saw few meadows. The cows were in a long cow shed. They were fed thin slices of sugar cane. They must have liked that, as they looked very healthy. They were a mixture of Holstein, Gurnsey, and East Indian cows. Holstein and Gurnsey cows gave lots of milk but they could not stand tropical diseases carried by ticks. The East Indian brown, long horned cows gave very little milk, but they were very hardy. The mixture was a good stock for Jamaica. The main building was screened in against mosquitoes. It was quite a large mansion. There were a lot of houses for the help and stables for horses.

I did not have any time to waste. I had to get power. Motor car batteries gave 6 Volts D.C. in those days. I connected six of them in series and three in parallel so that I used a total of 18 batteries. I hooked them up to a 32 V generator. I connected it by a belt and clutch to the diesel engine which drove the cane cutter. I made a panel and mounted my ammeter and voltmeter on a wall. Next I wired the cow shed and the milk storage room for light. I installed the compressor unit with its 32 V motor. The container for the four 10 gallon milk cans had no cooling coil. I had to make one from 5/8" diameter copper tubing. A liquid expansion valve controlled the flow. The end of the coil was connected to the suction side of the compressor. The actual cooling of the stored milk was done by brine, saturated salt water. Next to the storage tank I installed the aerator. It consisted of a double sided set of corrugated stainless steel sheets which enclosed a refrigeration coil immersed in brine. The refrigerant was fed in from the bottom through another expansion valve and drawn off from the top and connected to the suction line with a Tee. The milk was poured over the top of the aerator at 100° F and flowed into the 10 gal. container at 50° F. A magnetic valve, operated by an ordinary switch, closed the flow to the expansion valve, when the milking was complete.

The refrigerant was methyl chloride. If sulfur dioxide would have been used, and the unit should ever have sprung a leak, the cows would surely have panicked, and who knows what would have happened then. Freon was not available to Kelvinator. Methyl chloride was a very satisfactory refrigerant. Its operating pressures were between those of the two other refrigerants. With the temperatures I used, there would never be a vacuum in the coils, therefore no chance of drawing air and moisture into the system. The gas had a sweet smell, so that a bad leak could readily be noticed. Unfortunately, it was a narcotic, chemically closely related to chloroform but slower in its effect. The cow shed was wide open, and a leak would not constitute any danger to any animal or man.

I wired the house for electricity while I was at it. Oskar Lord was very pleased. The first installation took me about two weeks working nights, Sundays and Saturdays after a half day's work at the Public Service. On Saturdays the Company allowed me to use one of their small English Fords to drive to Old Harbour and back on Sundays. I was 18 by then, and had obtained a driver's license.

I finished the first installation on a Saturday evening. Oskar had just brought a fine retired race horse in England as a riding horse for himself and as a stud for his stable. He had gone to England himself to select the steed. We sat on his covered and screened-in verandah, and he talked at great length of horses. I had a tough time to keep my eyes open. It never occurred to him who had ridden horses ever since he could walk that a city bred boy, like myself, knew next to nothing about horses and never had time to give them much thought.

Eventually he asked: "Do you like horses?" What could I say after his enthusiasm. I certainly would not want to offend him.

"Oh yes, I love horses."

"Wonderful! Then you must ride my new acquisition! We'll saddle him in the morning. You'll find it a thrill to ride that one!"

In the morning four men brought out the horse. Mr. Lord beamed all over his face. The beast did not seem to like the idea, and the four men had all they could do to pull the saddle girt on tight. I mounted. The owner said:

"Now don't slap it on its backside, or it will gallop with you all out."

"All right, I understand."

What a good thing that I had ridden a bit in Ashton near Sheffield, and that they had told me to squeeze my thighs together with all my might so that I would not be thrown off if it galloped. The thought gave me a little confidence.

There was no time to muse. A wagon approached, laden to the maximum with sugar cane. It was drawn by six huge white Brahmin steers with high humps over their shoulders and long, curved horns. My nervous horse had never seen anything like that before. It started to dance sideways and shake its head and seemed frightened. The busha (foreman) gave it a good natured pat on its backside. That horse took off like a bolt of lightning. It jumped over a ditch at the side of the road and galloped across a meadow at an unbelievable speed until it came to a banana field where it stood stock still. I was happy that I was still on it. I turned it around and hoped to ride it back in a walk but it just stood there. I would have to give it a command. For a minute I entertained the idea that I should and could determine both the direction and speed the horse was to go. I was certainly not going to even touch its hind quarters! I decided to hit my heels into its flank. At that it took off again at the same fantastic speed to the very spot where we had started, jumping right across the ditch at the end of the ride.

"Oh, you are a great rider, jumping and all!" Oskar exclaimed.

"A week before you came we had a fellow here from England. This horse threw him, and he got his heel caught in the stirrup. The horse dragged him halfway to town, before we could stop it. He's still in the hospital."

# ELECTRIC DAIRY FOR ERIC LORD

The next evening I started on Eric's plantation. Unfortunately, he had heard how I loved horses and what a great rider I was.

"I have a horse here that is bred and born right here in Old Harbour, and it is every bit as good as Oskar's."

I sensed a severe rivalry between the two brothers. Oskar being the much wealthier one.

"You'll be the judge."

"It will have to wait till I have finished the installation." I was buying time.

"Yes, yes, when you've finished the job."

I did pretty much what I had done for Oskar. On the last Sunday morning as I got up, there were Eric's five year old son and his three year old daughter riding at a gallop together on one horse bare back around the large diameter circular gravel driveway! The boy was holding on to the mane, and the girl embracing the boy's waist. I would never be able to do that.

After a couple of weeks I finished my work and tested everything by lunch time. Now they brought out their favorite stallion. They had no trouble saddling it. That was a plus in my mind. There was a six foot high barbed wire fence with a barbed wire door of the same height. They opened it, and I rode slowly into a freshly planted banana field. It was irrigated, so that most of the ground was covered with muddy brown water. The Busha told me that, if I wanted to gallop, all I had to do is clack my tongue.

I shook my reins. I used my heels. The horse would not move any faster than a slow walk. Finally, stupid me, I clacked my tongue. The horse took off like a bolt of lightning! There was a 36" irrigation pipe. The horse jumped right over it, and I almost dived over its head. We came to a field where the banana plants were over six feet high. The horse had the sense to stop. I no sooner had the beast turned around when it dashed right back at full gallop. We again jumped over the pipe. I saw the end of the field coming up. The gate was closed. The horse did not seem to see that. I pulled at the rein as hard as I could and yet keep my balance. This, I had been told, should stop a horse. I wished someone had let the horse know! Just before the gate it turned sideways and stopped. I almost continued on through the air on top of the barbed wire gate but, by marshaling all of my strength, I managed to stay in the saddle.

I was covered with mud. Eric came up to me. He did not seem to notice my mud spattered clothes, arms and face. All he wanted to know was, how his horse compared with that of Oskar's. I had not been able to control either. So, I could truthfully say, that they both had a powerful and independent spirit. I did not tell him that I hoped that I would never ride either one of them again. Next Monday would be George's turn.

# ELECTRIC DAIRY FOR GEORGE LORD

Fortunately, George Lord, the third brother did not go in for fancy horses. He told me that he liked bird shooting. "One day," he said, "I was walking through an irrigated banana field," (He described it as just like the one I rode across at Eric's.) "I had a double barreled shot gun under my arm. I was looking up for bald pates (a kind of dove) when I stepped on something. I thought it was a log. It was alive! It was a crocodile* which immediately went for my leg! I quickly rammed my gun into its mouth and fired both barrels! As it died, the beast bit, twisted, and bent the gun making it completely useless."

This third electric dairy installation did not go nearly as well as the other two. The Kelvinator factory had sent one fitting short. I needed it to connect the expansion valve to the coil inside the storage box which held the four 10 gallon cans. It was at an awkward location too. Half of the box was covered with a thick insulated rigid top, the other similar half of the cover was hinged to the rigid top. I had installed the expansion valve in the very top center of the back wall where the the rigid cover meets the back wall just above the brine overflow line.

The Public Service machine shop made me a new fitting. It looked just like the purchased one but when I installed it, it leaked. I took it back to the machine shop. They made me another fitting. The next night I installed it. It, too, leaked. I used shellac. It still leaked. I tried red lead, white lead, hemp impregnated with shellac, with oil paint. It leaked. It was 4:00 a.m.. I was all alone in the milk storage shed. I was inside the box. I gave up.

Suddenly I realized that I could hardly move. I could not get up! The methyl chloride! It is heavier than air. I made a big effort to get my head over the rim of the storage box. I vomited. After having my head over the rim for a while I eventually had enough air

---

*Many Jamaicans call their crocodiles: alligators. Crocodile is the correct zoological name.

and strength to climb out of the box. I just had enough time to get my pants down. I had terrible diarrhea right in the cow shed. I lay down for a while under the starry sky and had some fresh air. Then I got up and cleaned up the mess I had made in the milk storage room and the cow shed.

I had them make another fitting at the Public Service machine shop. I told them to check for taper. It would be all right if the thread were a couple of thousands smaller at the flare end but not the other way around.

The next day I drove out again, to install a third fitting. It was already dusk. Along the Spanish Town Rd. the cane fields were irrigated. I had a flat tire. No one in his right mind exposes his skin to mosquitoes at dusk near a swamp or an irrigated field in Jamaica. I had no choice. I had to change the tire. The enemy was out in force. Mosquitoes covered my face and arms. They did not even move when I brushed them off. They just made a black and red slime on my arms with their bodies, my blood and my sweat. I contracted malaria. The disease gave me time to finish the last job in Old Harbour but then it hit full throttle.

I remember lying in bed, covered with lots of blankets, freezing, my teeth chattering. I could not keep my jaws still. Gerhard and a doctor stood over me. They gave me quinine, the traditional medicine for malaria attacks. I became delirious and do not remember the next few days.

Gerhard wrote Papa. The Old Man knew that they were experimenting with a new malaria medicine in the Hamburg Tropical Hospital. It was called Atebrin. It was not yet released to the public. Papa put in some volunteer time at that hospital and was allowed to send me some of that new medicine. During a malaria attack the patient does not eat, but this new medicine had to be taken on a full stomach. The dosage and for number of days I was to take it was prescribed on the bottle. Between malaria attacks the patient usually feels fine. So, I had to take the medicine while I was feeling great. I followed the instructions to the letter. The malaria never recurred.

# PREJUDICE AND RAGE

Late in 1936, a clerk was put in charge of our little stock room of the service department of the Jamaica Public Service. Clerks in Jamaica were usually better educated and were considered to be of a class far superior to that of lowly men dressed in khaki and working with their hands. His name was Owen Laing. He was a son of a well-to-do family.

Usually the last ones to leave the shop in the evenings closed the many windows and locked the doors. Shortly after Laing had been promoted from a mere radio repair apprentice to gentleman clerk in charge of our stock of radio and refrigerator parts, he and I were the last in the shop one evening.

His prestigious white suit went to his head. He sat down on the Service Manager's chair and said in a very haughty tone of voice:

"Porten, close the windows."

"You close the ones on your side, and I'll close the ones on mine." I had finished closing my half of the windows and was about to walk out, when he blocked my way. He told me: "I am in charge and you must close all the windows or else I shall report you."

"Report me," I thought.

As I was about to pass him, he gave me the Nazi salute and held the fore finger of his left hand to his upper lip mimicking a mustache like Hitler's. He was about my age, a little taller and fatter than I. The Nazi salute infuriated me. I despised people, who equated all Germans with the hated Nazis. Hitler had just recently managed to make all Germans even more unpopular than ever, by helping Franco to power in Spain!

That is where the German High Command had their new weapons tested, in particular the new concept of dive bombers. Those *Stukas*, as they called them, sank the Spanish Navy. The Japanese paid attention. The British and Americans did not. (*Stuka* is an acronym for *Sturz-Kanone* = dive canon.)

At any rate, his gesture made it quite clear that he thought me to be a damned Nazi! I was thoroughly provoked!

I tried to hit his jaw. He shifted with an agility which I did not expect. He hit my jaw. I felt groggy. I lunged at him again and missed again. His next punch floored me. I got up and went at him. He backed away and told me very politely:

"Stop. I have no intention of hurting you."

I just wanted to hit him at least once! He blocked the blow and sent me sprawling on the concrete floor. I got up, determined to hit that arrogant, fat slob at least once! He again told me not to try to fight him. I would not listen. This time he hit me so hard that I could not get up again.

He got a pail of water. He wiped my face with a wet rag and told me to stay down for a few minutes. He closed the balance of the widows and stayed with me, dabbing my face with the wet rag. As I lay there, I noticed that his lightly starched white suit did not even suffer a wrinkle. His tie was not even crooked. He had not even worked up a sweat! He said:

"I am an amateur boxer. I am sorry that you got so annoyed."

Eventually I felt well enough to ride my bicycle home. Laing and I got on very well together in the future. His dad soon found a better job for him.

# THE JOB CAN BE UNPLEASANT

One afternoon I had taken a refrigerator to a customer. As usual, I drove the pick up truck. Four laborers and the refrigerator were in the back. My four laborers wanted overtime and dragged their feet in a most annoying way all afternoon. Laborers were not employees, they were hired for each job at a predetermined pay. After 5:00 p.m., they were entitled to overtime. I, as a weekly salaried man, was not.

We arrived at the deserted workshop after 5:00 p.m., and they demanded that I sign an overtime slip. I refused and told them to get out of the shop. They got out all right. They picked up sticks and waited for me in a narrow passage on the property through which I had to pass.

Normally, I would ride my bicycle through there at full speed. This time I walked my bicycle past them at a very slow pace, looking neither left nor right. No one moved. I was relieved. The next morning the men lodged a complaint against me. Mr. Metcalf, the Service Manager, wanted to know why I did not sign the overtime slip. I told him. I never heard another word about the incident. In the future the workers did not waste time deliberately.

# I MAKE A GREAT TEACHER

One day, right after lunch, I took a refrigerator to a couple with three little children. Their entire family was there to witness the arrival of the new electric icebox. My four laborers placed the unit, not into the kitchen, not into the pantry, no, into the dining room. I took out the hold down shipping bolts very expertly with at least a dozen family members watching me in awe. They included everybody from the old grandparents down to the newly born. They were all Syrians.

The proud new owner asked me: "How does it work?"

I explained to him that every substance had a definite latent heat and that that was the key to the principle of refrigeration. Since nobody knew what latent heat was, I gave the definition and went on from there to explain the latent heat of vaporization, the necessity of drawing a vacuum on the liquid sulfur dioxide how the evaporating $SO_2$ absorbed the heat in the freezing unit, called the evaporator, and thereby cooled the inside of the refrigerator. I had to tell them, of course, that $SO_2$ was the chemists' abbreviation for sulfur dioxide.

I went on to tell them how the compressor functioned, and why the head of the compressor became so hot. I explained that the hot gas had to flow through the condenser which was a copper coil with fins. As the fan blew ambient air over the coil the gas inside cooled down, giving up its heat of vaporization, which is measured in BTU's, and became a liquid. I had to explain what the term: ambient meant, of course. I also had to define a BTU and the difference between degrees Fahrenheit which measured the intensity of heat and BTU's which measured the quantity of heat, a big difference!

I told them that the liquid sulfur dioxide was stored in the liquid receiver which was a small tank. It had a float valve in it which released some liquid into the evaporator, and then, obviously, the process started all over again. I never had such a large, captive and attentive audience like that before. I was in my element. When I was quite finished, the old grandfather stepped forward and asked:

"And where do you put the ice?"

# NEON ILLUMINATES THE FUTURE

There was a new form of lighting being used for signs. I do not remember having ever seen it in Europe. It consisted of illuminated glass tubing. There was a  sign like that in Jamaica. It read: MOVIES. Gerhard said to me one day:

"Arnold, customers import neon signs but the glass tubes usually arrive broken or when inexperienced workmen try to install them, they break them."

"What are neon signs?"

"Signs like the one on the 'Movies'. They seem to be the signs of the future."

"How do they get the wire into that tubing from one end to the other?"

"They don't. There is no wire in that tubing. They have a gas. The gas is the conductor. When some gases, such as neon, are ionized between two electrodes they glow brightly. Electrodes are melted to each end of the tubing. Neon will not combine chemically with any substance. Therefore a well made sign should last a very long time. Because they use neon they call those bent glass tubes neon signs.

"I think if you went to our parents in New York and learnt how to repair those glass tubes, the Company might open a neon department for you. You would get at last a decent salary as its manager when you come back. It would be worthwhile to talk to the management."

I quickly agreed.

Mr. Clarke, the chief accountant (a Scotsman), Mr. Young, the chief engineer (an American), Gerhard, and I had a conference. It was agreed that the Company would put me in charge of a neon department if I learnt how to repair neon signs in the United States. I would have to travel at my own expense and receive no remuneration until I returned to Kingston. All decisions were subject to Mr. Nichols's approval. He was a vice president of Stone & Webster, a huge American and Canadian engineering company which managed at least 50 power companies south of the United States. Mr. Nichols was the manager for Jamaica. The main share holder of the Jamaica Public Service was Russel V. Bell, the son of Graham Bell, the inventor of the telephone. Mr. Nichols gave his stamp of approval.

Papa sent the affidavit that I would not become a burden to the U.S. taxpayer and after much red tape, I finally got my immigration visa. The thought of seeing my parents again, and the approaching sea voyage were all very exciting. I also had some apprehension as to how I would fit in, and how I would earn enough money.

Herbert wrote to warn me that our parents had very little money and that a terrible unemployment raged throughout the United States. He also made it clear that he could not help me as his job at the bank did not pay very much, and that he had a wife and two children to support. I never counted on him anyway.

# HAITI

On a sunny January day in 1937, I boarded a United Fruit Company banana boat bound for New York. It sailed east after it left Kingston harbor. We were heading to Haiti to load more bananas.

On the steamer I befriended a high school graduate from Wolmer's Boys' School, one of the best schools in Jamaica. He had earned a scholarship being top of his class. He had taken French as his foreign language. All the other passengers took the normal tourist sightseeing tours through Port au Prince.

My friend and I could not afford such tours. Besides, we wanted to see the real Haiti as the general population saw it, not the tourist traps. It soon became evident that the honor student of Wolmer's did not understand the people talking to him. Though I had an "F" in French four years earlier in high school in Hamburg, I found that I could understand most of what was said except the main words. When I asked John: "What does so and so mean?" he proved to be a veritable live dictionary. Neither of us alone would have been able to converse with the Haitians. It had to be a joint effort. We made a perfect team.

We walked to the Presidential Palace which was built from shining white stone. It looked beautiful in the brilliant sun light. It had a very high wrought iron fence surrounding it. One could not get very near to that, as armed soldiers kept everyone a good distance away.

From the palace we strolled over to the Roman Catholic Cathedral. It, too, was an impressive building made entirely of stone. When we went inside, however, there were very poor looking wooden benches in disrepair instead of carved pews as we were used to in Jamaica.

We went to the market. People took my Black companion for a Haitian guide. It was amusing to watch their faces when I did the translation for him from their Creole (which is near enough to French) to English. Yet, I had to ask him constantly what the key words meant.

Very few streets were paved. Almost all houses looked quite

old and ready to collapse. They all needed a coat of paint. Sewage ran down the middle of the streets. We passed a school. It had obviously been built as a home for a wealthy family many years ago. Now it badly needed repair, paint, washing, and it looked, as if it were ready to collapse. That old wooden structure looked far too rotten to support so many children.

The market was crowded. Unlike their counterparts in Kingston, there was no shelter anywhere. The market women squatted on the ground just as in Jamaica. Their vegetables spread out before them on jute bags but, unlike in Jamaica, donkeys were allowed to walk among them. Those beasts relieved themselves, splattering their urine all over the vegetables and the hapless, protesting women nearby. That was most amusing entertainment for the people a little further away.

What surprised us most was the poverty of dress. Many children ran about completely naked. Several full grown men had nothing on but a short Tee shirt. No one seemed to mind. Very few people wore anything on their feet. Those who did, had on sandals made from old motor car tires.

John and I were properly attired as if we were going to an office or store in Kingston. He wore a dark blue serge suit, white shirt, a nice tie, and of course, highly polished black leather shoes. I wore a white suit, white shirt, tie and my only pair of properly shined shoes.

We strolled back to the ship. There were no wharves in Haiti, then a country of four million people about four times as big with four times the population of Jamaica. The steamer was anchored in the bay. Tenders took off the passengers, and brought them back. Large barges full of bananas were rowed out to the ship, and fastened alongside. Booms of the ship lowered nets to the barges, then lifted the full nets to the holds of the ship. When we arrived on board the loading was completed.

The next morning we were anchored off Cap Haitien in the North of the Island. Barges full of bananas were rowed out to our vessel. We went ashore by a launch and had a long taxi ride to the Citadel. It was an immense castle erected by the first emperor of Haiti, Toussaint L'Ouverture.

He was described as a very powerful Black man who led a

slave rebellion against the French in the North. He had been armed by the British during their war with France shortly after the French revolution. A brown man (Mulatto) led the rebellion in, and around Port au Prince in the South. For a while a northern and a southern state existed. Eventually the Emperor of the North appealed to the huge number of Blacks in the South to rid themselves of their mulatto rulers. This they did. So, after all the White people had been killed, and after their brown descendants had ruled for a while, almost all Mulattos were killed, too.

By this time the Citadel near Cap Haitien was finished. When the American architect had completed his impressive work, he and the Emperor strolled on top of the wall. The American is reported to have said:

"Now you and I are the only people in the world who know all the secret passages and chambers in this castle."

"You mean only I know the secrets," and with that he pushed the American off the parapet to his death.

If Port au Prince looked poverty stricken, Cap Haitien looked like its poor relation. In the entire town there was not a building worth looking at. Not a single street was paved. The people wore next to no clothing and what they did wear was in a pitiful condition. I was glad to leave Haiti. Next stop was to be Manhattan.

# NEW YORK IS NOT A BED OF ROSES

Mama was overjoyed to see me. The rest of the family gave me a very cool reception. It was nice to see the old, familiar furniture from Hamburg. My parents and Irma had left Germany a year earlier, in 1936. They were allowed to take all their possessions with them, but no more than $M$ 100.oo ($ 25.oo) for each adult. At the border to the Netherlands they were strip-searched by the Germans. My mother thought that outrageous. Outside of that they had a smooth journey.

I did not know how my father got enough money to get the family settled in America. I did not ask. Money was a touchy subject. Many years later I found out that my father's brother, Walter, had bought Papa's house in Hamburg and gave it to my grandmother. He paid Papa in American dollars.

My Uncle Walter had retired to South Africa. He had migrated to England before the first World War and had made a lot of money.

After living in Brooklyn for six months Papa flunked the New York State medical exam because of English. He passed the exam three months later. His practice was doing quite well when I arrived.

There was a terrible unemployment in New York. Papa wanted to know how I was going to earn any money. Herbert rebuked me and told me that I did not have a chance of finding any job. He scolded that it was irresponsible of me to come to Brooklyn and expect Papa's earnings to feed me, a grown man of nineteen. Maria was nice enough, but I saw very little of her and her two nice little boys. Herbert, however, came almost every evening and on weekends to play Skat (a German three handed card game) with our parents.

Papa balked at sending me to school to learn how to make neon signs. So, I went to an employment agency in Manhattan the morning after I arrived. A gruff man told me to fill out a form after I had waited for hours to see him. At least he actually read what I had written.

"We'll call you when we have something. Good-bye."

I got up very slowly. The phone rang.

157

"Oh yes," said the man.

He grabbed me by the sleeve.

"We have a young German-American here (German-American! I was in the Country all of 24 hours). He learned refrigeration abroad. He speaks English very well. He will see you eight o'clock in the morning. He'll bring his work clothes. Yes Sir."

He hung up and said to me: "Eight o'clock to-morrow. See Mr. Goldman at Puro Filter corner 8th Street and Lafayette Ave. Dress nicely and bring your work clothes with you. Here, give him this card."

I had a job the second day I was in New York!

# BROOKLYN, IRMA AND HER CROWD

Irma had a nice little bed room. I had to sleep in the waiting room. Mama converted the couch into a bed every evening and then reconverted it to a couch every morning when I went to work.

Irma was still going to high school. Because of her thorough education in Germany, she was way ahead of her classmates. Her English was excellent, too, by the time I arrived in New York. She was the top student in her class and was not even trying. She was in a clique of German-Jewish high school and college students with whom we spoke German. There were also some youngsters from Brooklyn so everybody spoke English when they were present.

In those days there was no tuition payment at either the Brooklyn College or the City College. All the students whom I met were Communist-Zionist. I told some of them that I could not understand how anyone could be a Communist and a Zionist at the same time. I pointed out to them:

"The Communists made it clear (in those days) that in conformity with Karl Marx' doctrine Capitalism and Communism could not long exist side by side on this globe. Therefore all capitalist governments must be overthrown, by force if necessary, including the one which so generously paid for your education. I think that the bunch of you are extremely ungrateful! Furthermore the Communists forbid all religions especially the Jewish Faith where they have control. They also want to eliminate all international borders."

(China under Chiang Kai-shek was not Communist then. No one in the West had ever heard of Mao Tse-Tung who had not yet established himself in the far north-western provinces of China. This Communist was totally dependent on the Soviet Union for money and weapons. He was in no position to tell Stalin, nor anyone else, to put their preaching into practice and eliminate the Russo-Chinese border. Stalin did not allow Chinese Communists to cross freely into Russia in accordance with the avowed Communist doctrine then promulgated throughout the world.)

"In contrast the Zionists want to establish a theocracy with very definite national borders in Palestine and call it Israel. To me the terms Zionism and Communism are mutually exclusive."

They arrogantly answered me: "Oh, you could not understand," and broke off the conversation.

Did **they** really understand? I often thought of those youths in later years after Israel was created. The Soviet Union never recognized its existence officially from the day it was founded until Mikhail Gorbachov inadvertently broke up the Soviet Union. When Gorbachov renounced the international claims of Communism, allowed freedom of speech and of religion, then Russia recognized the State of Israel.

At that time, in early 1937, I strongly advocated that the former Allies, including America, make a preemptive strike against Nazi Germany. Clearly Hitler had decided to make war. Why else would he have started an arms race with the West? But people would not hear of it. Yes, Jewish people! I told them that I was absolutely sure that war was going to ensue and that time was on the side of Hitler. They said that I was over reacting and called me a warmonger.

It made me very happy, a few years later, when I heard that I shared that same derogatory appellation with Winston Churchill. I was in good company. Mr. Churchill was called a warmonger by most of the press and many powerful politicians on the Nazi side as well as on the Allied side. Though, when Great Britain and France eventually did declare war, it made me most unhappy. I knew that it came far too late to be a preemptive strike. Hitler had been given almost two more years to build a huge modern land force.

# WORK AT PURO FILTER

Puro Filter made and leased water coolers for offices and factories. It was then located in downtown Manhattan on 8th Street, just south of Union Square. There were employment agencies on Union Square and the unemployed jammed the length and breadth of the square. There was hardly space for a car to squeeze through it. In those days there was no unemployment insurance in the United States. When one had no job, one had to rely on relatives, on charity by a religious organization, or starve! Sick and handicapped people were allowed to go on welfare.

My job was to salvage the refrigeration equipment of returned units. The refrigerant was methyl chloride. With its poisonous effects I happened to be quite familiar. The charges were let go right in the cellar. Fortunately, it was fairly well ventilated. I worked nine hours, five days a week, and six hours on Saturdays. I took home $10.oo per week, four times as much as I had earned in Jamaica. I also got a social security card. It entitled me to a federal government pension at age 65. This was due to a brand new law advocated and signed by President Roosevelt who was just then starting his second term in office. The bad part of the job was the methyl chloride. I left work with a headache every day.

After a few months I was transferred to the assembly department on the main floor. I installed the refrigeration units in the new or reconditioned water coolers, charged them with gas and tested them for leaks.

In those days the subway fares were five cents, a gallon of gas nine cents, and a loaf of white bread three cents. A visit to the barber shop cost an hour's pay: twenty-five cents. A white shirt cost twenty-five cents and a tie ten cents. For one cent one could buy a little Hersheys chocolate bar from an Automat. The latter were fastened at every other column in the subway stations. A post card with 1¢ printed on it, cost just that: one cent. Letters within the United States cost two cents, and those to foreign countries, cost three cents.

Once in a while I splurged at lunch time. I went to an Italian restaurant next door to the factory and had a plate of spaghetti with tomato sauce for twenty-five cents. If I really wanted to treat myself, I had an additional two meat balls for another ten cents and, if I wanted real luxury, which I did very, very seldom, I added a glass of Chianti, a very good dry red wine for another ten cents. I never added the meat balls and the wine on the same day. It was either the one or the other. Usually I had just the sandwich which Mama put in the Frigidaire for me in the evening before she went to bed.

In those days an office call to Papa would cost a patient two dollars and a house call five. Papa also made house calls for the Welfare Dept. for fifty cents. One night, well after midnight, Papa was called out by one of his welfare patients. After climbing the stairs to the 4th floor, (Papa had a bad heart), he found his patient and a friend of his pretty well boozed up. "There ain't nothin' wrong with me, Doc. It's just that my buddy here bet me that my doctor would not make house calls."

There is an old German proverb (It came from Sparta, well over 2000 years ago): *"Lerne zu leiden, ohne zu klagen."* (Learn to suffer, without complaining.) For my father it would have been more appropriate: *"Lerne zu klagen, ohne zu leiden."* (Learn to complain, without suffering.) One day my Old Man met his match in complaining about suffering due to hard times. In one of the apartment buildings lived an old, shabbily dressed man whom Papa had to visit regularly. Since the patient complained more about the difficulty of making ends meet than about his failing health, Papa, the compassionate, charged him only $2.oo instead of the usual $5.oo for each house call.

One day the patient was really upset: "The city is adding a 'Snow Clearing Tax' to all building owners based on the length of curbs at the edge of the side walk."

"What do you care. Your rent won't go up that much."

"Rent?! I own these three city blocks!"

Evidently it pays to learn to complain without suffering.

# SCHOOLING FOR NEON

The reason for coming to New York was to learn how to make neon signs. I found Egani's Technical Institute, the only neon glass blowing school in New York. It was on 125th Street, the main street of Harlem. I did not have the money for the tuition. Papa paid it after much grumbling.

I had to get up at 6 a.m., take the subway from Fort Hamilton Parkway and Prospect Ave. in Brooklyn, to Lafayette Ave. and 8th St. in Manhattan. On Wednesdays, after work, I took the subway to 125th St. and walked right across Harlem from 8th Ave. to 3rd Ave. to the glass blowing school. I was on my feet practically the whole time. In the subway on my way to work I usually had to stand. The nine and a half hours at work, I could only sit down during the half hour lunch time. I always had to stand during the subway ride to 125th Street. At school, blowing glass I could not sit down either. I was glad that I once had those long bicycle rides to check all the refrigerators on the line for the Jamaica Public Service and of my intensive swimming training. The combination of those two experiences had made me into quite an athlete.

On the ride home from Harlem, I always got a seat. The Yiddish newspaper *Forwerts* (Forward) was printed in Hebrew characters. Many readers abandoned the paper in the subway. I knew the characters for *kosher*. With the six different letters in *forwerts* and the two additional ones: "c" and "sh" in *kosher*, I could soon read the entire paper without too much trouble. Yiddish is more or less like High German with a different word order. I read the paper on the long rides home from school. I got home around 11:30 p.m. That was quite exhausting, even for me, as I did not get enough time for a good sleep.

I enrolled in the New York Electrical School in Manhattan to learn drafting, motor rewinding, house wiring and the electrical fire code on Tuesday and Friday nights. On Monday and Thursday nights I went to Brooklyn Technical School which charged no tuition. There I learnt mechanical drafting and machining. Riding the subway trains home from Brooklyn Tech. or the N.Y. Electrical School, I usually did not get a seat. Some evenings the conductor woke me up at the end of the line. I had one hand on the strap and was standing up, soundly asleep all alone in the entire train. That made the night even later than it already was, as I had a long subway ride back home. And I had to pay again for it, too!

After a while I realized that I was not making enough progress to satisfy me in only two hours per week at the glass blowing school. It was in my interest to learn as much as I could in as short a time as possible. It was in Eddie's, my teacher's, interest for me to learn as slowly as possible, as then he could charge me more tuition. I got permission from him to blow glass on Saturday afternoons after work, if I paid him for the extra glass. So, I worked five and a half days and went to school six nights. Saturday nights I quit school at 7 p.m. and Sundays I slept most of the day.

Papa gave Mama very little household money, often a $5.oo bill for the week and Mama would lament: "Paul, don't give me such a large bill. None of the stores want to change anything larger than a $1.oo bill." Herbert kept nagging me about being such a "leech," living off my parents at my age. I was nineteen then. He made me feel guilty about something I could not very well change. Looking for a better job would have been very difficult. Where would I find the time? We were still in a very bad recession, some even called it a depression. Since Mama made all my sandwiches, I decided to pay her the money which I had left over after making my tuition payments, paying for the extra glass and the subway fares. It amounted to more than the cost of the food I ate. We kept that quiet, lest Papa cut her weekly allowance for which she had to practically beg. I often wondered how Mama could make such wonderful dinners with so little money.

Herbert often ate with us and he smoked Papa's cigars at times, but I never saw him contribute anything. In all fairness to my eldest brother, he gave Papa excellent advice how to invest his money. At coffee time on Sundays Mama would serve some wonderful pastry with lots of whipped cream from the German bakery, Tell's, on Church Ave. That pastry cook used only pure butter as its fat for baking. Mama wanted peace in the house more than anything and Papa adored Herbert, so I kept my mouth shut and left the room when Herbert became too obnoxious. I did not want to make a scene.

There were definite goals which made the exhausting schedule worth while to endure: My own department at the Public Service, the swimming pool at the Bournemouth Club, the cheerful company of the fellow swimmers and the blue Caribbean Sea. New York was purgatory and the future in Kingston, Heaven on earth.

# MY SOCIAL LIFE IN NEW YORK

Mama was worried because I had no social life. I never mentioned girls. This seemed unnatural to my dear mother. Mama had taught me how to waltz before I left Hamburg about four years ago. That was all of my dancing experience. She persuaded Irma to let me escort her to a birthday party. Irma told Mama that I did not fit in with her crowd but she finally agreed to let me accompany her.

At the party I met a girl named Pearl. It turned out that she lived in the same house I lived in. I dared to ask her to dance with me. She did. It was not difficult at all. She happened to be an excellent dancer and adjusted easily to my clumsy attempts to dance a fox-trot. She was almost my height and had a beautiful figure. I never knew what to say to a girl but I thought it was obligatory to say something.

So I said: "You have beautiful fingernails."

"You like them? Have one."

She very slowly pulled her fingernail off her left index finger. I almost vomited! I had never heard of celluloid fingernails before. It revealed that her real fingernail had been very thoroughly chewed to the very limit. It must have hurt her to chew it that far.

Pearl invited me to visit her home to meet her family. I did. She told me that she was a senior at Erasmus Hall High School, and that she had trouble in Physics. Being ever the helpful one, I explained to her in great detail how a refrigerator worked. I told her that Frigidaire used a low side float valve and Kelvinator a high side one. I told her the advantages and, of course, the disadvantages of the one system over the other. I did not really make a hit.

In the fall of 1937, I joined the New York Field Hockey Club. We had two men's teams and one girls' team. Except for one girl and one man, we were all German refugees. We practiced in Staaten Island (now written Staten Island). We played a British and a Hungarian team and a team of the Philadelphia Cricket Club.

We always practiced with the girls. There was one girl there whom we called the Tank, not in front of her face, of course. She played fullback. She was very powerfully built. She would charge right into her opponent and knock her or him off balance. If you

166

should pass her, and she could not catch you, she would hook her stick under your wrist and really hurt you. That effectively eliminated you as an opponent, as you could not hit a ball hard for the rest of the practice.

The Christmas dinner-dance was coming. I did not want to go, since I did not have a girlfriend and besides it cost money. Mama, always looking out for me, insisted that I go. I went stag. There was the Tank. She had brought with her the most beautiful girl I had ever seen. She had on a stunning long sky-blue silk evening dress with a silver tiara. I found out her name, Jean David. I changed the table cards around a little bit, so that she was going to be seated next to me. She was as charming and vivacious as she was beautiful. We danced together all night and I accompanied her home.

We sat in the elevator of her apartment building holding hands. She squeezed up very close to me. I did not dare put my arm around her or kiss her for fear that the doorman, who was also the elevator operator, would come in any second and embarrass her. When a good half hour had passed and he had not come, I went out to look for him. He was still standing at the door. When he saw me, his Black face lit up with a grin from ear to ear: "Did you finish?" he asked as he passed me. I felt like turning around and giving him a swift kick in his pants! I asked her out once and took her to a museum. She declined all further invitations.

In January 1938, it became bitter cold. The one and only American girl in the field hockey club, Betty, asked me if I would take her ice skating the following Saturday night. I agreed. It was the coldest day of the year. I walked to her house. It was only about a mile or so from ours. She lived in a very neat two story house. She was ready.

We walked to the rink and I rented some skates. I had not skated since I had left Hamburg. She was the much better skater. She told me to hold her two hands crossing our arms in front of us. After a while I gained sufficient confidence in my ability and we skated much faster together. She hardly ever had to prevent me from falling anymore. She did not mind the cold but I was frozen right to my spine!

There was an unexpected hole in the ice. I lost my balance.

She tried to support me but I had too much momentum and fell right on top of her. At first she could not get up. She lay there and cried. She told me that she thought that her hip was broken. I helped her up, and we managed to get to a bench together where we could take off our skates. Her hip joint hurt badly. She limped the half mile or so home, leaning heavily on me. I carried her skates and her handbag in one hand and put my other hand around her waist practically carrying her. I would not have minded, if it had not been so miserably cold. Even though I had on good gloves and a shawl, I lost all feeling in my hands and my face.

At her house I just could not face the mile long walk to our home without warming up a little first. She invited me into the kitchen and made a cup of cocoa for each of us. She told me that her parents slept upstairs and sat down on my lap. I had never kissed a girl before. She showed me how to kiss. She was quite an expert at that, and I proved an apt pupil. Suddenly she jumped up. Her brother had come through the front door and found her sitting quite demurely at the opposite side of the table from me as he entered the kitchen. It was time for me to trudge home through the bitter cold. At least I started out feeling enormously hot.

# MY NEW YORK DRIVER LICENSE

The only hope to get more money at Puro Filters, was to become a serviceman. For that position I would need a driver's license. One of my fellow mechanics at the factory had an old, very heavy car. He let me drive it for a few minutes and lent it to me a few days later to take my driver's license test. I had never read the booklet on the rules of the road. I had driven only a few minutes on the right hand side of the road. But here I was in Brooklyn taking my test. The inspector made me drive down a nice, quiet street.

"Make a left turn at the next block."

I crossed the traffic into a fairly broad one way street. At the end of the block was a very busy avenue.

"Make a left turn at the end of this block."

I got into the left lane before I reached the corner. I felt very comfortable there as everybody in Jamaica always drove on the left hand side of the road. I waited for an opportune moment and then made a sharp left turn into the avenue staying on the left side, just as I would have done in Kingston.

There were three right hand and three left hand lanes. I found myself in the middle of the three left hand lanes. I had to stop as cars facing me were whizzing by on both sides of me at terrific speeds tooting their horns. Their drivers were shaking their fists. This seemed to make my unfortunate inspector feel exceedingly uncomfortable. He had drawn his knees to his chin and made a most unhappy face. After what seemed forever, the light changed and no cars passed me anymore. I could move over to the right side of the road.

"Do you know that you went through a red light?"

"I did not see any traffic light."

"No, this is a light street."

"What is a light street?"

"Just drive me back to the station."

I did. As he was about to get out, I asked:

"Did I pass?"

He gave me a very dirty look and a booklet. I had the gut feeling that I did not pass. My hunch proved to be correct: I did not pass. I looked up: Light Street. It was a street, where only every other block has a traffic light but that traffic light governs all intersections of that street. The cross streets which do not have a traffic light, have a little plaque on a pole near the intersection marked: LIGHT STREET. Each driver is supposed to notice and read that little plaque, drive to the corner, look at the light a block away, then see if he may proceed. I had never heard of such a system in my life but then this was "the land of the limited impossibilities", as Papa called it.

I read the booklet carefully. I passed the test the next month. I had a different inspector. I doubt that the first one would have entrusted his life into my hands again. I never found an occasion to use my license.

# DISCOURAGEMENT, TENACITY, AND NEON

I had written Gerhard that I did not like it in New York and that my job held no promise for the future. He wrote me back a very sharp letter, scolding me for failing to pursue the original idea. He told me that I should take a job in a neon shop. What Gerhard wrote seemed to make a lot of sense.

Eddie had promised to get a job for me upon graduation from the neon school. I quit my job at Puro Filter. Eddie told me that neon in New York is controlled by Local 3 of the International Brotherhood of Electrical Workers and they would not allow me to work in the City. He sent me to a neon shop in Waterville, Maine. I was to be the only glass blower, get a room to sleep in, all my meals and $5.oo per week. That sounded like a good opportunity to get a lot of experience.

A train took all night to get me there. It was in the middle of February. Mr. Taylor received me with great joy. His large house had no running water. My room in the attic contained a bed, a small kerosene stove and a wash stand with a bowl and a jug of water. The water was frozen. Charles Taylor warned me to turn off the stove before I went to sleep as there was the danger of carbon monoxide poisoning. We had fish cakes and rice for dinner.

After a very cold night we had a very skimpy breakfast of bread with margarine and a cup of coffee. Mr. Taylor was a Native American. He distrusted everyone. He was a retired circus clown and named his business the Circus Sign Co. His red-haired wife with a middle age bulge never said a word in my presence. He had two teenage daughters. He watched them like a hawk. They were not to talk to me. They smiled at me when their parents were not looking. When I came into the workshop in the basement, it was full of broken neon tubing. I worked as hard as I could to repair all those broken signs. I had to install some of the tubes outside. It was -30° Fahrenheit. To handle the glass better, I took off my gloves. That was a mistake. My fingers immediately froze to the glass and I broke the tubing trying to get my fingers off.

No matter what I did, Mr. Taylor, the semi-literate clown, quarreled with me. He was the most miserable person I had ever met. The food was monotonous, fish cakes and rice. Since there was no running water in the house, there were no baths. At nights the temperature went down to -40° and I had to trudge through the deep snow to the YMCA at the outskirts of the town to get a shower. It cost 25 cents. The deep snow in the forest started at the Y. It was very beautiful but bitter cold. The situation I found myself in was very bad. I had to buy my own kerosene for the puny stove in my room. I turned it off before I went to sleep, and the wash water had a thin sheet of ice on it every morning as I got up.

Since I had no money, but wanted to stay warm, I spent my evenings in the library. I read Emile Zola, *The Downfall*. It was a world famous novel about the Franco-Prussian war of 1870/71. It was both very anti-French Government and also very anti-German. After that, I read another book by the same author, *Nana*. It was a novel about a whore who completely dominated a very high official at the Imperial Court of France and ruined him. It was a very anti-royalist book.

Zola was best known for the Captain Dreyfus affair. That is why I chose his books. Poor Captain Alfred Dreyfus, a Jew from Alsace who had served with distinction in the French Army, was accused of treason and sent to the Devil's Island Penal Colony in French Guiana for many years. Much to the disgust of the top French society, and especially the judiciary, Zola found the guilty spy among the French Nobility and Dreyfus had to be released. It was too late. Dreyfus was an old, sick man and his wife and daughters were completely ruined by that time. Zola wrote a book, *The Dreyfus Affair*, which weakened the cause of the royalists in the Second Republic. I had read the German translation of that book years earlier. The reading was the most peaceful and pleasant time I had in Waterville.

Since Mr. Taylor, (that is what I was supposed to call this decrepit, cantankerous old man), was too weak to work, he often had a young French speaking fellow, of about my age, working for him on an hourly basis. Pierre, who spoke very little English, lived in Winslow which was connected to Waterville by a bridge across the Kenebec River. In that town only French was spoken. I told Pierre that I wanted to live somewhere else. He invited me to live with his parents, his married sister and family, his brother and

172

family, and him in a big old one-family house. I insisted that Mr. Taylor pay me $10.oo per week, and I gave half to Pierre's father. They gave me a nice warm room. Except for Pierre, none of them spoke any English.

In the evenings when I came home, one of the family would hand me the newspaper. None of them could read, so I was elected to read their newspaper to them in French. Of course, my vocabulary was so insufficient that I could not understand the key words of what I was reading, but they were happy since none of them had ever gone to school. Without me, they could not find out what it said in the newspaper. I wished that I had a French dictionary and that I had paid more attention to Studienrat Unbehaun's urging to do my homework and study the French vocabulary five eventful years earlier.

In Maine there were bitter feelings between the Francophone vast majority and the Anglophone minority as the latter got all the good jobs. The former, who could hardly read English, or not read at all, not even their own language, did all the poorly paying menial work. Almost all the unemployed in the state were French speaking. Besides that, there was the difference in religion. Practically all the Anglophones were Protestant and all the Francophones were Roman Catholics. The French kept their children out of public schools, where they would have to learn and speak English, tending to estrange them from their parents and their religion. It did not totally stop the integration, but it slowed it down. It caused quite a bit of bad blood and kept the French poor. The ecumenical movement was still many years in the future. The Roman Catholic Church ran quite a few parochial schools, where the teaching was in French, but very few parents could afford to pay for the public schools with their taxes and for the parochial school with their tuition and their Church contributions.

After I had been in Waterville for about two months, there was only one repair left in the shop and no orders at all. Mr. Taylor insisted that I should do that repair on Saturday morning. He owed me $10.oo. so, I came in.

We were all alone in the basement shop. I did the repair. He usually left me alone at work but this morning he hung around, watching every move I made. I repaired the tube, spliced it to the

173

vacuum system and was connecting the electrodes to the 7,500 Volt 1,200 KVA (kilo Volt Ampere) bombarder, (a transformer). I had one wire in my hand and was about to touch the other one, when the Clown threw the switch! I was flung across the shop, hitting my back violently against the work bench on the opposite side of the room. I had only recently bought very thick rubber soled shoes because of the icy cold cellar floor. Those rubber soles now saved my life. If I had touched both terminals at the same time, I would have received a shock ten times that of the electric chair in Sing Sing.

I was shaking like a leaf. When the would be murderer saw, that I was still alive, he yelled: "It was an accident! It was an accident!" He quickly ran out of the shop. I followed him upstairs and demanded my $10.oo. He sat close to his wife in the kitchen. He promised to give me my money if I finished the job. All the unit needed was pumping, a quarter of an hour's work for me at the most. I refused. I demanded my money. He gave it to me. I walked backwards out of the kitchen watching him. I did not trust him out of my sight.

On the way down the stairs, I met his elder daughter. She had tears in her eyes. She whispered: "Now again we won't have a glass blower for months and no money will come into the house." Feeling sorry for her, I went into the cellar and pumped the unit. This proves again the old adage: The world's most efficient source of power is a woman's tears.

I knew that one customer wanted to have his sign hung differently. I went to him and rehung the sign. He paid me a few dollars. It helped for the train ticket back to New York.

Eddie, the owner of Egani's, later told me that he sent the Chinese student, who had started a few months after I had started, to the same shop. He married the eldest girl and opened a shop 15 miles north, in Skowhegan, well out of the way of the miserable old clown, yet not too far from Waterville. I never went back to Maine.

# WORK IN QUEENS AND BROOKLYN

Eddie found me a job as a second glass blower and pumper at a little non-union neon shop in Long Island City. From the outside it looked like an empty store. Its plate glass window was painted black from the inside. I had to use a special knock before anyone opened the door. All the people inside were afraid that members of Local 3 of the I.B.E.W. would find the shop and beat up everyone inside, even kill us or at the very least destroy all the equipment. It was the only neon job, Eddie could find. The pay was very little. The risk of bodily harm very great. Worst of all, there was only one set of burners, so that I got next to no glass blowing experience. They did not have a good designer, so I did a bit of design work. I was very unhappy there. After a couple of months the shop closed down.

Papa introduced me to a patient of his who claimed that he did refrigeration work. He had a big repair job in a bar. He promised me a big share of the profits, if I helped him. I took the job. He took me to the basement underneath a bar. There was a large unit which was supposed to keep the beer cold on the floor above. The stench in the basement was terrible. The owner kept cats down there to keep the rat population down. There were no boxes with cat sand. There was no disposal of dead rats either. From time to time a man would enter from the street and roll a barrel of beer down a ramp and take an empty one out. He also brought in a lot of bitter cold winter air. That was the extent of ventilation for this pest hole. Besides that, there was the smell of stale beer. I almost became sick when I first entered that cellar.

There was a two cylinder refrigeration compressor. I had never seen one as big as that. I put on my gauges and found that one of the heads had no compression at all. When I took off the cylinder head, it was obvious that some fool had completely ruined the valve plate and valves. The part numbers were engraved on the parts. I gave my new employer the part numbers and he purchased the needed parts. I made new gaskets, drew a vacuum on the compressor, flushed the compressor with the refrigerant, and it worked very well, just like new.

Earlier my employer had told me that he would be working right along with me. I never saw him in work clothes. That should have opened my eyes. I worked three days in that filthy, stinking cellar. My employer promised to pay me. He never did. What a perfect partnership! He got the money and I gained the experience. His name be forgotten. Forever!

# LIFE IN BROOKLYN AFTER MAINE

Papa and Herbert scolded me at least once a week for having given up my job at Puro Filter. Herbert called me a leech and blamed me for "sitting on the pocket of my aging father." Papa was 59 at that time and he kept complaining bitterly how hard he had it. His practice was not very busy but years later I found out that he was doing quite well financially at that time.

Once in a while I went upstairs in our apartment building to visit Pearl Keysler and her family. One evening Pearl, who was by now going to New York University, told me that she had to write how a refrigerator worked for her Physics Class. Would I write the paper for her? I did. She copied it word for word. She phoned me a few days later that she got an "A" for that paper. That made me feel great. I, who had left high school in the middle of the tenth grade five years earlier, got an "A" at the prestigious New York University. At that university students were required to pay tuition, unlike Brooklyn College or City College which were free.

Irma took me to the birthday party for Reba Weiner. She was a shy girl and did not seem to fit in with the rest of the crowd. She was very friendly to me when she heard that I could draw since she was a commercial art student. She asked me to visit her and give her pointers on her drawings. I visited her several times and I did help her with her drawings. I did not think her very talented but she was a real lady. I liked her and I felt that the feeling was mutual. I was very conscious of my being unemployed and poor. Besides, we both were very shy and never kissed each other. I felt that I had no right to encourage any amorous feelings as I wanted to go back to Jamaica as soon as I had some more neon experience.

Some Sundays in the summer I went to the beach at Coney Island with two of Irma's girl friends, Romie Margolin and Alice Goldstein and my second cousin, Kenneth Von Der Porten. The girls and Kenneth sat mostly on a blanket on the crowded beach, while I, disliking crowds, swam out having the lifeguards chasing me. They never caught me.

The girls often visited Irma. They lived on the opposite side of Prospect Park. There were no street lights in that park then. They walked home as late as midnight right across the park. The thought of danger never occurred to them. Once in a while I would walk them home. It was the time when J. Edgar Hoover was the head of the F.B.I. There were about four murders a year in New York then. Now, there are between five and six a day.

Papa had a way of yelling at Mama. Mama tried hard to please everybody and especially my Old Man but he had a total lack of sensitivity. I could see that Mama was very unhappy. She still missed Hamburg and the way of life there. She took English lessons at a school across the park. She had to walk, while Papa drove everywhere in his vintage Dodge. At times I accompanied her. We set out to go to her school but more often than not, we ended up at a movie, especially if it featured Greta Garbo, her favorite actress. "One learns English in a movie, too," she would rationalize.

One evening, at dinner, Papa yelled at Mama for some very petty reason. I said to him quietly that he could have said the same thing in a polite way, too. He turned on me and shouted that he was talking to his wife, and that I had no right to interfere. That particular evening I was in no mood to take it. I got up, stood over him and made sure that he was aware that he was no match for me. "You don't yell at my mother and let me hear it or of it! Do you understand?!"

He did, and he never yelled at my dear Mama again in my presence. Herbert seemed to have heard of the confrontation and was impressed. He never said anything unpleasant to me or of me, at least not in my presence, for the rest of my stay in Brooklyn. I should have done this much earlier.

It was the time of the Nazi threat to Germany's neighbors in Eastern Europe. By this time the Germans had a modern and mighty military force. Most Americans were very "isolationist." They had a loose organization called: America First. Their leader was a very popular American hero: Charles Lindbergh, who had made the first solo flight across the Atlantic. They felt that the Europeans should stew in their own fat and that America should keep out of any armed conflict that might develop over there. There were also three major and distinct pro-Nazi organizations in the U.S.: The German Bund with mostly German and pro-Nazi

American members; the Ku Klux Klan (KKK), a residue from the Civil War (1861 to 1865) which was mainly against the non-whites, Jews, and Roman Catholics; and Father Coughlin's Silver Shirts mostly in the Mid-West who were also against non-Whites and Jews, but also against Protestants. The three groups applauded Hitler and his racial violence but fortunately for America, the last two organizations hated each other.

In downtown Manhattan there was a naval recruiting office. I always had a love for the sea, and New York was a hateful place as far as I was concerned. I stood in front of that office for a very long time but I did not go in. I took the subway home again. I found a seat. A young man, about my age and build, entered the car. There were no more seats. He stood up exactly in front of me. He was neatly dressed and wore a tie clip with the insignia of the Bund, dominated by a large swastika. It identified him as member of the German-American Nazi organization.

I had a really hard time to control myself. This filthy Nazi movement was the reason why I found myself in this poverty stricken situation in a city where I did not fit in, where I could not find a career. It all boiled up in me as this symbol of malevolence was flaunted only inches from my nose for the half hour subway ride! If I had followed my desire, I would have gotten myself into deep trouble by punching this guy in his face with all my might. Fortunately I listened to my brain and not to my feelings. I did not touch him.

One evening when the subway train passed the Brooklyn Navy Yard about twenty sailors entered the car. They were all paired. Each American sat next to one in a French Navy uniform. I asked the American who sat next to me why that was so. He told me that the Americans had been ordered to show the French the town, but he spoke no French and the Frenchman spoke no English. That seemed to be true for the rest of the pairs judging by their silence.

I tried my little bit of school French on the chap in front of me. He spotted my German accent right away.

He said in perfect German: "You might as well speak German to me if you prefer that to French. I am from near Strassburg in Alsace. We speak German at home."

"I am from the Elb-Sandsteingebirge. I was a Sudeten German

before I became an American Citizen!" said the American also in flawless German. "We, too, spoke German at home!"

(He was from a mountain range which is the border between the Czech Republic and Saxony. He was from the German speaking area just south of the German-Czechoslovakian border.) The three of us had a lively conversation in German until I had reached my destination.

If it had not been for me the two of them would never have found out that they had a language in common, their Mother tongue. They would have been as mute and dull as the rest of the pairs. I had done my good deed for the day. I felt certain that in the not far distant future both of them would be called upon to fight the people who spoke the language which united them. I often wondered how they fared in the War but I am sure that I shall never find out. I never even asked their names.

# A FATAL ACCIDENT

Early in August 1938, out of the blue, an air mail letter arrived from the Jamaica Public Service, signed by Mr. Caithness, the sales manager. There had been a motor car accident killing one serviceman and sending another to the hospital in serious condition with a broken hip. (Sulfa drugs had not yet been discovered and antibiotics were even further in the distant future.) The prognosis was: Several months in the hospital for the broken hip to heal.

Norris Spencer was the one in the hospital. He had been the service man who taught me refrigeration. He was the top refrigeration mechanic in the entire Colony. I felt truly sorry for him. I did not even know the one who died.

The letter stated that if I still wanted my job I had to come back to Jamaica right away. The joy I felt that I would soon go back to Jamaica overshadowed all other feelings. But there was a hitch: My German passport had expired. I had to go to the German Consulate to get a new one. I had heard rumors that the Nazis, if they wanted Germans hostile to them, had abducted them as soon as their targets had stepped on German soil, such as German ships or embassies. I told Papa: "If I don't call you by 2:00 p.m., call the police and get me out of there."

The consulate was facing Battery Park on the southern end of Manhattan, a few flights up in a typical office building. I walked in. A well dressed clerk at the desk greeted me saying:

*"Heil Hitler*, what can I do for you?" in very good English.

I answered him in German: *"Guten Tag,* I want my passport renewed."

He called out: *"Fräulein* Petersen."

A well dressed, pretty young lady came at once.

*"Heil Hitler,* follow me please."

We went into her office. and she looked at my expired passport. It still had the old Weimar Republic eagle on it. The photo inside was taken when I was 12. There were no marks to indicate that I was a refugee.

She said: "I can't renew this. I would have to issue a new one, but you can go home on the expired one."

181

"I have to visit another country first. That's why I want a valid passport."

"But you have not yet served in the military. All right, I'll give you a new passport and expect you to return to Germany before it expires. I can only issue it for three months. If you do not return to the *Reich* by then, you will lose your citizenship."

I gave her my photos which were taken on my way to the consulate only minutes earlier. She typed out the necessary forms, dated the passport, stapled in one photo and took me into a larger office.

The man at the desk signed the passport and repeated more or less what Miss Peterson had already told me. He handed me my key to return to Jamaica, said:

*"Heil Hitler."*

I said: *"Auf Wiedersehn."* Miss Petersen led me out of the room, shook my hand, said:

*"Heil Hitler."*

I said: *"Auf Wiedersehn."*

As I passed the receptionist he said: *"Heil Hitler."*

I said: *"Auf Wiedersehn,"*

went out of the door and raced to the nearest pay phone, as it was almost 2:00 p.m. and called Papa and told him that I had my passport and that I was O.K.

I did not care that the new passport had the hated swastika underneath the eagle on its cover. It unlocked the door to take me home to Kingston! Away from Brooklyn, from misery, where I could never feel at home, though Mama had certainly tried to make me feel loved.

I went to the United Fruit Co. office. They had only one berth left in the first class, and I had to share the cabin with an elderly man. That was certainly acceptable to me.

The last day in Brooklyn at 135 Prospect Park SW was a Sunday in August, 1938. Herbert had come over to play Skat with our parents. I had to discuss money with Papa, so I said:

"After this round, can I see you for a few minutes in your office?"

"Be reasonable. Don't you see that we are playing Skat?!"

Skat had become more important than anything, anybody and

especially me. I got up and went for a walk. Mama opened the window and tried to call me back but I walked for hours trying to get calm. It was late at night when I went back and to bed and slept in Brooklyn for the last time for a long time to come.

# BACK TO JAMAICA

It was a wonderful feeling to see the modern, little United Fruit Co. motor ship. Diesel engines had replaced coal fired steam engines on recently built ships. Old King Coal had been dethroned and oil was becoming the dominant source of energy. The thought occurred to me that the need for coal had been the reason that the World War of 1914 had been fought, spilling so much blood only 24 to 20 years earlier, and now the demand for coal was being pushed aside as oil was becoming the dominant source of energy. It showed how unnecessary that War was, and the subsequent bitter feelings and political turmoil it still provoked.

I did not dwell long on the economic power of oil that would soon embroil us in another World War. I was on board a banana boat, going to Jamaica, the blue Caribbean and a good job! There were hardly any male passengers on board and I was lionized by the ladies but I was still too naïve to take advantage of the situation.

In Kingston I was put in charge of commercial refrigeration. Gerhard concentrated his sales mainly on commercial customers. He sold especially to the much neglected Chinese customers. He was thoroughly familiar with who was who in the Chinese Community through his work with Tai Ten-Quee. Up to that time only Mr. Abner had made ice cream commercially. He had brought his equipment from Chicago. He sold ice cream only through his restaurant in King Street and his night club, *The Glass Bucket.*

Gerhard sold an ice cream maker to a Chinese restaurant. There are several rival Chinese groups in Jamaica. What the one has, the others have to get right away. Thus quite a few ice cream makers and storage cabinets were sold. Some large Chinese groceries bought refrigerated display cases from Gerhard. I had lots of installation and commercial repair work to do. I made very sure that all installations were done as well as possible. They benefited Gerhard's sales. I trained two apprentices. One was Henriques. He had started just before I had left Jamaica a year and eight months earlier. He was a particularly bright young man. He was Black and not related to the two well known and rich Henriques families.

# "PEACE IN OUR TIME"

Hitler had always wanted to reunite Germany with Austria. After all, Vienna had been the official capital, not only of Austria, but also of Germany until 1866, when Prussia wrested the title of being the predominant German State away from Austria in the short war over the government of Schleswig-Holstein. Until that time the Hapsburg Emperors in Vienna had been the titular monarchs over all of the German states. Their power was very limited, however, because of a very weak constitution and the fact that every state in Germany had its own army.

The Kingdom of Prussia, which was technically not a part of the German Empire, and the State of Brandenburg which very definitely was, were ruled by the Hohenzollern family for more than two centuries. On January 18, 1871, King Wilhelm III of Prussia, Prince Elector of Brandenburg, had himself crowned Kaiser Wilhelm I, Emperor of the Germans, thanks to the genius of Otto v.Bismarck. All German speaking states were included in this union except Austria, Liechtenstein, Luxenburg, and Switzerland. The latter country had fought a war of independence from the Empire in the 13th century and had remained a republic ever since.

The armies of the other German states were too weak to represent any challenge to the Prussian forces. How much Prussia dominated the other states can be seen by the choice of the colors for the new national flag of the united Germany: black-white-red. Black-white was the flag of Prussia and white-red the flag of Brandenburg. Colors of any other state were not represented in the new Empire's flag. Nevertheless, almost all German states had at least one of those colors in its state flag.

After Hitler had formed his Government in 1933, he had all Communist delegates to the *Reichstag* (House of Representatives) arrested. With that stroke he had an absolute majority in the parliament. He needed control of the army to be able to abolish the Weimar Constitution. v.Schleicher, the Minister for Defense, who had been supported by President Paul v.Hindenburg, was an obstacle. He was murdered. There was no investigation. v.Neurath, the foreign minister, a holdover from the v.Paapen

185

government, joined the Nazi party and remained in his office. He was the voice for caution and for peace. Naturally, he never enjoyed Hitler's confidence. v.Ribbentrop, the former champagne salesman and a member of Hitler's innermost circle, became the ambassador to London.

Engelbert Dollfuss was the popular, if strong armed President of Austria. In 1934, about a year after I left Germany, he was murdered. Nazis were suspected, but a proper investigation could have led to armed unrest. Kurt v.Schuschnigg took over that country's government. He did not have the political strength of Dollfuss, yet he fought the Nazis in his country valiantly until early in 1938, despite enormous pressure from his northern neighbor. Though the Nazis were mostly youthful and very noisy, they did not represent the majority. Union with Germany was a very popular idea in Austria and much more so in Germany, but rule by the Nazis was not what many people wanted in Austria. To prove this, Schuschnigg ordered a referendum to show the voters' choice to the world and especially to the Nazis.

Hitler must have known that his Nazis in Austria would lose an honest election. He handed the Austrians an ultimatum on March 11, 1938. The Austrian Army was no match for the German's. Schuschnigg turned over the reins of government to Artur Seyss-Inquart, a Nazi, the next day, rather than fight a hopeless war against Germany. The election was never held. Schuschnigg was imprisoned until the Allies freed him in 1945. The German Army marched into Austria to cheering crowds.

This bloodless victory emboldened Hitler. About four million Germans lived in Czechoslovakia. They or their parents had been Austrian citizens before Czechoslovakia was founded after World War I. Now Hitler put unbearable pressure on the Czech President Emil Hácha until that poor man called on France and Great Britain for help. Mr. Neville Chamberlain, the British Prime Minister, and M. Edouard Daladier, the French Premier, consulted with each other. As a result Mr. Chamberlain was dispatched to Munich where Hitler treated him very arrogantly. An agreement, "the Munich Agreement," was reached.

The Germans were to take over the mountains which had made a natural border of Czechoslovakia and where German was still spoken. Those mountains had been heavily fortified by the considerable, modern Czechoslovakian Army. Without those fortifications Czechoslovakia was defenseless. In return Hitler promised that he would let the rest of Czechoslovakia alone and make no more demands for any land acquisition.

Mr. Chamberlain flew home to England. The *News Reel*, which was usually shown before any movie started in the English speaking world, including Kingston, Jamaica, where I saw it, showed Mr. Chamberlain standing on top of the stairs which had been wheeled to his plane. The large black umbrella, which was the Prime Minister's trademark-like companion at all times, was held over his head by an attendant. He waved a piece of paper over his head and shouted in his thin, high pitched voice: "Peace in our time!"

A few days later Hitler marched into Czechoslovakia past the unmanned fortifications right into the capital of Prague. The Munich Agreement had served the Nazis well. It allowed them to march past the fortifications without losing a man. As for the part where it said to stay in the mountains, that was completely ignored by Hitler. Poor President Hácha was brought to Berlin and subjected to so much pressure, until the poor man eventually signed the Chechoslovakian independence away. All other Czechoslovakian political figures of importance disappeared, never to be heard from again. It was not at all unusual for Hitler to break his word.

France and Great Britain did nothing. They did not even rearm. France felt safe behind the Maginot line, the mighty fortifications, which it had built in the Vosges Mountains, and Britain was secure on the far side of the Channel. The Belgians had built an "impregnable" defense line with the broad Prince Albert Canal as its center piece. The whole world knew that all the bridges across that canal were mined and could be blown up at the first sign of a threat.

Papa's brother, my Uncle Ernst, and his wife, Aunt Friedl, certainly trusted those defenses. They had fled to Antwerp. Marianne, their youngest daughter, had fled to Amsterdam and had married a Dutch Jew by the name of Svart. The Netherlands had always been able to remain neutral since Napoleon's time. She, too, felt safe. Her husband was drafted into the Dutch Army. Holland's main defense was the breaching of the dikes, to drown invading forces.

The popularity of Germans was at its lowest point possible among the vast majority of the people in the civilized world. Dorrie and Gerhard applied to become British Subjects. I would have applied, too, at this point but one had to be five years in the Country. With my year and a half interruption in the United States, I had been only three and a half years in Jamaica though I had landed there the first time on November 15th, 1933, almost five years ago. Many people expressed the hope that the Germans would push too far East, and that the Russian Communists and the German Nazis would destroy each other, thus save the Western World the trauma of any armed involvement.

The French and British governments eliminated that possibility, however, when they guaranteed the Polish borders. Chamberlain and Daladier declared that they would go to war if the Polish borders were violated. Hitler mistook that statement for a bluff. Poland was the next obvious target of the Nazis. Its independence and its borders were the result of the Treaty of Versailles. The very treaty, which Hitler had said, was not worth the paper it was written on. As a deterrent for the French and the British to make good on their word, Hitler had the "Siegfried Line" built just east of the Rhine. It was his defense line using a lot of concrete for pillboxes, tank traps and under ground command centers, should the Western Allies try to come to the aid of his targeted enemies on the eastern front.

General Charles de Gaulle, then only one of many French Generals, had written a text book on future offensive warfare. It required dive bombers and self propelled artillery. The Germans followed the book's suggestions for their modern army. It was as new a concept to modern warfare as Alexander the Great's phalanx was to armies of 340 B.C.

Though the British and French guaranteed the border of Poland, they did nothing to show that they were willing to translate their word of honor into action if Hitler dared to challenge their sacred resolve. The Allies failed to prepare themselves for a quick, powerful thrust into Germany which would be the only conceivable way to come to Poland's rescue. A poorly concealed build up of an attack force in Eastern France, preferably including British soldiers, would have been the only way which might have convinced Hitler that the two Western Powers were serious, when they made the threat. Even building a powerful air force might have helped.

The British did not even start to build an army from their tiny nucleus of land forces. Their soldiers, as well as those of the French, still had World War I bolt action seven shot rifles. The British had a navy which was far superior to the German Navy, but that could not relieve pressure on Poland. The shallow mud flats along the German North Sea coast had been good defenses from when the Romans had tried to land and they still were in 1938. The mouths of the Rivers Weser and Elbe were, by then, defended with long range canons and the rocky island off the German coast in the North Sea, Heligoland, was also fortified with powerful guns.

The entrance to the Baltic Sea could easily be blocked with submarines, minefields and land based planes. The French had an army which was at least as large as the German *Wehrmacht* but it had no offensive capabilities. Its powerful artillery was mounted in fixed pill boxes called the Maginot line a good distance west of the Rhine. Neither the British nor the French Air Forces had sufficient fighter planes to defend against the new German dive bombers, and they certainly had no bombers to bomb any German Army which might invade Poland. The range of bombers, at that time, was not great enough to fly against German troops at the Polish border and return to French bases. If I could see that clearly just from *The Daily Gleaner* and the *News Reel* reports in peaceful little Jamaica, it must certainly have been obvious to Hitler and his gang.

v.Neurath, the German foreign minister, and Admiral Raeder, the commander of Germany's Naval Forces, warned Hitler not to provoke a war with Great Britain as the German Navy was no match for the British as yet. The German Navy was just building its first air craft carrier. (That carrier was never completed.) Besides, Germany had nowhere near enough submarines to starve out the British Isles. Hitler was a land lubber, and none who surrounded him were from the coast. He never did understand naval warfare and greatly underestimated its importance.

Admiral Raeder was a proponent of a high sea fleet to be strong enough to fight the British. Admiral Dönitz, the commander of the submarines, wanted enough submarines to blockade Great Britain effectively, but the bulk of the naval budget went to the high sea fleet, and his submarines never numbered more than 60. This tug of war over the budget prevented Germany from having either. It wound up with too small a high sea fleet to fight the British, as well as too small a submarine fleet to blockade the British Isles decisively.

When one looked at the *News Reels* and read the papers it seemed pretty clear that Hitler did not expect to fight the British. He built up an enormous land force. Clearly, he was preparing to make war in the East with Poland and Russia. He seemed to count on British and French neutrality. The German fleet did not seem important to him.

Roosevelt appointed Joseph P. Kennedy, a Boston Irishman, who had made a fortune with his Scotch Whiskey monopoly, as the American Ambassador to Great Britain. v.Ribbentrop, also a former alcohol salesman, and Kennedy became fast friends. v.Ribbentrop is reported to have told Hitler that Great Britain would never fight without America's backing and that America would never support Britain in another war. That was made perfectly clear by President Roosevelt's sending an anti-British Irishman to the Court of St. James.

v.Ribbentrop was admitted to King George VI. He did not make the customary bow but stretched out his arm in a Nazi salute and yelled: "Heil Hitler!" turned and left for Germany to replace v.Neurath. The latter was demoted to be the *Gauleiter* (Governor) of Bohemia (now the Czech Republic). Slovakia was severed into a separate dependent state with a Slovak Nazi at its helm. Now Hitler had no one to advise him against bold moves that might plunge Germany into the abyss of war.

The Hungarians did not want to be conquered by the huge German Army. They elected Admiral Miclós Horthy, who made a pact of alliance with Germany. In that way they kept foreign troops out of their country for the time being.

In scandal ridden Romania, the British owned the all important oil wells. The fascist, very anti-Semitic party, caused a lot of unrest. King Carol and his well publicized mistress became very unpopular.

The couple left for Brazil and his son, Michael, became King. Unfortunately, that teenager could not stem the rising tide which washed that unfortunate country into chaos. With Hitler's money and arms the Romanian Fascist Party took over and allied itself with Germany.

It was a tragedy for all mankind and especially for the millions of Europeans who were killed in the coming war that America took an isolationist position, but it was even more deplorable that Britain and France failed to start to build a believable, highly mobile offensive force in Alsace and Lorraine so that Hitler could not possibly mistake the French-British guarantee of the Polish border for an idle threat.

Winston Churchill, a conservative member of parliament, kept criticizing his party's leadership for its appeasement of Hitler. He kept saying that it was a policy of weakness which Hitler kept exploiting. Churchill was considered a dangerous rival for the Prime Minister's office by Chamberlain and his close friend, the ex-Prime Minister Baldwin. The two, Chamberlain and Baldwin, spent all their political power and resources on fighting the threat of a possible Churchill victory in Parliament rather than on concentrating on a national effort concerning European politics. When Baldwin had been made Prime Minister earlier, before Chamberlain, Churchill had gotten up in Parliament, imitating a country fair barker and shouted: "Hear ye! Hear ye! Come to see the greatest wonder of the world: The first and only British Prime Minister who is able to stand up, even though he has not got any spine at all!"

Danzig (now Gdansk) was an old Hansa City, a republic within the German Reich, until the end of World War I. Its population was almost 100% German. The Treaty of Versailles made it an independent republic. Poland guaranteed that it should remain that way. Poland declared that if the Germans marched into Danzig, there would be war. Poland had practically no air force. Their armed forces were every bit as large as the German but they still had horse drawn artillery and cavalry with carbines and lances. Most of it consisted of a militia where the soldiers worked in other jobs during the days and had their uniforms hanging in their closets. Their army was not a cohesive, professional force. When they dared to threaten Germany they must have relied on the British-French guarantee of their border.

There is the ancient German foreign policy goal: *"Drang nach Osten."* "Pressing towards the East." As the Anglo-French Treaty with Poland had the possibility of a western front, Hitler decided to protect himself against Russian intervention. Vyacheslav Molotov, the tough Soviet Foreign Minister, came to Berlin, bringing a lot of bodyguards with him. He signed a treaty of friendship with v.Ribbentrop, the Nazi Foreign Minister, and a member of Hitler's innermost circle.

Ever since one had first heard of Hitler, his name had been associated with a fierce anti-Communist and anti-Russian propaganda. Now, suddenly, he formed a treaty of alliance with his former sworn enemy. The world was surprised and shocked.

# LIFE IN KINGSTON IN 1938

One afternoon only Mr. Metcalf, the service manager, and I were alone in the workshop, when Mr. Goetz, a German, the chief tanner of Harty's Leather, walked into the department. He first talked to Mr. Metcalf, then he came over to where I was working.

"Why are you always badmouthing Germany?!" he demanded to know in a loud voice and in German.

I answered: "I never do. I only speak out against the Nazis."

"There is no difference. Germans and *National Sozialisten* (derisively called: Nazis) are one and the same, and 'who is not for us, is against us and must be wiped out from the face of the earth!' (A popular Nazi slogan) You son of a bitch of a traitor!"

I was about to go at him when I saw Mr. Metcalf get up. So, I just turned my back on him. The firm Goetz represented, Harty's Leather, was an important customer, and if I attacked that Nazi, I would most likely have lost my job. He was not worth that risk. I let it ride. It was most unfortunate and infuriating for people like me that the damned Nazis were most successful in their quest to make the concept of Nazi synonymous with that of German. Mr. Metcalf was an Englishman. He spoke no German and could not have understood what was said. He asked what it was all about. I told him that Mr. Goetz had insulted me because I was not a Nazi. I heard no more about it in the Company.

Marie Eisenmenger, Meis for short, had come from Offenbach to visit her elder sister, Dorrie, Gerhard's wife. Meis had a very cheerful disposition and charm. She was engaged to a Willie Müller in Germany. I took her swimming and hiking. She liked both of those sports. We got on very well together.

Once when I took her swimming at the Springfield Club, I introduced her to John Silvera, Jamaica's long distance swimming champion. He had arrived at the club with his cat boat. It consisted of a hollowed out "cotton tree" (kapok tree) with a mast, boom, and sail. It had no keel. He invited us to go sailing in the harbor with him. There was a very nice breeze, ideal weather for sailing. It was late afternoon. We sailed out a good distance. Meis had done a lot of paddling with Willie on German rivers and canals and felt very comfortable in the little boat. She was lying as close as she could on the luff where I was sitting in the bow and John sat in the stern holding the line controlling the sail in one hand and the tiller in the other.

The sun was turning red and was low on the horizon when John decided to return to the pier at the Springfield club. I saw Dorrie and Gerhard walking toward the pier. To stop the boat one has to turn into the wind. So, John gave the warning: "Coming about." He and I changed sides as the boom passed over Meis's head. She, being a landlubber, did not shift her weight to the opposite side, and the boat capsized. Meis was covered by the little sail. She reappeared laughing about fifteen seconds later, and we all swam to the pier only a few feet away, towing the boat behind us.

Poor Dorrie, she saw her unfortunate little sister submerge in the "shark infested" waters of the Kingston Harbour! She almost died of fright. She gave me a really terrible tongue lashing for leading her little sister to her doom! Well, almost. Meis tried to calm Dorrie down. But Dorrie held this "disaster" against me for years. Yet, Meis was more than three years older than I and was certainly fully responsible for her own actions. I could not accept or reject the offer to go into the boat for her. It was thoughtless of us not to tell her that one has to watch the boom and shift one's weight to the opposite side of the boat when the helmsman says: "Coming about."

There was a swimming meet for the Jamaican championships. I was to compete for the two hundred meter breast stroke junior championship. The favorite was the schoolboy champion, Douglas Bird. We had trained together and he was good. We both belonged to the Jamaica Amateur Swimming Club. There were five contestants. In the last minute three of them decided to drop out. They had all raced against Douglas before and lost. I was asked to concede the race to Douglas to speed up the affairs of the evening but I decided to race.

We stood at the pool's edge. My knees felt so weak, I wondered if I could find the strength to even push off. When the starter's pistol went off, I suddenly flew! I let Douglas set the pace. I stayed behind him just a head's length. We were to swim six 33 1/3 m laps. During the fourth lap I heard Walter Rogers, the

194

announcer, say: "The race is already decided, Von der Porten cannot pass Bird." Turning for the fifth lap, I started to make my move. I quickly passed Douglas and the race really speeded up. The crowd screamed: "Douglas, Douglas!" He tried, but I increased my lead, and I was Junior Champion of Jamaica for 200 m Breast Stroke! It was a wonderful feeling!

GOAL KEEPER

GETTING READY TO RACE

# MY FIRST WRESTLING LESSON

One evening, while training, I found myself swimming laps with Victor Khalil, the Light Weight Wrestling Champion of Jamaica. I had not forgotten the embarrassment when I had wrestled with Spencer. So, I asked Victor:

"Can you give me a lesson in wrestling?"

With all of his huge muscles he was still a slow swimmer. I had given him tips on how to improve his style and consequently boost his speed.

"Sure. Hey fellows, everybody come to my yard. Von der Porten wants me to show him how to wrestle!"

I just wanted some tips privately. Now the entire elite of Jamaican swimmers and lots of their girlfriends trouped to Victor's house up the street in their swimsuits to watch him show me how to wrestle. He got a wrestling mat out of the house, spread it on the lawn and told me: "Grab me anywhere you want."

I put his head in a head lock by squeezing my arms around his powerful neck as hard as I could. He put his arm behind my knees, lifted me high into the air and, as my arms slid off his neck and head, he flung me on the mat. I thought all my bones were broken. The fellows yelled and the girls screeched applause. He gave me no time to muse. He came at me again. I put the head lock on even harder. The result was no different. I flew through the air and landed on the exact same bones I had landed on before. The pain was terrific! The applause got even worse, (as far as I was concerned). He came at me again but this time he had his arms away from his chest. I put my head under his right arm pit, grabbed his right arm with both hands and threw him up into the air. He doubled up his knees. One caught me on my left eye brow. I fell on top of him. He was covered with blood. All the cheering stopped.

"Victor! you are bleeding!"

"No is you!"

I felt with my index finger above my left eye. I felt the bone. There was no skin, just bone and blood. They made me lie down.

197

Victor got a bottle of rum, the Jamaican all purpose medicine. He washed out the wound.

"Do you feel anything?"

"No."

My head was far too numb for any sensation. They bandaged me up the best they could. I had to go back to the Bournemouth Club to get my pants and shirt and then walk home to Arlington Ave., change into a white suit, walk back to Windward Rd. to take a tram car, change to another one at King Street, get off at North Street to walk to the Public Hospital, and all that with a bandage over one eye.

Dorrie and Gerhard had moved to a rented house in Bournemouth Gardens, but Dorrie still worked long hours in the factory where I still lived upstairs. At home, Dorrie spotted me just as I was about to sneak out. I certainly did not want to frighten her with my face! I turned my good side to her thereby facing a window. "There, look there is a plane!" Planes were very rare in Jamaica in those days. Dorrie looked and I cleared out fast.

It was over an hour after the end of the wrestling lesson by the time I reached the hospital. My head was pounding. A pretty Black student nurse spotted me in the packed waiting room. She took off my bandage and took me to the doctor on duty in the emergency room. He glanced at me and said: "Stitch him up." She took me to a bench, where another nurse was stitching up a stab wound in a woman's hand. I sat next to that woman, and the two nurses chatted amicably about a date, while they were stitching away. My beauty did an admirable job. Today there is hardly a noticeable scar.

When she had finished she ushered me into a little room.

"You have to have a tetanus shot." I started to take off my jacket. "You can keep on yo jacket, Sah. Please take off yo pants, Sah!" She said that with a very nice smile.

"What? Me take off my pants in front of you? No, certainly not!"

I had never exposed myself in front of a woman, and I was definitely not going to do so in front of this slim, young girl!

"Yo gwain take off yo pants, Sah, or I'm gwain take off yo pants, Sah."

The audacity of this teenager! Threatening my dignity! And

198

doing that with the most disarming grin from ear to ear showing perfect rows of brilliantly white teeth. I looked at that frail girl. How could she hope to force me.

"You are joking. You and who is going to take off my pants?" I said contemptuously.

"Me and four otha lady, Sah."

She beckoned outside the little room. Four husky nurses pounced on me. With tremendous speed and excellent team work they pulled me by my arms, and laid my torso helpless over a cushioned table. I was destined to lose every wrestling match that day. With much giggling and laughing and amazing speed and expertise they unbuckled my belt, unbuttoned my pants and underpants (zippers had not yet been invented), pulled them down and rammed a large syringe into my gluteus maximus. They obviously enjoyed their work. I tried to get up but the five jumped on me and begged me: "Don't get up, Sah. You gwain break off the needle inside, and that would be real trouble, Sah." Finally they pulled out the needle, I pulled up my pants. They all gave me a big smile, wished me a speedy recovery, and the slim one walked me to the door. "Come back in five days. I'll take out the sutures, Sah." She gave me a really nice smile and on my long trek home I thought: She was certainly a pleasant young lady and very competent in her field too.

I slept well that night. The next morning I was blind! It was very frightening! The face had such a hematocyst that my eyes were swollen shut. Ruby, the faithful factory worker who always seemed to be there when one needed her, found me. She had wondered why I had not come downstairs to go to work as I usually did. I begged her not to let anyone know that I was in my room and not at work.

She fixed me some breakfast and put cold compresses on my face. By lunch time my eyes could open a slit. I looked in a mirror. Horrors! My face was a huge black balloon with a white spot in the middle! That spot was the tip of my nose. I hid in my room for a week. Ruby brought me food regularly, and the swelling went down. Five days later I looked almost normal when I went back to the hospital. I never saw that slim little nurse again. Some other smiling nurse took out my stitches. I did not plan on any more wrestling lessons and I stuck to that resolve to this day. It was not hard.

# A SWEET SIXTEEN PARTY

1939 started very nicely for me. Eric Hill, a friend of mine in the swimming club, invited me to his sister Elise's "Sweet Sixteen Party" on January 23rd. I was delighted. In Jamaica, as in Germany, schools were not co-educational, so, brothers usually had to rustle up boys for the parties of their sisters.

The living room had been cleared to make a dance floor. Chairs were arranged against the walls. A bar had been built on the lawn. Tables and chairs were near the bar where John Hill, Eric's elder brother, served rum punch, rum, Scotch, beer and an assortment of aerated waters (sodas in American).

Many of the boys preferred drinking to dancing, and girls could not dance with girls in those days, that would have been considered very improper! So several girls just sat there and chatted with each other. They did not stand up at the bar either as that, too, would have been improper. I had not taken a drink since alcohol had made me so sick at the Continental Club, in 1934, but I was not a good dancer either. So, I stood there and watched all the pretty girls.

Mrs. Hill came up to me: "Arnold, dance with that one. She is 15 now. It is time for her to dance. She is a real wall flower. No one has asked her to dance all afternoon yet." She directed my glances to a tall skinny, physically underdeveloped, dark haired girl in a very pretty dress. She was listening to an animated talk by her neighbor, a very well developed and attractive girl. I had watched that girl dance with about every boy in the party. She was in great demand.

I approached the girls and bowed very politely in front of the skinny girl. The popular one got up and led me to the dance floor. She was a most excellent dancer and could compensate for my deficiencies in that field with ease. She told me that her name was Mary Moyston, and that she lived in Morant Bay. I enjoyed that dance very much. No wonder that she was so popular.

After the dance was over, and I had accompanied Mary back to her seat, Mama Hill came up to me: "Not that one, you dope. That is Mary Moyston. She is very popular."

"I know, but what am I to do? I go to the girls and bow to the one and the other one gets up."

"You don't do it right. Just go up to her, hold her by her arm and lead her to the dance floor."

"Me? Grab her by the arm?" I was horrified.

"No, no, not grab her, just touch her gently. She'll follow you, you'll see." I had my doubts and was afraid that I would make a fool of myself but I had been in worse situations and had survived.

I barely touched her arm, she got up just as Mama Hill said she would, and I followed her to the dance floor. They were playing a two-step. There was great embarrassment: She stepped on my toe, and I stepped heavily on hers. She did not even wince. She was a good sport but it was evident that we could not dance with each other.

In desperation I said: "I have just come back from the States and just learnt a new step." I knew that none of them had ever been in America to point out that there was no such dance. "It goes like this:" I flung my leg high first to one side and then to the other of the girl. That way I could not step on her toe. The obliging girl did the same. No one had seen a dance like that before. No wonder, it was my very own invention, spawned by dire need.

Everybody stopped dancing. All the boys deserted the bar. They all formed a ring around us and clapped in rhythm. The poor girl turned red and redder, and I felt my ear tips burning. The music stopped. A distinguished looking man stood in the doorway, a pipe was tightly clamped in his mouth. The girl spotted him. She said, the very first word she ever said to me: "Bye." She dashed past the crowd into the waiting car. The gentleman followed and they were gone.

Eric and several other boys came up to me and congratulated me: "Boy, I never knew you were such a great dancer!"

"Jolly good show."

"Three tigers and all that!" I really wondered who she was. They were making fun of me, saying that I was "sweet" on that girl, etc. I did not want to aggravate the teasing by asking her name. Besides, she was far too young for me anyway.

ASKING THAT SLIM GIRL TO DANCE

THE IMPROVISED DANCE

G'BYE

205

# EVENTFUL 1939

Early in 1939, I often visited the Myers family. The boys went swimming at the club and Rose seemed to like me. We would sit under a lignum vitae tree in the moonlight and hold hands. She was certainly very good looking. She was blond and blue eyed. She was very well proportioned, and she was of German descent. In all the months I never even kissed her, not even once.

My inhibition was prompted by my acute awareness of my poverty. I would certainly not want my sister to be kissed by a fellow who could not possibly marry and support her. I felt sure that Rose's many brothers thought along similar lines. It would have been very selfish of me to try to take advantage of that very nice girl. It could only have led to unhappiness, trouble and hostility, especially by the local boys toward the "damned" foreigner and a German at that. Then those war clouds hung over the world.

The political horizon had darkened since the take over of Czechoslovakia. Meis went home to marry her Willie. Dorrie, Gerhard, and I missed her very much. We had begged her to stay. We all feared that there would be war. Many Jamaicans, too, sensed that war could break out any day. We did not want her to go to a war zone. She was very much liked by all who came in contact with her. But there was Willie. She went.

Since my return from America I installed ice cream machinery, soda fountains, walk-in-colds for meat storage and all sorts of other machinery using refrigeration. My pay was £2.10.oo ($12.50) per week, a pittance! It did not nearly correspond to the responsibility that went with the job. I still lived upstairs the Jamaica Macaroni Factory with Dorrie and Gerhard.

I had gone to America with the promise by the Company that, if I learnt how to make neon signs, I would head my own department and would get a department manager's pay. On my return I had obliged the Company by taking over commercial refrigeration within the refrigeration department because they were in a pinch. In the meantime I had trained in two men. I felt that I had kept more than my end of the bargain, and that the Company should let me set up my neon department. It surely was their obligation! Gerhard advised me to take up the matter with my superiors.

Mr. Metcalf, the service manager, an Englishman, made an appointment for me with Mr. Young, the chief engineer of the Jamaica Public Service Company, an American. I reminded Mr. Young of our meeting of just about two years ago. I wanted to know just how and where the Company would let me install a neon shop.

Mr. Young told me: "You know Mr. Nichols died and our policy concerning all departments, except that which produces electric power, has changed. We intend to get rid of all departments, radio, refrigeration, all other appliances, and wiring, except for Company installations. We are certainly not going to start a neon department for you."

I was stunned! I sat still for a minute or two and then I said: "Mr. Nichols did not make me the promise as Mr. Nichols but as the Manager of the Jamaica Public Service. My parents and I spent a lot of money because of that promise. I certainly expect the Company to live up to its word."

"There is no contract. So none was broken. We are not going to start a new department. What you learnt is a valuable education for you, so you have not lost anything."

"If you will not start a new department for me, what about a promotion? My pay here does not correspond to the work I do."

"We have two sets of pay scales, one for those who were employed from abroad, and one for those who were employed locally. You were employed locally. If you were an American, from the British Isles, or a Canadian, you could certainly hope for a promotion, but as a German, forget it." I blushed till my ear tips burned. The Nazis had succeeded only too well equating themselves with all Germans. I got up and left his office. I never felt more defeated.

I felt cheated. I had invested a lot of time and money because of the promise of getting my own neon department. Then my parents helped me in the hopes that I would finally be able to stand on my own feet. I had to pay for the regular fare on the United Fruit Co. ship. The Company only paid for the difference between the regular and the first class ticket. Better, Papa paid for my journey, and I had hoped to pay him back by now.

A few days passed when Mr. Metcalf called me to the phone: "Mr. J. C. Campbell wants to talk to you." Old Mr. Campbell, a very light colored Jamaican, and Mr. Foster-Davis, a Scotsman, were the two founders of the Company. They had introduced electric power to Jamaica. When they ran out of capital, they had sold the Company to Russel V. Bell, the son of Graham Bell, the inventor of the telephone. Mr. R. V. Bell employed Stone & Webster to manage and expand the power company. Mr. Foster-Davis was dead for a long time but Mr. Campbell stayed on as he was the man who really knew all the engineering intricacies of the power network.

It was Stone & Webster's policy to have an American, Canadian or one from the British Islands as chief engineer, even though that person would depend on Mr. Campbell to teach him the system of the Company, local customs and to explain to his foreign boss who is who in the business community. Management who was employed from abroad lived in Company housing within walking distance from the office. Local people were not welcome in that walled in group of houses. Stone & Webster in its far away offices on Broad St., N.Y., did more for the independence movement in Jamaica than all the firebrand rabble-rousers could do in the slums, yes, more than the leading intelligentsia of the PNP could do in the top meeting places in the Island.

Be that as it may, Mr. Campbell wanted to talk to me. I had seen him before, but I had never spoken to him. Now he said: "Could you come to my office, I want to talk to you."

"Yes, Sir." I told Mr. Metcalf that Mr. Campbell wanted to see me, and I went to the office next door to that of Mr. Young's.

"Sit down, please. We have a new policy in the Company where we encourage people or companies to sell electricity consuming products. We are willing to lend them money to help them get started. You want to sell neon signs which consume electricity. Would you be prepared to start your own shop, and if so, how much money would you need?"

"I would certainly love to start my own shop, Sir. I would need £800.-.- ($4,000.oo)"

"Alright, I shall arrange with our purchasing department so that you can purchase your equipment. We shall pay for it. You will receive copies of all purchase expenses, and you pay us back as you sell signs. There will be no interest charges. We'll make our money from the electricity we sell."

"Thank you very much, Sir."

He stood up, shook my hand and said: "Good luck." That was certainly a most dramatic turn of events for the better.

# GLASSLITE CO.

While still in New York, I had visited the Tube Light Co., the best known neon sign supply company. Mr. Müller, the old German glass blower who had founded the company, showed me around his lab where he experimented with all sorts of new ideas of his. He gave me a catalogue and a list of all items which would be needed to start a new shop. Now I got out the list and ordered every item.

In the evenings and weekends I built work benches in the room next to my bedroom upstairs of the macaroni factory at 4 Arlington Ave. All the shops, I had seen in the States, had four foot wide work benches. The glass tubes arrived in four foot lengths and could easily be stored under a four foot wide bench with their ends easily accessible. The width proved very practical for layout work. The asbestos paper, with which I covered the tables, was also four feet wide. I strung wire from wall to wall and made "S" hooks from a little thicker wire to hang up finished glass letters. When the equipment and materials arrived, I was ready.

On March 1, 1939, I quit the Public Service and started the Glasslite Co., the only neon shop in the British West Indies. I was 21 years and 3 months old. The first sign I made read: "Dora Macaroni." A reporter from *The Daily Gleaner* came in to photograph the sign and interview me. I showed him how I bent the glass tubing. He wrote a very nice article about my work. Gerhard rented an outdoor sign opposite the end of South Camp Rd. on East Queen St. I put up a Dora Macaroni sign there. The sign was made of wood. I lettered Dora Macaroni in white on a very dark blue background. The neon tubing was red, which did not reflect the dark blue back ground, so that the lettering seemed to be in midair after dark.

I had offered to repair the sign reading: *MOVIES* to Mr. Richards of the Palace Amusement Co. He told me that he had ordered replacement glass from England, and that he would not need my services. He was very arrogant. When the neon tubing arrived broken, he asked me to repair it. I tried. It was made from soda glass. I could not join my lead glass to the English glass. I had

210

to replace the two broken letters. He suspected that I did that so that I could ask for more money.

At the installation he was in the control room where the switch for the sign was while I stood on the 18" wide parapet of the building out of sight from where he was. In front of me was the wall on which the sign was mounted. Behind me, and just below me, were the high tension lines of the Public Service Company.

Before I made the high voltage connections from the 10,000 Volt 30 milli amp. transformer to the glass letters, I yelled: "Make sure that no one switches the sign on!"

The next thing I knew, I was flung violently against the wall and a half inch long blue spark crackled between my elbow and the wall. I was relieved that I was not flung on top of those high tension lines. I was very angry with Mr. Richards. His explanation was that he understood that I wanted him to switch the sign on. In the future I had to deal with Mr. Richards several times. We never liked each other.

That was a close one! I learnt one lesson: Always install a switch in sight of the sign. Whenever I serviced one of the few imported signs I took out the fuse and put it in my pocket before I touched any wire.

Most of my signs were indoor signs but the Swiss Consul who was the manager for Jamaica of the Swiss Rum Co. and an importer of many different items, had me put up a "Rolex Watches" sign on a roof top at Cross Roads. I did not make much money but my work became known.

In July Mr. Blumenthal from Brooklyn N.Y., the manager of the Machado Tobacco Co., a division of the Anglo-American Tobacco Co., Ltd., called me into his office. He wanted me to convert his 22ft x 11ft bulb sign on a roof on South Parade into a neon sign advertising "Four Aces" cigarettes. I submitted a drawing and I told him that I could repair his flasher and animate the sign. He was very happy and gave me the order.

Masterton Ltd. made the metal parts for me. I repaired the flasher. First came on a white cigarette with a red line showing the fire and blue smoke 8ft tall in the shape of an "S". Then came on "moke" to complete the word "Smoke," then "Four" in green, then

THE FIRST NEON SIGN MADE IN JAMAICA

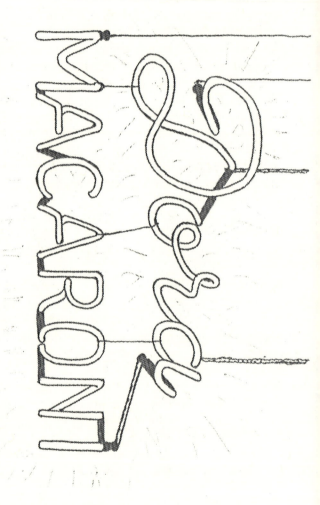

"Aces" also in green, then "cigarettes" in blue, then two red borders one after the other. The sign went out, the entire sign went on again, then out again, and the entire cycle repeated. It was my first big job. Mr. Blumenthal, Mr. Masterton, Dorrie, Gerhard and I were there when the timer turned on the sign for the first time. It was a great moment for me. They all praised me. I felt really good on that balmy evening near the end of August, 1939. Machado Tobacco Co. paid, and I could make a pretty decent payment to the Public Service.

For some time I had felt that upstairs of the macaroni factory was too crowded for the neon shop, Dorrie and Gerhard's and also my residence. I was earning enough money to rent a room with a Syrian man near the Bournemouth Club and Sirgani's Beach. I could run down to Sirgani's and swim a mile before breakfast in the company of three fellow club members, have breakfast and then go to work.

Louis Khouri, his three nephews and another boarder were all very nice people. Louis was an excellent cook. He always made a scrumptious breakfast on Sundays. He knew that khibbi was my favorite. It was a meat ball consisting of raw lamb with olive oil, raw onion, garlic, pepper, and several other spices. Breakfast and all meals on Sundays were included in my rent. The other meals I had at the macaroni factory nearby.

Louis was head of the shoe sales department at one of the Hanna Stores on King Street. Louis looked after every need I could possibly have. He was more than a landlord. He was a friend. The youngsters, all in high school, were all very good boxers. They showed me how to box. We put on 12 oz gloves and never hit hard. I was certainly no match for them. They could hit me anywhere they wanted, and I could never get to score a point. It was all in good fun. I really started to enjoy life. The future looked really promising.

> *Doch, mit des Geschickes Mächten*
> *Ist kein ew'ger Bund zu flechten.*
> Friedrich v. Schiller

But of the mighty powers of fate
Good fortune is a fickle mate!
Translated by Arnold Von der Porten

# GERHARD'S BIG CHALLENGE

In the meantime Gerhard had embarked on a huge endeavor which dwarfed all other sales projects he had done before. He intended to extend the power net of the Jamaica Public Service Company beyond its existing limits of Spanish Town past Old Harbour into May Pen. Mr. Caithness, the sales manager of the Company, had told him how much power he had to sell before they would expand their net to almost twice its present size. They promised him a very handsome commission for every kilo Watt connected, plus one shilling and six pence for every outlet or lamp. They believed that nobody could possibly sell that much power.

President Roosevelt of the U.S.A. and Sir Stafford Cripps, the British Labour Party leader, unwittingly helped Gerhard enormously. Both of those men sharply criticized the United Fruit Company, Jamaica's best and most civic minded employer by far, as well all other Whites in the Colonies, for exploiting the poor Negroes. They certainly helped tremendously to make the Whites most unpopular. The Whites made up only two percent of the population and therefore were obliged to conduct themselves in such a way that they would be liked.

The President's and Sir Stafford Cripps's faces were always shown on the *News Reels* and the press took up their cause. The result was that there was so much sabotage on United Fruit Company installations that the Company sold out to Tate & Lyle, a British sugar company. The latter uprooted all the banana plantations and planted sugar cane. They sold all of the employees' housing, the Myrtle Bank Hotel, turned over the company maintained hospital, schools, their three railway piers, and streets to the Jamaican Government to be maintained and paid for by the tax payers henceforth.

Fortunately Tate & Lyle did not like that their irrigation pumps, which they had inherited from the United Fruit Co., were diesel driven. They wanted them electrically powered to reduce the number of maintenance employees. That is where Gerhard came in. He sold them enough electric motors to fill the required power consumption quota which the Jamaica Public Service had set him, and all were located between Spanish Town and May Pen. Consequently the Jamaica Public Service started to expand their net as rapidly as they could.

Lots of business was done in Jamaica just on verbal agreements. Any businessman breaking his word might as well close his office. The report of a broken promise would ruin him. Gerhard never suspected that the all powerful Public Service, with its American, Canadian and English management, proved to be very untrustworthy.

After my experience with Mr. Young, Gerhard should at least have followed up with a memorandum stating the terms of the agreement. He should have mailed a carbon copy to himself and left the envelop sealed, making sure that the postal date stamp was clearly legible on the envelope. Even better, he might have asked for a written copy of the company policy covering remuneration for sales adding to the power grid. It proved to be a great mistake that he trusted his employer.

# WAR!

Mr. Norman MacDonald, a salesman at the Jamaica Public Service, who had often shown that he was very jealous of Gerhard, told me that the Army was preparing a prison camp for Gerhard and me, and all the other Germans in Jamaica. I told him that we were refugees from the Nazis, and that we, therefore, would surely not be interned. Besides, Dorrie and Gerhard had been assured by the Colonial Secretary's Office that their application to become British Subjects had been approved and had been sent to London for the final signature, a mere formality. Surely, they would not intern British Subjects. He just grinned sardonically and walked off. It was a very disquieting conversation, to say the least.

I took the warning seriously and discussed it with Gerhard. We decided that I should turn over the ownership of all neon equipment and materials to Gerhard in writing since he was a British Subject and since all Germans in Jamaica had lost all of their possessions in World War I. We could justify such an act if we had to as I had never paid Gerhard any rent. So, the equipment was turned over to him in lieu of rent. We carefully put that in writing.

In the peace negotiations of 1919 the people of Danzig (now Gdansk) had been promised a plebiscite in 20 years to determine, whether they wanted to rejoin Germany, remain independent, or join Poland. The Polish Government declared that there would be war if the citizens of the old Hansa City would rejoin the German Reich. The air was thick with war clouds when the plebiscite was held. The vote was over 90% in favor of joining the Third Reich. People had wild celebrations throughout the city and all over Germany.

Before dawn of September 1, 1939, the German Army marched, not only into Danzig, but also across the Polish border in many places at a very rapid pace. As could be expected the horse drawn Polish artillery never had a chance to get itself into position before the new *Stukas* (short for *Sturzkanonen,* diving canons) annihilated them. The archaic squadrons of horsemen were machine gunned from the air. To make the Polish defenses even more chaotic thousands of refugees plugged the highways.

I did not know all the details which I described in the above paragraph. At that time, the papers reported "Polish victories" only 30 miles from the German border. The next day *The Daily Gleaner* reported: "Poles mount a devastating attack on the Nazi forces in Krakow." Anyone knowing even a little bit of geography could see that the Poles were retreating as fast as they could. Obviously Poland was doomed unless the French mounted a quick, powerful attack across Germany's western borders to draw off most of the German Forces from the Polish front. They could at least have struck North from Lorraine into the Saarland which was West of the Rhine and the Siegfried Line. But even a determined action there might not have made Hitler reconsider and pull out of Poland. Time had run out. It was too late.

Everybody in the world, except Hitler and his gang, seemed to know that there would be a major war with the West as well as with the East if the Nazis attacked Poland. Hitler was pursuing the old German dream of expansion to the East.

On September the 2nd, early in the morning, Mr. Chamberlain issued an ultimatum to Germany demanding the immediate withdrawal of all German Troops out of Poland and Danzig. Daladier of France followed suit a few hours later.

On September the 3rd, at 6:00 a.m. Eastern Standard Time, the Khouri household, including me, sat around the radio. Mr. Chamberlain's voice was clear and serious. His announcement ended with, "....therefore, a state of war now exists between the United Kingdom and Germany." Everybody, but I, cheered loudly and wildly. I felt sick to the stomach. I felt that they should have done that six years ago. Hitler would have been a pushover then. Now, he had had plenty of time to prepare. I felt that. But why say it and spoil their enthusiasm.

I went to my room and thought of my recent disquieting conversation with that idiot, MacDonald. He might just be right. I dressed in my best suit. Louis made khibbi. He knew that I liked that. He called me to join them for breakfast. All, except I, were chatting very excitedly.

I packed a very small suitcase of what I would absolutely need if I should be arrested. I sat down on my bed and listened to the lively teenagers talking at the top of their voices in the living room next-door.

I did not sit there long. A station wagon drove up. Four policemen came out. One of them had his hand on his automatic pistol. "You are under arrest." Louis excitedly jumped between them and me. He tried to reason with them. He offered to be responsible for me that I would not do anything to hurt the British. He soon saw that his efforts were in vain.

He turned to me: "Don't worry, Arnold, once the British and the French get going this War will be over in three to six weeks. It will be a very short War. You mark my words."

"No, Louis," I said. "They should have done this six years ago when Hitler started to re-arm Germany. Now it is too late for a quick victory. This War will last four to five years (prophetic words!) and it will be very bloody. Hitler will lose. Just look at a map. Compare the size of Germany against the rest of the world. But I tell you; many, many will die."

I felt very sad and had to fight hard to suppress my tears. I was not going to show that much emotion and cry in front of those officious policemen. The cheering had stopped, and they all bid me a speedy return. They looked genuinely sad.

I took with me my little suitcase containing a change of clothes, a razor and a toothbrush. I left my opera glasses which Uncle Leo and Aunt Anna had given me as a farewell present, my little coin collection and the medals, which I had won as a swimmer in my room. (I am still sorry that I did that.)

I sat squeezed between two policemen.

The driver said: "Direct me to your brother."

"But he is a British Subject."

"You do as you are told!"

We drove to 4 Arlington Ave. Dorrie and Gerhard were dressed. They had heard that war had been declared. Dorrie quickly packed some clothes for Gerhard. He fetched a pack of 500 "Polo" cigarettes and matches. The good-byes were very short and emotional. Both tried to be brave and not shed any tears in front of the watchful eyes of those gleefully victorious policemen.

We were driven to the Criminal Investigation Department (C.I.D.) head quarters on East Street, just a few doors north of North

Street. We were not the first in the room of about 15ft x 15ft. An armed policeman sat in each window and one stood in the doorway. They effectively blocked all air circulation so that it was oppressively hot. I knew what most of the Germans there were doing. Some of them I knew by name. At least half of them were Jewish refugees who had recently arrived with wives and children to escape from Hitler's gangster regime. Some were in tears. Others were old residents. Almost all smoked. Gerhard lit each cigarette from the butt of the last one. After a while the room was so thick with smoke, one could hardly see across as the room filled up with more and more people.

The smoke was burning my eyes. I got very thirsty and soon got very hungry, too. Having never smoked (except for one fateful day 10 years ago), the smoke made me physically sick, and I most certainly felt mentally deeply depressed.

At about noon a man was brought in who was very drunk and disgustingly loud. His entire luggage consisted of two bottles of Scotch Whiskey. He promptly dropped one on the floor. It broke and added Scotch flavor to the already horrible stench in the packed room. He immediately demanded to see Mr. Higgins, the Chief of Police. All of the policemen seemed to know him and humored him. He opened the second bottle of Scotch successfully and drank from it liberally.

I asked to go to the bathroom. A policeman escorted me to a disgustingly filthy place. It seemed that it had not been cleaned since it was built in the beginning of the century. Nevertheless, it was a most welcome relief from the stench of the smoke, the whiskey, and the oppressive heat in that close room.

We were led one after the other into an adjoining room. I knew the Administrator General, Mr. Ritchie, well. I once had dinner at his house and I had played Ping-Pong with him and his daughters. He was interviewing the very loud mouthed drunkard. All prisoners were interviewed standing up. There were two other men interviewing. The drunkard told the policeman to get him a chair. The policeman pretended not to hear. Mr. Ritchie got up and furiously yelled at the officer: "Mr. Freimann wants a chair! Get one and hurry up!" The poor policeman rushed to give the drunkard a comfortable chair. Amazing! What was the hold this noisy fellow had over the powerful Mr. Ritchie?

I stood in front of a man who had a pipe firmly clamped between his teeth. I had seen that man before, but, since girls and sweet sixteen parties were far from my mind, I could not place him. He spoke very politely and asked what I had in my pockets. I gave him my wallet with my little bit of money, the silver watch, which I had inherited from my grandfather Rübner, my pen knife, and my driver's license. He put it all into a manila envelope, sealed it, and made me sign across the flap. He asked me where I was born, next of kin, etc. I had resolved to complain about the inhumane conditions in the adjoining room but I could see that this official would be powerless to do anything about it. So I kept my mouth shut. I was escorted back into the oppressive room.

The thirst, hunger, heat, and, above all, the tobacco smoke, had made me so sick, I was afraid that I was going to faint. At about 4:00 p.m., we were 22 by now, we were herded into the court yard and loaded into the "Black Maria." The outside of this ugly, black police van was so hot that one would burn ones fingers touching it. A few could sit but most of us were squeezed in standing together so tightly that I was seriously worried that my knees would break. We were driven to the "Stockade" in Up Park Camp. The British had a battalion of some 500 men of the Shropshire Rifles there. The stockade was normally used for soldiers who had broken the rules.

We were sent into an area of about 1,000 ft. x 1,000 ft. surrounded by a very high, spiked wrought iron fence. In the S.E. corner there was the administration building. It was divided into two equally sized rooms. One was for two English staff sergeants and two English privates and the other for Major Saulters, the camp commander. Three days before he had been a civilian and the manager of the South Camp Road Hotel. There was a little space between buildings, and in the S.W. corner there was a store room with iron doors and no windows. In the middle of the compound was a row of 10 cells side by side. Behind them, there was an out building with toilets and two wash stands. In the N.W. corner was the kitchen and in the N.E. corner was an open shed. In it were five cleanly scrubbed tables and ten wooden benches. Each table consisted of two supports like saw horses and a loose 5 ft. x 3 ft. table top. The benches could be folded up.

We sat down. Four soldiers, under the watchful eyes of the two staff sergeants, served us mugs of very sweet tea with milk and white bread with a mixture of some butter and margarine, topped with very sweet strawberry jam. We had not eaten all day, and this sweet stuff almost made me sick to vomit. I could see on the faces of several others that they, too, had a difficult time keeping the food down. As we were eating, the sergeant asked in a cheerful voice:

"Is everybody happy?"

We were glad that the fast was broken and some answered, not too convincingly: "Yes."

The soldiers cleared away the jugs of tea, the mugs and the plates. The sergeant lined us up in front of the cell block facing the office. "My name is Sergeant Hutchinson. I'll call the roll. You answer: 'Present.' " That done he said: "Now count off and remember your number. That will be your name in the future." Gerhard was No.9 and I No.10. "Now I want you to select a spokesman to represent you in the office and through whom we can communicate to all of you."

We automatically formed two groups of eleven each. The Nazis elected Mr. Deters, the unofficial German Consul. He was a very pleasant gentleman. He had joined the Nazi party as it was a requirement to represent German exporters to Jamaica. He actually employed a Jewish salesman and was on good terms with people of all races, religions, and nationalities. He was especially friendly with the American Consul. They were long time drinking buddies.

In our group Dr. Ernst Lobbenberg, the Jewish dentist from Hamburg, was the best known. We elected him. The vote was deadlocked: 11 : 11. The sergeant took both men into the office. The result was that Deters represented the Nazis, and Dr. Lobbenberg represented our group which was immediately dubbed the Jew Group. Major Saulters came out of the office to greet us. He was very cordial and told us that we all were caught in a very unpleasant situation, and he hoped that the War would soon be over, and that we all would go home. In the meantime we should try to live as normal a life as is possible under the unfortunate circumstances.

Two of us were assigned to each cell. Two were housed in a tent as we were 22 and there were only 10 cells. The cell block was elevated about 8" above the ground and a 4 ft. wide covered sidewalk was in front of the doors. As it grew dark, we noticed that the area around the compound was flood lit, and guards with fixed bayonets were posted at each corner. They marched around the stockade at regular time intervals.

At 9:00 p.m. we were told to go into our cells. Staff Sergeant Griffith locked first the door consisting of iron bars, and then he slammed a heavy wooden door shut and bolted it from the outside. Being locked up like that I felt degraded and unexplainably horrified.

The cell was 7 ft. wide and 10 ft. long. Inside there were two beds. Each consisted of two 3" high wooden supports with three 6 ft. long boards laid side by side, together they were 2 ft. wide. The mattress consisted of three pieces, each 2 ft. x 2 ft. These "biscuits," as the soldiers called them, were stuffed with coir (the fluffed up husk of coconuts.) The stuffing was most uneven, so that there was practically nothing in the center of each "biscuit." The pillow was a 6" diameter by 2 ft. long canvass tube, stuffed tightly with coir. It was so hard that it was completely unusable for the purpose for which it was intended. Over each bed was a mosquito net. That was good.

About 2'-6" up, on the long West wall, was a board cemented into the wall. It was wide enough to rest a writing pad on. The stool in front of it had a single leg. It was cemented rigidly into the floor. Just under the ceiling, on the North side, opposite the door, there was a small opening with iron bars welded together. There was one bulb in the middle of the ceiling. It was enclosed in a glass cover which was clamped to the ceiling with fairly heavy wire. The light was turned off from the office at 10 p.m. sharp.

There were no toilet facilities, not even a chamber pot. Each internee had been given two bed sheets, a pillow case, and an army blanket. I made a pillow out of my clothes and lay down on my bed. I took the one under the window. It was at right angles to Gerhard's. His was against the East wall. The unevenness of the "biscuits" made the bed most uncomfortable. I could not help staring at the shadow of the bars over the opening near the ceiling.

It was a most depressing sight, reminding me of my total helplessness as a prisoner with a number for his name! Hitler had correctly prophesied that those who were against him, would never be happy, even if they fled to the end of the earth. Again, he had judged the stupidity and prejudice of the decision-making people correctly!

It had been a long day, this first day of the Second World War. I had listened to the radio at 6 a.m. It was now way past 10 p.m. A lot had happened in those past 16 hours! Mercifully, Morphëus finally took me in his arms, and let me escape from the real world till 6 a.m. the next day.

# LIFE IN THE INTERNMENT CAMP

In the morning the cell doors were opened. We found that the toilets were filthy! Ludwig Klein, an accountant from Vienna, one of the Jews in our group, was covered with red wales from head to toe. His mattresses were infested with bedbugs. His roommate, too, had some wales on his body but they were not nearly as many as those on Mr. Klein.

The mattresses, all the bedding, and the mosquito nets were exchanged and the cell was sprayed with Flit, the usual kerosene based insecticide of those days. Then we had to line up for a roll call. Surprise, surprise! Not one of us had escaped during the night.

Each group had to furnish an equal amount of men for work details. Freimann, who had been so drunk the day before, grabbed me by the arm and volunteered both of us for cooking. What I had taken for a kitchen the evening before was really nothing but a pantry without a stove. We had to do our cooking outside of the stockade in the kitchen of our guards. I had no objection to this assignment and I was very happy that I had not been assigned to clean those filthy toilets!

Freimann spoke Polish, Yiddish and a heavily Yiddish accented English. He could understand German when he wanted to but he could not speak it.

I asked: "Why did you volunteer us for this?"

"Believe me, I had a lot of experience in Polish jails. One always has the best and sufficient grub in the kitchen."

"What are you doing here, you are a Polish Jew, aren't you?"

He sighed: "Yes, I was drafted into the Polish Army. The conditions there, especially for a Jew, were terrible! I just had to escape. I bought myself a forged Austrian passport with the name of Freimann. I traveled with it ever since and entered Jamaica with it. My real name is Pivnicza (pronounced: Pivnitsa). This is the best prison I have ever been in. I'm getting out of here soon. You watch."

For breakfast we were given three sticks of margarine and one of butter. We were supposed to mix them for our group and butter our slices of bread with that mixture. While I sliced, Pivnicza buttered the bread: All margarine for the other tables and all butter for ours. Now I fully understood why he volunteered for the kitchen detail so quickly. The soldiers got bacon and eggs. We all got the same mixture of overly sweet tea.

The soldiers in the kitchen apparently had orders not to "fraternize." They never said a word to us and answered only if the questions had to be answered and then as short as possible. The cooking was done on a wood burning Franklin stove. The wood was all chopped and ready to use. Mr. Huber, a cook by profession, who had bought Meyer's Restaurant from the creditors, was the cook for the Nazis along with another volunteer. We did not speak to each other, unless it had to do with cooking. There being only one stove, we had to cooperate.

As the dinner was carried into the stockade, we stayed there. Three more people had arrived. One was a Mr. Bauer. He had been transported from the insane asylum. He went to sleep with Deters and Goetz in the tent. The next person was Mr. Schönbeck. He was the chief sugar chemist at Frome Estates, the only sugar refinery in Jamaica. He claimed that he was related to me. He was from a Christian mother and a Jewish father in Berlin. He had been baptized Lutheran just like me. The third was Willy Gertig. He was the Handicraft teacher at the Friends' College, a Quaker technical school in Highgate in the mountains, halfway between Kingston and Port Maria on the North Coast. Though Willy wore a signet ring, showing that he was from a family of noblemen, he wanted to be in our group.

Another tent had to be erected, and the two newcomers to our group were assigned to it. Schönbeck did not like the idea. I dreaded to look at the shadow of the grill over the window in our cell for another night and volunteered to swap places with Schönbeck. Willy and I hit it off from the start. We selected the highest spot within the area to which we were assigned and built a little dike on the inner fringe of our eight foot diameter tent. The room we had, was no smaller than that of a cell. We put our cots near the outer periphery and our few belongings next to the center post. Willy was about Gerhard's age and had a very friendly disposition.

Dorrie brought belongings to Gerhard, mostly clothes and

cigarettes. Louis Khouri brought me all the clothes which I had left in my room. He asked if he could bring me something. The visitors were allowed only to the outside door of the guardhouse and we were not allowed to see them or talk to them directly. I told the guard to tell Louis that I needed some exercise, as I no longer went swimming and I asked him for boxing gloves. I knew that he had several pairs of worn ones which he no longer used and hoped that he would bring me two pairs of them. Instead, he brought me two brand new pairs of 12 oz. gloves the very next day.

There was always one guard assigned to patrol inside the camp. The Quakers from the college traveled all the way to Kingston to bring Willy his clothes, grapes, and lots of other fruit and delicacies. The guards, just homesick young prewar volunteers, had no such things. They soon came to our tent and were very friendly, as Willy readily shared with them and me. The internment did not seem to bother Willy very much. He said that he was glad that he was alive and this was better than his fate would have been if he had been caught by the Nazis. One has to count ones blessings and look at the bright side of every situation.

Gertig was born in Pomerania. He went to Berlin and joined the Quakers there and was active in an anti-war movement. He went to study at the Technical Teachers' College in Halle, Thuringia, and got a diploma as a Handicraft Teacher. While he was teaching at an orphanage, the Nazis tapped him to go to the leadership school. He was tall, blond, intelligent, and "Arian." He looked the type people would obey. He went to the school and quickly found out that the Nazi Movement had nothing in common with the Quakers. He deserted.

He walked through Munich, past the memorial for a number of Nazis (sixteen, if I remember correctly), who were shot by the police during Hitler's 1923 attempted take over of the government. He was followed by a plainclothed man when he refused to give the mandatory Nazi salute to the memorial. He eluded the man and hiked during the nights and slept in haystacks during the days, until he crossed the Dutch border. The Quakers sent him to Ireland where he learnt English. The Friends College of Jamaica ran an ad in an Irish Friends' publication. Willy answered it and got the job. He loved it there but now he was locked up.

The Friends College was an important part of the Quaker Mission in Jamaica. It was financed jointly by the Friends Five Yearly Meeting in Richmond, Indiana; the Friends Service Committee of the Philadelphia (Pennsylvania) Yearly Meeting; the Friends Service Committee of London, England; donations in Jamaica; and above all, by a wealthy resident American Quaker woman, Dorothea Simmons.

Dr. Lobbenberg and Mr. Deters went to the Camp Commander together and achieved that the cells would no longer be locked at nights. That was certainly a step in the right direction.

I went into the office and also asked to see the Camp Commander. I got as far as Staff Sergeant Griffith. He was of enormous girth. He had to wear a special belt. The Army did not have one long enough to fit him. He was the ranking non-commissioned officer and the person who really ran the camp. Later I found out from the guards that he was the heavyweight boxing champion of the British Army.

I told him that I wanted to volunteer to join the British forces. He was very pleased. He had the necessary forms handy. I signed them. I wanted to act an anti-Nazi and not be one only with my mouth. The Allies proclaimed that they were fighting to make the world safe for democracy. I wanted to be part of that fight. Now the staff sergeant said that my application would have to be approved in England. My hopes to get out of this stockade in a hurry were dashed.

At least I was the cook for our group and spent much of my time outside of the camp. The soldiers in the kitchen were all from the Shropshire Rifles and were a gruff bunch, but I did get a few valuable tips on cooking from them. It was a totally new trade for me. Of course, I had often cooked for myself but now I had to do it for a lot of people.

We kept the hemp ropes which supported our tent pretty taut. It looked nice that way. One afternoon, one of the guards with whom Willy had shared his goodies, came into our tent and told us: "A severe rain storm has been predicted for tonight. The hemp absorbs water, swells, and thereby the ropes become shorter and pull the tent pegs right out of the ground. You'd better slacken those ropes now before the rain starts." We did, and made sure that our dike, just

228

inside the tent, was high enough. I went outside to tell Deters. He had always been very decent to me before the War.

I saw Deters's hands. He was fixing his dike. So he knew about the weather. There was Goetz, loudly making remarks to Deters, telling him, how sloppy the Jew tent looked. Though Goetz addressed Deters, I knew that I was meant to hear that criticism of the Jew Group and me in particular. I changed my mind. I kept my mouth shut. Some will have to learn by experience and Goetz is one of them. The men of the Nazi group did not talk to us since the beginning of the internment, and we did not talk to them, except in the kitchen, where we had to share the same stove and cooperation was to our mutual benefit. Goetz would never have warned me. Did he not tell me once that people like me should be wiped from the surface of the earth? So, why should I be nice to him?

The thunderstorm broke, and it poured as predicted. Our little dike held. At about 4 a.m. we heard a loud: "Woosh" followed by a lot of angry words. We peeked from under our tent flaps. There were Deters, Goetz and Bauer crawling from under their collapsed tent into the pouring rain. We looked at our ropes they were very taut but the pegs were still deeply and firmly in the ground. It took them at least half an hour in the tropical downpour to get their tent erected again.

# THE BRITISH NAVY IN ACTION

Malcolm Finleyson, the captain of the Jamaica Amateurs Swimming Club, had once asked me to join his club and be the goalie of his "A" team. That is how I got on that team. He was one of the most superb swimmers I had ever met. Besides he also was a very decent, polite and honorable young gentleman. He sailed on the passenger ship, the *M.S. Athenia* to his native England to volunteer to fight for his country. The ship never arrived. It was ironic that such a marvelous swimmer should have drowned. The loss of ships, due to German "U" boats, was staggering.

What the British Navy obviously needed was a resounding victory! That is where Mr. Caithness, the sales manager of the Jamaica Public Service, came in. He donned his brand new, heavily starched, white British Navy Officer's uniform with all of those shiny, highly polished brass buttons, new glittering brass on his cap, epaulettes and sleeves. He was tall, had a trim figure, and must have looked very handsome and imposing.

Followed by a detective sergeant, another detective, both in plainclothes, and two Public Service mechanics, he entered 4 Arlington Ave. where the Jamaica Macaroni Factory was noisily making its products, and where the Glasslite Co. had its idle work shop on the upper floor. He was met by a mere woman, weighing between 90 and 100 lbs. She was dressed in shorts, a faded gray-green blouse, socks, flat heeled shoes, and on her head she hid her beautiful, chestnut-brown hair under a voluminous white baker's cap. All of her was dusted with flour. Not much to overpower for five men, except, perhaps, those piercing, dark-brown eyes.

Mr. Caithness, the commander of the task force, demanded to have a look at that little 10 ft. x 16 ft. neon workshop. Once there, he imperiously ordered the enemy property seized. The mechanics were about to rip out the precious equipment, which no one but I could use, when Dorrie, the lady with the piercing eyes, showed that she also had a fighting spirit and a mouth to match:

"This is my and my husband's property. We hold the title to it. We are British Subjects. If you as much as touch it, I shall have our lawyer take action against you, both for criminal trespassing and

230

civil action for damages! Get out! And the next time you come on my property, you'd better have a search warrant and a court order!"

The commander simply ignored her: "Take out this equipment!"

The detective sergeant stepped between the mechanics and the equipment and said to the workmen: "Wait na man."

And to Mr. Caithness: "Do you have a court order, Sar?"

The Navy executed a tack of 180°, then quick marched with the four others in his wake, down the steps and off the property. The Navy suffered its first ever defeat in Jamaica. It should have stuck to the high seas.

One day a week, there was visitors' day at the stockade. That is when Dorrie told Gerhard. Only one prisoner per visitor was permitted under the watchful eyes of one of the two staff sergeants. I could not see Dorrie myself.

# CHANCES TO GET OUT

Louis Khouri visited regularly every visitors' day. He always brought me something. He complained about a nagging stomach pain. He had done that from time to time when I lived there. I told him that it was due to the terribly hot peppers he loved to eat with his meals. "My stomach is used to them. I have eaten them all my life."

Rabbi Silvermann came to visit with the Jews in the camp. Only recently three of them had been in Nazi Concentration camps and looked it: Max Ebersohn from Vienna, Robert Hirsch, and Fritz Lobbenberg from Hamburg, the brother of Ernst. The Rabbi told the Jews that he had done all he could for them and that any further effort to free them would be useless. There would be no hope to get out until the War was ended. He would do no more. He never came back.

Mrs. Simmons, the most prominent Quaker in Jamaica, visited Willy, and told him that the Quakers would make every effort to get him and all the internees of the Jew group out. We did not know if Rabbi Silvermann from Brooklyn thought it cruel to give us false hope of regaining our freedom and let us hope in vain when he himself was convinced that all efforts were hopeless. Dorothea Simmons was not one to ever give up hope. I am sure that she really saw everybody who would admit her and who had influence.

Toward the end of September Gerhard was called into the office. His and Dorrie's papers had come back from England. They had been approved. He and Dorrie were officially British Subjects and he was free! He packed his belongings and told me that he would try everything to get me and all of our group out. Mr. Chen came and picked him up.

Among the guards, who were regularly assigned to patrol the inside of the camp, was a skinny chap whom his fellow soldiers called by the unflattering name of Pissy. He came to our tent as all the others did. He spotted my boxing gloves.

"Want some tips on boxing?"

"I certainly do."

He was about my height, 5'-9", but he could not have weighed more than 120 lbs. I weighed 135 lbs by now and did not have an ounce of fat. My chest was 41" and my waist 29".

We put on the gloves. He said: "I'm the flyweight champion of the British Army." I hoped that he was not another Victor Khalil. He said: "Try to hit me." I tried. I missed every time or hit his guard. "Now hit me on my jaw." He put his hands behind his back and stuck out his jaw. All members of our group and some of the Nazis had by now formed a big ring around us. I hesitated, and then hit him pretty hard right on the button. He did not flinch. He said: "No, no! Hit with all your might." I hesitated again, and then I really hit that jaw.

He just grinned. "Now guard your jaw." I most certainly tried. Within seconds he gave me one blow, and it was right on the jaw. I went down like a bag of flour. Everybody laughed. He waited till I felt all right again. "Guard your heart." I kept my right hand over it and jabbed at him with my left. In seconds he hit me so hard on my left chest that I went down again to the loud amusement of the crowd.

I was amazed that I could neither hit him even once, nor guard myself against him, yet, he could hit me every time exactly where he told me that he would hit me. My arms felt too lame to go on. We shook hands and he promised to teach me some more at another time. He did, every time he came on duty. People laughed at my clumsy attempts to box but I got my exercise and quite a few pointers on boxing. The crowd got a few good laughs at a time when there was not much to be happy about. It was good all around.

# THE EARLY PERIOD OF THE WAR

The War was going very badly. The Germans were feverishly completing their western defenses, the Siegfried Line, on the opposite side of the Rhine from the "impregnable" Maginot Line. Those fixed defense lines were more or less a more advanced form of the World War I trench warfare. The Nazis did not need soldiers nor money to do this. They had plenty of political, Czech, Slovakian, and Polish forced laborers to do the work, and all were expendable. The French certainly did not disturb them. The British sent some soldiers over to France. It was but a token force. Nothing to scare Hitler.

On the eastern front the Polish resistance was collapsing. The secret pact between Molotov and v.Ribbentrop revealed itself. Soviet forces marched into Estonia, Latvia, Lithuania, and the Eastern half of Poland. All of Poland was divided between Germany and the Soviet Union. For good measure the Russians marched into all of Romania which was east of the Prutul and Prut rivers and called it the Soviet Republic of Moldova. Though the Russians lost hardly a man, they had gained more territory than Germany annexed, when it took Austria, Czechoslovakia, Danzig, and half of Poland.

The press constantly heralded Allied victories. It made itself most unbelievable. So, when it did report a real victory, no one believed it. The War in the Atlantic went very badly for the greatest naval power on earth. A submarine sank one of her only two aircraft carriers the *H.M.S. Courageous* at anchor at her naval base of Scapa Flow. The aircraft carrier was sorely missed in Britain's fight against submarines in the Atlantic. Also in the Orkney Islands, north of Scotland, the mighty battleship *H.M.S. Royal Oak* was sunk by a daring submarine attack in its own naval base.

The submarines proved very effective against the British merchant fleet, despite their sailing in convoys and using all kinds of other precautions. The U-boats ("U" for Underwater) escaped sonar detection by staying on the surface at nights. They were hard to see after dark. That is when they attacked, dived and turned off everything that might create a sound and waited until they no longer heard the screws of war ships. The destroyers escorting the convoys used depth charges but usually missed. The Germans had greatly improved their technology, especially that which was needed to stay underwater for a long time after an attack.

Though the Americans officially maintained their neutrality, they helped the British very extensively with intelligence on the Atlantic, and they enjoyed the luxury of not running any risk of being torpedoed. British as well as American companies spent a lot on research to find and destroy submarines.

Early in October we heard the rumor that the crew of a submarine supply ship had been captured. The rumor proved to be a fact and the sailors were sent to our camp. Most of them had on nothing but British navy pants and shoes. The camp was very small for so many people.

The story a sailor told me before he knew that I belonged to the forbidden group was that they were a German freighter ordered to supply submarines. One day they found themselves shadowed by an American cruiser. That night they sharply changed direction. While completely blacked out, they repainted the stack and masts to resemble a ship of a neutral line. The next day the cruiser was still following them. They changed the length of the stack, the masts, repainted the superstructure at nights but they could not shake the spy.

As was to be expected, a British destroyer appeared and ordered them to heave to. The German captain had the ship stopped, ordered the crew into the life boats and opened the sea cocks to scuttle the ship. The British destroyer was on one side of the ship, the American cruiser on the other. The American may have stopped to take *News Reel* pictures. It turned out very badly, as the Germans naturally headed for the neutral ship with a promise of freedom in the U.S.

The British ordered them to head for their destroyer. When the crew did not obey, the British machine gunned the sailors and sank one life boat. Three men were killed and several wounded. The crew was picked up by the destroyer. Many had stripped so that they could swim better, hence the British navy pants and shoes.

They paraded a teenage boy around the camp. A bullet had glanced off his head. The impact had blinded him. The feelings in the camp, never very cozy, became very bitter. Tents were erected for them. We, in our group, were a bit afraid of them. They were obviously navy reserve and hand picked Nazis. Fortunately, they had strict orders from the Gestapo (Secret Sate Police) among them, not to talk to us under any circumstances. We liked that, because we would not have insults hurled at us or be goaded into a fight. We had every reason to keep our distance from them. We were outnumbered 4 : 1.

Soon several more sailors arrived, their wounds having healed sufficiently to be released from the army hospital. The blinded boy regained his sight after a few days. I felt that the British had over reacted. All they had to do was, tell the Americans not to take the Germans on board and get under way again. The British navy apparel was eventually exchanged for brown pants and white shirts. They also received socks and heavy brown boots.

A few days later another crew arrived. This camp got really crowded. A rumor circulated that the army was building a much larger camp for us and that we would soon be moved.

# FREEDOM !

All the local internees were interrogated, one at a time, by a local Board of Review. It was headed by a British official who seemed to have the final say. There were three prominent Jamaican members to advise him and Gerhard was their interpreter. One of the Jamaicans whom everybody, including me, knew, was Mr. Norman Manley. He was said to be the most prominent defense barrister in the British Empire. He was also the founder and leader of the Peoples National Party (PNP), the socialist party which demanded independence from the British Empire, or, at the minimum, Dominion Status uniting all British Colonies in the Americas from Br. Guiana northward, including all the British Island Colonies, and British Honduras (Belize today) forming the northernmost end.

A few days after the hearing, most of our group, including me, but not Willy, were released on November 15, 1939, exactly on the sixth anniversary of my first landing in Jamaica. I was given back my manila envelop with my little bit of money, my watch and penknife.

I went to the Khouris. My room had been ransacked by the detectives. They had taken my opera glasses, my little coin collection and, what really hurt, my medals which I had received for swimming. It was sad. But, compared to the long loss of freedom of 73 days, it was nothing. Louis was as fat as ever. But he was going to a doctor who did not seem to be able to diagnose the reason for his stomach complaints. Louis was relatively young, about Gerhard's age (31), so we did not worry too much. The prejudice against all Germans was everywhere. It was sickening! To save Louis possible embarrassment, I decided to move back to the macaroni factory at 4 Arlington Ave. Prejudice is a form of stupidity. It is the most difficult form to fight.

Gerhard was again working for the Jamaica Public Service. In the office he felt a lot of animosity from his fellow salesman, MacDonald, and his immediate superior, Mr. Caithness, the Sales Manager who came to work in his beautiful, decorative, imposing, and dazzling white Naval Officer's Uniform. MacDonald donned an Army uniform with corporal chevrons in the afternoons. He and two others, one wearing sergeant's chevrons, organized cadet corps in the high schools. Naturally, the two idiots had to find someone on whom they could let out their hostility. With "safety first" in mind, they picked an "enemy" who could not, and even if he could, would not retaliate. It was good for Gerhard that he did not have to be near those two pains in the neck. Fortunately, he could almost always be out on sales calls, and his customers were sensible people.

I started up my neon shop again. I still had it, thanks to Dorrie's courageous stand. Of course, because of blackout restrictions, I could only do indoor signs and decorative lighting in stores. I had enough to do, so that I could hire an apprentice. George Minott's father was a small contractor, and George was very good with tools. He was a great help. I also maintained Dorrie's macaroni factory. It was terribly noisy. From time to time, I asked Gerhard to change the gear drive to a chain drive. He said: "As long as it works, leave it alone. Noisy or silent, such a change will not increase production, costs money, and shuts down the machines while you change the drive."

It was the first time in my life, that I found "Production" vs. "Maintenance" on opposite sides of an argument. I did not know then that this controversy existed in all factories which I ever saw and worked at in later years.

Sometimes, when I walked along the streets, old acquaintances whom I once considered to be my friends, crossed the street rather than meet me and say hello to me. Well, the British spent millions of pounds to vilify all Germans. The propaganda was bound to have some effect. I visited Rose again once in a while. She had found others to be friendly with and did not seem to be interested in any one in particular.

The goalkeeper of the water polo "A" team of the Kingston Swimming Club, who was also the All Star Goalie of Jamaica, went home to his native Cuba. Now I was considered to be the best goalie of the Island, and I played on the All Star Team whenever a foreign team came to play Jamaica. I was to retain that honor for a little over 13 years, from 1939 to early 1953 when I left the Island.

Just around my 22nd birthday, November 30, 1939, the British light cruiser *H.M.S. Ajax* was in port. Its water polo team was the British Navy Champions. We played against them. Early in the game it became obvious that they could not possibly score against us. In our captain's sporting manner, he told me to give up the goal and play fullback. We still beat them but we held down the score so that they did not look too bad.

No one knew then that many of the crew who were watching and maybe some of the players who played against our team would be dead or wounded by December 14, after their ship, her sister ship, the *H.M.S. Archilles* and the heavy cruiser *H.M.S. Exeter* forced the German pocket battleship *Graf Spee* out of action on December 13, with the result that the once powerful German raider was scuttled by her Captain Langsdorff a few days after the battle near the mouth of the River Plate. The British casualties in dead and wounded were much higher than those of the Germans but the British attained their objective and got rid of the threat to their life line in the South Atlantic. The *H.M.S. Ajax,* however, never made it to port. She managed to cross the Atlantic but she was then beached and abandoned.

Sometimes other swimmers would invite me to a party. That was very nice of them. Unfortunately, when I went, there were always some fellows who wanted to fight "the damned German" after they had a few drinks, so I went home early.

"Mama Hill" and all of her family were especially nice to me, and I spent many very enjoyable evenings at their hospitable house arguing about the pros and cons of independence and other local issues. I avoided talking about the War. It was still called the Phony War because of the lack of action along the Rhine. The first stanza of the most popular song was:

> We will hang out our washing on the Siegfried Line.
> Have you got any washing Mama, dear?
> We will hang out our washing on the Siegfried Line.
> Is the Siegfried Line still there?

Eustace Chen, the sales agent of the Dora Macaroni brand for Dorrie's factory, was especially nice to me. It was a pleasure to go into his warehouse. His secretary was Iris Alexander. She later married Noel Ramsey. They all did their best to make me comfortable when I visited them. We are still the best of friends with the Ramseys to this day in 1996. Mr. Chen died long ago.

I did not see people doing too much as a war effort. Some were saving silver paper for its tin content. Aluminum foil or plastic wrap had not yet been invented. Toothpaste tubes were made out of thin tin tubes. One had to squeeze them from the bottom. Those who would squeeze them from the top, broke them and would get the paste all over their hands. Another item people saved for the Red Cross, was string. They rolled it up in big balls. String was usually made from brown paper, cotton, or hemp. Up to now, I am still wondering what the Red Cross ever did with all those balls of string.

# BREAK DOWN AT THE MACARONI FACTORY

As before, I did all the maintenance at the Jamaica Macaroni Factory. When Dorrie and Gerhard were away, I was in charge when anything unusual happened. The factory had become very busy as foreign imports of pasta had been stopped completely. Shipping space had to be reserved for more essential and less bulky items. Flour from Australia was still imported by Chinese merchants and sold to bakeries, groceries, and the macaroni factory. The latter ran two shifts to keep up with the orders.

One Friday Dorrie and Gerhard had taken off for one of their frequent hikes in the Blue Mountains. Early the next Saturday morning, the girls in the factory had just finished making all the dough for the day and had started pressing out the macaroni, when the line shaft broke next to the driven gear. Mazie, who had worked for Gerhard already five years ago in the Continental Club, told me that the dough would only keep for 24 hours at the most. She wrapped it in damp flour bags to keep it from drying out. The loss of all dough for a whole day's production threatened to become a terrible financial loss. Money was very scarce among the three of us.

There were several flaws which I had always wanted to correct but Gerhard never allowed me to shut down the machines long enough to do the work. Because the pulley on the line shaft and belt were only four inches wide, the belt slipped so badly that two girls had to grab the belt and help it move. This was a very inefficient and dangerous practice. I had wanted to change that to a six inch pulley and belt for a long time. Work would be safer and save the wages of two girls per shift.

The line shaft broke because of metal fatigue resulting from the heavy bull gear driving it. The hammering by that gear was also the reason why the motor, from time to time, had to have its bearings replaced in a hurry. There were no new 3 Horse Power, 3 Phase, 40 Hertz motors to be had anywhere. It looked as if even replacement bearings would soon no longer be available for civilian use.

241

Gerhard had always maintained that I should not change the gear drive as long as it worked. Now, that it did not work, was my chance to set things right without losing extra time and next to no extra cost. A chain drive would eliminate the ear splitting noise, prevent bearing failure, metal fatigue of the line shaft and a wider belt at the press would make the place safer and free two girls per shift to do other work.

I sent a telegram to Gerhard. A bearer would have to walk four miles steeply up hill with it and find Gerhard. He could not possibly be back for 10 hours at the earliest. I dismantled the line shaft and phoned Masterton Ltd. that we had an emergency. I hired a hand cart and loaded the broken shaft on it after taking off all the pulleys. By this time I was covered with black, tar-like gear grease.

I helped push the load with the cart owner all the way from Arlington Ave., along Windward Rd., down Hanover Street to Masterton's elaborate workshop. Mr. Forbes looked up in an industrial catalogue what size chain and sprockets I would need. Fortunately they were in stock. He had the sprockets bored out to the correct sizes. I knew that we had six inch wide crowned pulleys on the shaft of the press, so we did not need anything new there. He had a new drive pulley turned out of lignum vitae for the new line shaft. They gave me their best quality six inch wide rubberized belt for the best possible traction. I watched like a hawk that no one would waste any time.

It was evening when I helped push the heavy hand cart back in my dirty and torn clothes. I got a lot of stares from the people riding the open trolley cars home from work. "Decent people" do no physical work and let others see them, and then certainly not in filthy rags! At last I got back to Arlington Ave. The girls, thoughtfully, had made me a good supper. I was very hungry, and I took time out to eat. The girls had removed all the old, tar-like grease from the concrete floor. They had washed down the machinery. They had really done all they could, to make things easier for me and to please me. They all went home. I had to fasten old and new pulleys on the line shaft, install the assembly, cut the new belt to length, line up the motor and exchange the gear on the motor for the new sprocket. I had to reverse two wires in the switch, to reverse the rotation of the motor.

My work had started early in the morning about 7:00 a.m.  Now it was well past 2:00 a.m. the next day, 19 hours later.  The factory was almost ready to run.  All the parts were so heavy, and I felt really exhausted, when Gerhard arrived.  He saw at once that I had changed the drive from gear to chain.  He was furious!  He told me to get out and stay out and never set foot into the factory again.  I was so tired, I could not care less.  I went upstairs and slept on the floor of the neon shop, as my clothes were too dirty to go to bed, and I was too tired to undress.

When I awoke, I went down into the factory.  Gerhard, who had walked through half the night to his car in Mavis Bank and then finished up the few things which were left to be done when I went to sleep, had gone to bed.  I was greeted with smiles everywhere.  The dough had been saved and for the first time the factory ran so silently that a whisper could be heard across the room.  The six inch belt made the hated, dangerous job of pulling on the belt unnecessary.  The bearings of the motor would last as long as the rest of the factory.  The cost of the repairs were next to nothing.  The silence alone was a most welcome improvement for all concerned.  The wages saved, for two girls per shift, was a substantial improvement in the profit picture.  Neither Gerhard nor I ever mentioned his furious outburst to one another as long as he lived.

# IN QUEST OF AN EDUCATION

It was early 1940 now. The so called Phony War droned on. It seemed that the French and British had no stomach to attack the Siegfried Line, and the Germans seemed to fear horrible losses if they tried to cross the Rhine and attempt to storm the Maginot fortifications across rising terrain, where all cover had been carefully removed by the French. The War on the Atlantic Ocean went on with increasing losses to British shipping. The reports of the sinking of German submarines became more and more frequent. Because of the many exaggerated claims of Allied victories in the past, no one now believed that the Allies were really improving their ability to destroy enemy U-boats.

Russia had invaded Finland. The Finns were excellent winter fighters. Instead of trying to defend the fixed positions of their Mannerheim Line, they carried the fight to the Russians. The Finns wore white uniforms and were mounted on skis. They out maneuvered the Soviets and attacked where they were least expected. Everybody cheered for the brave followers of their President and the military genius, Marshall Mannerheim. The British were getting an expeditionary force ready to assist the tiny, democratic nation of about four million inhabitants.

That was the situation when I met an eighteen year old girl in the neighborhood who told me that she was about to take the London Matric Exam. She obviously feared this very objective empire-wide college admission test. The written part was graded in London. There could be no favoritism. I asked her to show me the books which she had used to prepare for it. I browsed through the books and told her that I could probably pass that exam. She laughed at me and taunted me to try. I had told her that I had left school halfway through the tenth grade when I was only fifteen. I intended to take her up on it. I always wanted a certificate that would show that I was an educated person.

I thought that it was a good time to continue my education. Rev. Lewis Davidson, a Presbyterian Minister, was the Principal of Wolmer's High School for Boys, one of the most prestigious schools in Jamaica. He advertised that he would start college level evening classes and invited applicants.

He gave me an appointment for 7 p.m. one evening. It was already dark. When I arrived exactly on time, I saw MacDonald and two other men in army uniforms waiting outside of his office. One of the men was a sergeant and the other two were corporals. Rev. Davidson, a Scotsman, opened the door. As they had come before me, I motioned to them to go in. But Rev. Davidson stopped the three and beckoned to me to come in. That really surprised me.

The Reverend was about five years older than I was. He offered me a chair opposite him at his desk. He made me feel very comfortable by telling me of his plans to start a college from the bottom up. He went into my educational background. He hoped that I would attend his classes as soon as he had signed up enough students to get started. We chatted about all sorts of things, never touching on the War. The fact that I was born in Germany did not seem to make any difference to him. That alone made me feel great and, on top of that, I was to attend college courses. We must have talked for an hour. I forgot the world around me. He made me feel so good. I felt that he was a real friend. When I left, I passed the three men who had waited outside all this while. I said good night to them. They ignored me. I was back in the harsh real world.

Once a month I went to the Public Service Store in King St. and paid back a little bit of my debt to them.

MacDonald saw me and asked me: "What did you tell Rev. Davidson? We wanted him to allow us to start a cadet corps at Wolmer's, and he turned us down flat. You must have a tremendous influence over him!"

"Who, me? Influence? All I wanted was to get admission for the evening college courses he intends to start at that school."

MacDonald obviously did not believe me. As far as he was concerned, every German was an enemy. Unfortunately, he was not the only one who was so stupidly narrow minded.

# THE BLITZKRIEG

Suddenly, the war heated up white hot! The German Army marched through Denmark practically unopposed. The German Navy, Army, and Air Force invaded Norway very successfully, because a powerful Norwegian politician, Quisling, a former Norwegian Prime Minister, prepared the invasion route and bases for them with his Norwegian Nazis.

The Nazi *Luftwaffe* (air force) bombarded the Netherlands. Especially, the important port of Rotterdam was almost obliterated, killing thousands of civilians. In the confusion, the Dutch failed to open the dikes to drown the invading Germans, and the entire country was taken with very few military casualties. It is possible that Dutch fifth columnists prevented the opening of those dikes.

In the middle of the night, while the *Luftwaffe* attacked Rotterdam, German sentries suddenly attacked their Belgian counterparts, so that the latter could not sound any alarm. German engineers raced across the bridges of the Albert Canal, Belgium's main defense line, and disarmed the explosives which the Belgians had placed under all of the canal's bridges. They had intended to detonate them in case of a German attack. German paratroopers blew up the Belgian Command Center, and thereby brought total confusion to the Belgian Forces. Most were captured or killed, before they knew that the Nazis were invading their country.

At the same time, the German Army broke through the Ardennes Forest, where the French and Belgian defense lines meet at Sedan. They broke through at the same area, where they had surprised the French in 1870, and again in 1914. Since it worked so well then, they surprised them equally well in May of 1940.

During World War I armies, and especially navies, had used black smoke screens to obscure themselves from enemy view. Now, 22 to 26 years later, in May of 1940, the Germans used lots of black smoke one night and climbed unseen on top of the Maginot Line and threw explosives into the air shafts. Paratroopers landed behind the fortifications and stormed them. All the heavy guns of the French pointed in the wrong direction and were practically useless. In one night the vaunted, "impregnable" Maginot Line had been overpowered. The Line, that had taken many millions of francs and endless years to build and to perfect, fell in one night. The German press called the astounding success of their warfare the *"Blitzkrieg"* (lightning war). The world press apparently liked that term, and had that German word enter its vocabulary.

The Dutch, Belgian, French, and the British expeditionary forces in France were in total disarray. The Daladier government resigned. Laval took over and Maréchal Pétain, the great, victorious national hero of Word War I, became President of France. The Germans marched into Paris, and the French established a government in Vichy under Nazi supervision. Almost all Dutch, Belgian, and French forces surrendered.

The British retreated to the beaches of Dunkirk. Hundreds of small boats bravely crossed the Channel from Britain to pick up their imperiled countrymen at Dunkirk. Fog prevented attacks from the air. The fact that the main forces of the Germans did not pursue them saved the British expeditionary force. The German soldiers headed south, to prevent a possible regrouping of a viable French Army.

Surprisingly, very few French, Belgian and Dutch Naval Forces crossed to England. Some soldiers of France crossed the Channel by fishing boats to fight with the "Free French" led by General Charles De Gaulle who had fled by plane. Since the General was from Lorraine, their flag was the French Tricolor with the red double barred cross of Lorraine in the white center.

My favorite cousin, Marianne, had fled from Hamburg to Amsterdam just before the War. She was half a year older than I was. I worried about her. After the War I found out, that she had married a Dutch Jew by the name of Svart who was drafted into the Dutch Army. Marianne was on an outing with some other ladies, when Nazis searched her train. They took her and sent her to the concentration camp at Oranienburg. She was pregnant at the time. She was burnt there.

Her parents, my father's brother, Ernst, and his wife, Friedl, had fled to Antverp in Belgium. They had to flee again. In France they were arrested by the French and sent to a concentration camp in the South of that Country. Uncle Ernst was made camp doctor. The conditions of the place were so depressing that Aunt Friedl and he took an overdose of morphine and thus ended their sufferings. I did not find that out until after the War.

The German victories, which even *The Daily Gleaner* and the *News Reels* could not camouflage as Allied victories aroused great surprise and frustration among the educated in Jamaica, especially among those who came from the British Isles. The general population did not seem to care. The poor, especially, were delighted that they could get bananas free from the government as there was no shipping space available. The government bought the bananas to save the growers from total ruin. One man even told me with a big smile: "Me like Hitler, Sah. Him make the govamen' give we free banana."

One of the reasons, why the Germans were so successful, was the fact that the native Nazis in all of those countries, which they attacked, had prepared landing sites for German parachute borne soldiers and had given valuable intelligence to the attackers. Hungary and Romania had established Fascist Governments and allied themselves with the Nazis. In Germany, as well as in all the conquered countries, in Hungary and in Romania the Jews were rounded up. Some of those, who were good workers, were used as slave labor, and all others were killed by the millions!

During the Spanish Civil War Generalissimo Franco was interviewed by a foreign correspondent who asked how he hoped to win against the government with such a small force. The Spanish armies in those days marched in columns of four men abreast. Franco boasted that he had an invisible fifth column marching with his troops, and that this fifth column would make him win. He explained that his sympathizers among the government forces, behind the enemy lines, were that fifth column, and were the ones who would make the difference.

The press made the term: "Fifth column" household words. It was made clear, that the fifth column in Denmark were Danish Nazis. Those in Norway were Norwegian. The name of their leader: Quisling, became synonymous with the word: Traitor. There were strong fifth columns in Holland. They were Dutch Nazis. Those in Belgium were Belgium Nazis. Those in France were French Nazis. There they called their organization: Croix de Feu (Cross of Fire).

The British Fascist Party was led by Sir Oswald Mosley. He was a member of the House of Lords. When he got married, he took his bride to Germany, so that Hitler and Goering, the No.2 man in the Nazi Party, could be the witnesses at his marriage ceremony. The British Fascists were uncomfortably strong, until one day Sir Oswald entered the House of Lords, stood still at the entrance and gave the outstretched arm salute. There was an embarrassed silence until one of the Lords, mimicking the female voice of a school marm, said: "Yes, Ozzy, you may go to the bathroom now." The laughter was hearty, loud, and prolonged. The press ridiculed the British Führer mercilessly, and the British Nazi Party disappeared from public view. Sir Oswald was interned at the beginning of the War.

The very fact that there were Nazi sympathizers in the Allied Countries, should have made it easy for a reasonably intelligent person to understand that the reverse was also true. There were lots of people in Germany, and many more Germans, like myself, who had fled to Allied Countries who were fervently hoping for an Allied victory.

The Russians moved a huge army against Finland and threatened its capital, Helsinki. The Finns surrendered a large chunk of their land to the Russians for peace. All became quiet now on all land fronts. Only the British Empire was still fighting the monstrous Hitler.

The British had developed the Lancaster Bomber. It was a very light, wooden framed plane with a canvas skin. It had a greater range than any other plane, could fly far out over the Atlantic, search for submarines and thus make it safer for convoys. The German sailors, according to the press, called their U-boats "iron coffins," and service in them, became very unpopular in the German Navy.

# INTERNED AGAIN

Mr. Dorr, of the London Shop, had given me my biggest order, since the beginning of the War, to illuminate the store's ceiling with curved neon tubing. My loyal and capable apprentice, George Minott, and I were standing on ladders and had just about finished installing the last tubes, when three men walked into the shop. One flashed a crown shaped badge mounted on a piece of leather, tapped me on my leg, and said: "You are under arrest." I knew habeas corpus, the center piece of the Magna Carta, and of British Justice, had been "suspended" since the beginning of the War. It made no sense to ask: "On what charge?" They would not have answered. Denmark and Norway had just been invaded, and the Allies needed a victory, so they arrested me and some ten or so other, mostly Jewish, refugees.

I asked George to finish the job and to tell Gerhard about my arrest. He would pay him. He did, and Gerhard was able to collect for the job. One detective had waited in the station wagon. I must have seemed like a real threat to their very lives that it took four armed detectives to transport me to the new internment camp.

It had been erected just east of the military camp and a good distance west of Long Mountain Rd. Just north-east of the camp was the military cemetery. There were 50 ft. long by 20 ft. wide wooden huts, on creosoted wooden supports, standing side by side about 20 ft. apart. There was only one entrance in the middle of the long side. Three steps led up to the door. There was expanded metal over all the windows, and a wooden cover could be let down over each window. The roofs had enough overhang to keep light rain out without the use of the wooden window covers.

At the entrance of the camp was a similar hut. It was the administration building. It was partitioned into several small offices with real glass windows and a store room. All of the "Jew Group" was together again, except Mr. Hirsch. He, and his family, had migrated to Brazil. Wise move! No one ever heard of him again. Four from our group, Richard Kahn, Richard Kaiser, Ludwig Klein, and Willy Gertig had never been released. The first three were Jewish. It made no sense but then no reason was ever given why we were interned. Any question by any of us, was answered: "The Government is not required to give a reason and, therefore, shall not." Any lawyer for us had no point whatsoever to argue.

I picked a spot in the corner. I had the identical bed as I described earlier. Besides the bed was a little locker. When I examined my mosquito net, I found bed bugs in it. They had been waiting impatiently for me. The cots were separated by two feet. Richard Kahn had the bed next to mine. This time they had also arrested his 17 year old son, Wolfgang. His 14 year old, Hans, was free with his mother. There were two tables and four benches. That was the total furniture.

The entire camp was surrounded by two 10 ft. high barbed wire fences. The inner one had its top five strands extended inward at a 45° angle. The bottom four feet were bolstered by coils of barbed wire. They were pegged into the ground by hooks. The outer fence, 10 ft. away, did not sport all those reinforcements. Guards, with fixed bayonets, walked in the space between the fences at regular intervals. When they were not walking, they stood at the corners of the camp. At each of the four corners, there was a 20 ft. high tower, manned by a guard with a machine gun. The entire outside was flood lit all night. The soldiers were still from the Shropshire Rifles. They were very professional looking prewar volunteers.

One hut was the hospital hut. It had a separate kitchen and separate rooms for each of the ship doctors who practiced there. There was one large kitchen shed for all the rest of the prisoners. The Nazis refused to cook for us, allow us to share the wash stands, and toilets with them. The camp authorities assigned separate facilities to us and had another kitchen shed built exactly like, and parallel to the hospital's. It was about 20 ft. away and both kitchens were 20 ft. from the fence.

Many of our group were very depressed. To most of us Democracy was our religion. None of us seemed to be much church or synagogue going religious. Four of us were not Jewish: Willy Gertig (both parents were Lutheran), Walter Schönbeck, Wolfgang Kahn, and I (our fathers had married Lutherans). We felt it ironic and most unjust that we should be interned with our worst enemies, the Nazis, in a country that claimed to fight for democracy

WILLY AND I, THE GUESTS OF THE KING

and justice!  Especially, Richard Kahn took it to heart.  He had been a Captain in the German Army in Word War I.  He lay on his cot all day and cried.  Most of us, and especially those who had a wife outside, were not in a much better shape.  It hurt that we were just numbers to the authorities.  My new number was 206.

We were told to furnish two cooks for our kitchen.  No one wanted the job, not even Pivnicza.  I did not volunteer because some said that they wanted a "good cook."  I felt that I did not qualify.  Finally Max Ebersohn, from Vienna, volunteered if I would help him.

Ebersohn had fought the first two years in World War I in the Austrian Army.  During a retreat he was shot through the leg and was captured.  He spent four years in a Siberian prisoners' camp, never knowing that the War was over for two years already.  He escaped during the confusion caused by the civil war between the Red and the White Armies in Russia.  He was held for a night in Moscow then released, and traveled north of Leningrad (St. Petersburg) through Finland, Germany, and then home to Vienna, just to have his mother slam the door in his face, as she yelled, that he was a very cruel impostor, one man had seen her son fall, and he was dead!

He had to go downtown to a delousing facility, had his full beard shaven off, and get some Central European clothes from a charity, before his parents recognized him.  After the *"Anschluss"*, as Austria's union with Germany in May, 1938, was called, he, being a Jew, was arrested by the Nazis, and spent almost a year in a concentration camp.  Someone paid to have him freed.  He fled with his wife, his 10 year old daughter and his brother-in-law, Fred Löffler, to Jamaica, just in time to be interned again.  He was 43 years old, had never done any crime but had spent one of every eight and a half days of his life as a prisoner.

He was very clever.  He knew his way around.  He never intended to serve in the kitchen, but this way he got me to be the cook.  He quit after the first day, saying that it was a one-man job and I could do it alone.  I did not mind at all as boredom is a prisoner's worst enemy.  It threatens his sanity.

The camp furnished us with fire wood for our Caledonia cast iron stove, our only cooking facility.  This firewood was a lignum vitae root. One root filled the entire two ton truck. If one hit it with an ax, the ax handle broke before the blade made any impression on the tough grain. We had to use a 12 lb. sledge hammer and wedges, to splinter some of that wood off to do the cooking. This is some tough cross grained wood. It is heavier than water. Fortunately it burnt very hot and slowly and had a delightful smell. I held the wedge while Willy Gertig hit it with a hammer.

We found some loose wood in the camp which the contractors had left when they cast the concrete platforms for the kitchens, wash stands, showers, and toilets. The camp had been enlarged, and some unused barbed wire was within the camp. We pulled out some pegs, heated the sharp ends in the kitchen fire and burnt a large hole through two wooden 1 x 3's. We made a dowel out of another piece of wood, and joined the first two pieces to make a crude pair of tongs. Now one of us was able to hold the wedge in place, while the other wielded the sledge hammer without fear of smashing anybody's hand.

One of the rooms, in the practically empty hospital, was furnished as a dental clinic. It was all Ernst Lobbenberg's equipment. Ernst and Fritz Lobbenberg got the room next to the clinic. The military dentist was not qualified to do oral operations. So, Lobbenberg performed root canal, impacted wisdom tooth and all other complicated operations on soldiers and prisoners alike in that little clinic, while Fritz pedaled to keep the drill going.

One of the sailors had a badly impacted wisdom tooth. Ernst realized that he had to chip away part of the jaw bone. The military dentist gave the narcosis. And Ernst did the operation. While the man was in slumber land, he kept yelling at the top of his voice, to be heard all over the camp: *"Heil Hitler, heil Hitler, und immer nur heil Hitler!"* (and nothing but hail Hitler!). It was magnanimous of Dr. Lobbenberg, that he did not drill him through his throat.

Fortunately, I received regular visitors once a month. Sybil Hill, at whose little sister's "sweet sixteen" birthday party, I had performed the outrageous dance, came to visit regularly. She never came empty handed. She brought me cake, sewing thread and needles upon my request. Louis Khouri came regularly almost every visiting day. He told me that he was taking a ship to New York to have his persistent pain in the stomach examined. I gave him my parents' and Toni's addresses and phone numbers. I also wrote them about Louis.

Toni had come to New York from England via Canada as the "Battle of Britain", the air war, had started. German bombers, escorted by fighter planes, were bombing Royal Air Force hangars, factories, air fields and were about to conquer the R.A.F., when one British pilot bombed a civilian area in Berlin. Hitler, in retaliation ordered London to be set on fire. That saved the British Air Force, and thereby possibly the total collapse of all of the British war effort. The Royal Air Force was the only defense, preventing the Germans from shutting down all shipping and food supply with their submarines. Hitler's cruel, impulsive but ill-advised order caused many civilian casualties in all of the English cities. It allowed the British, however, to build and fly reconnaissance planes to spot U-boats. In those dark days America and Canada could not help effectively as bombers which could fly across the Atlantic, had not yet been heard of.

Toni had evacuated four children to Canada, two of them, her own, Harald, 8, and Helen, 6. They arrived in Brooklyn August 18, 1940. They had been on the last westbound convoy which got through. The next convoy was shot up disastrously by submarines. From then on the British Government did not evacuate any more children overseas but sent them to rural areas in Britain.

Maria was taking Toni for her first trolley car ride in Brooklyn to go shopping. There was a turnstile in the front of the car. It would not budge, though Toni kept bumping it with increasing force. Just as the car started moving with very fast acceleration, Maria dropped a dime into the slot by the turnstile. Toni bumped again with force. The turnstile opened, and Toni lay full length on the floor with surprising speed. What a tiny dime could do in those days!

Louis Khouri was visited and comforted by my father and especially, Toni, practically everyday, while he was dying of stomach cancer in New York. Toni, Papa, and most certainly I, felt that we lost a very good friend.

In the meantime the camp population grew. One day, if I remember correctly, six ship crews arrived at the same time. Before they had been told by their *Gestapo* not to talk to us, one of them told me: "When the War broke out, several German ships in the vicinity sought shelter in the Dutch islands of Aruba and Curaçao. We had a good time there in the neutral port. Suddenly, the Dutch were at War with us.

"The police arrested us, confiscated our ships, took all our belts away and cut all buttons off our pants, so that we had to use both hands to hold them up. Then they paraded us through the streets of Willemstad, the people spat at us and pelted us with rotten fruit. We could not even protect ourselves, as we had to hold up our pants!" The man was very emotional and indignant over the incident. In a way I could not blame him. He did not make the War. He had been glad that he had escaped it. Nevertheless, he chose to be with the Nazi internees.

At times I felt very frustrated being interned with the Nazis as more and more ship crews arrived. I would go to the lignum vitae root, which was lying behind the kitchen, and chop away at it until my hands were bleeding from open blisters. I possessed one good shirt, one suit, three boxer type underpants (which one of the factory girls had sewn for me out of bleached flour bags. Those were cheaper and much stronger than any which could be bought in a store), two sleeveless under shirts (called merinos in Jamaica,) two white shirts, which I had to wear with the sleeves rolled up, as I did not want to show that the elbows were worn through, several ties, a pair of good khaki shorts, two oil stained khaki work pants, two equally stained khaki work shirts, my bright red shorts from the New York Field Hockey Club uniform, three pairs of darned socks, two pairs of darned knee socks, and one pair of shoes.

The uncertainty as to what would happen to us, whether we would be interned for a very long time, released, or shipped away, made me very conscious of the paucity of my wardrobe and the lack of money. We were not allowed to have any cash, and our bank accounts were frozen. To conserve what little I had, I wore nothing but my red shorts, no socks, no shoes. Only during visiting hours would I wear my good white shirt, my khaki shorts, knee socks and well polished shoes.

256

# THE QUAKER

The only furniture we had were four benches and two tables. Willy suggested that we make ourselves some furniture. I could not see how. There were lots of little pieces of wood around which the laborers had left when they cast the concrete foundations. Willy and I collected enough for a folding chair. The camp had been enlarged to double the original size and some of the barbed wire was left inside the camp. We picked up some of the iron pegs which held down the barbed wire. They were of several diameters, varying from 1/4" to 5/8". We also pulled out one of the 4 x 4 uprights. It was made of bullet wood, a very hard, termite proof local wood. We borrowed a saw, which had a lot of its teeth missing, from the store room. We had to return it at 5:00 p.m. every afternoon.

We sawed the pieces of wood to the lengths and widths we wanted and used shards of a broken bottle as a plane to smooth the cuts. We also used the concrete kitchen floor to grind the edges round. The iron pegs from the fence were heated in the kitchen fire until they were red hot and could burn holes through the furniture pieces. We rounded the pieces which were to be at right angles to the pieces with the holes until they fitted snugly into the holes. To fasten the dowel like end really tightly in the hole we sawed a slot into the end, soaked it over night in a cooking pot, fitted it into the hole, and hammered in a wedge made of bullet wood. We used the blunt end of an ax as a hammer.

The Quakers, who visited Willy regularly about twice a month, brought him some string. Willy knotted the string like a fish net to make the seat and the back rest. To my great surprise Willy did not keep the chair but gave it to one of the most depressed members of our group, Fritz Lackenbach from Vienna.

I asked: "Why did you do that? How is it, that all of us are so depressed and miserable, and you work and sing all the live long day? Nothing seems to get you down."

"You know, Arnold, I am a Quaker. I dedicated my life to serve man, to do my little part to make this a better world for all of us to live in. Where would you find a better place to serve than in an internment camp?"

I was flabbergasted. It made sense. It was probably the longest speech Willy had ever made.

"How does one become a Quaker?"

"You go to a Quaker Meeting. We can have one right here."

Sunday morning, right after breakfast, before we started cooking our lunch, we sat very quietly, one on a bucket with a board over it, the other on a stool which was part of the kitchen equipment, behind the kitchen shed for about half an hour. As he shook my hand, signifying the end of the meditation, I told him that I did not feel anything, and that I did not understand why it was called: Meditation. He told me that the feeling would come with time. That was my first Quaker Meeting.

It may not have been much of a meeting but Willy had changed my outlook on life drastically. I no longer fumed against the injustice of my internment and the underlying stupidity of prejudice which I could do nothing about but looked at it as an educational opportunity. I certainly learnt about people. They were not what they seemed. In the Bible there is the story of Salome and her seven veils. She dropped one after the other until, at last, she danced with just one of them revealing herself. In the internment camp, men drop their veils one after the other from their souls, until they reveal their hearts quite naked.

The barbed wire did not seem to be quite as forbidding as before. I helped Willy to make folding chairs and deck chairs for the rest of the group, so that we could all sit down comfortably. The Quakers were allowed to bring us some tools. They made work much easier. We had to turn them in at 5:00 p.m. to the British corporal in charge of the camp store room. The Quakers were the only religious group that seemed to care for any of us.

Willy also started a garden to spruce up the appearance of our hut and at the same time grow some fresh vegetables. He tried to get everybody involved to do something. He knew that occupying oneself was essential for one's mental health.

Every Thursday Willy and I scrubbed the inside walls of our hut from the ceiling to the flooring and the floor itself to combat the bed bugs. All others carried buckets of water from the wash stands.

Everything was taken out of the hut and placed in the glaring sun. Bugs do not like sun. Before sun down all was put back. The hut had dried by then. We also washed our mosquito nets that day. We really cleaned house. Even with all that cleaning we still found bed bugs in our mosquito nets every Thursday.

# STAYING BUSY

Ludwig Klein was a particularly nice man. He was Viennese. After the Anschluss he had fled to Italy. He could not work there as an accountant as he did not speak the language. He played the piano in a silent movie house. He had to sit right under the screen and play something that was appropriate for the action above. He learnt Italian but he decided to get out of Europe. The signs were ominously bad. Shortly after he arrived in Kingston he was interned. I asked him to teach me book keeping. He readily agreed. That kept both of us occupied for a while.

Fred Löffler, Mrs. Ebersohn's brother, was a year older and a little heavier than I was. He had liked skiing and bicycle riding in Vienna. He could do neither of them in camp. He had a very friendly disposition and a good sense of humor. We boxed for three rounds every day. We did not really hit but just touched with my heavy gloves. There was no hurt nor bruises and certainly no knock downs but we did get a bit winded, and that was the purpose. It kept us in shape.

In my duties as the chef I was particularly lucky. The camp received a carcass of a cow every day. There was only one certified butcher among all the German ship cooks. He was Polish and had been forced to serve on a German ship. He had somehow let Ebersohn know that he hated the Germans. Ebersohn had succeeded Lobbenberg as our representative to the camp authorities. The butcher always gave us the fillet mignon. The very best piece of the cow. The portions were small but very good.

At 10:30 a.m. I scrubbed the kitchen. At 11:00 a.m. was inspection. All internees had to line up before their huts except the cooks. We had to stay at our kitchens. I used that opportunity to pick all the weeds, which were not poisonous which grew around our kitchen due to the abundant water from my scrubbing, and put them in our soup. The guys always wondered how I managed to serve such deliciously flavored soup. I never let on.

The food was not bad but I, and most of us younger ones, still felt hungry, and could have eaten a lot more. Some of the older ones saved their bread from breakfast in case they should feel hungry later. Often it got covered with mildew and sported green, red, and white growths. I collected that bread, soaked it in water, added milk powder, cinnamon, and sugar, cut up an orange, skin and all, into little dice, added raisins, if I could get any from the corporal inspecting the kitchens and a lime also cut into little pieces. I mixed it all up, greased a pan, put it into the oven till the top turned brown, and all loved it. I ate, too. Fortunately, they did not see the raw material nor the preparation. I followed the sagacious Jamaican proverb: Not ebryting good fe eat, good fe talk. I eventually got Gerhard to send us a 10 lb. box of macaroni or spaghetti every day. That way we had plenty to eat.

Among other chores in the camp I was the barber for the group. The concrete platform behind the kitchen served as the barber shop. It amazed me how particular some of the men were about their hair cuts. After all we were in an internment camp and only very few of us ever had visitors. Willy cut my hair. He did a good job.

# A CRITICAL OPERATION

Unfortunately, always going barefoot, I got an abscess in my heel. It swelled and the pain extended into the bone. I suffered from a terrible headache. Dr. Lobbenberg, our dentist and fellow internee, looked at it: "You are getting blood poison. It has to be lanced. Speak to the military doctor about it." I knew that he was the only doctor in the camp who had a license to practice in Jamaica, though the few ship doctors were probably much more experienced practitioners. I made an appointment with Dr. Ward. He looked at my heel and said that it was nothing, and that he did not like my clumsy attempt to get out of the camp. He was just a young doctor fresh out of an English medical school. What he lacked in knowledge, he tried to make up in arrogance.

The throbbing was very bad now. I asked Dr. Lobbenberg to lance it for me. "I am not licensed to practice medicine in Jamaica. Suppose you should die then I'd be in real trouble if it should become known that I lanced your heel." I was amazed at the absolute selfishness of the man!

In those days artificial fibers, such as nylon, dacron, orlon, kevlar, etc., were not yet invented. So, all clothes were made out of cotton, wool, linen, silk or any blend of them. Rayon was a form of cotton. I tore my shabbiest white cotton shirt into narrow strips, boiled them and a razor blade in one of our cook pots. I hung the strips on a line and they dried very rapidly.

I waited till roll call time between 10:30 and 11:30 when I was alone and unobserved in the kitchen. I put my heel into as hot a water as I could stand, until it became quite numb. My heel became yellow where the pus had concentrated. With my razor I shaved the skin as thin as I dared, to allow the pus to push toward the outside rather than up my leg. I again put my heel into the hot water. At last I took the sterilized razor blade and lanced the skin. It was so numb I felt no pain at all. A lot of pus just poured out. Then I squeezed the heel until only blood came out.

My headache stopped. The pulsing up my leg stopped. I bandaged my heel with the shirt strips. Now I had to wash out the pot in which I had heated my heel. I would need it the next day to boil our macaroni in it. I made myself some wooden clogs. I contoured the inside to match my foot soles. I kept washing my bandages at the wash stand and then boiled them during roll call time. After drying the strips on a line, I rolled them as tightly as I could to minimize the chances of contamination. I made sure that I washed and boiled the inside of the pot I used quite thoroughly. My incision healed perfectly. The rest of the guys did not have to know that the pot in which I served their food had been used to sterilize my bandages only an hour earlier. What alternative did I have?

# THE SITUATION GETS WORSE

Since my run in with Dr. Ward I felt very rebellious. One of the rules of the camp was: "All internees will appear washed and shaven at roll calls." I told the other inmates that I would not shave as long as I was in camp, and if the authorities did not like that, they could throw me out of the camp. I grew a full brown beard. The authorities did not do a thing about it but almost all of my comrades, especially Dr. Lobbenberg, begged me to shave it off. One trait of mine is that I am resolute, (some call it stubborn.) My beard grew magnificently.

On the far side of the administration building three more huts were being built. All kinds of speculations arose as to who would occupy them. Besides those, the camp was being enlarged to twice the size again, and two more machine gun towers were being erected.

Mussolini had entered the War on the side of the Germans. From Libya, then an Italian Colony, he attacked the British forces in Egypt which was then a British Protectorate. The Italians had by far the most beautiful uniforms of any soldiers on either side in the entire War. Unfortunately, for the Axis Powers, as Germany, Hungary, and Italy were called, the soldiers of Il Duce (pronounced: Dootshe) had no desire to fight. They surrendered by the thousands upon contact with the enemy.

A couple of Italians now joined our group. One had a Jamaican wife with three very beautiful children, the other was a sailor who had served on a neutral ship. The vessel was stopped by a British destroyer, searched, and he was arrested, quite illegally as the ship was neutral, taken to Kingston and sent to the camp. He decided not to join the Nazis and Fascists, so he came to us.

The huts on the far side of the administration building were complete and all male naturalized British of German and Italian birth were interned. That included Gerhard. What was worse, all German women, whether Jewish, Christian, naturalized British or not, were interned in a building in Hanover Street. That street was also the main street for prostitutes. Choosing it for the women's internment camp, was a disgusting insult to the internees! The malicious men who made that choice must have wanted to add insult to injury.

The hurt, defenseless women obviously included Dorrie. The other naturalized British were: Dr. Stamm, Dr. Hans Stamm's wife (he was Jewish, she was not), Mrs. Kronecker from Vienna, and the wives of men from our group: Mrs. Ebersohn from Vienna, Fred Löffler's sister with her ten year old daughter, Mrs. Kahn and her 14 year old boy, and Mrs. Lackenbach also from Vienna. Those from Vienna had never been German citizens.

Thus Dorrie, Gerhard, and I found ourselves in three different camps. Communication between the three camps was strictly forbidden. All letters I wrote to Dorrie or Gerhard were confiscated. We were allowed to write only one letter per week. Thus my only letter of one page per week was confiscated without my knowledge. This was absolute madness! It was quite unnecessary cruelty. All internees of all the three camps were very much upset.

Ebersohn, who had his wife and his little daughter in that house, went to the commander of our camp, Major Saulters, who told him that he did not make the rules, he only abided by them. The rules were formulated in the Colonial Secretary's Office. I wrote to the Right Honourable, the Colonial Secretary but it was a vain effort. There was Gerhard only a few yards away and I was not even allowed to write him, much less see him! Even more ridiculously, he was not even allowed to write Dorrie, his wife, or receive letters from her! It was absolutely preposterous!

After a few weeks the ban on writing each other was canceled. However, the letters were strictly censored. One day I was told that I could visit my brother for one hour once a week. When I went through the door from the office into the Britishers' compound. Gerhard took one look at my full beard and said: "Arnold, you look like a rabbi!" The only rabbi I knew was Rev. Silvermann who had told us that it was of no use asking for our release, because it had been denied already, and that he would not try for us again. The man disgusted me. I certainly did not want to "look like a rabbi!" The next words by both of us were greetings.

Gerhard told me that the conditions in the women's camp were deplorable. The woman in charge was a warden from the women's prison. She had other Black women under her. She and her helpers made it quite clear in words and actions that they hated all Whites. There were Black men with loaded rifles lounging and walking about in the camp and there was no privacy for the internees. I knew, of course, that the house in Hanover Street was in the hottest part of all Jamaica, but I did not know that the house was surrounded by a very high brick wall which effectively kept out any sea breeze. The heat was oppressive.

Gerhard was most depressed. He was not a man ever to show any emotions but, though his voice was very normal, I saw that he had tears in his eyes when he told me. My visit to him cheered him up momentarily but it was only a short one hour.

The camp for the British was nicer than ours. Each internee had his own room. I knew most of the men there. Bernhard Koht, a commission agent in private life with a Jamaican wife, was related to the prominent Campbell family. They had three lovely, little boys. He proved to be an excellent cook, and so were Captains Amadeo and Rinaldo Doro. Each of the brothers had commanded one of the Webster Line freighters. This shipping line had its headquarters at the East end of Harbour Street. The naturalized British brothers, Amadeo and Rinaldo, were of Italian birth. Now they were interned.

If I remember right, there were only ten internees: Heise, the general manager of the Shell Oil Co. for the West Indies, had diabetes. He had a Haitian wife. American Jesuit Priests came to visit him regularly. Joseph Stephens had been the German Consul under the Weimar Republic. He resigned that office, when Hitler took over in Germany. He was a commission agent. He had a Jamaican wife and two lovely teenaged daughters. Stephens was also a superb cook. Hans Schnorr had a wharf with a ware house and a very good import business. He was married to a lady from a wealthy Jamaican family. Louis Kronecker was a buyer for the world famous Myers Rum Co. He and his wife were from Vienna. She was in the women's camp. Dr. Hans Stamm and his charming wife had a practice in Kingston. Hans' wife was the only medical doctor in the women's camp. Then there was a third Italian, Paracchini. He was apparently a bon vivant of independent means. He did not work. He was socializing with the Governor and his wife. He was released very shortly after I met him. These were all people who had been highly respected in the Kingston business world. If the British Empire would get hurt, Jamaica would get hurt which would certainly be very detrimental to them. As it was, they were all great assets to the poverty stricken Colony. None of them had anything to gain from a British defeat.

Gerhard told me that there was a real fifth column hysteria gripping the Island. Gerhard's colleague, a fellow salesman who had always considered Gerhard to be his arch rival, Norman MacDonald, had taken the opportunity to fan the flames of this madness. He circulated a petition throughout the Jamaica Public Service, asking fellow employees to sign that it was "outrageous" to ask them to serve the Company side by side with a German enemy. Shortly after the petition had been sent to the management with a copy to the Colonial Secretary, all the Naturalized British were interned.

Immediately, when I got back to our hut after my first visit to Gerhard, I grabbed my long neglected razor, went to the wash stand and shaved off my rabbinical beard. Dr. Lobbenberg scolded me: "We all have been after you to shave off that horrible beard of yours just about every day, and you did not do it. Your brother tells you to do so once and off comes the beard! You are a real, little, nothing, little brother. When will you ever make a decision for yourself without asking your big brother for his permission? Anyway, I am glad that the beard is gone." I could not answer him, Though I knew that he had no use for Rabbi Silvermann either. I had no intention to let anyone in the hut know what Gerhard had said to convince me to shave cleanly from then on.

The next time I visited Gerhard, he was very depressed. The women from the internment camp had been transported to visit their husbands for an hour in the camp office. Dorrie had looked sick. She obviously suffered both mentally from the degrading situation and physically from the constant heat. Dorrie had not complained. She did not want Gerhard to worry about her. That is how she was. She was always protective of Gerhard. It was her drawn looks which gave her away. The other women were less delicate about their husbands' feelings and described the inhumane conditions of the Hanover Street prison minutely. That is how Gerhard knew the details. Susan Ebersohn, the ten year old girl, had been released and was allowed to live with Jewish refugees from Czechoslovakia who knew German.

# INTERNEES FROM AFRICA

In the meantime the camp had again doubled in size. It was now eight times the size it was when I was interned in May of 1940. They had built several huts to house 50 internees and there were six machine gun towers now. The British had made raids throughout all of the British and French Colonies south of the Sahara from Spanish Morocco to the Sudan. They arrested all German and Italian citizens and shipped them in a troop ship to Kingston. There were about 300 Germans and 400 Italians. Four joined our group. One was a weird little Italian Jew from Kano in northern Nigeria by the name of Levi. He refused to take part in any chores in which we all shared. Ebersohn told him that we would not cook for him. He insisted to take his food raw. He soaked dried peas in water over night, let his coffee stand in water and drank it the next day. But nothing could persuade him to share his chores with us. He was a real loner.

Another new member, with whom I became good friends and who remained my doctor until I left Jamaica, was Dr. Rudolf Aub. Our group had grown to 22 members now. Before these new arrivals our camp housed about 500, mostly German ship crews. The new 300 German internees were mostly well-off, middle-class people, some planters, thirteen Catholic priests led by a Monsignor, two Protestant missionaries, merchants and one Dr. Marschall who had been sent to Africa by the Hamburg Tropical Hospital. They all knuckled under the rule of not daring to talk to us. The medical doctors all got individual rooms in the hospital hut just like the one the Lobbenberg brothers occupied.

Despite serious threats by the *Gestapo*, Dr. Marschall became quite friendly with Dr. and Fritz Lobbenberg, Hamburgians all. Fritz decided to study English. He had a very thick, comprehensive dictionary. He got as far as learning all the words under "A" and most under "B". He used some words which no one had ever heard of, and they all started with either "A" or "B". As a matter of fact, most of the words he used when he spoke English, started with those two letters.

British Colonial Governments and mining companies had hired

a lot of the Italians as laborers, building roads or working in mines. These men were used to camp life and were quite happy that they did not have to fight, had plenty to eat, and certainly could enjoy a much more pleasant climate than they once had to endure in Africa. They comprised more than half of the new Italian arrivals. Among the rest of the Italians were quite a few-better off, middle-class people.

# WORK THAT COUNTS

Lieutenant Walker was one of the few officers in the Camp Administration. We knew each other from the Continental Club days. His hobby was butterfly collecting. He had been instrumental in allowing the Quakers to bring in wood and tools for us to use. We had to turn them in to be locked up in the store room at 5:00 p.m., of course. Lt. Walker needed a special cabinet to house his collection. Moth balls destroy the pigment in the butterfly wings. He needed a cabinet made out of Honduras cedar, as that has a very good aroma, insects will not go near specimens stored in it, it will not discolor, and, besides, it is a beautiful red wood with a beautiful grain.

I knew that Mr. Karl Sauerlender had a factory making cigar boxes out of that wood for the Garcia Tobacco Co. Lt. Walker bought enough from Mr. Sauerlender to make the insides and drawers from that wood. One of the German internees had a beautiful mahogany bed shipped for him from his home in Africa. It arrived all broken up, and he discarded it. Willy and I took it over and made the top, sides and doors for the cabinet from it. Willy excelled himself. There was a very long and quite wide headboard made from a solid piece of mahogany. To get matching grain door panels, Willy cut the 3/4" thick board in two to get two panels more than 1/4" thick. That took some real sawing skill!

All drawers had invisible dovetailing in their fronts, and I carved all the handles into the drawers. The drawers fitted so well, that one could easily slide them open, yet, one could not slide a piece of paper over their tops when they were closed. Willy, of course, was the master craftsman, but I certainly did my share of the job. It was a great antidote to boredom for a long while. Lt. Walker had very good reason to be very pleased with the cabinet.

The Quakers brought Willy a book on handicrafts. It contained a picture of a weaving loom. There were no looms in Jamaica that we ever heard of. We had started to construct a loom, even before we had real tools to work with. I had straightened out well over 100 ft. of barbed wire by laying the wire on a stone and hitting it with another. We had constructed most of the main frame by burning holes through pieces of wood and by making dowels to fit. The contractors, making the forms for the concrete castings, had left some bent nails. I straightened them between two stones and used them as well.

Now we had real tools. We made the heddles and the comb from the straightened barbed wire, six pedals and hinges for them. Out of bullet wood I made a six-toothed ratchet wheel and pawl and mounted the ratchet on the warp beam to keep the warp tightly. We made several heddles to be able to make a great variety of patterns.

The loom could make a blanket 2'-6" wide. By sewing two together we could make a good sized blanket.

Now, that the loom was complete, we needed wool, a card, (a kind of comb to prepare the wool for spinning,) and a spinning wheel. The Quakers managed to find us a card cover, i. e. two sheets of rubber with hundreds of stainless steel wires sticking out. We had to make a roll, bearings and a handle to mount one sheet on, so that it could have a combing action against the other sheet. We also received a broken spinning wheel which we repaired to work like new.

The wool was "butchers' wool", i. e. from sheep which had recently been slaughtered. We had to wash it and dry it. We combed it on the card and Willy spun it excellently. I, too, learnt how to spin wool yarn. We made a shuttle for the loom and made several blankets. I still have the very first two blankets made in the internment camp, yes, maybe the very first in Jamaica in modern times.

Clifford Meridith was a plant pathologist from Iowa. He was a prominent Quaker. He had been called to Jamaica to fight the Panama disease, threatening the banana crops. He thought that the sansevera (called "donkey's ears" colloquially), a wild agave, had beautiful fibers. He dried their leaves into silky white strands. He sent them to us. Gertig and I spun them into threads and wove a cloth from them. Probably the only one of its kind in the world. The threads were too brittle to be practical for commercial use. But Clifford thought, given a little time, he could probably treat them to make the fibers more pliable. At any rate, the cloth shone like silver and was really beautiful. Unfortunately, Clifford never found the time to pursue his research on the sansevera fiber.

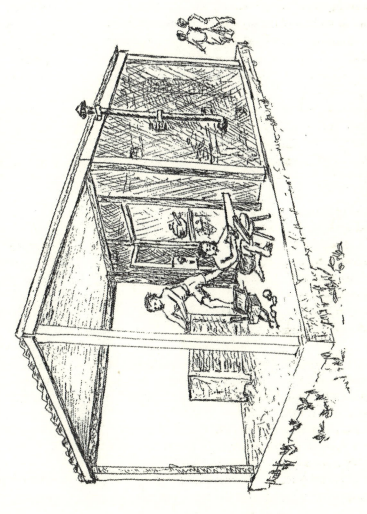

The Quakers sent in all sorts of bark and vines. Willy boiled them and got dyes out of them to give the wool different colors. Now he had three colors: red, blue and the natural cream of the sheep. After the war, this first loom would be copied at the Friends' College many times, and it would develop into a significant cottage industry under Willy's guidance. Being a true missionary, he never tried to make any money from it for himself.

# AROUND THE KITCHEN

As mentioned earlier, every morning at 11:00 a.m. there was roll call. All internees had to stand in line in front of their huts, except the cooks who had to stay in their kitchens. My kitchen was about 20 ft. from the hospital kitchen. It was also identical. Both kitchens were 20 ft. from the fence. It was built on a 20 ft. x 10 ft. concrete slab. Six wooden posts supported a corrugated zinc roof which covered the entire length. 10 ft. x 10 ft. were enclosed by expanded metal. The enclosure had an expanded metal door which was locked at nights.

Inside was a cupboard for pots, pans, plates, cups, knives, forks, spoons, and kitchen utensils. All cutlery had to be turned into the camp store room every night. It was always counted at that time. We had a Caledonia cast iron wood stove, (fashioned after the Franklin stove principle with air access from under the flame,) a table, and a stool.

Before inspection I scrubbed all utensils so that they shone and the floor thoroughly. The floor was clean enough that one could have eaten from it. I wanted no one to be able to say that the "Jew kitchen" was dirty.

Just before inspection the sanitation inspector, a corporal, went around, and checked all facilities including the kitchens. We had a new corporal. He was an out and out Nazi. I had often seen him go into the ship captains' hut, give the Nazi salute as he entered and later come out smoking a big cigar. He seemed very much at home with those who really controlled the camp population with the exception of the "Jew Group." It seemed like a good bet, at that time, that Britain would lose the War. This corporal made it a point to walk through the black mud created by washing the kitchen floor and then to trample all over my clean kitchen floor at a time, when I did not have a chance to clean up after him before inspection. I noted that he did not do that to the ship's cook in charge of the hospital kitchen next door.

The inspection itself was done by the camp commander, Major Saulter, another officer, a sergeant major and a ship's captain who had been chosen by the Nazis to represent them. The latter never entered my kitchen. I said: "How do you do gentlemen," the Major acknowledged my greeting with a wagging of his swagger stick against his sun helmet, walked in and out of the kitchen, and that was the inspection.

Even though I went to meditate every Sunday morning with Willy behind the kitchen shed for half an hour, and though I kept myself busy, I did have times of ugly moods.

One day while I was scrubbing the kitchen floor, I was contemplating that here I was, a convinced democrat, held captive in a country that claimed to be fighting for democracy. Worse, I was locked up with my very worst mortal enemies who would love to see me dead! On top of that, I was guarded by a Nazi in a British Army uniform with two stripes!

Just then he appeared. He again made his detour through the mud as usual. I stood at the end of the concrete slab blocking his entrance. He was a good six feet tall and weighed at least 200 lbs. By his standing on the muddy ground, and my standing on the concrete slab, our eyes were at about the same height and very close to each other.

"You are not going to walk with your muddy boots on this floor."

"Out of my way you dirty Jew."

With that he started to push me out of his way. My 135 lb. body was all muscle and bone. His carried a lot of fat. I grabbed his arm, spun around and threw him over my shoulder into the mud.

The right side of his uniform was black from the mud. He got up, never said a word and limped away. A feeling of terror came over me. What had I done? I threw a British soldier! I was wondering if that would mean solitary confinement in one of those cells which were built like brick ovens with a black tar roof and only a tiny window, or worse, if it would adversely affect my application to be released from the internment camp.

As it had been roll call time, we had been all alone. I never told anyone about it, and, to my great surprise, I never heard a word about it. I never saw that British Nazi corporal again.

The Germans had strict orders from their police not to talk to us. The Italians did not talk to us either. One day during roll call time, when we were all alone, I asked the ship's cook at the hospital

276

kitchen, only 20 ft. away, how to spice the meat to give it variety. He was very friendly and told me. We got into a conversation and he told me that he had been the cook on a little tramp steamer. He had left Hamburg long before the Nazis had come to power. For the last seven years, his little vessel had hauled freight from one little Caribbean port to another. There had been only three Germans aboard, the captain, the chief engineer, and himself, the cook. All the other crew were Latinos.

They had just started on their way home, and he was anxious to see his daughter for the first time and his wife, when the War broke out. They were intercepted by a British destroyer and taken off their ship. He sounded very sad. That was very understandable. He was obviously not very political minded, but politics catches up with us, whether we are interested in politics or not.

The next day I said, "Hello," to him. He ignored me completely. I thought: "You conceited jackass. To hell with you!" As I washed my kitchen floor, he sat on his stool at the near end of his kitchen platform.

He said: "Don't look at me but keep on washing the floor."

I could hardly hear him, he spoke so softly.

"They threatened the life of my wife and daughter in Germany if I ever talked to you again. So, don't hold it against me if I don't talk to you again."

"I understand."

It was courageous of him to even tell me. I thought: "What a mean bunch, those Nazis! They threaten to take two lives just for talking to a democrat and then not even on politics! Besides, how could I possibly harm the Nazi movement in the slightest here in a British internment camp?!" We never talked again.

# CHANGING OF THE GUARDS

The well trained Shropshire Rifles left Jamaica for home. We could see the convoys assemble in the Kingston Harbour. It is a nature made, perfect place for that purpose. Kingston is on the South Coast of Jamaica. The bay is very large and can accommodate many ships at anchor at the same time. The entrance of the harbor, at Port Royal, faces south at the western end of a long narrow peninsula called: the Palisadoes. Ships approaching have to do so close to the shore, coming from the east, as there are reefs and small islands south of the channel. There are gun emplacements at Newcastle, well over 1,500 ft. high in the mountains, overlooking the harbor and its approaches. I was not sorry to see the English battalion go. They kept themselves very aloof. The newly recruited West India Regiment took over the guard duty between the barbed wire and on the machine gun towers.

After we gave up our tools at 5:00 p.m. Willy and I walked up and down on the parade ground in the afternoons, talking, just as many other internees did. We turned around, usually about ten feet away from the fence. It was a rule, which nobody observed, that internees were not to go closer to the fence than ten feet after six in the evenings. As we turned one evening, we may have been a little closer than ten feet, I heard a breach bolt click. I turned around and looked at the black face of the guard over the barrel of his rifle! He was aiming at me! As I walked away he lowered his gun. How blood thirsty! The man was ready to shoot me without warning if I had walked one step closer to the fence. It had just turned six o'clock. It was bright day light. I had made no move that could have remotely resembled an attempt to escape over two sets of ten foot high barbed wire, guarded by men carrying rifles and manning machine guns on a tower nearby.

After a very short time the Winnipeg Grenadiers from Canada replaced the Jamaicans. They were recently recruited volunteers. Their uniforms did not fit them very well. Their clothes and helmets looked as if they had been bought in a pawn shop. They took over some duties inside the camp. They proved to be very congenial and informal human beings.

The new sanitation corporal was in his late 40s. He grumbled: "This Imperial Army consists of red tape and tea." I immediately made him a good cup of Blue Mountain coffee. His face lit up with a big smile. "Your pots and pans look pretty worn and shabby. After roll call, bring them to the store. I'll give you all new kitchen utensils." He was as good as his word. At every inspection time a cup of coffee was waiting for him.

The fence was only 20 ft. from my kitchen platform. One of the rifle carrying guards must have talked with the corporal. He asked me for a cup of coffee every time he came on duty. I handed it to him through the fence. Jamaica is a coffee exporting country. What would it have taken the Canadian supply officer to obtain coffee for his men on a regular basis?

One Canadian guard, he could not have been more than 18, complained to me as he drank his hot cup of coffee:

"As I walk my rounds between these fences, I see all those Nazi flags in the huts. After all, this is British soil! There is one in particular which annoys me. It is a very large flag, hanging exactly opposite the open entrance of a hut as if it were intended to mock the soldiers. It is fastened by a cord."

"I agree with you," I told him. "That constituted a provocation. The military should not allow the enemy flag or pictures of Hitler and Mussolini to be displayed on British soil."

I never considered that conversation of much consequence.

One night we heard a shot! We all thought that some fool might have tried to escape. The wooden walls of our huts were not thick enough to prevent a bullet from penetrating. We were a bit scared. Fortunately there were no more shots.

The next morning we heard the news that a Canadian guard, who had just heard that his brother had been killed in battle in North Africa, had been arrested for shooting through the cord which held up the big Nazi flag. An officer walked briskly around the camp with a sergeant and a couple of soldiers. They collected all German and Italian flags and all pictures of Hitler and Mussolini.

Another sanitary inspector took over for a while. He was a tall, powerful-looking, young Jew. Unfortunately, I forgot this admirable man's name. When he saw our group, he was outraged.

Jews interned in a British internment camp! and then with 1,200 Nazis and Fascists! That was too much.

He contacted his superior officers, his chaplain, and Rabbi Silvermann. When he got nowhere, he petitioned to be released as a conscientious objector, as he could not guard Jews in good conscience. He was discharged and sent home. This, incidentally, might have saved his life, as the regiment was sent to Hong Kong a few months afterwards.

When the War broke out with Japan a little over a year later, about 70% of the regiment were killed and the rest imprisoned, and who knows how few did survive Japanese imprisonment. It made me very sad, when I heard that long after my release, because I felt very sympathetic to those men. There were some very nice and friendly young men in that regiment.

# WORKING WITH THE CENSOR

Walter Lowe was an incredibly successful swimming and water polo coach. He had made the Jamaican water polo team a world class team, the best in the Western Hemisphere. He took over the cooking for a while. The office requested that one of our group register outgoing letters. I volunteered. I dressed up every day wearing my white shirt, my khaki shorts, knee socks and my only pair of shoes. I went into the censor's office and registered all outgoing mail in a book. The censor, Sergeant Lee, had been a bank clerk in London before the War, and that was all he ever told me about himself. He was exactly my age, very polite and diligent. I was more or less a live dictionary for him. He was apparently under orders not to have any private conversations with any internees. When I talked about myself, he listened politely, but he never talked to me, unless it had to do with our work.

The Italian censor was a sergeant from the Winnipeg Grenadiers. He was a second generation Canadian of Italian parents. He wanted help, too. I told him that Ludwig Klein spoke Italian. Klein was asked to join us in that little office. Every now and again Sergeant Gentelucci would get into a very friendly conversation with Klein and myself. After a short while, Sergeant Lee would catch his Canadian counterpart's eye and the conversation would stop.

I must have worked there for two or three months, when Ebersohn pointed out to me that he had observed that the mess room boys who cleaned out the offices every evening collected all the contents of the waste baskets. They carried them into the ship captains' hut. I warned Sergeant Lee not to leave anything that was not the Nazis' business in his waste basket, but to burn it before he left his office.

The next day, as I walked into the office, I was sent into the office of a major whom I had never seen before. I was accompanied by a sergeant and a private. Only the major was seated. The sergeant introduced me to the major.

The major nodded to the sergent. The sergent said to me:

"The ship captain, the representative for the internees, has complained that you burnt their mail. The clean up crew had found the ashes in the waste basket."

I answered: "I would never have done such a thing as a law abiding resident of Jamaica, as burning Royal Mail is a crime in Jamaica, and any mail in the office was Royal Mail as far as I am concerned. I had told Sergeant Lee that the clean up crew carried the contents of the waste baskets to the captains' hut. I had suggested to Sergeant Lee to burn all scraps of paper which he did not want the Nazis to see. Sergeant Lee had probably followed my advice and had burnt his scrap paper after I had left the office. Furthermore, I could not have done it, as I had never been alone in the office for a minute. Besides, I never carried matches.

"I hereby formally request to face the person in this office who had made the charges in the tradition of British Justice where the accused has the right to face the accuser."

The major denied my request by shaking his head and said:

"That is all," to the sergeant who then led the way out of the office.

I never heard anything more about it, but Klein and I were dismissed from the office "for our own safety." That was a pity, as I liked our little group in there. The garbage from the office was henceforth collected by soldiers.

# THE WOMEN INTERNEES

Rumors started that the women in the Hanover Street Internment House were being ill-treated. The internees from Africa had swelled the population of that formally, one-family residence, to 60 women and about 100 babies under three years old. The husbands and fathers of the women internees kept petitioning the Colonial Secretary to be allowed to see their wives and daughters. As a result, the husbands were bussed down to Hanover Street. They came back with shocking stories.

The high wall around the building prevented any cool breeze from relieving the oppressive heat and the stench from that terribly overcrowded compound. The woman, who had originally been in charge of the women's prison, was in charge of the camp. She and several other former women's prison guards had told the German women that they now had a chance to pay back the White people for making their ancestors slaves. Black male prison guards, with their rifles, were stationed inside the compound and walked around as they pleased, robbing the internees of the least bit of privacy.

The food was barely edible. The babies got only saltine crackers and water, no milk nor baby food. As a result, they were all hungry and crying and in a very poor condition. The two doctors, Dr. Stamm and a Roman Catholic Mission doctor from Africa, and the Lutheran Sister, a nurse from a Lutheran Mission in Africa, had been given no medicines. They were at their wit's end.

Dorrie's "room" was a broom closet underneath the staircase. She could stand up only in one end. The rest of the floor space was taken up by the bed. Every time any one went up or down the stair case, it sounded like thunder in her little cubby hole.

Eventually, six women committed suicide, 10% of the adult population. One was the Lutheran Sister. Hitler himself threatened in a radio broadcast that he would take revenge on British prisoners if the German women imprisoned in Jamaica were not treated more humanely. He must have gotten a report via some Church, probably the Roman Catholic Church.

The Swiss Consul, the local representative of the International Red Cross, was asked by the Red Cross to investigate. He and his staff took a stroll through the three internment camps: The women's, that of the naturalized British, and our big one of approximately 1,200 guests of His Majesty King George VI.

The Jamaican Government reacted. A deaconess from the Methodist Church, a well respected lady of English descent, was put in charge. The house next door was added, thus doubling the space for the internees. No armed guards, nor any other males, were allowed inside the compound.

It turned out that good food rations, including proper baby food, had been issued to the camp but the internees never received it. All of it had been sold on the black market, and much inferior food had been bought by the thieves with some of the money.

*The Daily Gleaner*, the popular newspaper of Kingston, published stories that Black people were replaced by Whites on Hitler's orders. This was welcome propaganda for the anti-British independence movement. The racial issue has always been a delicate one in a country, where only about 2% of the population was White. The article made no mention of the fact that some fifty mothers were losing their minds seeing their babies crying because they were slowly dying from malnutrition! The *Gleaner* did not mention either that perfectly good food had been bought for the unfortunate women and their babies by the Jamaican Government, but that the appropriated food never reached the internees. No mention was made that the proper distribution of the food had been one of the matron's most important responsibilities! It was kept quiet that six interned women had been driven to commit suicide. It was quite obvious from the facts, but not from the newspaper article, that the matron was totally unqualified to be responsible for the lives of some 160 civilian internees. *The Daily Gleaner* proved to be a disgrace not only to its country, but to the entire newspaper profession as a whole. As for the discharged matron, there are no words mean enough to describe her.

# VISITING THE BRITISH INTERNEES

I visited Gerhard regularly. All internees in this camp had their own room. They all had arranged to have their own beds shipped into the camp, so that they had many more creature comforts than we had. The atmosphere among the British prisoners was much more friendly toward one another, though they all were very bitter, because of their internment. Those whose wives were also interned, were especially bitter and depressed. Since most were pretty wealthy, they had all kinds of food sent into the camp. Bernhard Koht, Joseph Stephens, Amadeo and Rinaldo Doro were excellent cooks. They took turns making delicious meals.

No wonder that Dr. Stamm complained that he was getting too fat. He was at least six feet tall and weighed well over 200 lbs. Gerhard had the ideal solution. "Arnold, the next time you come over, bring your boxing gloves along." I did. Hans Stamm was about Gerhard's age, a little over 30. We put on the gloves.

"Here, Arnold, are the rules: You box three three minute rounds with one minute breaks between rounds. You must not hit Hans but he must try to hit you."

"Who ever boxed with rules like that?"

"Go!"

The good doctor lunged at me with a wide swing. By this time I had learned a little about boxing. I had time to duck under the blow. The more he missed me, the harder he swung. After one round, Hans was bathed in perspiration. We rested a minute. Not long after the second round started, he gave up. We did that quite a few visits. The fact that he was never able to hit me, was great for me but it was an embarrassment to him. After a while, he could continue for two rounds but he felt that he looked foolish and gave up after a few weeks.

# BUSTAMANTE INTERNED !

One day, to our great amazement, they brought in Bustamante, the most powerful leader of the Bustamante Labour Union and President of the newly formed Jamaica Labour Party. We had read in the *Gleaner* that he had recently fomented a very successful strike of the sugar workers. He knew that the British desperately needed sugar to manufacture explosives and also to be consumed as food. He must have realized that the government could not tolerate a long strike, and he must have hoped that the sugar estates would accede to his demands. He probably did not expect to be interned. He never gave a hint as to what were his thoughts. He was a tough man, used to strife.

He was the illegitimate son of a well-to-do man. He was tall, imposing, thin, and very light-skinned with flowing, graying curly hair. He always dressed in black pants and a white shirt. He always tore the sleeves off, just above the elbows. He had been totally neglected as a child, his barefoot days. His name had been Williams then. He could neither read nor write. He had been away from Jamaica learning Spanish and "Revolution" in Spain on the Loyalist side. He changed his name to Bustamante. The poor people referred to him affectionately as "Busta." Franco won. He had to get out of Spain. Home in Jamaica, he became a usurer on the waterfront. He organized the longshoremen into a powerful union and led strikes.

His brilliant, well educated cousin, of the prosperous Manley family, Norman Manley, was probably the best known barrister in the British Empire. He practically always won his cases. He would fly to the remote corners of the Empire to defend a leftist man of color without charge and usually get him off. Mr. Manley was very anti-British and pro-Soviet Union. His dream was, quite clearly, forming an independent, socialist, federation of all the British West Indian Islands, and of the two large British colonies, British Guyana, and British Honduras (Belize today, named after its former capital). The British seemed to be losing the War, and no educated British West Indian politician would want the Nazis to gain a

286

foothold in any part of the Caribbean. It seemed to be the right time to start pushing.

Manley, like so many intellectuals, thought himself much more popular than he really was. He had surrounded himself with a bunch of flatterers who made him think that he could not fail. Hardly any of the business, estate, and factory owners had the slightest use for Socialism. Manley ignored that fact. Manley just knew that Busta, being illiterate, would always depend on his leadership. Manley was the founder and leader of the People's National Party, the P.N.P. It seemed to be a great arrangement. Manley was the political party leader, and Busta supplied a plentiful membership with his labor unions.

Being illiterate does not mean that a person is stupid nor unduly dependent. Manley quickly found that out when he took the Teacher's Union, with Mr. Glasspole as its head, under the wing of his party. Busta did not like that at all. He wanted to be the boss of all unions. He promptly founded the Jamaica Labour Party, the J.L.P., in competition to the P.N.P.

Busta was a pragmatist. His right-hand-man was a very highly respected and successful lawyer by the name of Douglas Judah of the firm of Judah & Randall. His constant companion, his former secretary, and then common-law wife, was Miss Longbridge. She was self-effacing and absolutely devoted to Busta. She read to him what was important and dumped what she thought trivial. Busta had no intention to offend any one with any "-ism" theories. He did not inspire as much fear as Manley did among the business elite of the Island, nor did his ambitions extend beyond the shores of Jamaica. His English had a very limited vocabulary but he was an electrifying orator in the Jamaican dialect. What he said was not really profound but his delivery was spine chilling!

Seeing that rivalry develop, it was not too surprising that Busta was interned, and that Manley apparently did not move a finger to get him released. Busta remembered me from the old Sirgani's Beach swimming days and he greeted me warmly. There were Jamaican workers in ragged clothes outside the internment camp mowing the grass with their sickles and widening the road to the camp. Busta stood near the fence. He crossed his arms majestically over his chest. His graying hair flowed behind him. He fixed one after the other laborer with his eyes. As their eyes met, without saying a word, one after the other of the workers walked off the job. Soon there was not one Jamaican laborer to be seen, and one could see for a very long distance. I was impressed with the power of the man.

Conflict arose almost immediately. Bustamante refused to do any manual work. He refused to help clean the common areas, such as the dining room, toilet, or yard. He would not help to chop wood for the kitchen fire. Heise, whom the fellow British internees had chosen as their spokesman to the camp authorities, told Busta that he could not use their bathroom nor share in any meals. The two had dealings with each other when Heise was still the manager for all West Indian Shell installations and Bustamante had organized his workers at the Jamaican installation and Heise had to increase their wages steeply to avoid a strike. There was no love lost between the two of them. When I visited, we always greeted each other in a very friendly way.

Busta had a commode sent into the camp. Soldiers cleaned it and his room. His meals were sent in. He had his civilian barber come to trim his hair. It was a surprise to all of us to find out that the great labor leader was illiterate. A newspaper was sent to him everyday and Kronecker would read it to him.

# BRITAIN'S DARKEST HOUR

Soon after Bustamante's internment a group of about five P.N.P. organizers (or rabble-rousers, depending on your point of view) were also interned. They were very articulate, inciting their listeners to violence against the Whites, especially against the British. They occupied a new hut on the other side of the administration building. Though everyone knew why they had been locked up, they were never given any reason officially, just as we were never given any reason why we were interned. The authorities took advantage of the fact that the *habeas corpus* clause in the *Magna Carta* of the year of 1215 was suspended for the duration of the War throughout the British Empire. The *Magna Carta* had set a laudable example to all legal systems throughout the world.

Actually, I could not blame the British-Jamaican Government for locking them up without giving them an official reason. An official charge would most certainly have resulted in a trial. For the British to win the War seemed absolutely hopeless at that time. Their soldiers in North Africa, and especially their sailors crossing the Atlantic were dying in a desperate fight against the odds. And the last thing they needed was a court case that would give the most radical and articulate members of the P.N.P. a forum to incite the people with their poison of wanton violence.

The "Axis" forces, Germany, Italy, Hungary, and Romania, had occupied all European countries which had been allied to the British: France, Luxembourg, Belgium, Holland, Denmark, Norway, Poland, Czechoslovakia, and in North Africa: Libya. Tunisia, Algiers, and Morocco were under Vichy France. The section of France left under a French government, headed by Maréchal Pétain, was the south-eastern third of the nation, stretching roughly from the Swiss border at Mont Blanc in a quarter circle to the middle of the Pyrénées, with Vichy as its capital.

The General whom Pétain had put in charge of the French forces in North Africa, had the very German name of König (meaning: King). Half of the French Navy was in Oran, the main port of Algiers under the Vichy French. The other half of the French Navy was in Toulon, on the French Mediterranean coast.

No one knew which side, if any, the French Admiral Darlan would support. That fleet posed a potential, and then, severe threat for the supply route to the British forces in Egypt. Spain was still neutral but Franco, its dictator, was indebted to Hitler and Mussolini for helping him to overthrow the elected government only a few years earlier. No one could predict if or when Spain would join the Axis forces.

The American Government under President Roosevelt was helpful enough, but the Congress was against re-arming that country, and there was the powerful, popular "America First" movement, led by Charles Lindbergh, the national hero because he was the first man to fly solo across the Atlantic. He was always assured of a huge audience. He now preached absolute neutrality.

The Ku Klux Klan (KKK), the German-American Bund which had by no means only German members but also many right wing radical Americans, and Father Coughlin's Silver Shirts were outspoken and potentially violent proponents of the Nazi movement in the U.S. They would probably have become the fifth column for Hitler should America have officially joined the British in their desperate hour by declaring war against Germany and Italy. Even the Communists, who had a lot of adherents in America in those days, especially in the colleges, sounded like friends of Hitler, since Molotov and v.Ribbentrop (the Soviet and German foreign ministers) had signed a friendship pact.

The famous "Cash and Carry" policy helped the British at a price. That policy, proposed by Roosevelt and approved by the Congress, specified that the British could buy American weapons and supplies for cash only. They had to be transported by British ships. Many of the big American companies had British owners. They had to sell their shares to Americans to buy food, ammunition, ships, weapons, and especially war planes to be shipped to England on British ships. Trans-Atlantic flights were far in the future.

Though the British still controlled the oceans more or less, the Germans now had access to the west coast of France which allowed them to launch raiders into the Atlantic. They were German merchant ships which had a camouflaged canon and a navy crew on board. They approached unsuspecting British ships, ordered the crew to maintain radio silence and to abandon their ship. Often they would send a prize crew on board the British merchant man, take what they could use and then sink the vessel. If radio silence had not been maintained, the raider would sink the merchant ship without further warning with gun fire.

The Germans had a very powerful "pocket battleship", the *Graf Spee* in the South Atlantic. It was called, "pocket battleship", because it had guns of greater range and a faster speed, than British war ships of that size. The *Graf Spee* did a lot of damage to British shipping. Even when its location was known, it could always outrun its pursuer. These raiders would also re-supply German submarines, often from captured prizes, thus extending the U-boats' range to become a threat to shipping headed for, or from, the Strait of Gibraltar.

It was very fortunate for the British that, though the Italians had many more submarines than the Germans, they never attacked anything or any one. There were a few attacks by Italian two-man submarines. They were launched near British ports, such as Gibraltar. Frogmen would then attach an explosive device and a timer on a target ship, take off to their glorified under water scooter and return to their mother submarine.

This was a time where all "friends" had abandoned the British Empire and where disloyal elements within, such as powerful politicians, especially in Egypt and India, tried to flex their muscles and sever the bonds which tied them to England. It was a time where it seemed that, never too friendly neutrals, like Spain, Ireland, and Turkey, might be tempted to try to share in the spoils of a soon to be destroyed British Empire and declare war on Great Britain. Fortunately that did not happen but we feared it then.

It was very uncomfortable as the general feeling in camp was: "It won't be long now." I dreaded the idea of being in this camp at a time when the British gave up and the Nazis might go into a victory frenzy and kill all of us in the process. I tried one more time to persuade the government to release me. I wrote a very polite letter to the "Right Honourable the Colonial Secretary", the head of the civil service under His Excellency the Governor. I even got an answer, not under the Jamaican coat of arms, but under the British coat of arms with its motto in French which stems from the time, as Shakespeare once put it with its double negative: "No King of

England is not also King of France!" That boast looked pretty pitiful at the end of the first half of 1940: *"Dieux et mon Droit."* "God and my Right."

So, under "God and my Right" he wrote as best as I can remember:

"Mr. Arnold P. Von der Porten,
Internment Camp, Jamaica.

Sir,

His Excellency the Governor has directed me to inform you that he sincerely regrets, after careful consideration, that he is unable to grant you your request at this time.

I remain, Sir, your most obedient servant The Colonial Secretary of Jamaica."

(then his signature above his typed name and titles.)

Someone must have typed that with tongue in cheek. At least they retained the proper form. And that, as is well known, is the important part to officialdom. I could not help but laugh at this letter. I could just imagine Sir John Huggins, His Excellency the Governor, having tears in his eyes with "regret" that he cannot set me free. Some "obedient servant!" "God and my Right!"

It was the time when Britain's great Prime Minister, Winston Churchill, made his famous, defiant speech stating that Great Britain would never give up but should it ever succumb fighting the enemy, then let it be said by the world that this was Britain's finest hour. It was a rousing speech. Those well chosen words did wonders to my moral. It made people, regardless of nationality, race, or station in life who had a desire for a free society, feel proud and open their hearts to their undaunted leader.

# THE CULTURAL LIFE IN THE INTERNMENT CAMP

Churchill's most powerful and defiant speech gave us great hope. We felt assured that Britain would go it alone for a long, long time if necessary. Though it seemed impossible that Britain could win, it also seemed equally impossible that the Germans could cross that natural moat, called the English Channel.

We were given some seeds by Dorothea Simmons, the wealthy Quaker woman from Boston, Massachusetts. She was probably the one who was most responsible for financing the Quaker Mission in Jamaica at that time. The Quaker presence was originally established by George Fox himself, the founder of the movement, which has been officially called: The Religious Society of Friends of Jesus, Friends, for short. In the 17th century George Fox had traveled to Barbados to minister to the Irish slaves. From there he traveled to the western end of Jamaica and founded a mission there. I do not know how long that mission was functioning. The centers of the modern Friends, during my time in Jamaica, were in Highgate and Hectors River.

Willy was the one who was most responsible for our gardening. We planted a hedge of castor oil bushes against the hut and neat, straight rows of various vegetables. We also planted some flowers in front of the vegetables.

It was easy to see by the gardens, as to who lived in the huts next to them. In front of all the German huts were extremely neat rows of vegetables, spaced at exactly the same distances from each other. In front of the Italian huts the vegetables were planted in the most intricate patterns, to be most pleasing to the eye. They usually had a mosaic as a centerpiece. The stones to create them were picked up in the camp. The colors ranged from shiny white to very dark brown. The subjects of this fine art work were usually Jesus, the Madonna with the Christ Child, or Mussolini. Where the P.N.P. organizers lived, not even a blade of grass grew. The yard was strewn with paper and other garbage. The sanitary corporal had them clean it up once in a while.

The camp had some fairly large areas which were not built up.

The internees made a full-sized soccer field. They formed leagues and several games were played every day. The competition to win the championship seemed to have been taken very seriously. The Italians leveled several areas as boccie fields. They were so perfect that water would not form puddles after it rained. Either all of each field would be inundated or all of each field would be perfectly dry. They too had their leagues. All sports were of great importance to the men.

Some of the Germans had brought harmonicas with them. They were the only musical instruments they had. They gathered pieces of scrap wood, just as Willy and I had done. They made excellent xylophones from them. They were tuned to each other. There was an empty hut near ours which served as a sort of community center. Exactly at 6 p.m., you could set your watch by it, their orchestra would start there. All spectators brought benches from their own huts to sit and listen. Our quarters were nearby, so we could listen by just staying in, or near our place. Their selections were light classical music by Strauss, Mozart and some old folk songs. Considering the lack of proper materials and work shop facilities, the music was really of a very high quality.

The Italians were quite different. Many had accordions, concertinas or banjos. There was a big shade tree near the parade ground, the only tree in the camp. One guy would go there and start playing his instrument. Others would saunter up and start singing or bring their own instruments and play the harmony. They sang mostly arias from operas or folk songs which were quite different from the German songs. Soon one man would conduct, more fellows would join in, and others would leave. That would go on most of every evening. Sometimes our loner from Kano, Nigeria, Mr. Levi would join in. He had a most beautiful tenor voice and knew many arias from Italian operas. The Fascist Italians did not seem to mind.

The Germans decided that the education of the sailors, especially the young ones, should not be neglected. They had English courses, lessons in Steam and Diesel Engineering, Mathematics, Physics, Chemistry, and History, the Nazi version.

The thirteen Priests, who were led by their Bishop, were busy writing alphabets, grammars, and dictionaries for not well known

African tribal languages. On Sundays and Catholic Holidays they also celebrated several masses for the Germans and one for the Italians. Since there were also two Protestant German Missionaries among the prisoners from Africa, there was also a Protestant Service. But it was very poorly attended, as the Missionaries were from some very obscure sect, and not Lutheran as most Germans are. It is also well known that church attendance in the Lutheran parts of Germany is minute. The censors had to attend. Sergeant Lee told me that all services started with a prayer for Hitler or Mussolini respectively, so that he did not really experience a religious feeling, though he had to be present physically.

# LEARNING ITALIAN

We, in our hut, were getting on each other's nerves. We were thrown together by fate. We came from quite different backgrounds, walks of life, and ranged widely in age. We had different temperaments. We did not choose each other as company. Worst of all, we had no privacy whatsoever. The beds were far too close together. We could not even be uninterrupted in the shower or on the toilet, as there were no doors.

I decided to talk to an Italian loner. I had noticed that he was walking up and down all alone on the parade ground just as Willy and I did. He was only a few years older than I was, blond, blue eyed and about my height and build. He stopped at the big tree and listened to the music. I went next to him and said that I appreciated the way the Italians performed. He was quite friendly. He spoke excellent English. He told me that he had a hotel in Lagos. Suddenly the police came in one day and arrested him. He was wondering whatever became of his hotel and his belongings. He had not heard. It seemed to me by the way he spoke that he was quite well educated.

He told me that all the other men in his hut were very coarse, semi-literate miners. They had been shipped to Nigeria under contract by big mining companies. They were used to camp life and did not mind the internment at all. They thanked their lucky stars that they were not in the Italian Army in Libya and could sit out the War in the much nicer climate of Jamaica and not in the oppressively hot and muggy climate of southern Nigeria. They had nothing to lose.

I suggested that he should teach me Italian and I would teach him German. We should meet alternate evenings in each other's hut. Unfortunately, most of my hut mates objected. So, we met in his hut every evening at 9:00 p.m. till "lights out" at 10:00 p.m. I divided pages in half vertically with pencil lines. I wrote a story in English on the left half and in German on the right. Then I wrote the same story again in English on the left side on another page. He had to write the Italian translation on the right. I also wrote the vocabulary the same way, one half in English and one half in

German and another page the left side in English only for him to put down the Italian. I gave him the English-German pages to study. We made good progress for a while. He learnt a bit of German.

As soon as his roommates found out that I could understand some Italian, they started to tease me about the handful of Germans in my hut who were hoping for the impossible, a British victory. It was light weight banter and not intended to hurt my feelings. I responded in kind and teased them that Mussolini was just like a little puppy dog to Hitler. That Il Duce wagged his tail when the Führer praised him and crawled under the table when his master scolded. If I seemed to get the upper hand, they drowned me out with their concertinas, accordions and banjos playing *Giuvinetsa, giuvinetsa,* the Fascist Anthem or just a folk song very much fortissimo.

These evenings were a very good, light diversion, and I really learnt enough Italian to understand what they said and make myself understood. Unfortunately, my friend did not learn much German. He did not seem to mind. He helped me out when I did not understand a word and I asked him in English what it meant. The entire crew seemed to look forward to my visits, as they always had a barb at the English ready as I entered their hut. They were obviously waiting as to how I would rebut them.

# ARROGANT, INCOMPETENT DR. WARD

Since I no longer worked in the censor's office, I again took over as cook. One day the sanitation corporal told me: "Dr. Ward, the stupid English doctor, has killed two Canadian soldiers. He had given them castor oil for a stomach ache. It turned out that they had appendicitis. They both died within a few hours of each other!"

The internment camp lay close to the route from the South Camp to the military cemetery. We watched the funeral procession. They awarded the two soldiers full military honors, with the regimental band, slow march and the firing of salvoes. Dr. Ward still visited our internment camp regularly but he had himself accompanied by a few English soldiers of the permanent camp maintenance staff. He seemed to avoid the Canadian soldiers.

Shortly after this incident, two Italians who had been brought over from Africa, came down with black water fever. It is a potentially fatal disease, a form of malaria which causes bleeding of the kidneys. It is transmitted by mosquitoes. There was no medicine for it in those days. It is easily diagnosed. The urine is black, and the fever is very high. It does not occur in Jamaica.

Dr. Marschall, the German specialist for tropical diseases who had come with the contingent from Africa, ordered that the patients not be moved but that a mosquito net be kept over them at all times. He insisted that they not get up, or sit up to eat, or to pass any body waste. The good doctor ordered cups with spouts to feed the patients and bed pans for their body waste.

The store room sergeant alerted Dr. Ward, when he got the request for the special cups and bed pans. Dr. Ward ordered the patients removed to the military hospital. Dr. Marschall vehemently objected. Dr. Ward told his German colleague that he did not even have a license to practice medicine in Jamaica and that if he wanted advice he would ask for it. Dr. Marschall and the German ship doctors were outraged. They told Dr. Ward plainly that he was committing MURDER!

The patients were removed to the military hospital where they got worse. Dr. Ward had them moved again to the Kingston Public Hospital where they soon died. The fury of the internees, not only of the Italians, was very much discernible. Dr. Ward did not show himself in the camp for several months.

Dr. Marschall, a very sensitive man who obeyed his conscience rather than any political authority and who was already ostracized by the Nazis, as he kept having friendly conversations with Dr. Lobbenberg, became very depressed. Soon after my release, I heard that the very humane and decent Dr. Marschall had committed suicide.

I believe that the arrogant and childish show of superior authority by Dr. Ward, and the consequent deaths of the two Italians, was the beginning of the good Hamburgian's depression. After the War, Dr. Ward became the Chief Medical Officer of Jamaica. It seems that his only qualification for that post was that his mother gave birth to him in England.

# CHRISTMAS 1940

Nothing very exciting happened in the camp for the rest of the year. I still visited Gerhard regularly. The wives from the women's internment camp were bussed to the men's camp once a month. There they could converse in the visitors' room. The conditions in the women's camp seemed tolerable now; no more suicides.

The news we got from the War concerned mainly the submarine warfare. Even we saw the evidence that the British had turned the tables on the Nazis. From the camp we could see captured German ships in the harbor. The interior of one of them had been burnt out by the crew before it abandoned ship. It was being refitted to serve the British. Instead of it supplying submarines to stop Britain's imports, it had itself become a carrier for those imports. The crew was in the internment camp with us. Large huts had been built to house about 50 inmates each.

These British victories at sea certainly made it less likely that they would give up, but it did not influence anything on the European mainland. In North Africa the Germans had been fought to a stand still in Libya. The Axis did not seem to have enough power to control the Mediterranean Sea, and, therefore, their supply ships were often sunk. The likelihood that they would ever reach the crucial Middle East oil fields seemed more remote than ever. Still those victories were a far cry from any decisive action which could only occur on the European Continent.

It was time to think of Christmas. Willy thought that it would be a good idea to make linoleum cuts and print Christmas cards from them. The Quakers sent in the necessary tools and linoleum scraps. We made a variety of cuts. I drew a self portrait with the help of a mirror, drew two strands of barbed wire across my face, transferred the picture onto the linoleum and made a very good cut. I printed a few dozen cards on soft paper twice as wide as the picture to fold them over and write greetings on the inside: "Merry Christmas from the internment camp." We were allowed one letter per week. So we started early. None of the cards ever reached their destinations. They were confiscated, as there was a rule that no

300

pictures were allowed to be sent out of the camp. We found that out long after Christmas.

My parents sent Gerhard and me a tie each! That showed us the extent of their comprehension of our situation. I usually walked around in my red sports shorts only, Gerhard in his khaki shorts. Now that we received a tie each, we wore them around our necks and had them dangle down our naked chests for a few days.

In every letter my father complained vehemently about the shortages in New York, and how prices were shooting up beyond the reach of ordinary people. The lamentations achieved their purpose, I assume. I never asked him for money. Yet a dollar per month would have done wonders for me. I could have bought raisins to put into our bread puddings, bananas, oranges and other little luxuries. I needed needle and thread. Fortunately, Sybil Hill asked me once if she could bring me anything. I asked for a sewing kit which she promptly brought me the next visiting day.

Years after the War, Papa told me that he never before or afterwards earned so much money as he did during the War. A dollar a month would not even have been noticeable as far as he was concerned. I did not say a word. I was too disgusted!

Visitors became less and less frequent. Willy's Friends still came as often as they could find transportation. Iris and Noel Ramsey and Sybil Hill, Sam Francis' fiancee, still came to visit me regularly. Very few others came once to cheer me up, or possibly just to see what an internment camp looked like. I had become a bit cynical. That was the background as Christmas, 1940, approached.

Christmas Eve found all of us, Christians, Jews and atheists alike, in a very depressed mood. Even Willy looked pretty down. We got up at sunrise as usual, and had the early roll call at 7:00 a.m. I did not have anything special to give the group for breakfast. At 10:00 a.m. I was called into the office. There were two dozen of the most gorgeous roses for me with a card from Sybil Hill. It read:

301

"Smile a while
and while you smile
another smiles,
and soon there's miles
and miles of smiles,
and life's worthwhile
because you smile!"

This was so thoughtful and touching of Sybil. I was overjoyed! This was Christmas Eve, time for happy thoughts, and she thought of me in this dismal place. What is more, she made the considerable effort to get these roses, select the most suitable card and went to the camp to deliver these gifts at a time when there was no gasoline for civilians. She must have walked to Windward Rd., taken a tram to South Camp Rd., taken another tram towards Cross Roads and walked from there through the entire military camp to the internment camp, just to be nice to me and all of my group. Then she had to take the journey all the way back in the broiling tropical sun.

I got back to our hut bearing the two dozen magnificent roses. I read the poem to the smiling bunch of *misérables*. It was exactly what we needed. Some got busy washing bed sheets. Willy, Walter Lowe, and I went into the kitchen. I asked the sanitation inspector in the store room if he could get me some raisins, oranges and/or limes. He did. He threw in a pound of cocoa, flour, icing sugar and green and red food coloring. He had caught the Christmas spirit. We made the best possible dinner we could. Lowe baked a cake. As we did not have any baking powder, it turned out hard as a rock. That did not phase us. I covered it with white icing, wrote "Merry Christmas" on it with red icing and made pine branches with green icing. Dipped into a little cocoa that cake would make a great dessert.

When all was done, we carried the gourmet dinner into the hut. Ebersohn had gotten busy. He did very little physical work himself if he could help it. He had organized. The two tables had been shifted together. They were laid with freshly washed, white table cloths, (later to be used as bed sheets again). The table silver had been polished, and the two dozen roses were decorating the banquet

302

table very artistically. We all dressed our very best with the clothes we normally reserved for visitors' day. We were all in a festive mood. All praised Willy's and my cooking and had good things to say about Lowe's cake. It did taste great soaked in a lot of cocoa. What a Christmas!

# MAJOR AXIS BLUNDERS

The countries, Germany and Italy, run north-south like an axis through Europe. The two dictators, Hitler and Mussolini, once hoped that the world or, at a minimum, Europe would spin around this axis. The press seemed to like this term and named all countries which were opposed to the Allies, the Axis Powers.

The first major blunder of the Germans was not to follow the advice of Admiral Raeder and Admiral Dönitz. Those two never made Hitler's inner circle. They advocated to concentrate on naval and air warfare in the North Sea and North Atlantic to reduce supplies to Britain to a point where their industries would stand still and severe hunger would grip the cities.

The Italians' campaign in North Africa proved to be a total disaster for Mussolini. That was the Italians' first and the Axis's second major mistake. The German General Rommel and his powerful Afrika-Corps had to rescue the Italian Army and the Colony of Libya. Rommel was dubbed the Desert Fox because he cleverly outmaneuvered the British. He was marshaling his forces to attack Egypt.

Hitler and his gang, never understanding the importance of the sea, failed to make a serious effort to occupy Malta. It was a refueling base for British bombers and a base for spy planes to watch German and Italian transports. If needed, British convoys could also shelter there against Axis attacks on their way to or from Egypt and Gibraltar. It seems that the Axis insisted on making the same mistakes over and over again. This was the Axis's third major mistake. Malta's fortifications and air bases saved Egypt and the Arabian oil fields.

In the first place, Hitler apparently did not understand that he simply could not win if he did not knock out Great Britain. His Generals seemed to understand that. They concentrated to eliminate the Royal Air Force (R.A.F.) by bombing their bases, hangars, and factories. The British had only very few planes left. They were the vital defence against the submarines. In a fit of rage, the Führer ordered the attacks on the R.A.F. discontinued in order to start, militarily unsound, terror attacks on London. This stupidity allowed the British Air Force to rebound with a vengeance. That was the Axis's fourth major blunder.

These mistakes did not really threaten the very existence of the Axis. However, they saved Great Britain from defeat. It spread the Axis forces very thin, while the British could use Colonial and Dominion Forces in Africa. It seemed that all Winston Churchill had to do, was to avoid similar blunders and wait till the Axis made a mistake that would hurt them to a point that would make them lose the War.

They did not have to wait long. Mussolini occupied Albania against very light resistance. The Albanians did not like their communist masters and readily surrendered to the Italians. Mussolini was in his glory. He should have rested on his laurels but he was not satisfied with that. He attacked Greece. The tiny Greek Army did not only stop the Duce's forces, they drove them deep into Albania.

One of the jokes of that time was: "News flash! A Greek company of 100 men captured two Italian mountain regiments of 4,000 men and a pack train of 50 mules, despite the stiff resistance put up by the 50 mules."

Another: "Swiss Authorities put up signs along their southern border, reading: Greeks please stop here. You are entering Swiss territory."

The Italian Navy ventured forth to attack the Greek coast. Off Cape Matapán they suffered a humiliating and decisive defeat by the British Mediterranean Fleet. This persuaded the Italian Fleet to stay in port for the duration of the War. So far it would have been a minor setback for the Italians and not anything of such major consequences that it would effect the outcome of the War.

After subduing Norway, Hitler shifted his major fighting forces east. It was spring of 1941. His powerful Panzer units rumbled into Yugoslavia to rescue their desperate Axis partner in the mountains of Albania. Then the *Wehrmacht* crunched the Allies in Greece. Crete was taken by paratroopers. It was a first. Never before had such a large territory been taken just by paratroopers alone. There were two British sapper regiments working on fortifications. They were unarmed German (mostly Jewish) refugees in British uniforms. The British had not trusted them enough to allow them to carry arms. They were not even given British citizenship. When the paratroopers captured them, they were all shot as traitors.

We, in camp, did not perceive this as another blunder by the Nazis. Yet, this fifth blunder would prove fatal for the Axis. We thought the *Gleaner's* jubilation that Yugoslavia was fighting on the side of the British stupid and misdirected. The newspaper should have expressed sympathy for the unfortunate civilians of Yugoslavia and sadness to see another big country crushed by the Nazi war machine. In a mere three weeks of ruthless and destructive advances, the formerly peaceful territory was under the German heel. But the paper, which was usually wrong, pointed out, quite correctly this time, that it spread the Axis Forces even thinner. We thought this fact insignificant at the time.

We could not have anticipated that Germany and Russia would shortly go to war with one another. In that coming hostility, those three weeks which Germany used early in that very year to fight in the Balkans, made it impossible for the Axis Powers to take Leningrad, Moscow, Stalingrad, and Sevastopol before winter. The deadly, traditional ally of the Russians, and a determined Russian counter attack stopped all further advances. I still believe that a counter attack would not have dislodged the Nazi forces, if they had been able to establish themselves in the four major cities before winter.

*The Daily Gleaner,* the only newspaper which we received occasionally, had, besides reliable local news, most unreliable foreign news. It constantly reported glorious British victories by land and sea. Anybody who had the slightest knowledge of European and North African geography knew right away that the British were losing ground everywhere.

The British did win the air battle over London, called the Battle of Britain. Due to the inventions of more sophisticated detection devices, "smart torpedoes," magnetic mines, more powerful depth charges, and stepped up American intelligence, they were successfully sinking German submarines. Yet, no-one believed any news of British victories anymore because of the former false reporting of British successes.

The Nazis had their own hand-written news service in camp. They pieced the stories from the *Gleaner* together. With their

306

knowledge of geography, they could easily deduct and report how badly the British and their Allies were being pushed around on land. Their stories of German victories at sea were pure fantasy but who could check the facts?

# RUSSIA IS IN THE WAR!

Among the Nazis there were four men who defiantly declared that they were not Nazis. They should have come to our group, but did not want to join the "Jew Group" either. They wanted to be considered neutral, neither for a German, nor for an Allied victory or defeat. The Nazis labeled them Communists, the only non-Nazi political affiliation tolerated since the Molotov-v.Ribbentrop friendship pact. The Soviet Union was considered a potential ally of the Nazis ever since their division of Poland between the two dictatorships.

In the evening of the 2nd of June, 1941, we heard that the German Army had made a surprise attack on the Russians in Poland. The Nazi *Camp News* reported that the attackers were the Soviets. None in our hut believed that the Russians would have attacked the Germans after the tiny Finnish Army had defeated the Red Army again and again.

After dark, four groups of twenty sailors each, beat up the four unfortunate men whom they had labeled Communists. The screams were heart rending, piercing, and lasted for a long time. Fear seemed to drain the blood right out of my face. Freddie Löffler and I, the best fighters in our group, stood by our door, the narrowest space by which to attack us. We resolved to fight anyone who might want to enter, though we both felt pretty scared. We thought that this would be our best location to defend ourselves if need be.

When the British soldiers with fixed bayonets, led by Captain Hatton, finally stormed into the camp to free the four men, the Nazis made a short circuit to plunge the camp into darkness. Captain Hatton had brought a flash light. One of the victims had been hanged with electric wire from the rafters in one of the huts. One of the soldiers cut the wire with a bayonet in time to save the man's life.

Another poor soul had been wrapped in barbed wire. He was bleeding profusely. The other two were just beaten up terribly. After a day's stay in the hospital hut, the first two came into our hut. The man who had been hanged, became completely insane. He was removed to the Mental Hospital where he died soon afterwards.

The fellow who had been wrapped in barbed wire told me that he had migrated to Argentina in the great depression of 1930. He had worked as a sheep shearer in the country. About a year and a half ago (1939), his mother wrote him that she was not going to live much longer and begged him to come home. He sailed for home on a Norwegian ship. While at sea a few days, the War broke out. A British war ship stopped the merchant ship, boarded it, and arrested him, quite against international law. He had tears in his eyes. "I was on a Norwegian, a neutral ship! They had no right to take me off that ship!" He became more confused daily and became mentally ill, I assume, from the beatings. After a week it became so bad that he was sent to the Mental Hospital. I do not know what became of him. The other two men were housed in the hospital hut. They often came to visit us for company until I left the internment camp.

The mood of the Nazis changed. Though they could figure out from the names of the towns which the *Gleaner* mentioned that the *Wehrmacht* penetrated deeply into Russia, they were no longer so sure that they would win the War in a hurry and "be home before Christmas" as they had prophesied earlier.

Their letters from home reported casualties. They realized that they might never again see their brothers and fathers. As they became increasingly bitter, they wrote our names on the rafters in the neighboring hut in big enough letters that we could read them from ours. We were going to hang there as a victory celebration.

The Canadian guard who told us, said: "Now, I am sure that they know that the Allies will win. That's an act of desperation. They wrote your names because they want to convince themselves that they would win, even though they know deep down in their hearts that they no longer have a chance. Germany is finished! And they know it!"

The horrible beatings which had been so cowardly administered to the four men could not possibly influence the outcome of the War. They only demonstrated the power of the *Gestapo* inside the camp. They used terror to show their determination to maintain that power. It might be noted that the priests and the Protestant ministers were conspicuously absent during the turmoil. They were the only ones who had an outside chance to stop the murderous beatings and to restore tranquillity before the British soldiers rushed into the camp. Sadly, the clergy made no effort.

# ENCOUNTER IN THE DARK

I asked my Italian friend if it would be all right if I continued coming to his hut in the evenings. He assured me that it was. He was most disgusted with the recent beatings. He told me that the *Gestapo* had no power over the Italians. There were, of course, a number of fanatical *Fascisti* among the Italians, most of the rest cheered when they were told to cheer, booed when they were supposed to boo, but were exceedingly happy that they could sit out the War. They all professed loyalty to Mussolini but were elated that their loyalty was not put to a test, like having to fight. Who knows what thoughts they kept to themselves as far as politics were concerned. So, I continued with my lessons. The light bantering continued, just as if nothing extraordinary had happened.

Among those miners in the hut was a giant of a man. He reminded me of Primo Carnera, the recent World Heavyweight Boxing Champion from Italy, who was over six feet tall. He had won his crown in Madison Square Garden. Eventually he was defeated by Max Bear.

Carnera clearly had the upper hand during that fight. Max Bear slumped against the ropes. Carnera, relaxing his guard, came in for the coup de grace. Bear had faked the weakness in his knees. He jumped and shot a mighty right hook to Carnera's jaw. The giant fell very hard to the canvass and did not get up during the rest of the *News Reel* which I saw just before the War started.

Carnera's apparent twin also had a very loud voice, and when he could not think of a smart answer to give me, he loudly sang the Fascist anthem. He accompanied it on his tiny concertina which seemed far too small for his huge fists. He seemed to be a sort of leader, as what he did or said was usually followed by the rest of the men.

One night the banter became exceedingly lively and noisy. We were all in great form, and I did not leave the hut as usual at lights out time but stayed for a good quarter of an hour. On my way to my hut I had to pass by the sailors' quarters, where the terrible beatings had taken place. It was about in the middle of the camp.

311

The fence and its lights were far away. It was pitch dark where I passed the Nazi huts.

Suddenly, right before me stood the huge form of "Primo Carnera!" He was too near to me to turn and run. It would have been worse if I had screamed for help, as I was practically at the entrance of the sailors' hut.

Sweat poured down from my forehead as I squared off for my last fight. He said something to me in Italian. His voice was a soft whisper. It did not seem hostile. I realized that he wanted to tell me something. I did not comprehend what he said right away but eventually I understood. He told me that he had a cousin in America. If he could, he would go to that cousin. He told me that I should not take his defense of Mussolini too seriously. He really had no use for those dictators, not for Mussolini nor for Hitler. He hoped that the British would win. "But, please," he begged me, "please, don't tell the others in my group."

You could have knocked me down with a feather. I was totally wet with perspiration. I was certainly happy to promise him. At that moment I would have promised him anything! I was so happy to be alive! It was certainly wonderful and useful that I had learned enough Italian to understand that much.

I discontinued my walk to our hut. I had to make a detour to the bathroom. Happily, I reached my bed eventually. I lay awake for a long time, thinking: The guy had no idea that he had almost caused me heart failure with his urge to tell me that he was secretly on my side! Why was that so terribly important to him? If he was afraid that any of his countrymen might find out that he was secretly rooting for a British victory, why did he tell me or anybody else for that matter? A good thing that I did not throw a punch when he suddenly stood before me! It was almost morning when sleep finally released the tension.

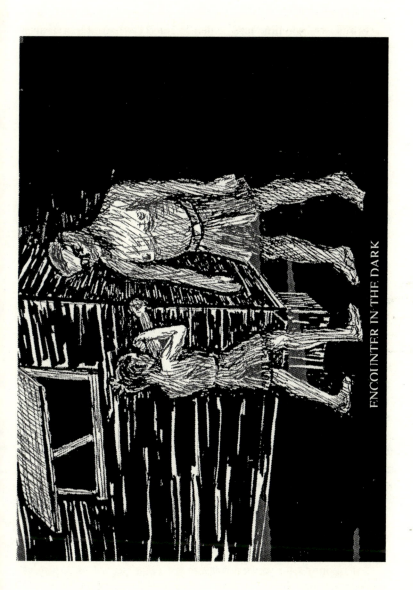

ENCOUNTER IN THE DARK

# GERHARD IS ILL

For quite some time now, when I visited Gerhard, I had noticed that he was limping. It got worse and worse. His right leg had a bluish tint. Dr. Stamm told me that my brother had phlebitis, a disease of the vein in his leg. He had to stay in bed. Dr. Ward said that it was just pretense, as Gerhard wanted a pretext to get out of the camp. He refused to give Dr. Stamm any medicines to treat my brother.

Gerhard could hardly walk, yet Dr. Ward refused Dr. Stamm's request for a chamber pot, let alone a bedpan to be placed into Gerhard's room. This dragged on for several months. The camp commander eventually allowed me to stay with my brother day and night. It got so bad that I had to carry Gerhard to and from the bathroom.

Fortunately Mr. Heise, the former manager for the West Indian Shell installations, was the group leader of the British internees. The Heises were staunch Roman Catholics. American Jesuit Priests came to visit Heise regularly.

One day one of the priests was given permission to leave the visitors' room and visit the compound of the British. He went straight to Gerhard's room in the company of Dr. Stamm. He was shocked and promised to intercede with the Government on Gerhard's behalf. He wanted Gerhard sent to the St. Joseph's Hospital, where the nuns and a competent doctor would look after him. That visit gave us some hope for a while but nothing happened, at least, we did not hear of anything happening.

Not long after the visit Dr. Stamm came into the room. He had a grave face.

"I have done all I can for you, Gerhard, you are going to die. There is just one more thing we can try: Stop smoking."

In his fear, Gerhard had been smoking more than ever. He had always been a very heavy smoker ever since he came to Jamaica eleven years ago. He smoked at least 40 cigarettes a day.

At midnight he snuffed out the last cigarette with the resolve, never to smoke again. He had terrible withdrawal symptoms. He would get up in his sleep at nights and limping on his good leg, he would use angry words at somebody I did not know and start to fight with me. I had no difficulty in subduing him in his weakened condition. He never remembered the incidents the next morning, and I never told him. After only a few days, he slept through the nights and his health improved remarkably. I was amazed. Hans Stamm was pleased, but Gerhard still had to lie in his bed with his leg propped up. He still dreamt of smoking. I saw him pursing his lips, drawing in air through his mouth in his sleep.

I was glad that I had never taken up this dirty, expensive, and unhealthy habit. I had ruled it out for myself, as I so much wanted to be the breast stroke swimming champion of Jamaica. What a blessing! I was only junior champion. The internment prevented my training for the championship.

The priests were as good as their words. The Jesuits took it upon themselves to guarantee to the Jamaican Government that Gerhard would not leave the Hospital as long as he was still officially interned. An ambulance drove up to the camp, and Gerhard was taken to the St. Joseph's Hospital, where caring nuns nursed him back to health.

The Hospital had been a gift by a very wealthy German noble woman. She herself had taken a nun's vow and remained the Mother Superior of the Hospital. In 1941, she was very frail and old. She still made policy but a young Irish nun, Sister Catherine, managed the institution and made all the routine decisions. The main remedy for Gerhard was the fact that he had given up smoking. There were also some medicines given to him. Above all, there was loving care. With it, hope was restored, and a reason to keep on living.

# BOXING AND RICHARD KAISER

Richard Kaiser was by far the most inconsiderate, often obnoxious, and least liked person in our group. It did not seem to bother him. He was hyperactive, and though everybody told him to leave them alone, he kept on pestering people. He did not seem to have any pride. You could tell him to get lost in the most insulting way, he came back as if nothing had been said to him. After several months, we had formed little cliques of friends. He belonged to none. We were all very polite to each other and cooperated in our daily chores but were really friendly only with our little clique.

Richard Kaiser, who was much shorter than I, had taken boxing lessons at the Y.M.C.A. regularly before the War. He asked me to go three rounds with him, three minutes each with one minute breaks. I agreed to box with him under the same conditions as I boxed with Löffler. We had no sooner started, when I noticed that he was hitting pretty hard. I had no intention to hurt him and did not retaliate in kind. I also noticed that due to my longer reach, he was no match for me.

Towards the end of the second round, I faked a hard left to his jaw. He parried it with his right elbow. I felt a very sharp pain in the knuckle of my forefinger of my left hand. I felt sick and could no longer use the left hand to guard, let alone hit. I certainly did not want this little squirt to know that he had hurt me, so I did go into the third round and finished it mostly backing away from him. He was triumphant that he had beaten me. It made him happy.

I went to the Hospital hut as it was too painful to take off my left glove. The ship doctor who was on duty was very polite to me. After all, the *Gestapo* was not watching. He took off the glove as carefully as he could but I felt nauseated and vomited. He felt my hand and told me that I had a hair line fracture, and that I should not use my left hand until it healed. He made me sit down in the little room until I felt better. This fracture healed, but to this day it hurts when I grip a wrench really hard to loosen or tighten a bolt.

A couple of months passed. In that time the Winnipeg Grenadiers had been replaced by the Argyle Highlanders from western Canada. They paraded in kilts and had a glengarry on their heads. They marched to the unique tunes played by their band with bag pipes and drums. They looked very smart and their uniforms fitted them properly. In the internment camp and outside, while on guard duty, they wore the usual shorts, khaki knee socks and sun helmets, on their heads.

First the P.N.P. and then Bustamante had been released. Toward the end of Busta's internment, the poor fellow had some real mood swings. He would walk up and down crying loudly, complaining bitterly of the injustice done to him. Then again he would boast about the good he had done for the poor Jamaicans and that he would gladly remain interned if that would help the cause of the people of Jamaica. He made it clear that the people would follow him and not the government. He proved to be right. He won every election before and after Jamaica became independent.

His internment had been truly a life saver for him. He suffered very badly from a chronic desease. He refused to take medicine for it. Soldiers forced him to take it by threatening him to cut off his meals and all visitors from outside. We would never have known, if he had taken his medicine quietly without making big scenes over and over again. Two soldiers stood there and made sure that Busta swallowed his pill and did not spit it out. He was cured and was glad for it. The *Gleaner* reported that Miss Longbridge, who later became his wife, checked into the St. Joseph's Hospital for an undisclosed reason at the same time. Busta's illness was kept very secret from the public.

Somehow Kaiser scrounged up some very nice wood and built himself a desk. It looked nice but it did not look very strong. It was obviously his first attempt at cabinet making. Give credit where credit is due. He did not ask for help. He only borrowed some tools from Willy. He had a right to be proud that he accomplished something all by himself. That was more than most of our group had done.

Thursday rolled around. It was our weekly hut washing day. Everybody had carried all his belongings outside into the sun. The hut was completely empty except for Kaiser's desk. It stood in the middle of the hut with books and pictures standing up on it.

Willy and I came in with our brooms, and the rest of our dormitory mates had gone to the washstand to carry buckets of water. Seeing the desk, I said to Willy: "Let us pitch it out of the door, so that no two pieces of wood will stick together!"

"No, no. We'll carry it outside as if it were a crate of eggs, so that not a picture nor a book will fall over. We'll also carry it back in the same way after the hut is washed."

There was the Quaker way again. I grumpily agreed, and we did carry it out without turning over a picture or a book.

We took over the buckets of water as the first men arrived from the washstand. Kaiser arrived on the scene. He saw his beloved desk standing outside.

He screamed: "Nazi methods! Taking private property away from us Jews! You two don't belong in our hut! You are nothing but stinking Nazis. I'm going in the office and demand that you be removed from our hut, you Nazis!"

All of us had applied for release, and our applications were still pending. This wart could certainly ruin our chances for the duration of the War. Calling me a Nazi had always been enough to get my blood boiling. It certainly boiled now! I saw red! Without saying a word, I dumped the full bucket of water over that idiot's head, so that the rim came down hard on his shoulders. Willy said, "you can have one from me, too." We all wore nothing but shorts, the ones carrying buckets, also wore shoes. Willy's bucket of water washed Kaiser from the feet up to his head.

The bucket came flying off the big mouth's head, and his fists came punching. I shifted to let his attack hit nothing but air. Three hard jabs to the nose sent Kaiser reeling, first against his desk which promptly collapsed, and then he fell backward over a locker, so that his Adam's apple and jaw were widely exposed. I was going to tear that head right off his neck with a straight right from the shoulder! I wanted to kill him! Four men jumped on top of me: Willy Gertig, Fred Löffler, Max Ebersohn, and Ludwig Klein, the least physical man I ever met. I struggled but soon gave up. They were right. I was about to make a very bad situation an awful lot worse. Kaiser had slumped to the ground. There was no skin on the bridge of his nose. Dr. Aub was washing it and eventually bandaged it. It never left a scar.

Willy and I washed the hut as usual. I thanked the four men who held me back from doing irrevocable harm to Kaiser and myself. It was the only time in my life where I really wanted to kill somebody. Willy, true to his convictions, put the desk back together. It was now in a much better shape than it had ever been. He and Kaiser carried it inside after the floor had dried.

Kaiser told Ebersohn later that he had obtained special permission from the camp authorities to leave the desk in the hut while we washed it. He had told none of us. We had always made our own common sense rules by consensus. These rules mostly concerned chores, such as whose turn it was to chop wood for the kitchen, who was to clean the washstand, shower, or toilet, etc. We obeyed them, too. This was necessary to maintain peace and tranquillity in our crowded dormitory.

We had all agreed to let Max Ebersohn represent us in all official acts. No one had ever gone over his head to the authorities. There was absolutely no need for that. This sneakily obtaining permission behind our backs, to oppose our rules, did not endear Kaiser to any of us, but it was true to his lack of character. Kaiser wore a bandage over his nose for a while but there were no repercussions resulting from that brief but fierce fight.

# THE PLIGHT OF THE SOVIET UNION

*The Daily Gleaner* reported news about "tremendous victories by our good Russian Allies." Again, anybody who knew even a little bit of geography realized from the cities and rivers mentioned that the Soviets did not put up too much of a resistance to the unstoppable *Wehrmacht*. In the North, the Finns were cutting off supplies to the city of Leningrad, (now again St. Petersburg), and the Germans were at the southern approaches to the city.

There had been a battle by the Moskva River, just west of Moscow. It was reported that the Germans had been stopped there decisively, mainly by the political police forces who were fanatical Communists. Who would believe that? Were not similar reports announced in 1812, 128 years earlier, almost to the day, that the Russians had defeated Napoleon at pretty nearly the same spot? Then why did the Czar's armies retreat through Moscow and then burn down the city rather than leave it to give shelter to the enemy? No one in the camp believed the truth: Victories by the Red Army which had not even been able to defeat the Finns, the little nation of a mere four million people? How could anybody believe in Russian victories now?!

Still further south, the army of the German General Paulus was in the important industrial city of Stalingrad. That city had supplied the Russians with much needed weapons. "Fierce street fighting" was reported in the city itself. In the extreme South the Germans were in or at, that was not clear from the reports, the Crimea. Obviously the main thrust was towards the Baku oil fields, still a few 100 km away over mountainous territory.

All the news were depressing. All seemed so hopeless. Who believed that the old reliable ally would again come to Mother Russia's aid? Reports came in that the temperatures at the Russian Front had dropped 100° F in a few hours and that the German soldiers wore only light summer uniforms and leather boots. Leather, as the Russians well knew, was not sufficient insulation for the feet. I could not believe that the *Wehrmacht* who had always planned every attack to the tiniest detail, would have allowed German soldiers to face the Russian winter unprepared.

Yet, the reports did not change as far as geographical names were concerned. In Russia, winter was definitely there. Germans were not in Leningrad and not in Moscow. Russians and Germans were street fighting in Stalingrad. That city was reported to be so badly destroyed that it would never give anyone shelter for a long time to come.

I should have realized then and there that the three weeks' campaign to conquer Yugoslavia was not only a mistake, it was the most decidedly fatal mistake that would eliminate any possibility that the Nazis could overwhelm the big Russian cities. Without the big population centers the Axis armies would have no chance to win the War in Russia.

If the German forces had started their invasion of Russia three weeks earlier, they would almost certainly have taken Leningrad, Moscow, Stalingrad, the entire Crimea, and possibly even the Baku oil fields during warm weather. The Russians might have given up. They would most likely not have been able to mount a serious campaign to regain their lost territory. Who knows how the Moslem Soviet Republics would have reacted if practically all of the European Russia would have been under German domination?

As it turned out in fact, the oil froze to grease in the German weapons. They could not be fired until the soldiers figured out how to adjust them for the cold weather. The Russians wore thick felt boots over their shoes and mittens over their gloves. The Germans lost any amount of men due to frozen fingers and feet. After the War, Eckart's mother told me that Eckart was hospitalized because of frozen feet towards the end of 1941.

We saw newspaper reports that Russian cavalry behind the German lines would dismount, waylay supply trains, destroy them and disappear into the thick pine forests, where they could not be pursued by motorized columns. After the war, I found out that my cousin Rudi Lampe's son, Herbert, who was my age, was a motor cycle currier. He was shot by a Russian partisan far behind the German lines. The Germans ran out of gas for their tanks and trucks. They converted many to run on wood which was plentiful in Russia.

We, in sunny Jamaica, believed that all those reports were either not true or greatly exaggerated. Reporting had been so unreliable before that no one knew what to believe or reject. Imagine, horse cavalry seriously hampering the invincible Nazi thrust east! Ridiculous! But then truth, is sometimes stranger than fiction.

# BILL SCOTTER, THE POWER OF THE PEN

Kingston is supposed to be the world's sixth largest natural harbor. It is also easily defended with a battery about 1,500 ft. high up in the mountains at Newcastle which gives one a splendid view of the harbor and its approaches. We, too, could see the harbor very well from our camp. Quite a few ships would assemble there periodically, and then, one morning, they would all be gone. British war ships would escort the convoys across the Atlantic to United Kingdom ports.

The British desperately needed more destroyers to protect this life line across the ocean. America had most of its World War I fleet "moth balled" on the Tappan Zee up the Hudson River. America sold the British 50 old destroyers for Goats Island for a naval base off Jamaica's South Coast and land for an air base opposite that island on the mainland west of Old Harbour.

The *Gleaner* employed Bill Scotter, an Irishman, as a newspaper reporter. He was formerly an Inspector of the Jamaican Constabulary. He had the unfortunate habit of speaking his mind emphatically, especially when he had acceded to his love for imbibing a few too many inebriating beverages. He did not like the idea that good crown colony land should be turned over to the neutral Americans for a "few rusty old tubs which the Yankees wanted to get rid of because they cost them too much to maintain."

Scotter was very vocal about his views concerning the "cowardice of the Americans letting the valiant few British fight it out to defend the freedom of the world, while the Americans only tried to make as much money from arms sales as possible and stay away from where the bullets fly. Now, that the British were running out of cash, the greedy Yanks took away British land."

All this talk took place in a bar where the highest British Officers had been assigned to make visiting American Naval Officers and civilian officials feel comfortable and welcome in Jamaica! At that time Gerhard had not yet been transferred to the St. Joseph's Hospital.

The next morning Bill Scotter found himself interned along with Gerhard, Heise, Dr. Stamm and all the other British internees.

Scotter had known all of them in better days. All pointed out to their newest fellow inmate that everyone of them had sworn loyalty to the British Crown when they became British Subjects. Furthermore none of them had ever broken their solemn oath, nor had they acted in any way that might suggest that they might do so. As a matter of fact, it could never have served the interest of any of them in any way, to go against the new home land of their choice.

As I was there to look after Gerhard, I, too, let him know how stupid, unjust, unnecessarily expensive, and hurtful it was to lock us refugees up with our worst enemies, the Nazis. We had probably lost our families in Europe already. In Gerhard's and my case that was certainly true but we did not know it yet. Everyone of us had more to lose from the Nazis than anyone I could think of in all of Jamaica. Yet we were endangered in this miserable camp! Scotter knew me from the bar of the Continental Club from seven years ago. He listened very attentively. What a story!

Neither a police inspector nor a veteran newspaper reporter is easily shaken, and Scotter had been in both of those professions. He told us that he was outraged that so many good British Subjects were interned without ever being given a reason verbally or in writing why they were locked up. He was also appalled at Gerhard's condition. Gerhard was taken to the hospital just a few days after these conversations.

Scotter told us that he had influential friends in England and that the *Gleaner* would soon get him freed. He said that he would see to it that charges would have to be filed against all the British Subjects and the refugees, or the Government would set them free. If they did not listen to him, he would write a column per day in the *Gleaner*.

# FREE AGAIN !

Scotter was certainly right that he would be released soon. Though he was born in Ireland, he had remained a British Subject when that Country became a republic. A column appeared in the newspaper promising to reveal some sordid conditions "right here in Jamaica." It was authored by Scotter. No more was written about it. I was no longer allowed to visit the British as Gerhard was no longer there.

A few days later Schönbeck, of our hut, was released. He resumed his position as Chief Sugar Chemist at the Frome Estate. Sugar was a most important commodity, not only for food, but also as an ingredient for ammunition. One after the other of our hut and of the British compound was released several days apart.

On October 28, 1941, I was called into the office. I was told to pack my things. I was a free man! I phoned Eustace Chen. He told me that "Sonny," his brother, would call for me at 4:00 p.m. with a van.

On my way out the Canadian sanitation inspector told me: "Get out o' here or we'll charge you rent!"

I was walking on a cloud! No one can appreciate freedom as much as anyone who has lost it even for a short time! My total time as an internee had been one year and nine months. It was not really wasted. I had gone in as a boy, I came out as a man. I do not think that I could have learnt as much about men in any sociology or psychology class. My religion was no longer democracy, I had become a Quaker. That changed my attitude toward people. It prevented me from becoming permanently embittered.

It seemed that the Jamaican Authorities had received orders from London to let all refugees go, provided that their papers were in order. In England, no naturalized British had been interned, so no order came through for those in Jamaica. The result, Dorrie and Gerhard remained interned for another half year. Dorrie was originally interned two weeks after Gerhard. He spent all of two years in the camp.

Unfortunately, both, Dorrie and Gerhard, remained very bitter and suspicious of everybody with whom they came into contact for

325

the rest of their lives. They had become very religious Roman Catholics but they never recovered from the injustice done to them. Dorrie, especially, could not forget the inhumane treatment she and the other women received at the early stages of their internment, which drove six women, 10% of all the interned women, to suicide.

Actually, my original assumption, concerning the time difference between my and Dorrie's and Gerhard's releases, was wrong. Many years later my father-in-law told me that Dorrie's and Gerhard's releases lay on someone's desk in the Colonial Secretary's office for a whole year, awaiting that man's signature. Mine had arrived there at the same time and lay there, too, but "only" for half a year. As Administrator General and Custodian of Enemy Property, my father-in-law had excellent connections to that office. He had made it his business to know what was going on in that all important policy making department.

He made it quite clear to me: I was interned half a year, and Dorrie and Gerhard a full year, because some prejudiced, sadistic middle-level clerk let these papers lie on his desk for all that time! This story always disturbed me. I could not verify it, and my father-in-law never talked about it again. I never told Dorrie nor Gerhard, as none of us could do anything about it. It would only have served to make them more bitter than they were already.

# COMING HOME .

Sonny dropped me off at 4 Arlington Ave. I was home! All the factory girls, there was faithful, old Betsy, the ever helpful Ruby, Mazie still from the Continental Club days, Cynthia, Hermina, Blanche, Madge, Wilhel, and Lissa, and the only male employee, Winston, came to greet me with the biggest, heartwarming smiles ever. There were tears in our eyes and smiles from ear to ear on all of us. They had not known that I was coming. Yet, the place sparkled with cleanliness.

I put my clothes into my bedroom which was upstairs. It was the smallest room, only 10' x 12' at the north-east corner of the very big house. North of it was a little bathroom and a small kitchen. The girls had kept everything perfectly clean. The pitch pine floors in all the rooms were polished to perfection. I wandered into the neon shop which was adjoining my bedroom at the south-east of the house. I was glad that Dorrie had saved its equipment from those idiots at the Public Service. This work shop, 10' x 16', too, had been dusted and swept. It warmed my heart to see it.

I opened the door at the right side of the south end of the shop, stepped down one step to the landing and opening the door on the opposite side. I stepped up one step into Dorrie and Gerhard's large living room which doubled as the office during the days. It was the south-west room, 20' x 16'. The north-west room, 20' x 12,' was Dorrie and Gerhard's bedroom. It had a door to my bedroom. The beds were made up. I was still surprised that I had been released before them. I expected their release any minute. As it developed, I expected their release any minute for another half a year!

I stepped on the south verandah, walked to the west verandah which had a staircase to the ground floor and then went to the south verandah. All the verandahs were a good 6' wide. I opened the door which led to the staircase in the middle of the house and went down. I turned right into the long room which ran from the front door, underneath the neon shop, my bedroom and the little bathroom and kitchen. The east side of this room housed three wind tunnels. In front of each was a quarter horse power Delco motor with a 30" diameter fan blade, blowing air over drying vermicelli. They were resting on trays of flour bags, each stretched over a wooden frame. The tops and sides of the tunnels were made of plywood and could be removed easily. I checked the motors and oiled them. The blades had obviously been cleaned. On the west side of the room were six foot high drying racks for macaroni or spaghetti.

Back to the bottom of the stairs. Under Dorrie and Gerhard's bedroom was a dark room. It was the first drying room with fans whirring. When the pasta came fresh from the machine, they were hung on three foot long sticks from six foot high drying racks. On the North end of that room was a door leading to a very large concrete block bathroom. It extended all the way to the end of the verandah upstairs. This was certainly a change from the bath room in the camp where the shower and the toilet were separate cubby holes and did not even have doors. I walked back to the stairs, turned right into a corridor and left into the south-west front room.

The girls were busy breaking macaroni to length and packing them. The breaking device was Gerhard's design. Going back through the door through which I had come in, crossing the hallway, I came into the factory itself. In front of me was a concrete sink and the back door about 16' away. It was a large irregularly shaped, concrete block room, about 26' x 20,' with a concrete work bench running along the entire north wall, fresh dough and freshly sterilized flour bags rested on it. On the south wall was a door, leading to the 8' wide red concrete west verandah. I had once cut that door in half horizontally. We kept the lower half closed and the upper open for ventilation. A line shaft ran along the entire south side. The 3 H.P., 3 phase, 40 Hz, 220 V motor drove the line shaft. Its pulleys drove the kneader on the west end, the mixer in the middle, and the press nearest to the entrance door.

I stepped through the back door on to a large concrete patio. There to the right, behind our large bath room, was the employees' bathroom. I checked it. It was very clean. Looking into the large backyard, there were the magnificent old lignum vitae trees. To the west of the patio was a storeroom. In about half a year it became my office and storeroom for my material. It was about 10' x 22'. West of that was the double garage, about 50' x 22'. West of the garage was room for a car to drive into the backyard. On the east side of the house was even more room to the fence. In the front, running the full length of the south side of the house, was an eight foot wide red concrete verandah. In about the middle of the 70' deep frontyard stood a good sized coconut palm and a pretty poorly looking lime tree. There was a personnel gate at the east side of the fence to the street and a double gate to the west for trucks to drive through. There was a low hedge against the ornamental wire fence to Arlington Ave.

Rice was still shipped regularly to Jamaica from the Orient at a very low price. It hurt the pasta sales very badly. There was only one shift working. I had to look for work. With black-out restrictions on out-door signs, and the emphasis to conserve current, I did not foresee many neon sales. Besides, there were so many shortages that there was no need to advertise with neon or anything else. Except for cars and trucks, all goods sold as soon as they were displayed. Gasoline and tires were very severely rationed and transportation became a problem.

# MURALS

The Springfield Club was within an easy bicycle ride from the Jamaica Macaroni Factory. It had a very large shark enclosure and was one of the better swimming places and night clubs. It was owned by Murray Jacobs, a locksmith from the city of Worms (rhymes with forms) on the Rhine. He had told the authorities that he was French. He must have known someone very important. He was as German or as Jamaican as I was. He did not speak a word of French. He probably was the only German who was never interned. I do not know if he was Jewish. He was only a very few years older than I was. I was glad for him that he escaped that miserable and humiliating experience. I wondered how he had done it! But I did not dare ask.

Each lunch time there were Bustamante; his lawyer, Mr. Pixley; and Chief Inspector Higgins, the man in charge of the Criminal Investigation Dept. (CID) and the Immigration Dept. They stood by the bar. Murray boasted that it was the longest bar in Jamaica, made of pure Honduras mahogany. The three men had quite a few drinks with Murray. Then they all sat down and had a sumptuous meal together.

I asked Murray to allow me to paint murals along the 100' long wall behind the bar and around the corner another 20' at the entrance. We agreed that they should depict the history of Jamaica. I went to the large reference library at the Institute of Jamaica to read the history of the Island, sketch a portrait of Columbus and study pictures of the *Santa Maria,* the Spanish flag of the time, the uniforms and clothing, the flag of Cromwell's republican Great Britain with its horse head in its center, the uniforms of the conquering Englishmen, the buildings, clothing, later uniforms, etc. I made watercolor sketches of the proposed murals to scale. Murray was greatly impressed. He paid me very little money but I had very good meals.

The first panel, 8' x 8' depicted the Santa Maria arriving in Jamaica in 1494, and a life size portrait of Columbus at eye level at the top left hand corner of the mural. The history unfolded on the ten other panels which were 8' x 3'. The last panel, 8' x 8' depicted the coat of arms of Jamaica with a dark skinned, almost life size woman wearing a feather headdress and little else, holding a cornucopia on the left of the coat of arms and a matching man on the other side with a more luxurious feather headdress, holding a bow and with a quiver strapped to his back. The girl was quite a bit more alluring, and the man a lot more powerfully built than the ones on the official stationery of government correspondence.

While I was at it, I also designed some attractive stationery for Murray, depicting the club with the harbor in front and the mountains as a back drop.

# SOCIAL LIFE DURING THE WAR

Time of adversity is good for one very important thing: It shows who is really your friend, and who was only a fine weather friend. Mama Hill and all of her children were wonderful. I was always welcome at their home. The Alexanders were another family who went out of their way to be nice to me. However, several people made it quite clear that they would not have anything to do with "a damned German." Some went so far that, when we were approaching each other in the street, they rather crossed the street, so that they would not have to say hello to me.

Every now and then I was invited to a party but invariably had to leave early, as there were always a few boys who, after a few drinks, wanted to pick a fight with me to show their patriotism. That had not changed since 1939. Two in particular come to mind, Foster and Tibbits. Both came from the Cayman Islands.

Tibbits was especially annoyed with me. He was a water polo player of an opposing club. He had one of the most powerful shots. It infuriated him that he never could score against me. He always showed his wrist when he took a shot at the goal, so that I could see exactly where the ball was going, and of course, then I could stop it.

When he had a few drinks, he and Foster always wanted to gang up on me. I had no intention to make myself conspicuous with a fight. The internment camp immediately loomed before my mind's eye. Tibbits was the only swimmer who showed some animosity toward me. The water polo league chose me to be their all star goalie again, just as I was after the first release.

Two years earlier, when I was released on November 15, 1939, the War was still very popular and so was the sarcastic song:

"We shall hang out our washing on the Siegfried Line,
Have you got any washing, Mama dear?
We shall hang out our washing on the Siegfried Line,
Is the Siegfried line still there?"

After my release on October 28, 1941 the enthusiasm had vanished. The Siegfried Line had not. There was no more talk of idealism, such as: "We are fighting to make the world safe for democracy." That phrase had been borrowed from the Athenian

332

Government when that doomed city-state needed recruits to fight powerful Sparta in the disastrous Peleponesian War 480 to 430 B.C.

Finland, which fought for its life on the side of the Germans, was every bit as democratic as Great Britain, while Russia, the British Empire's only fighting Ally worth talking about, was every bit as totalitarian as Nazi Germany, though that was not a popular fact to mention in Jamaica at that time. It brought to mind the well known Jamaican proverb: Not every ting good fe eat, good fe talk.

As the War broke out Sir Oswald Mosley was interned for quite a while and justly so. He was the leader of the British Nazi Party, the leader of the potential fifth column. I could see no reason why they should ever have released him. Now, in 1941, he was no longer interned. This really upset me.

Chief Inspector Higgins's deputy, I believe he was in charge of all police matters concerning the War, came to pay me a visit at 4 Arlington Ave. I asked him to come upstairs into Gerhard's office and offered him a seat. He preferred to stand as he said that he only had a minute to talk to me. So I, too, stood during our conversation. He was quite a bit taller than I. He looked very smart in his khaki officer's uniform.

He told me: "Your application to join the British Forces has come back from England. It is approved. Do you still want to go?"

I knew that in England naturalized British and refugees, people like Dorrie, Gerhard, and I, would never have been interned. So I was not surprised that they would like me to serve in their army.

I said: "My brother and his wife are still interned. The aim of the War has changed. There is no longer any idealism, but the aim is now to completely dismember the Axis Powers. I am still willing to translate any document for you free of charge, and to help you in any way I can right here in Jamaica, but I am no longer willing to go abroad to fight, especially now that you have released Sir Oswald Mosley."

Then he asked me how I felt about my former fellow inmates who are still interned. He named them: Gertig, Kahn, Klein, and Kaiser. I said something nice about all of them, yes, even Kaiser, and told him that I considered it a disgrace to keep them interned as they would never pose a threat to anybody, or do anything that might cause him to regret releasing them. Each one of them had more to fear from a German victory than he, or anyone else in Jamaica. He told me that he had no power to release them. He could only report what he heard. That was most likely true. I liked the man. He acted every bit a perfect gentleman and did not seem a bit haughty but spoke in a very friendly tone. A pity that I forgot his name. I believe that he was from South Africa. I knew that he spoke German fluently, but he spoke only English with me. I regretted that he never took me up on the offer to translate for him.

Practically all educated Jamaicans were solidly for a British victory. People greeted each other with the "V" sign by making a fist of the right hand, except straightening the index and the middle fingers and spreading them apart. This symbol was made popular by Winston Churchill himself. Store windows caught your eye by three dots and a dash, Morse code for the letter "V" for victory. Radio broadcasts would start with the sound of the Morse code "V". All the high schools for boys now had cadet corps. The boys drilled with great enthusiasm after school.

My much admired friend, Rev. Lewis Davidson, the ardent pacifist, had resigned his post of headmaster of the Wolmer's Boys' School. He did not want to introduce a cadet corps in his school. He became headmaster of the Friend's College in Highgate. His leadership in that school was a boon for the entire Quaker Mission in Jamaica. Highgate is in a most beautiful mountain region, about 30 miles by road north of Kingston.

Many of the educated men of Kingston had joined the Jamaica Defense Force, a para military organization which trained after work without weapons. The West Indies Regiment was reactivated. Its volunteers came from the Jamaican poor, illiterate, and semiliterate. They trained full-time, were actually issued rifles and learnt how to fire weapons. The Victoria League consisted of nice looking young, well educated girls who attended dances with British and American Navy officers to boost their morale. These dances were chaperoned by elder ladies of the "society."

The poor Jamaicans, and there were a lot of poor, were generally fed up with the War. They were particularly annoyed with the kerosene shortage. There was no electric power in Jamaica except in Kingston, Spanish Town, and the large net westward past May Pen, thanks to Gerhard. Montego Bay, Port Antonio, and

Morant Bay had power plants, but the rural areas and small towns did not have electricity in their homes. The power nets mentioned, only covered a very small part of the Island. Most people still used kerosene lamps after dark, yes, even within the power net, the poor could not afford to have electricity connected to their homes.

Due to the lack of shipping space, most of the staples the poor were used to, were in very short supply. When a ship load of rice came in from the Orient, one could buy rice. The government subsidized the price to make it affordable for the poor. Dried and salted cod fish came from Canada. This very important food was also subsidized but it was in very short supply. Fortunately, for the population, bananas were not classified as essential and no shipping space was made available for them. The government subsidized them, too.

The people ate them green boiled, like boiled potatoes; boiled and then fried like home fried potatoes; ripe, raw, of course; and when too ripe, fried with sugar and flour, corn meal or cassava flour as delicious banana fritters. I was told by many workers that they liked Hitler, because he made the English give them so many bananas so cheaply and sometimes even free! The Marxist independence movement, headed by Norman Manley, grew very rapidly.

During all that time the news from Europe was terrible! The Germans were rapidly advancing toward all the major cities in Russia. U-boats still menaced British shipping and supplies. Convoys to Murmansk and Archangels by the British to the Russians were often attacked and sometimes sunk by German naval forces or aircraft based in Norway. There were reports of victories in Africa and on the high seas, but they did not seem decisive.

The Vichy French with their large fleets in Oran and in Toulon were a serious potential threat to the British control of the Mediterranean Sea. Who could guess which way Admiral Darlan of Vichy France would point his guns? The good news was that the Americans now made bombers which could fly across the Atlantic, stopping for refueling at the New Foundland base of Gander. They no longer had to be sent by ship to be assembled in England. America was now mass-producing them and was selling them to the British.

Jamaica experienced a big influx of American money. The Americans were building a huge base at Goat Island. They blew up a lime stone mountain, bulldozed it into a huge swamp to build an airport on it. By doing that, they also eliminated malaria from that area. Then they bulldozed the rest of the mountain into the sea to make a long breakwater to accommodate supply ships and to set up refueling stations for their war ships. That was a good distance west of Kingston. No one had ever seen such huge earth moving equipment in Jamaica. The pick-ax and shovel were the only tools used for digging up to then. Dynamite had been used at times, but no one ever thought of blowing up a whole limestone mountain and of bulldozing it away! The Americans changed geography!

They built a road into the Kingston Harbour around Rockfort as the gate through that historic monument was too small for their trucks. Above all, they built the military airport on the Palisadoes over a huge swamp. That airport is today (1997) the Manley International Airport, serving Kingston. For the first time land planes could service Jamaica. As far as I remember, till the end of the War, the Pan American Clipper, the seaplane that landed at Harbour Head, was still the only air connection to America for civilians. There was no air connection to any other country.

# A GALA PERFORMANCE

There were a lot of merchant marine sailors who had survived their ships being sunk by enemy action. Money had to be raised for them. The government decided to put on a gala ball for all important people in the Island to raise money, and boost the morale for the war effort as well. The Bournemouth Club was the best location for such an event.

It was a beautiful building overlooking the sea and our specially built water polo pool. It was 33 1/3 m x 20 m (109' x 66' approximately). The pool was 2 m (6'-7") deep at the shallow end. No player could touch bottom. At the other end, near the harbor, it was very deep, so that divers from the 30' tower would not hit the bottom. On the long east side were cabanas. Above them was the dance floor, a band stand, a bar, tables, and chairs. On the shorter north side, forming an "L" with the east side, were more tables and chairs. West of the pool was a well kept park. Halfway along the east and west sides stood poles supporting a steel cable across the pool. From the cable hung rings on chains for those who felt ready to show off their strength by swinging the 66' across the pool. In the south beyond the 30' diving tower was the harbor and far away, beyond the narrow strip of land, called the Palisadoes, was the Caribbean.

Walter Lowe, our great swimming coach, my former fellow internee, had been put in charge of the water entertainment. It was a most gorgeous, full moon night. The moon light over the harbor seemed blue in contrast with the many electric lights of the club. (Fluorescent lights had not yet been invented.) The first order of the evening was a water polo game.

The Governor and his top staff had been given the best seats in the house in the middle of the east side. All the top military officers, such as the General in charge of all the British troops in Jamaica, the highest naval officers of the British Caribbean Fleet, his American counterpart and all the civilian department heads attended. There was Mr. Easton, in charge of Education; Mr. H.F. Barry with his family. The latter had superseded Mr. Ritchie (who had died) as the Administrator General and Administrator of Enemy

Property and many more. Who was who in the commercial world were also invited with their families for the grand occasion. I suppose, they were the main financial contributors.

The fourteen best water polo players opened the evening with an exhibition game. Walter Rogers, the former center forward of the Kingston Swimming Club, the league champions, operated the flood lights. I was the goalie of the Jamaica Amateurs Swimming Club. We had lost to Kingston by only one goal. This evening we were evenly matched teams from all clubs. I played goalie for the winning team. At the end of the game the lights went out. My goal was at the foot of the diving tower.

The next item on the program was a water ballet to be performed by all the prettiest girls who could swim well. I had not seen any pretty girls in a year and nine months. I was not going to pass up this opportunity. Instead of retiring to the showers with the rest of the players, I climbed the 30' tower in the cover of darkness.

The lights went on and there, in the middle of the pool, were all those bathing beauties, and I had the best seat in the house. Actually, I was lying on my stomach with my head over the edge of the top platform. The band was playing beautiful music, and the lovely girls performed to its beat. The flood lights made them look even more attractive than they were already. What a perfect night! I wished that the water ballet had lasted a little bit longer but, alas, the flood lights were turned off and the girls swam out of the pool.

I got up to climb down the ladder, or so I hoped. A trumpet fanfare blasted from the band stand, drums rolled feverishly, and the flood light caught me standing on the 30' tower. Walter Rogers got his revenge for not letting him score against me in many a try. How could I climb down? The governor was clapping and so did the rest of the people! I tried a way out so that I might climb down and not lose face. I shouted: "Walter, I can't see the water. The flood light is blinding me!"

The drums kept rolling. The flood lights shone on the water and went up, back to me. My excuse had been shot down.

I had never dived from anything higher than the ten foot high spring board. The crème de la crème of Jamaica's society was waiting for me to do something. I had no choice. I had to dive! I made a swan dive. I was concentrating so hard on entering the

338

water vertically that I forgot to hold my arms as stiffly straight as I could. When my hands touched the water at a speed of thirty feet per second, they were forced against my head which descended also at thirty feet per second. The sad result was that I got a bump on the center of my skull that prevented me from daring to use a comb on it for three weeks. When I came up for air, all were clapping and the lights went out. I was a little dizzy from the blow on my head. I swam out in the dark and took a shower. Wow! what an experience! What a headache!

I could not afford to go upstairs. All the money I possessed in this world was one solitary one pound note (U.S.$ 4.00). It was safely stowed in the pocket of my jacket. The jacket of my only good suit. It was the one I was now wearing. I was not going to waste my money on a drink. It was too beautiful a night to go home. The moon reflected on the still water of the harbor. Lights shone almost orange in contrast to the moonlight. The band played most beautiful Bing Crosby music. It was hard to believe that there was a war on. I leaned against one of the poles which supported the chain with the rings. On the opposite side of the pool was the Club, people dancing and spending money lavishly. I thought, I must paint this scene one day.

I was thus minding my own business, when Winnie Chen and another pretty Chinese girl, Orange Blossom, came along.

"Hi Arnold, why aren't you dancing?"

"It is so beautiful here tonight, much nicer than in the big crowd upstairs."

"You may be right. I haven't seen you around lately." (No wonder, I had been interned.)

"It must be hard to go across those rings," piped up the other charmer.

I followed her eyes to the rings spanning the pool.

"Naah, that's nothing."

"Nothing?! I bet you, you can't do it."

"Sure I can. Done it many times."

"Oh yea? Show me!"

"Not in my good clothes and shoes on my feet and the rope is so low, my feet would dangle in the water."

"Excuses, excuses, excuses," said Winnie.

"Then take off your shoes," said the other.

"No, I won't."

I had holes in my socks. I did not want those two pretty girls to laugh at me.

Now, it is well known, Chinese tend to bet. Winnie is Chinese.

"I bet you an ice cream, you can't do it."

"You are on!"

I climbed on the two foot platform and swung from the first ring. Drums rolled fortissimo. The flood lights from both ends of the pool caught me. As I approached the next ring, the drums sounded mezzo forte. When I touched the second ring, they resumed their crescendo. I had forgotten all about Walter. He reminded me that he was still there in his own inimitable way. I must have really looked comical, swinging with my knees raised so that the feet would not drag in the water, my jacket flapping wide open, and my tie swinging in rhythm with my arms.

The crowd went wild!

"He is going to fall in!"

"How much are you going to bet?!"

Girls screamed! The voices were just too many to distinguish. I did not know how my one and only pound note in my pocket would dry. I was not going to risk a wet pound note! In the meantime the drums reduced their volume when I came near the next ring and resumed their crescendo as a new swing started. I came to the second to last ring, when I noticed that Winnie had run around the pool and had the last ring firmly in her hand. I could not possibly land!

There was only one thing to do: Swing back the 66' to where I had started. The screams were louder than the drums. Because of the flood lights in my eyes I could not see further than to the next ring. I had not considered that there were two girls in the act. Not until I was practically back at the starting point, could I see that the other held on to the last ring. She had a mischievous smile on her face and seemed to amuse herself immensely. I begged her to let go of the ring. She shook her head and laughed out loud. It was no use. I had to swing back again. I knew the Chens to be kind people. Maybe Winnie, too, had a heart.

I stopped in the middle of the pool and puzzled as to what to do.

Why could I never resist a dare?! Ever since I was a little boy I had that fault! A smart person learns from the mistakes of others. The average learns from his own mistakes. Why did I have to belong to the extra stupid ones who do not even learn from their own mistakes?!

For a minute I thought I would dive straight in and get it over with. My hands were soft from swimming earlier. The rings were rusty and rough, and blood started to trickle onto my sleeves. The crowd was having a wonderful time at my expense! None were more delighted than Winnie, Orange Blossom, and Walter Rogers. They and I were the only people present who knew that this clown act was not planned. For every force there is a counter force.

The sum total of all the enjoyment of all the people present was counterbalanced by my feeling of frustration to even out the scale perfectly. I raised my legs high up into the air, toes pointing up, the jacket over the back of my head, and the cuffs of my pants sliding to my knees, with my head straight down, so that I hung there with straight arms and straight body.

Then I changed my mind and swung right toward Winnie. I begged her to let go of the ring. She must have seen the blood coming from my hands. She did have a heart. She let go the ring. It swung in the same direction I was swinging. I could not reach it. I had to stop my swing, hanging with both hands from one ring, and then start swinging in the opposite direction of the ring which the girl had let go. Eventually, I reached the platform to a wild applause.

I went into the shower room and washed my hands. They had very minor blisters which had opened. There were no Chinese girls to be seen anywhere near the pool. What about my ice cream?

Some ten years later I walked into the Jamaica Ice Cream Company office. I wanted to rent their roof to put a neon sign on it. There sat the secretary prim and proper at her desk. She saw me and burst out laughing.

"Winnie," I said, "you still owe me an ice cream!"

We both had a good laugh, and she handed me a five imperial gallon container of my choice to bring home to Amy.

CROSSING THE POOL THE HARD WAY

# AMERICA IS IN THE WAR

News came over the radio that the entire American Fleet had been sunk by aircraft carrier based bombers at their naval base of Pearl Harbor. It said that the port was in the Hawaiian Islands. I had never even heard of that port before. It was the 7th of December, 1941, just about two weeks before Christmas. I felt very sad.

The Americans had helped the British to escort convoys of merchant ships safely across the Atlantic. They also spotted German submarines and their supply ships and reported their locations to the British Forces. The German sailors in the internment camp were living proof of that. The British really needed this help in the Atlantic. Now with the American Pacific Fleet sunk, would the Americans withdraw their Atlantic Fleet and send it to the Pacific to prevent a Japanese invasion of Hawaii?

It was just before Christmas when Admiral Togo sent the fastest units of the Japanese Fleet to sink the enemy fleet at anchor at their own island naval base. They did a very thorough job! President Roosevelt in the Whitehouse in Washington cheered the audacity, cunning, and masterful ability of keeping the preparations secret from the rest of the world. He really admired "the little Nips," as he called them. Later, he presided over a conference where the Japanese had to get out of Korea and give the Russian Naval Base of Port Arthur back to the Chinese. It must have smarted the successful Admiral Togo to give up his conquest.

Prime Minister, General Tojo, the de facto ruler of Japan, had his revenge a mere 37 years, almost to the day, later. He ordered to do what the admiral of the very similar name to his own had done. At that time the future dictator Tojo was still a young man. He sent Admiral Yamamoto with the fastest units of the Japanese fleet to sink the enemy fleet at anchor on an island base at Christmas time, and he did it to a Roosevelt! Franklin was almost 23 when his cousin Teddy cheered "the little Nips", but later took away the spoils of war from the victorious Japanese. Franklin knew his cousin, Teddy, the President, very well in January of 1905.

A few days after Pearl Harbor I read parts of President Franklin Roosevelt's speech in the *Gleaner*.

He said: "The first time in history any nation performed such a 'cowardly' act...."

Had he never heard of the Trojan Horse? or more recently, of Washington's crossing the Delaware River to surprise the enemy at Trenton, NJ, on Christmas Day?

"This day will go down in history as the day of infamy! Never before in history, etc."

He was already a man when the Russian Fleet was sunk at its anchorage at Port Arthur in December, 1904, according to the Russian calendar and January, 1905, by our calendar. He became 23 that same month. That seems to me to have been a very artificial lapse of memory by F.D.R.

Every editor throughout the Allied world must have put that speech on the radio or in his newspaper with tongue in cheek. To this day I never heard a public ridicule of that part of the Roosevelt speech, nor did I ever hear any comparison mentioned between Port Arthur and Pearl Harbor.

What I did hear years later, was that Admiral James O. Richardson, the top Admiral of the American Pacific Fleet, had most strongly advised against the move of his ships from their San Diego base. That port could only be attacked from the West across busy shipping lanes. The new base in Hawaii could be approached from all directions. Admiral Richardson is said to have claimed, as it turned out, correctly, that the fleet would be too open to a surprise attack.

President Roosevelt saw to it that Admiral Husband E. Kimmel, a "yes man", replaced Admiral Richardson to command the Pacific Fleet. F.D.R., of course, blamed and fired the poor "yes man", and replaced him with Admiral Chester W. Nimitz. It was a most fortunate choice, as that officer was to become the winner of the Pacific War.

In 1941, I did not know those details. However, I certainly knew about Port Arthur, and I was amazed that President Roosevelt had the nerve to assume correctly that nobody would pick him up on the glaring parallel facts.

The radio and the *Gleaner* pointed out that the loss of the battleships, cruisers, torpedo boats, etc. was not too serious, as the aircraft carriers had not been in port at the time and were therefore still intact. Aircraft carriers were a new weapon. A German submarine had already sunk one British aircraft carrier at anchor in its home base. The Germans had not even bothered to finish their only one before they provoked the War with Britain.

Most of the Western World, and that includes military people, thought that the battleship was still the mainstay of any fleet. Pearl Harbor was a cruel awakening. Only a short time later, when a Japanese carrier sank the H.M.S. Prince of Wales and the H.M.S. Renoun, the heavy cruiser and the mighty battleship, the prides and main powers of the British Far-East Fleet, off the Malaya coast in two separate attacks, the importance of aircraft carriers could not escape even the greatest enthusiast for battleships.

President Roosevelt's speech was very grim. He promised the defeat of the Japanese, but with what?! His fleet was resting on the bottom of the harbor. I felt very despondent. I could not see any advantage gained for the near future by the fact that the U.S. was at War on the Allied side. It now had to fight in the Pacific, and had to reduce the Atlantic Fleet for that purpose. Of course, I was glad that the Americans could now squash all pro-Nazi movements in the U.S. and that there was no longer any danger that the U.S. Government would stop helping the British and Russians after the next election in the States. America was definitely committed. Their bombers could and did cross the Atlantic in great numbers. Bombers had proven to be a most effective weapon against submarines. There was at least a glimmer of hope that the Allies could yet win the War in the far distant future.

It was obvious to me that the War would last a long time to come. I had made the prediction to Louis Khouri that it would last five years. It had lasted two years and three months already. The Allies were still going downhill and the War was still spreading. Dorrie and Gerhard were still interned. I could not understand why. My neon shop was struggling. I could not get new material. Times were depressing!

The Japanese took Hong Kong. I knew that the Winnipeg Grenadiers had been transferred there. I had liked the men from that regiment. They were really enthusiastic and idealistic young men of more or less my age. I wondered what had become of them. I did not hear till much later that seven out of every ten men had been killed! The survivors were taken into Japanese prisoner of war camps. The poor chaps did not have a chance against the Japanese battleships bombarding them and bombers attacking them. They had no weapons which could compare.

Chiang Kai-shek put up a brave rearguard action against the Japanese invaders, making them pay dearly for every town they gained, at least according to the *Gleaner*. In the North, in Manchuria, or Manchuoko, as the short lived Japanese satellite republic was officially called, Mao Tse-tung seemed very successful hurting the invaders with his Communist peasant army. They used a hit and run tactic.

On the other hand the small American Army based in French Indo-China (now called Viet Nam, Laos and Cambodia), under the American General "Vinegar Joe" Stilwell, was chased across French Indo-China, Thailand, and Malaya into Burma, where the long supply lines, American trained Chinese, American reinforcements, and the Imperial-Indian Army (Indian soldiers with mostly British officers) finally halted the Japanese conquest. Meanwhile the French as well as the Thai Forces in the region avoided all fighting. They let the Japanese pass through.

The American General Douglas McArthur had learned nothing from the defeat of Hong Kong. The Japanese were most obviously in control of the Western Pacific. They had taken all of the South Sea Islands including the Dutch East Indies (Indonesia today).

The Japanese owned the sea and the sky for thousands of miles. They invaded the Philippine Islands, which was under the command of blustering, publicity seeking American General McArthur. The Americans were out gunned, but they had the local population on their side. McArthur retreated to a peninsula, to Bataan with the fortification called: Corrigador!

He knew that there was a very inadequate supply of food on the peninsula. It was surrounded by the sea on three sides. He was taken off by an American torpedo boat, but his forces were battered mercilessly by Japanese battleships, bombers and heavy land based artillery until they surrendered. 100,000 Americans and Philippinos surrendered to 50,000 Japanese. Many G.I.'s and local forces died during the infamous death march to their prisoners of war camps. More than half died later in the several starvation camps from malnutrition and disease. Some were murdered by the guards. There were also a lot of suicides.

To this day I cannot understand why the Americans did not retreat into the mountains and fight guerilla actions against the Japanese from easily defensible positions in the high mountains, where the Japanese could not transport heavy artillery, beyond the range of battleship guns, and where cloud cover made flying dangerous and useless because of the high trees shrouded in clouds. The Japanese committed the grave blunder of treating the local population terribly. Because of that American-Philippine guerilla warfare should have been sustainable for many years.

Many people have since tried to explain General McArthur's actions to me, but I am still convinced that McArthur sacrificed his troops to save his own skin. Some said that he received orders from Washington to retreat to the sea. Others told me that the retreat to Bataan was the contingency plan worked out long before the War started. To me that is all nonsense. The commander in the field has the obligation to do the best for his troops and hurt the enemy as much as he can. He alone has the ultimate responsibility, not someone thousands of miles away from the battlefield, not even the President who is not trained as a general.

The radio reported that the Americans were running out of rubber. Artificial rubber and plastics had not yet been invented. Rubber was normally imported from Vietnam and other Southeast Asian countries. The Japanese announced mockingly over the radio that their chemists had found a way to convert all of their surplus rubber to oil.

Farsighted Henry Ford had bought land in Brazil, the only country where the rubber tree was an indigenous plant. Ford Motors had planted huge rubber plantations though Asian rubber was cheaper. Now this hedge proved to be very much justified. It may have saved the Allies from defeat! It kept the American industry going for a little while longer. The rubber shortage threatened to shut down electric wire, vehicle, and plane production. It was very, very serious!

It was reported that I.G. Farben, the giant German chemical

347

corporation, had by then found a process to make rubber out of wood and foliage. Spies were able to supply the Americans with the process, and artificial rubber production developed rapidly in the U.S.

The news could hardly get much worse, when some good news arrived, though no one believed it at first. The Russians with their trusted ally, the winter, had fought the *Wehrmacht* to a standstill. Thousands of German soldiers had been incapacitated due to severe frost bite. Many had even frozen to death. Their supply lines were too long and were constantly interrupted. Their weapons could not fire in the extreme cold as they had used the wrong kinds of lubricants for the extremely cold weather.

The fighting was still most ferocious around Stalingrad (now Volgograd). The city was totally destroyed. Its factories could not produce anything for years to come. Even if the Germans should be able to take all of it, its ruins would not give any shelter to anyone. Beyond it lay the broad Volga. If the Germans should be foolish enough to cross it, they would cut themselves off from their supplies as there were no bridges anymore. During the ice melt, they could not bring strong and powerful enough ships there to help them. For all practical purposes the battle for that city had become useless. It destroyed huge armies on both sides. For what?!

From the Pacific the news came in; all bad. Australia and New Zealand were now threatened. The best Aussie (as Australian and New Zealand troops were called) were in Libya, facing Erwin Rommel's *Afrika Corps*. I am sure that the Dominion Governments wished that their boys were home! The Japanese were just across the straits from Darwin. In Singapore 75,000 British troops had surrendered to a force of 65,000 Japanese. The Japanese had the control of the sky. Their battleships were out of the range of the British guns and they pounded the British positions.

The Japanese called the Americans "paper tigers." The American Forces had lost every engagement with the Japanese so far. They had been of no help to their Allies in the Pacific. Many people in Jamaica thought that the Japanese naming the Americans "paper tigers" was very appropriate, disappointing, but factual. The prestige of the Americans never was at a lower ebb than in the years of 1942 and 1943.

348

The Americans stopped producing silk stockings. It may have diminished the women's ability to make their own conquests. Now that was doubly lamentable due to the shortage of eligible men. But flight crews and paratroopers needed silk parachutes. Silk, this most wonderful material, too, was in terribly short supply.

The invention of Nylon by Du Pont was not too far in the future but no one could have known that as yet. The invention of Nylon had much more far reaching consequences than could possibly have been anticipated by the Pentagon.

The production of Nylon thread far outstripped the need for parachutes. Nylon stockings for the ladies became the most popular item the American soldiers used to conquer women in all the territories they occupied. Nylon stockings became more valuable than currency in many cases.

# A GAP IN MY EDUCATION

Display of affection was considered very poor taste in Jamaica among the educated people. Kissing or hugging in front of a third person, let alone in public, was most certainly not done. I believed that girls did not want any close relationship with boys. Girls only wanted men because they wanted children. Without getting any pleasure out of it for themselves, they would give themselves to men only if they got married. My impression was that women did not really want physical contact with men but would want to please their men to make them happy, so that they would treat them well and be good fathers to their children. I supposed that a kiss was tantamount to a marriage proposal. I did not feel close enough to anyone to ask any questions about sex. In the movies, too, the men always wanted a reluctant woman. He usually succeeded and they got married. That was the extent of my sex education.

One afternoon, after swimming, Walter Lowe, the great swimming and water polo coach and former fellow internee, asked me for a chat, after training, upstairs of the Bournemouth Club. Walter was about twice my age. I was 23 at that time. As I went upstairs, Walter was sitting there with two ladies, slightly younger than he was. They were having a rum punch. He introduced them to me. I ordered a ginger ale. I never drank since the unfortunate incident at the Continental Club. Walter suggested that we go to the boarding house where he had a room. At first I did not want to go, but the women insisted that I should come, too. I could never refuse the wish of a girl.

It was getting late. To my surprise, after a nice cup of tea in the parlor, one of the women asked me to accompany her to her room. In front of the door she gave me, what I thought, a good-bye kiss. She pointed out that I needed practice in kissing and took me into the room with her. Once there, she gave me lessons for the whole night! I found out that she did enjoy the teaching every bit as much as I delighted in learning.

A few days later, I asked her for a date, but she told me that it was the wrong time of the month. I was disgusted. I did not like superstition.　How could a woman find the nerve to ask an astrologer when to have a relationship with a man.

As I found out years later, there again it was my lack of education which ended any further contact with this very sympathetic lady who really enjoyed teaching me.

# SYBIL, THE INSPIRATION FOR THE "MIRRORLITE"

Though I was not permitted to make any outdoor signs, I earned a little money doing indoor signs. Sybil Hill's birthday was coming up, and I wanted to show my gratitude to her for all the many visits she had made to me, while I was in the internment camp. It was a time when practically no one else ever came to see me. I was particularly keen to thank her for the wonderful two dozen roses which made our Christmas in 1940 a real celebration.

She had gotten herself a brand-new cedar vanity dresser with a 30" circular mirror. I made her a circular white neon light to fit around that mirror. Thus the first "Mirrorlite" was born. It was a tremendous success. All who saw it admired it. After all, it was unique. I had never seen anything like it in the States. I decided to commercialize it. I sold quite a few through Alexander's Furniture Store.

Neon is an inert gas, which means that it will not combine chemically with any other substance. When an electric arc is sent through neon, it gives off a practically pure red light. Only two gases are used for neon signs: Neon for red light, and argon, another inert gas, with a drop of mercury for blue light. All other colors are created by adding various fluorescent powders and sometimes also colored glass to blue light.

In those days white neon and fluorescent light was made by filling a clear glass tube, coated on the inside with white fluorescent powder, with argon gas and a drop of mercury. Fluorescent lamps had just recently been invented and were a much admired novelty in Jamaica. Unfortunately, all people who used my Mirrorlites and the new fluorescent lights looked ghostly pale with a sickly greenish hue. Consequently the ladies put on far too much rouge which then looked terribly overdone under ordinary incandescent light.

I went to Father Blatchford, the Jesuit Priest, who taught Physics and Chemistry at the St. George College, the Roman Catholic High School. I brought with me two sets of tubes of all the various fluorescent shades I could make. I had filled one set with the industry standard of argon and mercury and the other set with, my own idea, neon and mercury. The latter set was pink for the first fifteen seconds or so, but after that, there was no discernible difference in appearance between the two sets.

I had brought with me a little black box with a small horizontal slot. It held one tube at a time. Father Blatchford sent its beam of light through a prism to a screen in the otherwise totally dark room. It was a normal spectrum analysis. The ultra violet light inside my tubes was refracted by fluorescent powder to give white light. The tubes filled with argon and mercury had no red lines in their spectrum. On the other hand, the tubes which had neon instead of argon had lots of red lines in their spectrum. So, I was probably the first in the world who filled his white illumination tubes with neon and mercury.

Today all fluorescent and neon tubes, except red ones, are filled with a blend of neon and argon with a drop of mercury. Father Blatchford must have told all the lamp manufacturers of the entire world. I did not.

# STORE ILLUMINATION

Before the War, Nathan's was a large, prosperous dry goods store, catering mostly to the wealthy, preferably to the English and to freely spending American tourists who craved for a strong British flavor. They even imported English salesclerks to accentuate their Englishness. It had a very, very snooty English manager. He had imported an English neon sign with an English 50 Hertz transformer. Made for English stores indoors, obviously. He called me in as one of the two tubes of the sign had arrived broken.

He asked me if I could repair it. I told him that I could, but that it would not work with his 50 Hertz transformer.

He told me: "I had given all the electrical details to the experts in England. They, I am sure, must know better than you what would make our sign light."

I ignored the insult. I wanted to prove my point.

I told him: "I'll repair the sign. You won't have to pay me if it works with your transformer."

The broken tube was made from soda glass. I used lead glass, a much superior glass. The two glasses would not fuse. I made a completely new tube and brought it to Nathan's the next day. I also brought a 40 Hertz transformer with me. His highness deigned to grant me an audience. He brought an English dry goods purchaser with him. I connected his sign to the English transformer and, of course, it did not work. I then connected the tubing to my transformer and it did light very nicely.

His highness said to his crony: "This man is so desperate to sell us his transformer, so he fixes the sign in a way, so that it will only work with his transformer."

"Quite so, Sir, quite so."

The arrogance of those idiots! I almost said what I thought of them, but I controlled myself. I took my precious transformer (I could buy no more "for the duration," a popular phrase then, meaning as long as there is a war on,) and walked out of the store. His sign was never hung which was not bad, but I was never paid. That was bad.

Nathan's had imported a huge neon sign to be installed on the roof of the building. I knew where it was stored. I asked the warehouse manager if I could check it out and give him an estimate, how much its installation would cost. I knew, of course, that the sign could never be lit during the War. The aging Mr. Nathan must have smelled peace coming. I did not.

The sign was far too large for the building. If I anchored it on the roof, its wind surface would take away the roof and possibly collapse the building in even a mild storm. In a hurricane the entire building could possibly become air born with that huge sign on its roof. Hurricanes pass Jamaica several times annually, and sometimes hit full force. I could rent a perfect spot for such an immense sign. The warehouse manager referred me to his highness, the guy I could not do business with before. He made an appointment for me. As I got into the office of his Arrogance personified, he said sarcastically:

"You seem to know more about our Company and my business than I do."

"When it comes to neon, I most certainly do. I can assure you."

I know that the truth hurts. I intended to hurt him. That was not very polite, however, it was time that someone told him off. Besides I detested that man and his insufferable attitude.

"I think you should postpone all thoughts of having that sign installed until after the War. Good-bye."

I deliberately left out the customary: "Sir" after the: "Good-bye."

Nathan's clientele had been mostly the British overseas and wealthy tourists. The former had dwindled to a mere handful and the latter no longer existed. The store had to change its image. I was surprised when a girl, not with an English, but with the accent of the educated Jamaicans phoned me:

"Mr. Gordon would like to see you at Nathan's. When would it be convenient for you, Sir?"

"I could be there in half an hour."

"Fine, Sir."

Who was Mr. Gordon? I thought that I knew everyone who was who in business. I had never heard of Mr. Gordon.

Mr. Gordon received me in his office.

"Mr. Nathan hired me to manage this store. I have managed many department stores in my native Canada."

We walked to his shoe department.

"We want to emphasize children's shoes."

He gave me an order to paint a mural from a children's story book. Later he gave me orders to cut out wooden letters for the various departments. He was a most pleasant person to work for. The former manager, his name be forgotten, and most of his English staff had gone "home," as they always called the British Isles, even if they had a perfectly good home in Kingston.

One day Mr. Gordon called me in:

"We have a large wholesale business in dry goods. At present we are losing market share to Issa and Hanna. We have to find a way to get customers to come to our warehouse and find it so attractive that they don't want to go anywhere else. We are remodeling now. We want lighting that will knock them off their feet. Can you supply that?"

I submitted a scale drawing, done on black construction paper with tempera paints. It showed the proposed ceiling lights. The neon tubes were mainly a combination of red, green and blue lights in all sorts of shapes.

"We want to sell dry goods! The colors must appear true as in sunlight. How can you submit such a conglomeration of colors!"

This was long before T.V. was invented, but I remembered from my high school days, that Dr. Lichte, my physics teacher, had told us that white light could be obtained by combining red, green and blue light. I had experimented with the quantities in the mix. I concluded that I needed three units red, four green, and five blue.

"Mr. Gordon, let me install the lights. You do not have to pay me, if you do not get white light, and if the colors on your rolls of print do not look the same under sunlight as under my light."

He looked at me in astonishment:

"You make a big investment in time and material, and you may lose it, young man. You must be pretty sure of yourself". He looked at me probingly. "Go ahead."

We shook hands, and my shop was busy for more than a month. The order had included light in several show cases. In their tubes I used white fluorescent tubes filled with neon and mercury as in the Mirrorlites.

I put up the lights as per drawing. He took a bolt of cloth, looked at it, ran out into the lane behind the building, ran in again, out again and repeated the same procedure with bolts of many different colors. We went into his office.

"I have seen dozens of stores in Canada and the U.S. but I have never seen anything like this. If I had not seen it with my own eyes, I would not have believed it. There is nothing like this in the whole world! It's a knock-out!"

He wrote the check himself and thanked me most graciously. His recognition made me feel better than the check did. On the practical side, the check was what I needed the most.

Today, more than 40 years later, neon is used quite extensively in stores, but only as supplementary lighting, eye catchers and lettering, not as the main source of light. I noticed that the designers do not pay attention to the color light they create. Consequently the goods displayed near the neon do not show up in their proper colors. I have yet to see the proper mix, so that the resulting light is white as sunlight.

# CATCHING A THIEF

I often went downtown to Princess Street where Eustace Chen had his business, and where we delivered the products of the macaroni factory. One day I saw a man take a jar of freshly delivered Farquharson's Guava Jelly right out of a box in front of Mr. Chen's wholesale house.

I told the man to give it back. He kept right on walking. I told the man that I would walk with him until we passed a policeman, and that I would have him arrested. We walked about a block, when he suddenly turned on me. He had, innocent me, led me into the middle of his gang of thieves. Two powerful men grabbed my arms. One man in front and one behind me with a big stick between them rammed it repeatedly against my private parts in an excruciatingly painful way. A woman who had been hawking fish right where we stopped, held a very sharp looking 10" knife right against my throat, screaming:

"Kill de white man! Kill de White man!"

The thief himself had passed on the jar of jelly to an accomplice. His left hand held on to my shirt, and he was swinging his right in vicious circles as if he could not make up his mind, as to where exactly he would hit me.

This is the situation I suddenly found myself in a hostile gathering crowd: My arms were held behind me by two men. Two men rammed very sensitive parts viciously. The knife with the screaming witch on the hilt end, forced me to lean back as far as I could. The thief was tearing my shirt and was about to knock me out.

I yelled to the thief in front of me: "If you touch me, I'll kill you!"

To my great amazement he waved to the gang to let me go.

The fish woman had been the scariest. That was a horrible looking knife! I was shaking like a leaf. The whole episode had taken only a few seconds. I went to the police station to report the incident. My shirt was torn. I must have looked like a sailor who had missed his ship.

The policeman asked me: "Are you drunk?"

358

I was most disgusted and walked back to Eustace Chen's office. He looked at me and shook his head, listened to my story, and warned me: "Always look after your safety first in all unpleasant situations before you act." Good advice. I took it.

# MY THANK YOU TO THE JESUITS

Father Blatchford called me. I went to see him at the monastery on North Street, next to the Cathedral.

He told me: "In the last hurricane the shingles had been torn off the dining hall roof. Water has severely damaged a very large painting of Joseph holding the Christ Child in his arm. Can you restore it?"

I certainly could and would. Most of the paint which was still there, was loose and ready to peal off. I made a water color painting in proportion to the one in front of me. Then I removed all the flaking-off paint and painted from my water color until the entire painting was restored.

The priests praised my work very much. I did not want to take any money, but they insisted on paying me something. I took the cost of my material and donated my time to their order. They knew our story. After all, they had been able to have Gerhard saved at the St. Joseph's Hospital.

# DISAPPOINTING THE CHAUVINISTS

Fortunately, I was earning enough to make my regular repayments to the Jamaica Public Service Co., just as I had done before the War. Every end of the month I would dress up in my starched white suit and take the tram car (trolley) down to King Street and make my visit to the Public Service Store. I was always greeted very nicely by the staff in a most friendly fashion, but it was obvious that Mr. MacDonald and Mr. Caithness avoided meeting me.

One good day, in 1942 I made my entry into the store as usual, when all the ladies and MacDonald, who happened to be near the front door, stared at me as if they had encountered a ghost. I, of course, flashed my most winning smile and said a cheerful hello to them as I normally did. The cashier in the back of the store could not have seen me enter. When I suddenly stood before her, she jumped as if she had gotten an electric shock. She stared at me in disbelief.

A strange feeling crept over me. Was I about to be interned again? MacDonald, through his friends in the police and military, always seemed to know ahead of time what was about to happen to me. Did all of them know something that might harm me?

MacDonald came over to me and laid his hand on my shoulder in a most friendly gesture. That gave me the creeps, knowing full well how he felt about me:

"There is a rumor floating about that some German tried to steal an airplane from the new airport the Americans are building on the Palisadoes, and that the guards shot him dead. Ha, ha! And the rumor is that, ha, ha! it was you! Ha, ha, ha, ha! Of course, no one here believed that rumor, ha, ha, ha, ha!"

I was not a bit amused. I had more to lose from the Nazis than anyone Jamaican, except the very few who had gone to England to fight, could ever lose! I had been prevented from finishing high school! To secure my survival, I had to leave home at 15. I had been imprisoned one year and nine months! My brother and his wonderful wife who had originally come to Jamaica to nurse a seriously-ill little son of a British Army officer to health, were still

361

locked up. I would probably lose all my relatives on my father's side who had remained on the European Continent! That fear, unfortunately, materialized for Uncle Ernst; his wife, Frieda; their daughter, my favorite cousin of my age, Marianne; Aunt Anna and her husband, Leo Lippmann. They were all swept from this earth in, what has become the shame of the Nazis, the "Holocaust."

Knowing what depravity the Nazi movement could sink to from close up, on the day we heard that they had attacked the Soviet Union, I felt, though I could not know for sure at that time, that my fears would more than likely be justified. Yet, it was still constantly assumed and disseminated by these ignorant chauvinists that I should be a Nazi sympathizer. What is worse, they always found more simple minded subjects who believed them!

To keep the people's support for the war effort, the British Government spent millions of pounds on anti-German hate propaganda, such as: "The only good German is a dead German." It was reiterated in all the newspapers. You could hear it on the radio. It was self-evident to all Jamaicans, that if it was printed in the *Gleaner*, it was the absolute truth. At least that was the opinion of unthinking people and there seemed to be an awful lot of them!

I had come to this Island as a 15 year old boy. I had never even flown <u>in</u> an airplane. How could I even have learnt to fly a plane? Until the War started the "Pan-American Clipper", a seaplane, was the only aircraft which came to Kingston once a week. As Kingston did not have an airport until the Americans built one in 1941, only seaplanes could land at "Harbour Head."

I had worked at the Public Service for years as a refrigeration serviceman. Every move I made had been known to all of those people in the Public Service Store. How could they have been such simpletons as to believe such a farfetched rumor? How stupid could they get? I left the store as fast as I could. Another word, and I might have said or done something that might have proven hurtful to them, and worse, harmful to me.

Where ignorance is bliss,
't is folly to be wise.

William Shakespeare.

# DORRIE AND GERHARD ARE FREE AND ACTIVE

In the late spring of 1942, a rumor circulated that a ruling had come from England that all British internees must be told why they were being held. Rather than comply, the Jamaican Government released Dorrie and Gerhard and the few other British Subjects whom they still held. They came home. There was no celebration. Both were extremely bitter.

At the time Dorrie and Gerhard were released the importation of rice, the mainstay of almost everybody's diet, was severely curtailed. In the Reader's Column of the *Gleaner* a lady wrote that by breaking up spaghetti or macaroni into small pieces, one could make just about the same dishes as one could with rice. Even the Island's most popular dish, rice and peas, could be imitated that way.

No paid advertisement could have done for sales at the Jamaica Macaroni Factory what this letter did. Gerhard sent the lady a heartfelt thank you note and enclosed a very nice check with it. The factory went back on three shifts. Besides from the Chinese Shops, orders came in from the Jamaican Government for shipments to the Cayman Islands and the Turks Islands which were Jamaican Dependencies. Orders came in from various military purchasers: The Up Park Camp (the Canadian Battalion), the Internment Camp, the American Air and Naval Base, and ships' chandlers.

Suddenly, one evening, Gerhard became very ill. An ambulance took him to the Kingston Public Hospital. He was diagnosed with acute appendicitis. Poor Dorrie could not sleep (nor could I). I stayed at her bedside the entire night. Gerhard should have been operated on that very night, but they waited until after noon of the next day! They had almost waited too long. In those days before antibiotics, an appendicitis operation was a very serious matter because of the danger of bacterial infections. Antibiotics were not yet discovered.

We went to see Gerhard. Only Dorrie was allowed to see him after the operation. He was in a private room. Dorrie said that Gerhard was covered with bedbugs. They quickly cleaned him up and transferred him into a clean bed. Gerhard recovered very slowly. The next few nights were torture for poor Dorrie. I stayed with her until she finally went to sleep. She alone carried the burden of the Macaroni Factory. She refused all help from me. She had to prove to the girls in the factory that she was the person who gave the orders and no one else.

The recently discovered sulfa drugs worked wonders on Gerhard and he regained his strength soon after he got home. Dr. Stamm had once told me in the internment camp, almost a year earlier:

"He has a sub-acute infection somewhere in his body which perpetuates this phlebitis. Here in camp I cannot determine where it is located."

I reasoned now, after Gerhard's recent brush with death, that it must have been the sub-acute appendicitis all along. Fortunately, it became acute after his release. In camp, under Dr. Ward's jurisdiction, he would have died!

# THE GAS PRODUCER

The neon shop was as good as dead. I had to find other work. Gerhard had a brilliant idea:

"Make gas producers to run trucks on charcoal."

Mr. Henter, a Hungarian with a Czechoslovakian passport, and Mr. Gross, a German and Hungarian speaking Jew, also with a Czechoslovakian passport, were already experimenting to make one. They were financed by Mr. Hanna, one of the richest men in Jamaica, a Syrian dry goods merchant. I went to see them. They were both master machinists of the top education in technology. They could not employ me with the budget they had. They had abandoned the project "temporarily." They never restarted the project.

They were making dies to make door locks from the sheet metal of scrapped cars. They complained that the metal was not uniform enough to make interchangeable standard parts. They showed me a lock which they had made. It was a very neat job. They had wanted to mass produce it, but they needed uniformly thick metal with uniform hardness and spring back characteristics. There was no way to obtain that during the War.

It was virtually impossible to buy gasoline for civilian use. Gerhard bought a mule and a mule cart to deliver the macaroni, and everything else to Mr. Chen's wholesale house on Princess Street. The mule kept the grass down at 4 Arlington Ave.

I went to Bill Masterton, the second largest metal working firm and ship and car repair shop in Jamaica. Mr. Masterton was a former ship's engineer. He got drunk one day when his ship docked in Kingston. He did not make it back to his ship on time and he was left broke "on the beach." After a very difficult time Mr. daCosta, the extremely rich manager and main stock holder of La Selles, deMercado & Co., Ltd., financed a car repair shop for him. Masterton bought out his rich partner and expanded to be one of the most respected businessmen in Jamaica. He was one of the most decent and sympathetic human beings I have ever met.

He listened to me, and I built a gas producer there. But I soon felt the animosity of many of the other people who worked there, and since his main work was connected with ship repair, I had the opportunity to hear the names and sailing dates of vessels. I avoided all talk of ships, but I was afraid that I might arouse the suspicion of the Criminal Investigation Department and risk internment. I quit.

Gerhard introduced me to a Mr Hurani, a Syrian, who had a lucrative business of reconstructing and then selling wrecked cars until gasoline was rationed. There were no cars to sell nor to repair as gasoline was practically impossible to get, even on the black market. He made me an offer to go 50:50 in making and selling gas producers. He had a wide open yard in a good business location and just about enough equipment to do the job. We employed a welder and a mechanic.

To make a gas producer, I had two 55 gallon oil drums welded together. At the top a 10" diameter x 3" high x ¼" thick ring was welded to facilitate charcoal to be dumped into the drums. I had a cast iron cover made with a groove for an asbestos gasket. I attached a quick release mechanism, so that the furnace could be recharged without delay.

12" from the bottom of the lower drum, the "twyer" was inserted. It consisted of a double walled conical tube with a 1" opening inside, almost to the center of the drum, widening to a 2" opening outside. It had a "feather" inside the double wall which forced the water from the inlet on the bottom to go to the very tip of the innermost part of the tube, before it could go into the upper half of the double wall. The fire at the tip of the twyer would have melted the steel if the water were not led to the inside of the tip. A car radiator was fastened at the top of the furnace. The bottom of the radiator was connected to the bottom of the twyer and the top of the radiator to the top of the twyer. The radiator was filled with water which kept the tip of the twyer from melting.

On the opposite side of the inlet, there was a grill from a Franklin stove and a 2" diameter pipe. All welds had to be absolutely gas tight, or the charcoal inside would start to burn where air leaked into the furnace and melt the steel of the wall. The 2" pipe led to several filters under the truck body. The last one was filled with oil to trap the finest ash which might have eluded the earlier filters. In a "T" of the pipe, before it reached the engine, I

366

installed a regular globe valve. The inlet was open to the air. Between the carburetor and the intake manifold I installed a cast white metal "T" with a butterfly valve in the stream from the gas producer and straight through from the carburetor to the manifold. I had ordered the cast iron covers, all twyers and the "T"s with the butterfly valves from Masterton, Ltd. His shop made all those parts locally.

I moved the gas pedal connection from the carburetor to the butterfly valve, and the hand choke connection to the carburetor where the gas pedal connection was earlier. Once the furnace was filled with charcoal, the truck was ready to run. The carburetor was filled with gas, a man made a torch from a newspaper (hopefully the most unreliable War News of the *Gleaner*), lit it, the driver would start the car using the hand choke to give gas, the burning torch would be sucked in through the twyer and light the coal. Because of the very restricted air supply, the coal would burn to carbon monoxide. It burnt only in the center of the furnace at the twyer. The rest of the furnace was cool as coal is a good insulator. Mixed with air, the carbon monoxide would explode to carbon dioxide in the cylinders and drive the pistons of the engine. The driver would use the gas pedal and push in the hand choke. The first time the unit started, and only the first time, I had to adjust the air intake at the globe valve, until the engine sounded just right due to the correct air and gas mix. The proud owner paid Hurani, and off he would go. That owner would practically be the only one in his area who could move civilian goods outside of mule carts and head loads. His truck had 2/3 of the power it had when it was driven with gasoline.

# EXCURSION TO MORANT BAY

One day a little Syrian, Frank George, came to me. He had just been awarded a contract with the world famous Myers Rum Company to haul rum from their sugar estate and distillery, Duckensfield, near Morant Bay, to Myers Wharf at the west end of Kingston, about 30 miles each way. Mr. George had a beautiful, practically new German M.A.N. truck but the Competent Authority had ruled rum transport non-essential. No gasoline would be allotted for the purpose.

Mr. George's face lit up in a great big smile, when I told him that I could make him a gas producer to run his truck on charcoal. I started to work, when after two days Mr. George came to me in tears, literally in tears. The Sugar Board would not allow him to put rum on a truck with an open flame. I could understand the Sugar Board's concern. I could also sympathize with my poor little customer.

"All right," I said, "we'll put the furnace on a trailer."

Mr. George's tears dried up immediately.

The next day he came back beaming: "The Sugar Board will allow the furnace on a trailer!"

We bought a model "A" Ford car, stripped it down to the chassis, cut it in two, ripped the unessential gears out of the differential and mounted our furnace on the rear portion of the chassis.

An asbestos lined hose connected the furnace to the pipes under the truck body. Truck and trailer were ready to roll. I could not find a drill-bit small enough to drill a hole through the bolt for a cotter pin. The bolt with its castle nut connected the trailer to the truck. It was too late in the afternoon to buy anything. Rapid Vulcanizing, the hardware store, was closed already. Conditions for my release from the internment camp forbade me to go into the street after 7 p.m. and beyond a radius of five miles from my home at anytime. I had gotten permission from the police to drive beyond the five mile radius from my home for a trip to Morant Bay, just as a precaution.

Mr. George, Mr. Hurani and I stood together and looked at this weird monstrosity. Finally our customer voiced his misgiving:

"If you can drive that there thing to Morant Bay, load rum at Duckensfield Estate, and drive it to Myers Wharf, I'll pay you but not until then."

Both of the other men looked at me.

"All right, I'll drive you there and back."

I had never driven a big truck like that. I eased it out of the yard. It reacted to my foot on the gas pedal beautifully. We drove along the deserted Windward Road around Rockfort on the new bypass the Americans had built, across the Dry River, and the Yallahs River, past Roselle with its waterfall just to the left of the road and the coconut palm covered beach along the right of the road. The first test came at "White Horses." This area was given that name because of its two steep white lime stone cliffs rearing out of the Caribbean. From far out at sea, the cliffs look like two galloping snow white horses. The road led over the top of the cliffs. The truck climbed the hill nicely, went down the other side to go up again for the second hill and down.

Mr. George observed: "No problem, but then, the truck is empty."

It was late in the evening when we reached his home. We had done thirty miles. I was greeted like the Savior! Frank George's wife was a good looking Black woman. She shook my hand smilingly. She told me how much she had wanted to meet me after all the wonderful things Frank had told her about me. About a dozen of her children climbed all over me. All the neighbors came running. Kerosene lamps were hung from galvanized wire strung between coconut palms. 200 proof white rum mixed with coconut water flowed freely. I took one little sip. It was far too strong, and besides, it tasted horribly! My opinion did not count at all. They all imbibed liberally. After all, the gas producer and consequently the chance to work again, were an exellent reason to celebrate.

"We'll leave here at 4 a.m. in the morning," Mr. George told me.

I thought, but did not say: "Yea sure, with all that rum!"

I was given a small, very neat and clean room. I fell asleep almost immediately. I had had a long day. I had done physical work since 8 a.m. till it became dark and then drove to Morant Bay never having driven a truck before.

"Time to go!" It was Mr. George's voice. "Four o'clock, Sir."

I washed and shaved quickly. On the truck were several bags of charcoal. The gas producer was full and ready to be lit. We had a quick breakfast and drove off in the pitch darkness to Duckensfield Estate.

We arrived before sunrise. It was bright enough to be able to see that there were five East Indian laborers in front of the gate with shining two foot long machetes.

"No one g'wine enter, Sah. We's on strike!"

"All we want, is to load some rum," I said.

I had walked toward the men as I had to pass them to open the gate.

"Call the Busha (foreman)," said Mr. George.

I thought it wise to stop walking, seeing that the men had raised their machetes in a threatening manner. They seemed to mean what they said. One man went to get the Busha. We all stood motionless. The arms with machetes were hanging straight down. The Busha arrived. He was a neatly dressed brown man in a khaki pant and white shirt. He wore a sun helmet. He greeted all of us very politely. He turned to the most ferocious looking man:

"Oblige de genclemen, na. Dem come fram a lang way. All dey wan' is a load a rum."

I started to walk to the gate again. The man swung his machete over my head.

"Oblige?! noah! Settle de strike fi's', yah! Nobady g'wine pass!"

Even the familiar, friendly, broad Jamaican dialect failed to do the trick. To say that the machete swinging over my head gave me a most uncomfortable feeling, would be an understatement of Churchillian proportions.

Without saying another word the Busha turned around his mule and trotted off where he had come from. Frank George, an arm's length behind me, kept tugging at the back of my shirt.

"Nah bother, let's go. Don't excite the men."

"But you told me that you will not pay, unless I bring a load of rum to Myers Wharf."

"I'll pay you, I'll pay you."

That is all I wanted to hear. I wished the strikers good luck, flashed my best possible smile. They visibly relaxed their tension, so did I, incidentally. We got into the truck and took off, the rising sun behind us.

There came the White Horses again. The truck easily climbed the two hills. As we had coasted down the second one, I got no response as I stepped on the gas pedal. I looked in my rear view mirror. There was no trailer! I parked the truck and we trudged up the hill. On the top of the hill we saw the trailer on its side in the bush. Fortunately the bolt and nut lay on the road not far from each other.

We righted the trailer and pulled it back on the road. How to get this heavy thing down the hill? It had no brakes and the decline was steep. We tied a coconut bow to hang from its back. Mr. George walked in front and I behind. When the trailer went too fast, I jumped on the bough. That was a most effective brake. We hitched up the trailer, and filled the furnace while we were stopped anyhow. We reached Kingston in good time. While Mr. George went into Mr. Hurani's little office to pay, I got the needed small drill bit, drilled the hole through the bolt and installed the little cotter pin.

More than half a century later I met people from Morant Bay. They told me that Mr. Frank George became the richest man, by far, of that town, as he was the only one who could transport any civilian goods to and from there. He bought half of the town and lived happily ever after.

Shortly after the War was over, Mr. Birbari, another Syrian for whom I had made a gas producer, told me that he had bought half of King Street with the money he made from trucking due to his gas producer. He was the only one who had the Kingston-Maypen route (35 miles west of Kingston.). When I told him that I hardly made a living from it, he scolded me:

"You should have told me! I would have given you a truck, and we could have gone 50:50 on the freight you hauled!"

It was too late. I missed the boat and so did Gerhard. We could have been rich. We did not see the forest for the trees. We had the knowledge and the connections. Mr. Chen and his Chinese business friends would have given us all the freight we could possibly haul.

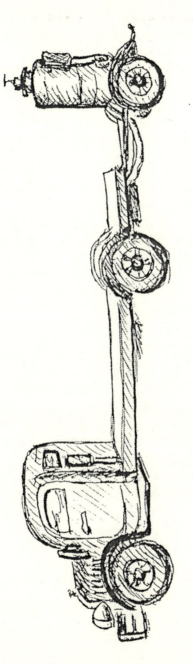

GETTING READY TO HAUL RUM

# A GAS PRODUCER IN GORDON TOWN

The Jamaica Public Service fueled its power plant with oil. They also used an about 72" diameter pipe, delivering water from the Rio Cobre to their original little hydroelectric power plant in Bogwalk. Unfortunately, its capacity was insignificant. As the War progressed, the Competent Authority started to ration power to non-essential industries, such as Chinese bakeries. The owners of two large bakeries in Kingston, Powell's and Huntington's apparently had pull. Their power was not rationed. But then, they were not owned by Chinese.

There was a thriving Chinese bakery in Gordon Town, some seven miles from and 1,200 ft. higher than my home at 4 Arlington Ave. We built a gas producer at Hurani's place in Duke Street, in Kingston. We used the Ford engine of the car which we had bought to make Mr. George's trailer. We supported the loose end of the drive shaft with a pillow block ball bearing. It worked fine. We dismantled the contraption and sent it by mule drawn dray to Gordon Town.

Every morning I rode my bicycle to Gordon Town to re-assemble the unit and to install pulleys and clutches to drive the mixer and kneader for the bakery. I took my meals there. They did not have any knives and forks. I had to use chopsticks. Fortunately, the rice tended to stick together. That was helpful until I became quite proficient in the use of those chopsticks. The job lasted about a week and was quite successful.

Mr. Hurani never told me how much he charged the customers, nor did he give me any accounting as to how he arrived at the paltry amounts which he claimed to be my just share. I felt sure that I was being cheated.

# MORIN'S ELECTRIC SHOE REPAIR SHOP

Mr. Eric Morin, the owner of one of the only three shoe factories in Jamaica, came to me and offered me the job of rescuing his foundering electric shoe repair shop. I was glad and told Mr. Hurani that I quit. Mr. Sasso, a Cuban, of about my age, gave up managing the repair shop and opened his own shoe store on East Queen Street, just east of East Parade.

The repair shop was on West Parade, a pretty rough section of the town. It was an unholy mess. It was on strike, and the strikers wanted more money. Mr. Morin told me that the shop had been losing money for some time, and that I should try to hire those back who were willing to work for the present rate. He told me that the only reason why he kept it open was to serve those customers who had bought new shoes from him.

I hired back the two women. The one was the cashier, the other, the very pretty young girl who painted the shoes with Duco. Several of the men, all skilled shoe repair men, came back to work. There was a tremendous animosity between those who came back and the strikers outside. All of the men always had their shoe maker's knives in their hands and seemed ready to cut each other up at the drop of a hat. Some strikers screamed at me that they would cut me to ribbons. I kept a very sharp shoe maker's knife in my hand whenever I left the store room/office. There were several men who had recently come back, to whom I never dared to turn my back.

It was a challenge to get this shop producing again. There were many pairs of repaired shoes without an order, name or price attached to them. They were not stacked alphabetically. Shoes had been taken in without proper identification. I had to organize a sensible system. Mrs. Evans, the cashier, was a great help. I pointed out to the workers that without their best effort the shop would never break even and therefore they could not hope for a raise as they could only be paid out of the money which came into the shop.

They have a saying in Jamaica: "Punctuality is a wayas' o' time." Hardly any of the men ever came on time in the mornings.

Some came more than an hour late. In Jamaica, employees were paid by the week. The American army base contractors paid very much better than any Jamaican employer, but they paid by the hour and deducted money from latecomers' pay in proportion to the time they were late. Jamaican workers resented that very much, but they started to come on time.

My crew felt that they were doing me a favor by coming to work at all. I warned them one Monday that as of the next week, I would introduce the American system and dock pay from latecomers in proportion to the time they were late. I repeated the warning every day for that week. I went to the men who were the worst offenders and warned them in person. I made sure that I had my back to the wall and had my knife in my hand.

Some paid attention, but others who did not, protested loudly when they received their pay the next payday. The next week punctuality became the norm. The shop started to pay for itself. Now, if I could only change the attitude of about half of the men, I would make it a reasonably good place to work in.

I noticed that one of the best shoemakers I had, was sweet on the girl who painted the shoes. I also knew that she resented his advances. I do not know exactly where he touched her while she had a tin of red brush duco in her hand. At any rate she splashed the entire contents of the tin over Stan. He grabbed her and threw the screaming girl backwards over the counter. His knife was raised high. I jumped him, spun him around, so that he was leaning backwards over the counter, my left hand grabbed his right in which he held his knife. My knife was at his throat.

"Drop the knife!" I yelled at the top of my voice.

It all happened so fast, nobody had much time to think. His knife dropped.

I let go of the man. I took the shaking man to the back of the shop and told him that I had done him a favor. For, if he had killed the girl, he would swing in Spanish Town. (The penitentiary with its grizzly gallows is in Spanish Town). I told him to sit still for a while and just consider what could have happened to him and the girl. The cashier took the shivering, sobbing girl in her arms. When she was calm, I sent her home. I told her, she would be paid in full for the day.

Somehow Mr. Morin always knew what went on in my shop. He was in the Hospital with some heart trouble at the time. He called me. He looked very pale in his hospital bed. He praised me for my efforts. He told me that I had accomplished what I had set out to do, make a profit. He also told me that there were men in the shop who had told others that they would kill me. He, Morin, knew the men. He also knew that they meant it. He could not have it on his conscience to expose me to so much danger. The doctor had told him to avoid stress. In the future the repair shop would never be much help to him financially, and it caused nothing but danger and trouble for all concerned. He was closing its doors as of that very day.

Though Mr. Morin thought that I had achieved my aim by making a profit for him, I felt unhappy. I had failed to reach my real objective, to make this, potentially lucrative shop, a happy place to work at, like the Jamaica Macaroni Factory. It must have been a sad moment for Mr. Morin to give the order to close the shop. It was his first, and in the beginning very successful enterprise which had made it possible for him to expand into a thriving shoe factory. Of all the many jobs I ever had, this had been the most stressful and most dangerous one.

# THE BIRTH OF THE JAMAICA MANUFACTURERS' ASSOCIATION

There was a group of Czechoslovakian and Hungarian (mostly Jewish) refugees. Some had money. They started the Jamaica Knitting Mills. They had brought the machinery with them from Czechoslovakia. From Cuba they hired some knitting mill foremen who knew how to set up the machinery and operate it.

Mr. Henter who had given up trying to make gas producers and door locks was the chief engineer at the Knitting Mills. He was in charge of all maintenance. He had a very comfortable job. His expertise was very much needed, as import of spare parts was impossible. All spare parts had to be made locally. Mr. Ebersohn, my former fellow internee who once had a small textile factory in Vienna, started the manufacture of ladies' undergarments with about 20 sewing machines in one part of the Knitting Mills. Henter was allowed to accept outside contracts on his own account.

Gerhard thought the world of Mr. Henter and the two started a prototype cement plant in the backyard of the Macaroni Factory. The project swallowed a lot of Dorrie and Gerhard's money, but it never made cement. Eventually they realized that the experiment would cost far more than they had anticipated. They questioned whether they would ever earn as much from the results as it had already cost them. They gave up. They remained good friends though.

Unfortunately, there was an enormous amount of prejudice against Jamaican made goods, though some were world famous, such as Jamaica rum, sugar, coffee, cocoa, ginger, coconut oil products, Farquharson's Guava Jelly and Orange Marmalade, and many others. Other Jamaican goods were for local consumption and of high quality, such as the products of the Jamaica Macaroni Factory, the Jamaica Knitting Mills, shoes, shirts, underwear, perfume, Red Stripe Beer, soft drinks, and many others.

There was a firm of wholesalers who marketed their goods under the brand name of Redd-O. All their packages sported that name in red, inside a big red "O". In competition to Mr. Chen they bought about 20% of the goods from the Jamaica Macaroni Factory.

Their boxes had been imported from America and were marked "Printed in America." That little print was enough to make some people believe that they were buying American goods.

One day a prominent Jamaican who did not know of Gerhard's connection to the Jamaica Macaroni Factory told Gerhard: "You know, with this rice shortage we buy a lot of spaghetti instead. We buy Redd-O now. It is so much better than that local stuff. There's just no comparison."

What the man did not know was that the "inferior local stuff" as he called it was made out of the same batch of flour, dried the same way, sterilized the same way, only put into different boxes as the "much superior" Redd-O. Gerhard wisely did not say a word.

The Jamaican Government doled out permits to members of the Jamaica Chamber of Commerce to import goods to be paid for with "hard currency," i.e. U.S. dollars or Canadian dollars. It was a sort of "old boys' club." The importers who got the coveted permits were usually of old Jamaican families and merchants from the British Isles and a few Syrians but hardly any Chinese. A few manufacturers were also members of the Chamber, but almost all were mainly merchants with only an insignificant income coming from producing anything.

The few Jamaican manufacturers who made their living by producing something, remonstrated with the authorities that there would be many more items available in the Island if they would be allowed the limited amount of dollars allotted to the Colony to purchase raw materials and then manufacture goods locally. Besides, they would employ a lot of Jamaicans gainfully. The Chamber had all the pull, and the manufacturers were not even organized.

Harry Vendreyes was a very interesting man. He was White with flowing white hair. He was a walking encyclopedia, an extremely capable mechanic, jeweler, gun smith, and plater. He had a house in Johns Lane with his shop on the ground floor. It was certainly eccentric in class conscious Jamaica for a man of above average means to live in downtown Johns Lane. Saturday afternoons he had a little chess club at his home, where Gerhard played chess with him.

Mr. Vendreyes was also the Vice President of the Jamaica

379

Chamber of Commerce. He was the very eloquent spokesman for the manufacturers. He founded a third political party, the Jamaica Democratic Party. It was opposed to independence, strongly capitalistic, and it wanted to retain the limited franchise where only tax payers were allowed to vote. His party was opposed to Manley's P.N.P. on all points, but only opposed to Bustamante's J.L.P. on the last point.

Gerhard and Harry got on very well.

There was also a perfume manufacturer on Princess Street who felt very strongly that manufacturers should organize. Harry, Gerhard, the perfume manufacturers and a few others got together to start the Jamaica Manufacturers Association. Mr. Tai Ten Quee with all his money was very happy to lend his support. Harry became the first President, Gerhard the director of the Food Group. Later, as I joined with my Glasslite Co., I became the director of the Miscellaneous Group. I also joined the Saturday afternoon Chess Club.

After the first few monthly meetings, we became a pretty large organization. It was decided that the duties charged on imported goods were illogical. The categories were divided into electrical goods, furniture, dry goods, chemicals, cosmetics, pharmaceuticals, etc. A tariff committee was formed, headed by Harry Vendreyes himself. Gerhard, the perfume manufacturer whose name I have forgotten, and I formed that committee. We went through every item mentioned in the existing tariff used by the customs department. We classified the items under: Absolute raw material, such as crude oil, cement, wheat, oats, hops, malt, (to make beer), undressed lumber, etc., no import duty; slightly manufactured, such as corrugated sheeting, dressed lumber, essential oils, syrups for the manufacture of soft drinks, bottles, crown corks, various packaging material, pipes, tubing, raw castings, cloth, etc., low duty; manufactured goods like refrigerators, clocks, finished clothing, furniture, cars, trucks, etc., a much higher duty; luxury goods, such as perfumes, silk dresses, speed boats, fancy cars, etc., a very high duty. Such a tariff would have gone a long way to alleviate Jamaica's unemployment problem. The Colonial Secretary's Office rejected our proposal. It was never submitted to the legislature.

One of the most essential needs of just any manufacturing

process is a reliable supply of water. While I was interned, a team of English engineers had come from England to study the problem and make a recommendation. They found a very substantial bed of clay in the Mona area north of the Long Mountain. Ideal! They went home to dreary, drizzly London and designed the Mona Reservoir and named it after the Governor, Richard's Reservoir.

Bulldozers came and made a high dam of clay around a large area. They scraped almost down to the bare limestone. They must have found statistics about the annual rain fall in the Kingston area. With a safety factor of four, they must have divided that figure of 365 by 4 and came up with 91, by which to divide the quantity of water. So they had an adequate canal built to take that much water to the reservoir.

A hurricane passed the island and dumped almost a year's supply of water in a day! The Hope River came down, rolling boulders weighing many tons. They blocked the pretty little canal. All of Hope Gardens was underwater but whatever water reached the Richard's Reservoir did not come via the canal. A very much wider canal was eventually built. The next rainy season, the canal did deliver enormous quantities of water into the reservoir. Unfortunately, it did not stay. The formally brown brush land all around the reservoir sported a verdure nobody ever expected to see in this dry, barren area. On the Caribbean side of the Long Mountain, bitter water springs appeared, where there had never been a spring before. The bottom of the reservoir grew a nice green lawn, but the limestone, of which almost all the island was formed was very porous and would never hold water. The wonderful clay the engineers had seen had all been bulldozed away to make the impressive high dam.

I wrote a memorandum, stating that just a few miles north, where the canal for the reservoir starts, there is the only area in Jamaica which is pure impervious granite, the Blue Mountain Range. Near the bridge, where the road forks, the left to Newcastle and the right to Gordon Town, the valley is very narrow. A dam should be built there, blocking the valley. It would be able to hold enormous quantities of water. The dam would, of course, have to be designed as earthquake proof as humanly possible. A properly designed dam would most certainly create a beautiful reservoir which would hold all the water they could ever use.

To this day I cannot understand why anyone could recommend building a reservoir on limestone, when there are miles of river running over a granite bed right there! My memorandum was copied on the Jamaica Manufacturers Association's best stationery, signed by our President, sent to the Colonial Secretary's Office and was never heard of again.

# THE JAMAICA KNITTING MILLS

Mr. Henter got me a job at the Jamaica Knitting Mills as his assistant. He told me: "Arnohld, de Eenglish dey lose ze Var because of ze eench seesteem. Vhot take von Yerman enyineer von hour to feeguur out, take von hondred Eenglish enyineer von hondred hour to feeguur out." He looked very sad. He would not touch a job if the dimensions were given in inches. I had to convert everything to the metric system before he gave out the work. It was a time long before the electronic calculator was invented, and I had no conversion charts. I had to use pencil and paper to get the needed results.

Fortunately for Henter, the machinery used metric fasteners and the Cuban foremen used the metric system exclusively. The men in the maintenance shop had to learn to work with the metric system. We seldom got work where the dimensions were given in inches. He had some pretty good help, one machinist, one millwright, and one apprentice, Sonny. Sonny was a very tall, good natured youngster. Just as in the old days at the bakery we needed a lot of languages to converse: English, Spanish, Slovak, Hungarian, and a little bit of German here and there.

One rainy morning as I came to work, Henter Ur, as he was respectfully called in his native Hungarian, sat in his chair by his desk. He stretched his clay covered boots toward me and asked: "Arnohld, vhot sis?"

"Dirt," I said.

"No, Arnohld, is mudsa."

"It's what? I never heard that word before. What language is that supposed to be?"

Mr. Henter was always afraid to lose face and be teased because of his very limited knowledge of English. He turned to Sonny: "Sohny, you tell me lie?!"

"Noa, Sah. Is mud, Sah."

"Mr. Arnohld tell me there is no mudsa. He never hear of mudsa! You fool me?!" The rest of the shop had some difficulty to suppress their laughter.

Poor Sonny was desperate: "Is trut me ah tell you, Sah. Is mud, Sah."

I had to explain to Henter Ur that "mud" and "Sir" were two different words, and that "mud" described the type of dirt on his boots very well. Tranquillity was restored.

As import of repair parts was absolutely impossible, all parts had to be made right in the shop. I learned how to recognize different qualities of steel, weld, harden steel and, if need be, redesign machines to accept our parts, and yet put out the same goods. Though the job did not pay very much, it was very helpful to learn under a real master tool maker. It was better than going to the finest technical school.

Henter obviously liked to augment his income by outside jobs. There was a little Slovakian-Jew, Dr. Weiss. He was a chemist and lawyer (in Czechoslovakia). He was unbelievably lazy. He played an excellent game of chess. He usually beat his opponent, even Vendreyes and Gerhard. This man had been blessed with a very diligent and talented little wife who tried to earn a living for the two by making very high quality artificial flowers. She came to Mr. Henter and ordered a little press from him, which was electrically heated and could shape pieces of rayon or silk into curved flower petals.

The Weisses lived on Old Hope Road, near Papine, and the Jamaica Knitting Mills were on West Street. Those two locations were on the diagonally opposite ends of Kingston. To get to us, she had to board the tram car near Papine for an almost two hour ride on wooden seats to the bottom of King street, then she had to take a half hour walk or more to West Street in the broiling sun. West Street was in a pretty rough neighborhood. Not many well dressed women would dare walk there alone.

We built a very neat looking press. It functioned perfectly. The day arrived when it was supposed to be finished. Mrs. Weiss walked into the shop. It was past midday and she looked very hot and exhausted. Henter had disassembled the press, and he told her that, unfortunately, the press was not ready. She should come back the next day. I could not really understand what they were saying, as the conversation was in either Slovak or Hungarian. I could not distinguish which. At any rate poor Mrs. Weiss looked very disappointed and sad. She rested for a little while. She obviously needed the rest and then took the long trek home.

After she had left, I remonstrated with Henter: "We tried the press. It worked fine. Why didn't you give it to her?"

"Arnohld," he looked very grave. "The press needs plaster of paris to hide the roughness of the welds and she need painting. The plate she need polishing." He showed me how to wrap sandpaper around a piece of dowel stick and polish the plate in a drill press so that it looked as if it had been milled. I had to round all welds with plaster of paris, paint the machine with glossy black enamel, and all bolt heads fire engine red. The parts most exposed to heat were painted with heat resistant aluminum paint.

When it was all done, I said: "This press will work no better now, than before it was painted. Besides, all this prettiness will burn off after a very few times the machine is heated, and for that you make the poor woman spend a whole day riding a tram and walk all the way from King Street."

Mr. Henter looked at me. He obviously pitied my ignorance. "Arnohld, the more she has to travel, the more she vants it. If I had given her ze machine so ugly and gray, she vhould have vondered, if she got her money's vorth. I could have charged her £4.-.- (U.S.$16.oo) (My pay was £2.-.- per week.) Now, vhen she come here tvice, she vont the machine tvice as much. She vill look at the pretty machine. She will smile very much vhen she see it. She vill be happy to pay me £8.-.-. You vill see."

The next day as Mrs. Weiss came in. Henter Ur handed her the little gadget very ceremoniously. It reminded me of a scene in a movie, where a South American President presents his successor with the sash of the office of President. Mrs. Weiss was all smiles. She could not possibly have looked happier. She went for her handbag and quickly paid him £8.-.-. This time she did not even need a rest. She traipsed out of the shop as happy as a lark. He was right.

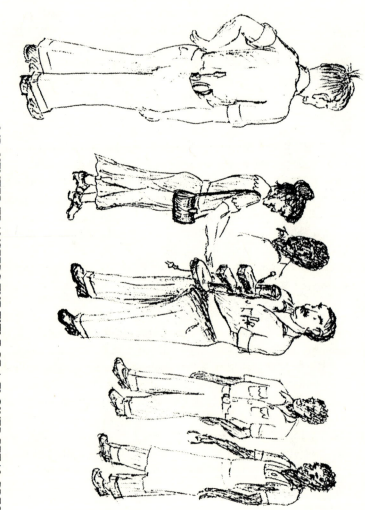

MR. HENTER TRANSFERS THE TITLE OF A FLOWER PETAL PRESS

Mr. Ebersohn's department made ladies' underwear in the Knitting Mills. That department had its own specialized "indispensable" maintenance man who kept the 20 or so sewing machines running. He was fully aware of his importance for his department. He came late just about every morning, repaired or adjusted the machines at his own time table, squeezed a very high rate of pay out of management, he took a lot of "sick leave", and he knew that he could not be fired.

The year before, I was not working there yet at that time, he demanded double pay rather than take his vacation. He got it. He took days off when he pleased anyway. As he got paid by the week, it cost him nothing. His vacation time came up again, and when he requested double pay instead of time off, Ebersohn told him: "No."

Monday morning came with a big commotion in the sewing department. None of the sewing machines could work. Max Ebersohn did not want to call the vacationing service man back. He told me that he had confidence in me as I had the (unfortunate) reputation of being able to fix anything. Who said that flattery will get you nowhere? Henter Ur bestowed the distinct honor upon me to get the 20 specialized and very different sewing machines into running order. He knew that I had never before worked on a sewing machine.

Almost all machines had broken springs. I could not find any spare ones. Henter told me to buy fishing wire of the same diameters of the springs. He showed me how to make coil springs, both compression springs and tension ones. The girls were very helpful with the adjusting process of their individual machines. By Monday evening I had almost all of the machines running. By Tuesday night all were running very well. I could not have done it without Henter's showing me how to make springs out of fishing wire, and the girls' familiarity with their specialized machines. Even so, the job presented quite a challenge. For instance, the knives of the button hole machines cut the holes in the wrong spots, the top and bottoms of the machines were out of line, etc.

Shortages became very acute. We could not buy any parts for the Knitting Mills. Some parts, especially some castings, were very complicated. I would sketch a broken casting and Mr. Henter would instruct me how to make the parts. The machinist would make the shafts out of scrapped motor car shafts. The welder would do his job of welding the pieces together. Thus, we would replace the castings with much stronger weldments. Worn shafts were replaced with shafts made from motor car parts of a much better quality steel than the original equipment. Almost all materials we used were once part of motor cars.

The top management at the Knitting Mills spoke either Slovak or Hungarian to each other. Henter spoke both of those very different languages very well. He understood and spoke English sufficiently to get by, but at times, when it suited him, he did not understand any English at all. He could act very dumb at times. He took advantage of the fact that many people equate the lack of being fluent in English with stupidity. He happily let people think that he was too stupid to understand them, when in reality, he wanted to get rid of them.

Max Ebersohn and I spoke German to each other when we could not be overheard by any Jamaicans. His English was still very poor but we spoke English when local people were around, as German was too unpopular. All the knitters and their foremen spoke Spanish to each other. The seamstresses, mechanics and laborers spoke Jamaican dialect. It was a very international atmosphere. I learned a lot and liked it there, but the pay was distressingly poor. Fortunately Dorrie and Gerhard paid me something to maintain the Jamaica Macaroni Factory.

# NO POWER FOR MACARONI!

Gerhard got a letter from the Competent Authority that macaroni were not considered essential for the war effort, therefore the power to the factory would be rationed to 10% of its consumption of the year of 1938. I visualized Mr. Caithness's beautifully manicured but dark hand behind this order. After all, the Jamaican Government was a major customer. It shipped Dorrie and Gerhard's products to the Cayman and the Turks Islands, bought goods for the prisons, the hospitals, and various other institutions. The British and American Forces were also major customers. Then why should one government department want to cut off the supplies to various other ones?

"Arnold, we will have to build a gas producer to run the machinery on charcoal. Ten percent of our average consumption of power will be just enough to keep the fans going." Gerhard told me to get Mr. Henter to weld up a unit at the Knitting Mills. Mr. Chen had an old Morris car. Somehow we managed to get enough gas to get it to Arlington Ave. We dismantled it there and cut the chassis in two. We mounted a sprocket on the drive shaft, held up the back end of that shaft with a ball bearing and mounted a larger sprocket on the line shaft which drove the machines. We drilled holes through the door to pass the chain through it.

We built the gas producer from a 10 imperial gallon milk can. It held enough charcoal for a four hour run. We put the air valve close to the engine and fed the gas-air mixture through the existing carburetor. We created the suction for the start by running the electric motor for a few seconds till the engine fired. Once the engine was up to speed, the gas pedal was set and the unit needed no more attention until it was out of charcoal.

The first morning we ran the motor car engine I watched, looking for unwanted surprises. It had rained and the girls, walking in and out of the factory, got the concrete floor wet. I could see that Cynthia, wanting to impress me, I suppose, being the brother-in-law of her boss, walked especially briskly, never minding the slippery mix of a little spilt flour and water on the floor. Just as she raced past the concrete hand basin, she slipped and fell. Going down, she hit the back of her head on the basin with a very loud, sickening thud! I thought that her skull must be broken! I was relieved, when I heard her cry. At least she was not dead. She was even conscious.

I ran over to her: "Stay down! Rest till you feel better!" It was of no use.

She got up, still crying.

"It hurt, Sah! It hurt!"

I looked at her head. She had not even lost her cap. "Where does it hurt?" She just kept on crying: "It hurt, Sah."

All the girls had come running to see what had happened to poor Cynthia. We all stood in a tight circle about her.

"Where does it hurt? Where?!"

"My foot, Sah!" she lamented.

"Your foot?" incredulous! "Your foot?!" I looked down on her feet. There seemed nothing wrong with them. We all looked at her feet. She just kept on crying.

"Show me, where does your foot hurt?"

"Right here, Sah." She held her right hand on the right cheek of her backside. All the girls, and I, too, turned away to hide our laughter. As comical as the scene seemed, she was really in pain, and we did not want to hurt her feelings, as we all felt sorry for her, but it was hard to suppress our laughter.

In Jamaican dialect the "hand" extends all the way to the shoulder, and the "foot" does extend to the buttocks, but none of us ever heard of it to include the buttocks itself. I admire the Black people for the toughness of their skulls. I doubt that I might have survived such a hit on the head! Certain parts of her were still very tender, so Cynthia chose to eat her lunch standing up. By late afternoon she did not even limp anymore and was her usual happy self.

# MUCH CLEANER CLEANSER

The Knitting Mill paid me very little. Gerhard had the brilliant idea to make cleanser. The favorite brand: Dutch Cleanser and its many competitors were no longer imported. The Competent Authority would no longer allocate shipping space. They ruled such products "nonessential for the war effort".

We bought a little hammer mill. I do not know where Gerhard found it. We rigged it up in the garage. Gerhard put me in charge on a profit sharing basis. We sent Tommy out with the mule cart to the quarry at Rockfort to buy a half ton of white limestone very cheaply twice a week. That took half of a day each time. Everyday after Tommy delivered the macaroni, spaghetti, and vermicelli to Mr. Chen with the mule cart, Tommy made the rounds of the Chinese bakeries and bought the wood ashes from the previous night's baking for next to nothing.

The hammer mill beat the limestone to powder as fine as flour. A girl mixed it in a special proportion with the ashes and filled the mixture into one pound bags. I had designed a blue label with a little man on it as a logo. It was glued to the bag. Eustace Chen distributed it for us. We sold all we could make. Our production was limited to the amount of ashes we could buy.

Since we could produce much more limestone powder than we needed for the cleanser, we bagged limestone powder in two pound bags and sold it as calcium additive for chicken and cattle feed. Mr. Chen, who raised chicken at the time, told us with a big smile that the egg shells were much stronger since he used our calcium additive. It sold well. The customers were happy with our products.

# BOARDING AT MRS. GENTILE

Dorrie, Gerhard, and I all thought it best that I move out of Arlington Avenue. I longed for a quiet room close to Sirgani's Beach in Bournemouth Gardens. Mrs. Gentile had such a room for rent. She was a charming lady in her early thirties, with a progressing middle age spread. She had a very well behaved little boy of about ten. She made her living by dress making.

There was another boarder, Mr. Bob Morris, an affable motor car salesman. He and I shared the love for Louise Bennett's poems. She had been for years the most humorous writer of Jamaica. Her witty poems were written in Jamaican dialect, and made light of political and every day life in the Island. My new landlady gave me a front room with my own entrance to the front porch and garden. This feature enabled me to run down to Sirgani's Beach at sun rise, before breakfast, swim a mile, run back, have breakfast, and go to work. I liked it there. The police restricted me to my home as of 7 p.m. There was no T.V. in those days and none of us could afford a radio. I was restricted to reading at nights. So, it was no wonder that I could get up very early and go swimming at the first light of day.

One Sunday a hurricane passed south of Kingston. We had some terrific winds. I stood by the window of my room and watched things flying through the air outside. It was afternoon, but the clouds and the driving rain made it fairly dark.

Opposite us lived Mr. and Mrs. Green. They had a beautiful lignum vitae tree in their front garden. The wood of that tree is so tough and hard that an ax cannot cut it. Its wood is so dense that it will sink in water. That tree did not sway nor bend like all the other trees. At the top of its trunk it divided into two main branches, where the crown started. Suddenly one of the limbs separated. I could not hear any sound over the roar of the storm. Half of the crown of this heavy, strong, and mighty tree floated in the air like a balloon. It sailed over the roof of the Greens' house and disappeared. If I had not seen it with my own eyes, I would never have believed it possible!

The next day I looked for broken neon signs. I removed

dangling glass and made sure that there were no fire hazards. Repairs had to wait till after the end of the War.

Next door to us lived Mrs. Gentile's friend Mrs. Smith. Her hard drinking son, Harry Smith, kept harping that Mrs. Gentile "harbored damned Germans." Early one Sunday afternoon, Harry called Mrs. Gentile to the garden gate. I begged her not to go, as I had heard from some swimmers that Harry wanted to harm me. I also suspected that the man was drunk already, even though it was early in the afternoon. But the trusting, sweet Mrs. Gentile went anyway.

They started to argue about me, and Harry got very loud and excited. I called out repeatedly from the verandah, imploring Mrs. Gentile to come in, but she had to defend her decision to rent a room to me. Mrs. Smith seeing her darling son getting so worked up came out and begged him vehemently, but in vain, to come in.

Suddenly Harry swung his right fist into poor Mrs. Gentile's eye, smashing her glasses embedding glass splinters in her skin all around her eye. Plastics had not yet been invented, much less plastic lenses. She staggered backwards. Harry opened the garden gate to attack her in her own garden. I rushed at him. He had a trim figure and was much taller than I am. He looked like a powerful opponent. I pushed him back into the street and told him to leave my landlady alone. He yelled: "I'm going to kill you, you damned Nazi!" With that he swung at me. I ducked and he missed. I wanted to avoid a fight if at all possible, but excited Mrs. Gentile would not go into the house. She stood there besides us with blood all around her left eye, explaining her position to little, old Mrs. Smith. Feeble, worried Mrs. Smith was not even listening. She was busily, but futilely tugging at her darling boy's sleeve, begging him to go home. I could not leave my defenseless landlady with this idiot reeking of rum. Not even his mother could influence him at this stage.

The fool came at me again. I ducked under his swing, clamped my arms around his waist and pressed my head against his chest. He fell backwards grabbing the back of my shirt with his left hand. As I did not want my good shirt torn, I went down on top of him. My right knee was on his chest and my left knee on his right arm. He could not move, and my hands were free. I

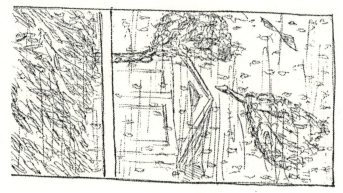

could have punched him anywhere I wanted to, if I had wanted to. I told him as calmly as I could: "Let go of my shirt, and I'll get up and let you go." But he held tightly onto my shirt as if that could alleviate his disadvantage.

His mother screamed at the top of her lungs: "The German is killing my son! Help! **Help! Murder! <u>Murder!</u>"** All the neighbors came running. I kept repeating to let go of my shirt. It was useless. A powerful neighbor, he runs a weekly magazine, lifted me off Harry, and thereby ripped my shirt very badly.

The last thing I wanted was a distorted version of the situation to get to the press! I went with the editor to his house and let him question me. He promised me not to publish the story. Fortunately, he had the good sense to keep his word.

Mrs. Gentile's eye was not damaged. I pulled glass splinters out of her skin all around the eye. She sported a good shiner for a week. She had to buy new glasses and I was minus a shirt. Mrs. Gentile told me that Mrs. Smith said that Harry complained about chest pains and was contemplating to sue me. I was happy that he did not. I would not have minded in peace time, but with all the war hysteria, the less publicity the better. Nevertheless, I was amazed at the nerve of that bum!

# TURNING POINTS OF THE WAR

Since the fall of 1942 the most devastating battle of Stalingrad (since renamed Volgograd) had raged. The full significance of that man devouring fire and ice horror did not become immediately clear to me. It was reported at that time that the Russians needed shoes more urgently than arms. British convoys got through at great cost of ships and lives, to bring shoes, ammunition, and arms. This battle of Stalingrad was the turning point of the War in Europe. From the Russian counter offensive of the winter of 1942/43, about a year after the Americans got into the War, the War in Europe had been decided against the Germans. The Nazis did not have a chance from that battle on to recoup their losses. The Red Army encircled and destroyed the retreating, freezing Germans by the tens of thousands.

America's role was to manufacture and to supply ammunition and food. The British Navy and Merchant Marine was delivering supplies by sea to Russia's arctic ports. They had to fight off the determined attacks by the German Navy and Air Force.

The stalled land war in Africa was no longer decisive for the outcome of the War. It became increasingly clear to all but the German people, whose press was strictly controlled, that Russia had won the War at Stalingrad. Hitler should have sued for peace at that time to save lives and the extensive destruction of Europe.

The Western Allies efforts could only be an anticlimactic mopping up operation. If one read the press, however, without knowing geography, one got the impression that the Western Allies did it all.

The Japanese and American entries into the War on December 7, 1941, while the Germans were stopped at Stalingrad, west of Moscow and at the gates of Leningrad (St. Petersburg today), was too late to make a meaningful difference in the defeat of Germany and Italy.

As I see it, America's entry into the War did reduce the length of the War and prevented that all of Germany, Italy and even the Netherlands, Belgium, and France be occupied by the Soviets and possibly become permanent satellites of Russia. Without the invasions of Italy and Normandy by a joint effort of the Americans and the British, the Russians would have taken over all the Countries which had been occupied by the Germans and Italians, including Italy and Germany and would have made each one of them a Soviet Republic under the iron fist of Stalin. The British alone would have been too weak to invade Italy and Normandy.

I am convinced that the bombing of Pearl Harbor, in the far away Hawaiian Island, prevented three quarters of Europe from becoming a part of the Soviet Union. That bombing attack brought America into the War. It made it possible to overcome the reluctance of the American Congress to go to war. It made it possible for a Western Allied Army to retake Western Europe. "If" is a very big word, when it comes to speculating what would have happened in history. It happened as it did, and one could argue on "if" forever without any practical results.

The bombing of Pearl Harbor was certainly a turning point in the War. Everybody saw right away that it was very bad for America, the British Dominions and Colonies, the Dutch and the French Colonies in the Pacific. The realization came later that America's entry into the War was a tremendous help for Chiang Kai-shek's China and far away Western Europe. The almost total destruction of the American Pacific Fleet and the poor performance of the minuscule American Army made it difficult to realize at that time that there were advantages for the British and Russians that America was in the War.

The Japanese seemed invincible in the Pacific. They took one island after the other and chased the American General "Vinegar Joe" Stilwell across Indo-China.

They were threatening Australia, when there came a report of an American Victory. It seemed that the Japanese had tried to take the two American Midway Islands. It was only two miserable square miles of land halfway between Hawaii and New Zealand. It seemed ludicrous to make such a big story over such small islands. Yet, as it turned out, it was the turning point of the War against Japan.

An American Navy officer, Roshford, had broken the top secret Japanese code. Admiral Yamamoto made an all out dash with his enormous fleet, which included all of his four large aircraft carriers, to capture Midway Islands. Up to then I had never even heard of that Island.

McArthur, now the Allied commander in Australia, had to stop the Japanese advance across New Guinea on Port Morseby, the big harbor town on the Australian controlled section of New Guinea. A large fleet of bombers was needed to prevent a significant troop build up and the assembly of a Japanese invasion fleet to attack Port Morseby, New Guinea (now: Papua). From there the Japanese could have readily invaded the North coast of Australia. That huge, almost empty country, desperately needed a large fleet of bombers. In those days, planes could not fly from Hawaii to New Zealand nor to Australia without refueling at Midway. For this reason the two tiny Midway Islands were such enormously important two square miles.

American bombers, based in Australia, the War's largest and longest naval battle in the Coral Sea, and a determined attack by amphibian American and Australian forces, all under General Douglas McArthur's command, stopped the Japanese from taking Port Morseby in New Guinea.

On June 4, 1942, the Midway Island based planes attacked the approaching Japanese Fleet ineffectively. The Japanese carrier based Zeros and anti-aircraft fire destroyed just about all of the American land based planes, killed their crews and made a shambles of the American installations on Midway.

Many of the Japanese planes, now low on fuel, landed on their own carriers. Others circled overhead waiting their turn to refuel, when the American carrier based bombers attacked. In minutes the Japanese carriers were sinking or burning from the unanticipated attacks from Admiral Nimitz's three carriers. The Japanese planes, though low on fuel, attacked the American carriers. They set the *U.S.S. Yorktown* on fire, but did not do any harm of consequence to the *U.S.S. Hornet* and the *U.S.S. Enterprise*. So all the American planes could land, but none of the Japanese planes could. All their carrier planes, and worse for them, all of their carrier trained pilots were lost.

The loss of the four large carriers decided the War in the Pacific. The margin was two American carriers on which planes could land and save the pilots as well. Her crew doused the flames of the burning carrier, *U.S.S. Yorktown,* but she was so disabled that she had to be towed toward Pearl Harbor. Two days later, before reaching her destination, she was torpedoed and sunk by a Japanese submarine.

All admirals, generals, and political leaders on both sides must have known that this battle for the lonely two square miles of Midway Islands was the turning point of the War in the Pacific. The Axis Powers should have sued for peace right then and there, but each of their leaders knew that he had his head in a noose and wanted to postpone the springing of the trap as long as possible. For this very selfish and personal reason they let millions of their own, as well as enemy people die in a, for their side, hopeless War.

# WHAT AN ARTICLE ON VINEGAR CAN DO

Toward the end of 1944, it looked as if the War would drag on forever. Gerhard believed that a lot of sugar could not be shipped and was piling up in Jamaica. He told me to investigate how to make vinegar from sugar. It might be practical to start a vinegar factory.

I rode my bicycle down to the Institute of Jamaica, the highest learning complex in Jamaica at that time. It was known to have an excellent science reference library. To my very pleasant surprise, the slender girl who had danced with me at Elise Hill's "Sweet Sixteen Party," now almost six years ago, was in charge of the science reference library. I had no idea as to how I could find anything in such a place. The girl came over to help me most cordially and efficiently. I could not help but notice that she had a most winning smile. She gave me a book with an article on how to make vinegar. Regulations required that I was to sign out the book, and she made me promise to return the volume in a week.

In the meantime, Gerhard found out that England needed sugar in the worst way, not only as food, but also as an ingredient of ammunition. Sugar commanded the top priority when it came to cargo space. Besides, there was no machinery to be bought to manufacture vinegar. Even if we succeeded in making the stuff, there were no bottles to be bought, nor bottling machinery to be had. After a short discussion, Gerhard advised me to return the book. I had not even read it. From the manufacturing point of view, it was a total waste of time. But then there are other sides to life besides just manufacturing.

When I entered the library, the slim girl whose name I did not know, gave me a very bright smile: "How do you do Mr. Von der Porten." She must have gotten my name from my signing out the book, and she took the trouble to learn it by heart, very flattering! I was encouraged and boldly asked her if I could take her to the Christmas dance at the Myrtle Bank Hotel, the event of the season. She told me that she already had a date.

She was wearing a nice looking blouse and skirt. Decorating her blouse was a large pin of the Victoria League which featured the white ensign, the British war flag. It showed that she was patriotic and served to advertise that she was doing her share in the War by going to dances with British and American Naval Officers under the chaperoning eyes of some more mature ladies. I realized that I could not compete. Those naval officers had lots of time and above all lots of money and were welcome in every household and club.

I had met Norma Sullivan, a very beautiful red head, at the swimming club. To my great surprise, this stunning beauty agreed to go to the dance at the Myrtle Bank with me. I had gotten permission from the police to go out that night. They had warned me to stay away from any Allied military people and certainly not socialize with them. The warning signified distrust. That irritated me but I did not say anything.

At the dance, the starched white navy officers' uniforms outnumbered the drab suits of the local young men. This fact alone dampened my spirits, besides it became increasingly obvious to me that Norma felt uncomfortable to be seen with that German. Just a couple of tables away sat that slim girl from the Institute with a British Navy Officer. She danced with him. He seemed to have indulged in imbibing quite a bit of rum, and it did appear that he could not handle it very well.

Norma seemed reluctant to dance with me, (I was still a very poor dancer besides being that "damned" German). I had saved my money and had looked forward to this evening with such a very pretty girl. Her coolness put me into a bad mood. Besides, that the girl a few tables away allowed herself to be fooled by a drunken sailor in a glittering uniform, annoyed me. I kept saying to myself: "That girl and that guy are none of my business. Forget that they even exist!" It now annoyed me that I allowed myself to be annoyed!

It did not help that another officer came over to them and wanted to dance with that girl. Both men seemed to have had too much of that smooth Jamaica rum. It looked as if a fight was in the making. The poor girl was right in the middle and was bound to get hurt, least so it seemed to me. I got up and was about to run over there and push the drunks away from that girl, when Norma held on to my arm and whispered: "Do you want to go back to the internment camp?" I at once saw the danger to me. Besides, that girl was positively, absolutely, and very definitely of no concern of mine. I did not even know her name. Why should I care? I turned my chair in such a way that I no longer saw them. It was a spoilt evening anyway. I took Norma home. We said good night to each other very formally and politely. That was the first and the last time that we went out together.

It was like this with all the girls I took out. I was shy. I usually talked about technical things, such as the advantage of 60 cycle (Hertz, now-a-days) electricity versus the local, antediluvian 40 cycles. The girls talked about Clark Gable or the latest song, and no spark would develop. The restriction by the police that I had to be home by 7 p.m. every night was no help to my social life either.

I came to the conclusion that no decent girl in Jamaica would want to be seen with a German. My assumption proved to be wrong, as all the other bachelors who were released from the internment camp at about the same time I was, married Jamaican girls. The real reason was that girls found me boring. For one, I liked hardly any of the modern music. I did not like to talk about, though I knew the names, of all the leading movie stars: Al Jolson, Charley Chaplain, Joe E. Brown, Buster Keaton, Eddy Cantor, Bob Hope, Red Skelton, Fred Astaire, Clark Gable, Don Amichie, Edgar G. Robinson, Oliver Hardie and Stanley Lawrence, Abott and Costello, Errol Flynn, Peter Lorrie, George Greene, Roy Rogers, W.C. Fields, Robert Young, Dick Powell, William Powell, Robert Taylor, Jim Cagney, Tyrone Power, George Burns, Bing Crosby, Humphry Bogart, John Wayne, Gary Cooper, Gene Kelley, Nelson Eddy, Frank Sinatra, Micky Roony, Spencer Tracey and the two French actors: Maurice Chevallier, Charles Boyer, etc.

Most certainly I liked the performances of the girls: Loretta Young was number one. I also loved to watch the others: Greta Garbo, Dolly Haas, June Allison, Ann Sheridan, Myrna Loy, Joan Crawford, Claudette Colbert, Marlene Dietrich, Alice Fay, Grace Kelly, Paty Page, Diana Durbin, Judy Garland, Hedie Lamar, Ginger Rogers, Betty Davis, Katherine Hepburn, Audrey Hepburn, then there was the very pretty little newcomer, Elizabeth Taylor, and of all the comediennes I loved Gracie Allen, the wife of George Burns. After seeing her, one had to be in a wonderful mood. I just loved the performances, sympathized with the characters they played, but did not want to know anything about the lives of any actors or actresses.

The seriousness of life had gotten to me. The lighthearted chat about modern songs, movie stars, and scandals bored me. I could not bring myself to listen to any girl talking about these things or talk about them myself. I found most male and to a lesser extent, female company flat and shallow. Life was just too serious for me at that time.

Then there also was the competition. I had a chronic lack of money to spend. The dashing navy officers, both British and American, in their pretty uniforms had loads of money and were out to have a good time, while they had nothing else to do in the evenings. They promised the girls anything they wanted to hear: Affidavits to go to the States or Britain after the War, marriage, you name it. They sounded great and the girls fell for it hook, line, sinker, and pole. The men would suddenly disappear and never be heard of again. They broke many a heart and ruined many a girl's reputation. Sex outside a proper, formal and religious marriage of middle class girls was still considered very degrading. Even rumors about it could ruin a girl's chances for a good marriage.

# GOING TO THE MOVIES AGAIN

As the War was going well for the Allies, I asked permission from the police to go out at nights. Happily, they granted me permission to do so. I was glad that I could visit friends in the evenings and go to see a movie once in a while. The *News Reel* before the feature film was a much more reliable source to get war news than the *Gleaner*.

One evening, after I had checked my bicycle at the Carib Theater, I saw those two girls again, the ones I had met at Elise's "Sweet Sixteen Party." I knew at least the name of one of them. It was Mary Moyston from Morant Bay. I followed them into the theater at a distance and sat down behind them. Mary spotted me after a very short time and alerted the one from the Institute, whose name I did not even know yet. She never turned around.

We chatted amicably after the movie, and I invited them to have an ice cream at the Rainbow at Half Way Tree. They drove there in a beautiful, dark brown, straight six cylinder Dodge sedan. I arrived on my bicycle shortly after. Mary was the more vivacious one. She told me that she was going to be in Kingston only for a few days. She was visiting her former classmate and friend. I finally found out the name of the tall slim girl. She was Amy Barry, the daughter of the Assistant Administrator General, (a high government post). She told me that her parents were in America at the time.

It was a beautiful night. At the Rainbow there was a tiled garden with hedges between the tables and colored bulbs strung across the garden in a very subdued way, so that they did not really compete with the moonlight. There were only very few other guests. We chatted cheerfully for quite a long time, then we shook hands, and the girls drove off in Amy's father's heavy car, and I rode home. Mary had done most of the talking, but there was something very intriguing about that slim Amy.

My experience with girls was extremely limited. Before the War, I visited Rose Myers regularly, but I was too shy to even try to kiss her. She seemed to have lost all interest in me, and I did not feel a compelling attraction to her. Besides, there were other very nice men interested in her. I did not have a sufficient income to support a wife. I felt it would be in Rose's interest to go out with men who had a sufficient income to be able to marry. I felt very much inferior. Still I visited her, and she was always very polite and friendly.

When the War broke out she visited me only once in the internment camp. I heard that when people asked her about me, she admitted that she knew me, "but only very superficially." When I heard that, it strengthened my conviction that she would not be the right partner for life for me. It seemed most unlikely that she would stick with me when things would not go smoothly. If past experiences should be an indication of the future, things would usually not go smoothly. Now that my curfew was lifted, I decided not to visit Rose again.

Everybody was getting used to the War, the feelings no longer ran so high. The Axis Powers were in full retreat. I decided that it was time that I should get myself a girlfriend. I went to the Science Museum, a major part of the Institute. I found out that Miss Barry was in charge of the Botany Section, the Science Reference Library, the Herbarium, the nonprofessional staff, and when Mr. Bernard Lewis, the Curator, was traveling or not in the building, Miss Barry was in charge of the entire museum which included a zoology section with a small zoo. I was impressed. She was obviously no lightweight, mentally that is. Physically, she could not weigh 100 lbs.

She received me in the public section, and I asked her for a date. She told me that it would not be proper for her to go out with a gentleman until he had been introduced to her family. That seemed like a lot to ask. I was not really interested in her family. I was interested in her!

As we talked, I noticed that she was very self-conscious about her hair. It had been dyed flaming red. She was obviously growing it out, so that the top half was very dark brown and the lower half was bright red. It puzzled me, as in very class-conscious Jamaica, in those days, it was considered vulgar for a young girl to dye her hair. Yet by her speech, position in the museum, and very proper formality, she quite clearly belonged to the upper class. So, how was it that she had dyed her hair? I was curious, but it would have

405

been very bad manners for me to ask. That paradox might never be revealed. She asked me if I would come to dinner the next Saturday night. She explained that her parents were in the States, but her Mother's sister was home. She told me that I would also meet her siblings. I agreed, 7 o'clock Saturday evening.

# MURPHY'S LAW

Barry and Murphy are both very Irish names and Barry and Murphy might have been friends. Murphy is the more prominent name, because of his often experienced law: What can go wrong, will.

Dressed in my best suit with a linen handkerchief in my breast pocket, wearing my best looking tie, my shoes polished to a bright shine, I arrived with my bicycle at the Barry residence at 22 Lady Musgrave Road at 7 p.m. sharp. I tried the central garden gate in the middle of the fence in the front garden. It was jammed. Its hinge holes were about an inch too high for the hooks in the cement pillar into which the hooks were firmly cast. The pin parts of the hooks were long enough, so that the gate could not fall down, but the eyes on the gate did not seat. It would take quite a bit of force to drag the heavy wrought iron gate along the cement walk to open it. Many people had used it. That was obvious from the deep scratches on the cement walk inside the gate.

I did not want to bother with that gate. I went to the double gate at the driveway toward the detached garage at the side of the property. It was partially open which looked unusually sloppy for this neighborhood. The hinged garage doors were wide open and the garage was empty. I walked inside. I heard some women's voices quarreling. I went to the verandah. There were six French double doors. Each one had 14 little glass panes. All 84 of them were broken! I turned around. Was I at the right house? Yes, there it was: 22. I hesitated. What was I going to let myself in for? This place certainly looked run down, most surprising in this neighborhood! My curiosity got the better of me. I had just done a three mile bicycle ride uphill, I was not going to turn around and not even look what was waiting for me in that house.

A dog barked fiercely, and Amy came out elegantly dressed and sporting a lovely smile. She led me through a large living room into the dining room and introduced me to her Aunt Beulah Litherland. Miss Litherland was nicely dressed but she made a face as if she smelt something very sour. I guessed that she was not going to be one of my friends. Two servants were busy laying a table with very fine dinnerware. I caught a glimpse of a little girl running into the backyard. Amy followed her. I did not want to be alone with that sour-looking aunt of hers and followed Amy. The little girl climbed on the "coolie plum" tree to join her brother. They began to sing at the top of their voices. Amy called them: "Kathleen, Alan please come to dinner." They kept right on singing and Amy looked unhappy and went back into the dining room.

Three of us sat down to dinner. Three places were not occupied. One was for John. He was sixteen and had just gotten his driver license. Mr. Barry was high enough in the Government to get gasoline. John used it to show off to his classmates and pretty girls. He was not home. We were having soup, when blond, curly-topped Kathleen came in. "How do you like my sister's hair, black or red?" I did not have to look at Amy to know that she was most embarrassed.

Nine year old Alan came in. He went for the chair opposite me. He had to show off his athletic prowess. He swung his leg over the back of his chair. Unfortunately, he did not quite make it. He hit the chair hard. The chair hit the table hard. That in turn dumped a pitcher of ice water over the beautiful linen table cloth, gushing its content in my direction. As a goalkeeper I had learnt to react quickly, and managed to push my chair back and get out of the way of the waterfall just in time. Two servants came to clear up the mess. Poor Amy kept looking imploringly at her two siblings. They pretended not to notice.

"My sister is not going to go out with any foreigner, especially not with a damned German!"

"Whom do you call a foreigner, Kathleen?"

"You, of course!"

"How long are you in Jamaica?"

"All my life!"

"How long is that?"

"Since 1934. I am ten years old."

"Well, I am longer in Jamaica than you are. I arrived here in 1933. So, I have more of a right to be here than you have." She looked perplexed and kept quiet for almost a whole minute. She turned on Amy: "I'm going to write Mama that you are using our best china!"

"Go ahead. We are having a guest, and I wish you would behave."

Aunt Beulah sat there the whole dinner through looking as inscrutable as a Buddha and never said a word. Alan supported his playmate sister, and Amy looked as if she wished that the floor would open up and swallow her. If Amy had ever heard of Murphy and his law, she must have considered him an incorrigible optimist.

Amy told me after dinner, when we were alone in the living room under the hostile eyes of the very protective dog, that the children never liked that she would meet a gentleman. When they heard that I was coming, they played ball on the verandah which they knew they were not supposed to do and broke every window. She discovered that when she came home from work.

"Where was your Aunt when they did that?"

"She has no control over them." It became clear to me, that Amy had a tough time with her siblings, running the household, having a very demanding full-time job and this ineffective Aunt of hers.

When we shook hands to say good night very formally, I noticed tears in her eyes. I assumed that she feared that after this disastrous dinner I would never want to see her family and her again. That was exactly my resolve. I had had enough of her family. I needed no more trouble. True, she had planned such an impressive evening for me, but then there was Murphy's Law.

Early Monday morning I rode up to 22 Lady Musgrave Road and measured the windows. From there I coasted down to Rapid Vulcanizing and had them cut 90 glass panes for me. I bought a tin of glazing putty and rode my bicycle uphill again to Lady Musgrave Rd. The children were at school. I was completely undisturbed. I do not know where Aunt Beulah was. All the servants were in the back. I was able to install all the glass. I felt that I owed this to the very unhappy Amy, as the children had done all that damage because of my being invited by her.

Never before did any girl ever go to so much trouble to impress me, and never before did anyone suffer so much humiliation because of me as Amy had done that night. That she had thought me important enough to go to prepare this fine dinner was definitely very flattering! I felt really sorry for the young lady when she looked so mortified when everything went wrong. I also knew that the family did not welcome me, and that I did not care to meet them ever again! I did not want Miss Barry to possibly suffer a rift between her family and herself because of me. I solemnly resolved **never**, and I meant <u>**never**</u>, to have anything to do with that family under any circumstances!

# POWER VERSUS RESOLVE

I was not home very long after I had fixed the glass panes three miles away at Lady Musgrave Road, when the phone rang. It was Amy. She thanked me profusely for putting the glass in the doors. She would be so happy to see me anytime. I remembered my resolve, but then I heard myself say to my own surprise: "How about tonight after dinner?"

"That would be nice."

So much for resolves. I did not suspect then, that Amy has a remarkable way to always get exactly what she sets out to get. This time I was the object she desired to acquire. So, I found myself riding the three miles uphill for the third time that day.

Amy greeted me on the verandah with a big smile. There were two comfortable chairs set up, ready for us. The very smooth red and white tiles on the verandah were polished to a mirror finish with bees wax. For a while, Amy managed to keep her two little siblings out of my hair, but then Kathleen came over: "And who is going to do my hair, when my sister gets married to you?" That dreadful word! I just wanted a girlfriend. I had no intention of marrying, ever! I was a confirmed bachelor. I had long since resolved never to get married! I could see the, now familiar, despondent look on Amy's face. Amy reminded the little brat, that she had homework to do, and that the desk to do it on, was inside. The girl took off.

I realized that it was of the utmost importance to get the two little ones to like me. But how? Then there was the frigid looking Aunt Beulah. John was mostly out with the car. It smoked terribly. I checked the oil. It was almost empty and had the viscosity of tar! I changed the oil, but it was too late. The cylinder rings and the cylinder walls must have been very worn by then. The thick black oil I drained out could have been used as grinding compound. It contained so much dirt. I used the heaviest oil I could buy, and still, it was used up in a very short time. Amy and John had used the car for months everyday but never thought of putting in oil, or more importantly, change the oil and oil filter.

Amy's parents were in the U.S. for a long time for health reasons. It was surprising how much could go wrong with a house in a few months. In Jamaica there is a variety of termites which does not need water, therefore it does not need access to soil. These chi-chi, (they have several local names for termites), love picture frames which are made of imported wood. I took one of the frames into my hand. It crumbled. I had to make a new one.

In those days, children had very few toys. Alan had a bicycle and some two inch tall lead soldiers. He loved those soldiers. That did not mean that he had treated them gently. They all had something missing. The officers lacked swords, rifles were broken off, some had even lost their heads and arms. I took one at a time without him noticing it.

I bought some pure tin and mixed it with regular solder, so that the melting temperature was lower than that of the soldiers. I used different size nails, tinned them, (i.e. covered them with solder,) and soldered them to the soldiers replacing their broken swords, guns or whatever they needed. I also attached lumps of solder to their shoulders and carved proper heads with helmets. I had fun. I told Alan: "The new weapons are made of real steel, the very material real guns and sabers are made of and they will not break." He was so happy. The words: "real steel, the very material real guns and sabers are made of," impressed him immensely. He became my friend for life. I was glad that I did not say: "Some odd nails which I found lying around."

I became a regular guest at the Barry residence. The family seemed to appreciate to have a free maintenance man look after things. Amy finally explained the red in her hair to me, as I kept on giving it puzzled glances despite myself. Her hairdresser had just come back from the States where she had learned new techniques on hair styling. She told Amy:

"Miss Barry, you have lovely hair. You have some natural reddish highlights in your hair. I just brought a rinse back from America which brings out such highlights. It would look so beautiful on you. I would love to let you sample it."

Such sweet talk. Amy was happy to have her put the rinse into her hair. It foamed mightily, and when it was all over, the hair was bright red! Amy stared into the mirror with horror!

"Take it all out immediately!"

"I can't. It looks beautiful."

"That's not a rinse, That's a dye!  Take it out!"

"I can't."

"Then how am I going to get rid of it?"

"You can only grow it out if you don't like it."  The result, unhappiness all around and embarrassment for Amy.

One evening, I went into the house to find Kathleen in tears and Amy near tears.  Kathleen was supposed to be learning New Math and she always got the answers wrong.  She went to Amy and Amy tried in vain to show her the new method.

I looked at the problem and told them the answer.  That Math was not new to me.  I used it all the time.

"How do you know?!" asked Kathleen.

"I just figured it out."

"You did not use any pencil and paper.  No one can figure that out in his head.  It can't be right!"

"Isn't the answer in the back of the book?  Look it up."  She did.  She was amazed that my answer was correct.

"How did you do that?"  Her tone was full of admiration and very friendly.  I showed her very patiently.  From then on, if Kathleen had any kind of problem she came to me.  I had overcome the worst hurdle.

Aunt Beulah was next.  As it was still War, one could not buy a lamp socket anywhere, and the one in her room did not work.  I noticed that the contact spring was broken.  I knew where to find a little piece of spring steel.  I drilled it, cut it to size and bent it to fit.  I took it to Lady Musgrave Road and put it into the socket.  In those days the socket contacts were bolted together, not riveted the way they are today.  For the first time since I visited, Aunt Beulah gave me a very big smile.  She has greeted me with a smile ever since.

On weekends the family went out to Cable Hut or some other beach.  Alan could not swim.  I taught Alan how.  I coached him so well that he later became the swimming champion of his high school in all strokes.  John could swim.  He was an all around athlete and boxing champion of all high schools.  He was a King's Scout (equivalent to Eagle Scout in America).  He was in the cadet corps, and became the youngest lieutenant in the British forces in Jamaica.  He asked me to coach him in breaststroke.  He came to the Bournemouth Club regularly.  I coached him and he became

413

breaststroke champion of Wolmer's Boys' School. Besides being a great athlete, he was also an outstanding student. He had excelled in biology. He had already decided that he was going to be a medical doctor. I started to feel very much at home with the Barry family. I liked everyone in the family and they in turn were very nice to me.

# DO I HAVE TO BEG LIKE FALAH?!

The stories of the War were very disturbing. The Russians were setting up governments in absentia for all European countries. The German Communist President was Wilhelm Piek. The commander of the Communist German Army, consisting mainly of German soldiers captured in Russia, was Paulus, the General who was in command in the attack on Stalingrad. He declared that Hitler had refused his advice to retreat in time. That proved to him that Hitler was incompetent and that Germany would be much better off in a very close alliance with the Soviets.

The Western Allies, on the other hand, had not set up a democratic Government in absentia to whom the disgruntled German Forces could rally. They talked about the "Morgentau Plan." Morgentau was the Secretary of the Treasury under Roosevelt. He was Jewish and had very good reason to hate Hitler. He was a very close friend of President Roosevelt. His plan was to castrate all German males, destroy all German cities and make Germany an agricultural land without any industries. This preposterous, hate-inspired plan was published in all the papers and all radios world wide and found credence everywhere. The fear of the Allies to go through with such a monstrous project, rallied the Germans, even those who hated Hitler. They resolved to fight to the last man. It prolonged the War unnecessarily for many months.

The Allies had created governments in absentia in London for Poland and France. The British supported a Serbian guerilla leader by the name of Mihajlovic. The Russians supported Broz Tito a Yugoslave Communist of a Slovanian mother and a Kroat father. He served in the Austrian Army in World War I, but joined the Communist revolutionaries against the Austrian Emperor toward the end of that War. When the British stopped supplying their ally, Tito captured Mihajlovic and had him and many of his followers executed.

The Russians stopped in Poland. Instead of pursuing the retreating Germans, Stalin's Army disarmed the Polish Army, which was loyal to the Polish Government set up in London, and executed thousands of Polish soldiers who had fought Hitler. The

Russians had stopped in Poland to consolidate their gains from the Balkans in the South to their border with Finnland in the North.

General Patton and his victorious troops stopped short at the Elbe River. Patton had implored Roosevelt to take all of Germany, Austria, and Czechoslovakia, but Roosevelt had made a deal with Stalin at Tehran, thus allowing the Russians to create Soviet Governments up to the Elbe River and beyond.

Winston Churchill was outvoted by Stalin and Roosevelt at the Tehran Conference and was reported to have exclaimed to the American President: "Must I beg like Falah?!" (The President's miniature dog.) He and General Patton had seen the instability-breeding stupidity of Roosevelt of dividing Germany and putting all the Slavic Countries under "democratic" governments with the Soviets defining the word "democratic".

In today's world the proclamation of the Morgentau Plan, the deliberate division of nations, the handing over of all the Slavic Countries of Europe, as well as Hungary and Romania to absolute soviet dictatorships seem preposterous and incongruous to any sane person. Yet, it was done by Franklin Delano Roosevelt and his successor Harry S Truman. Their chief advisor was Averell Harriman. Churchill's vehement protests were published in all papers and on the radios.

Harry Vendreys, the president of the Jamaica Manufacturers Association, said to me: "Dem swap black dawg fe monkey", a very apt Jamaican saying. It was concisely expressing the feelings of a few intelligent people. We knew that the long bitter War had merely swapped one horrible dictatorship for another most horrible dictatorship. What a disappointing result for the sacrifice of the lives of so many wonderful and brave, young men!

I do not have to explain what I thought of Harriman and the two presidents he served. The post war developments, the deaths in the labor camps, the extreme poverty in all the lands under Stalin, his successors and their stooges in the satellite Soviet Countries and, inevitably, the bloodbaths in the streets when the people in the Communist Dictatorships had more than enough, tell it all.

I was happy that the horrible War in Europe had finally ended and that the Soviet Union declared War on Japan. I, being the spiritual descendent of Cassandra, felt like she did (according to

Schiller's poem). When Apollo had given her the power to see into the future, she saw in a vision that her beloved city state, Troy, would burn to the ground; her father, the King, and all other men slain; all her sisters and all other women taken as slaves by the victorious Greeks.

The Cassandra in me visualized that Europe would have a very difficult post-war period because the West was handing more than half of Europe to the ruthless Communist Dictatorships. Like Cassandra, I had no one to talk to about my vision. My perceptions and views were so out of line with the general euphoria and wishful thinking of the rest of the people around me and the texts of all the media.

Roosevelt said that Stalin had promised him that Russia would become more democratic. Stalin was never asked: "What is your definition of 'democratic'?" Roosevelt, and later Truman, said that they had made a "gentlemen's agreement" with Stalin and had no reason to doubt his word. So, who was I to doubt Stalin's impeccable record of trustworthiness just because that former bank robber had betrayed and killed lots of others who had trusted him?

My great hope was that Stalin would soon die, that his successors would fight one another, and the satellites would then free themselves. Unfortunately, that did not happen immediately. He survived both Roosevelt and Churchill. After Stalin's death it took six successors and a long time before the Soviet Union imploded.

Of course, I had no way of knowing exactly what was going on in Winston Churchill's mind but he had proposed a United States of Europe under the Queen of England. I embraced that idea wholeheartedly but Charles de Gaulle objected, (I wished that I had been given a chance to talk sense to him), and the idea had to wait until it was far too late to prevent the Soviet take over of more than half of Europe.

To this day, the "European Union" is a very loosely defined organization with a practically ineffective central council. It still has a long way to go before it fits the definition of a government. It resembles the ineffective Continental Congress of the thirteen United States of America, the time between the Declaration of Independence in 1776 and the ratification of the Constitution when the legislature of New Hampshire eventually signed it as the ninth State in 1788. Yet the European States, to this day, fail to draw a comparison with the American history.

The thirteen American States remained weak and were ignored by the rest of the world until they gave up some of their own sovereignty to a central government which could then speak as one voice for all of the United States of America.

A cease fire came to a devastated Europe. For a while it seemed as if the Russians were going to fight the Western Allies. Several German units, especially *Luftwaffe* (air force) pilots, were told to be ready to fight under American command. The Western governments gave in. Patton withdrew from Czechoslovakia, Austria, and middle Germany far west of the Elbe beyond Magdeburg. Berlin was occupied by the four principal victors: Russia, America, Great Britain, and France. Vienna was occupied by the Russians and the Americans.

The War continued in the Pacific region. Since the Soviet Union had declared War on Japan, Russian troops flooded Manchuria like a tidal wave. American Marines landed in the North of China. They stayed at the coast. They fought to prevent the Japanese from being picked up by their troop ships. The Japanese retreated south. They engaged the Nationalist Chinese. The Russians dismantled factories in Manchuria and shipped them to their own country. They plundered everything that was of any value from the unfortunate Manchurians. Yet, they were supposed to liberate the people from the Japanese occupation.

I met a Chinese lady who was a scared teenager at that time in Changchun, Manchuria. She told me that the Russian soldiers raped, looted, and burned at will. There was absolutely no discipline. Girls cut off their hair and disguised themselves as boys in the hope of not being raped. She told me that though the rule by the Japanese was harsh and one had to be very careful not to say anything bad about them and their government, there was law and order, food, regulated life, and commerce.

Under the Soviets there was chaos. An armed Russian soldier robbed her father, who was a fur merchant, of everything of value he could carry. The family eventually moved to the South in the hope that things would be better there.

After the atomic bombs were dropped on Hiroshima and Nagasake, the Japanese armies surrendered to the Russians. Before leaving Manchuria, the Soviets gave the captured Japanese weapons to the primitively armed peasant followers of Mao Tse-tung. This Communist leader, armed with the best weapons of Japan, could now make great strides against Chiang Kai-shek. The Americans stopped supplying that valiant ally after the armistice with Japan and thus, shamefully abandoned him and his pro-Western Allied Chinese to the Communists.

# SPARE TIME AT THE BARRY'S

At Lady Musgrave Road life continued as usual. The War was far away. Reports of victories were standard fare from the beginning of the War, but now the announced geographical locations proved that the G.I.'s were really winning. One no longer heard the words "paper tiger" in reference to the Americans. There were naval, amphibian, and land battles. The casualties on both sides were terribly great. It seemed that the Japanese losses were exaggerated and the American under reported.

One day, Kathleen and Alan decided that it was great fun to swing on the gate which led from the driveway to the street. The maker of that gate did not anticipate this extra load and the hinge pulled out. Now the small personal gate and the large gate were out of commission. Amy was understandably annoyed and frustrated. Originally, the hinge on the large gate had just been riveted. It was too short to just stick it back into the hole it came out of and rivet it. I took the broken hinge to Henter's shop. I found a square block of mild steel and shaped it into an "eye bolt" and threaded it. I found an appropriate lock washer and nut.

In the evening, I took it to the house. I wanted to surprise Amy, but I could not lift the gate and put the thread through the hole on the gate at the same time all by myself. Alan came on the verandah. I motioned to him to help me.

He called out to me in a very loud voice: "What do you want?"

Amy came running: "Who is there?" She spotted me, and my fun was spoiled. She helped me straighten out the bar on the gate and put in the new hinge. She was very happy. That was enough satisfaction for me.

One day, I asked Amy to go swimming with me at Cable Hut. She said that she did not have a swimsuit. I bought her a very modest two piece bath suit. We drove her car out to the beach. We were the only ones at the beach. A hurricane had passed Jamaica. It was still very windy, therefore the breakers were unusually high, just as I loved it. I had bathed in much more formidable weather than this in the ice-cold pounding surf of the North Sea, but Amy was scared.

I explained to her: "When you lie down and stretch out with your arms over your head, the waves will roll right over you and give you a thrill in the bargain. Right after the breaker, the sea is calm, and it will give you time enough to get ready, before the next wave rolls in." Amy had a lot of confidence in me, but none in the sea.

We waded out towards the breakers, her left hand in my right. As the water towered over us, I yelled: "Now!" meaning, as I had explained to her before, lying flat face down, arms stretched over the head, legs straight toward the beach. Poor Amy panicked and did the worst thing possible: She pulled her hand free from mine and turned her back to the wave which was about to break! Of course, the breaker tumbled her over and over again and washed her onto the shore. She lay there face toward the land, feet toward the sea and did not move.

I rode the next wave in as fast as I could swim. She lay there quite motionless. The bottom part of her swimsuit had come down, so that it barely covered what it was designed to cover. I thought that she was dead! The thought made my heart race. It was imperative to move her to a spot where the waves could not wash over her. I decided to pick her up and carry her under the coconut palms.

I was about to pick her up, when I was made aware, in no uncertain terms, that she was still very much alive, that it was all my fault that she almost drowned and got frightened half to death! It was the worst tongue lashing I ever got from any girl. I never expected it from Amy. As time went on, she proved to be quite capable of dishing it out. Though the bawling out was quite loud and forceful, I was delighted and relieved by her proof that she was definitely alive and in full command of all her faculties.

My explanation that nothing would have happened to her if she had only followed my instructions and that I was absolutely sure that she would have very much enjoyed the feeling of having the huge wave roll over her, did not seem to make the least impression on her. She sat down under a coconut tree and would not even venture near the sea again for the whole afternoon. She never told me what her thoughts were while she sat there. That was probably just as well. I swam out a little beyond the breakers for a little

421

while, but the afternoon was spoiled. We drove to her house, and I rode my bicycle home.

BATHING WHEN THE BREAKERS ARE ROUGH

# THE FOCAL POINT ON LIFE CHANGES

Many credible reports of Allied victories buoyed the spirits of most people, but the reports of casualties were staggering. This was all very important to be sure, but Amy Barry was the major interest of mine at that time.

Unfortunately, she had the most disconcerting habit of humming the German national anthem when she was feeling good. She insisted that it was the melody of one of the hymns sung in her Presbyterian Church: *Glorious words of Thee are spoken...,* and that she had every right to hum it if it pleased her to do so. I pointed out that it would put my very liberty in jeopardy if someone should report to the police that my girlfriend hums the German national anthem.

"I am not YOUR girlfriend. I am my own person. I belong to nobody. I like that hymn, and I'll hum it if I want to."

"Aren't there some others in your repertoire which you could hum instead?"

It became very obvious to me that being interested in one particular girl can have its downside. I never expected that. She absolutely refused to see it my way. Her freedom of speech was not to be infringed upon!

After work, Amy would change to one of two white blouses on alternate days. The blouses were identical. They had long ago been part of her Wolmer's Girls' School uniform. Both were supposed to be fastened by two large buttons in front. Even the buttons were identical on both blouses. Each of the blouses lacked one button. On the one, the top button was missing, on the other, the lower one. To hold the blouses together, she wore the Victoria League pin where the buttons once were long, long ago. The white ensign of the British Navy was the center ornament of that pin. It reminded me that she still went out to dances sponsored by that League and also to dances promoted by the USO, its American counterpart. She considered it her "War Effort." A most delightful "War Effort" where the British and American Navy outnumbered the girls.

This Victoria League pin was a constant reminder that my freedom hung on a narrow thread. With this most ardent, and at the same time most inane spy scare, I was worried that someone might accuse me that I used Amy to find out the names and movements of ships. I had also become very active with the Quakers and this British white ensign just irritated me. The practically universal identification of all Germans with the Nazis was a constant threat to my freedom. I had to be careful that I did not go anywhere with people who were close to the military, especially the Navy.

I had hoped that the British Government would have formed a German Government in Absentia in London with which I could have identified and to whom the German Army could have surrendered. It would have sent a clear message to the general public that many Germans were on their side! That idea had become unthinkable since the Morgentau Doctrine had been announced in the U.S. and had found popular support by a lot of people. I was not at all enthusiastic concerning the rumored Allied War Aims of cutting Germany up into small pieces, destroying all factories, and making what would be left into a purely agricultural state. I considered such a solution as most impractical. Anyway, I kept my thoughts to myself. That Victoria League pin annoyed me. There was no getting away from that fact. It was quite natural that I resented that Amy still went to these dances.

With the humming of the German national anthem and the Victoria League dances, I was thinking that my association with Amy represented a danger to my freedom, besides we did not seem to have any interests in common. She was a scientist, and politics were not of the slightest interest to her. She did not understand that politics decided everybody's life including her own. In Jamaica she was considered upper class and that was quite natural to her and could not possibly change. She did not realize that the War changed the society around her drastically. "After the War" would never again be the same as "before the War." The song goes: "There'll always be an England....." and Jamaica will always be a Crown Colony immutably so!

With that revolutionary independence movement, she was dancing on a volcano. Happily, that never occurred to her. It did not erupt anyway. So, the thought was purely academic. What was I doing there? I had to give up seeing her! It was surely the most sensible thing to do. Amy obviously enjoyed those Victoria League parties. What could I offer her? It was silly to ride my bicycle uphill several evenings per week to Lady Musgrave Road. I had to give that up, definitely! How was it that despite my logical thinking to the contrary, I still found myself at Lady Musgrave Road. almost every evening?

The first of October, 1944, was coming, Amy's 21st birthday. She was to attain majority according to Jamaican law. I bought her a large silver filigree pin. I made a little gray box and laid it into it. I also drew a clown and colored him with watercolor paints. I bought two identical white, good looking buttons and sewed them onto the hands of the clown. One hand he held high over his head, the other low, because one blouse lacked the top button, the other the lower one. I made a false bottom fom the clown's painting and laid it over the silver pin, so that when one opened the box, one could only see the clown holding the buttons.

It rained that evening. I knew that Amy had nothing planned, not even a special dinner. I rode my bike the three miles through the rain. Amy was very appreciative and flattered that I braved the rain just to congratulate her for her birthday. She opened the box. I expected her to scold me for my obvious reference to the missing buttons on her blouses, but she found the clown very cute and was smiles all over. I could have saved myself the cost of the silver pin. She said that she liked it, after I removed the false bottom, but she hardly ever wore it.

# ART CLASSES, THE MANLEYS AND I

Ever since I was again allowed to go out after 7 p.m. I joined Mrs. Edna Manley's art class at the Institute of Jamaica. It was a great help as it improved my painting a lot. I admired Mrs. Manley. She was a wonderful teacher. Amy came one evening and modeled (fully clothed, of course). A fellow artist, Topper, made a very good, if unflattering, likeness of Amy. He gave me that painting. It now hangs in our living room in Gainesville, Florida. The painting which I made was very incomplete. I did not like it, and I reused the canvass at another session.

Mrs. Manley was by far the foremost sculptor and artist in Jamaica. She had exhibited not only in Jamaica, but also in London, England. She was without a doubt the best known woman in the Island. She was the wife of Norman Manley, the founder and leader of the Marxist Peoples National Party (PNP.)

Mr. Manley had a very strong dislike for British Conservatives. During World War I, he was an outstanding student and sprinter in England. He asked for an officer's commission equal to that of many other students with much poorer grades than he had. His grades entitled him to a commission in the Cold Stream Guard Regiment. Because he was colored, he was denied his right to serve in that regiment. That was the time when he decided that Jamaica must become independent from the British Isles.

He became an outstanding barrister. When a dark skinned man anywhere in the British Empire was accused of a capital offence, he traveled there, at his own expense, to defend him and usually got the release of the defendant. Norman Manley was probably the best known barrister in the entire British Empire.

The Manleys strove to unite the British Colonies around the Caribbean Sea: British Guyana, Trinidad, Barbados, and all the small islands of the British Antilles, Jamaica, the Cayman Islands, Turks Islands, and British Honduras (called Belize today after its erstwhile capital.) They negotiated with the powerful British Labour Party in London which had formed a "National Unity Government" with Winston Churchill's Conservative Party for the duration of the War. Sir Stafford Cripps, Bevin, Bevan, and Attlee

427

were sympathetic to the Manleys. Norman Manley wanted Dominion Status for the West Indian Federation, or even better, complete severance from the Mother Country, a republic, called the West Indian Federation. They already had a flag. The Manleys expected that Kingston, Jamaica, was going to be the capital, and that Norman Manley would be its first Prime Minister. Serious negotiations were going on. London would have to agree after the end of the War.

Both of the Manleys were great admirers of the Soviet Union which alone could withstand and repel the onslaught of the Nazi Armies.

Mrs. Manley invited me to their huge house, "Drumblair," where the elite of the PNP met every Sunday morning. I looked at the book case. There were a translation of *Das Kapital (Capital,)* the book Karl Marx had written, *The Communist Manifesto,* by Marx and Engels and many other works of socialist leaders. I soon found out that I did not fit in with that crowd and stayed away. The Manleys were very intelligent and highly educated people. It seemed a paradox to me that they could have believed that Socialism could work in Jamaica.

I asked Mrs. Manley to sit for me. She readily agreed. While I painted her, we got into a furious argument. By that time I was a Director of the progressive and capitalistic Jamaica Manufacturers Association. Our disagreement started out when she told me that the new flag had been designed for the coming West Indian Federation of all the Colonies. It had a blue field, a golden dot representing the sun, in the center, and four wavy white lines from end to end representing the sea.

She said that she did not like the design, but it had already been accepted by the PNP and independence parties in the other colonies. It was a *fait accompli.* I told Mrs. Manley, who could move anyone to willing submission with a sweet smile:

"Whether or not you liked the flag, is purely academic, as the West Indian Federation will never be ratified by any of the enthusiastic members."

That statement hit her like a bomb shell! Her eyes shot sparks at me.

"How can you say that?!"

"Even if King George, his cabinet, and the House of Parliament agree to allow a West Indian Federation, the various prospective members will not agree to several points: For one: Which town do you propose to be the capital?"

"Kingston, of course! My husband started the movement right here, Kingston is the most advanced town in all of the West Indies, and Jamaica is the most developed of any of the Islands."

"Yes, but will Mr. Williams in Trinidad see it that way? I doubt that very much. Besides Mr. Grayham, I believe is his name, in Barbados claimed that Georgetown, Barbados, should be the capital as a perfect compromise between Kingston, Jamaica, and Port of Spain, Trinidad."

"Nonsense! We here in Kingston have been the first line in the fight for independence from Great Britain. We have earned the right to have the capital here."

"British Guyana has a population of half East Indian and half Negro. The East Indians would not want to have their capital in an Island which has only one percent East Indians. Besides Guyana has more land mass than all the rest of the Federation put together including British Honduras.

"Talking of British Honduras. Guatemala claims that it was taken away from that Latin American Country by the British. The inland population speaks Spanish. Would they agree to be governed from Kingston? If Guatemalan troops march into British Honduras, who is going to defend it?"

"The Federation is certainly going to defend its territory!"

"Who will control a Federal Army and appoint its commander? What ships would be used to transport the troops? Where would the escorts come from to protect the troop ships? Who will be in charge of raising the taxes to finance such a defense? Whoever it will be, he will become most unpopular in a big hurry."

"Those are all problems my husband will solve once the Federation is established."

"Who will decide who will be the first Prime Minister?"

"That will most certainly be my husband! He started the whole independence movement. They would have to put him in charge!"

"If there will be voting based on equal votes for all over 21, Jamaica would be outvoted all the time, as British Guyana has a

429

larger population than all the rest of the Federation put together. They will most likely vote for a man from Georgetown, British Guyana. Mr. Manley will have a sizable opposition even here in Jamaica from the Jamaica Labour Party and its leader, Alexander Bustamante. Do you really believe that your husband could rally enough parties in the other proposed members together to govern the Federation, and make its capital Kingston?"

"I am convinced that he will succeed. He looms head and shoulder above all the others."

"That may be so. But will the people in all the other Islands, in Guyana and in British Honduras know? Where will be the Supreme Court? Who will control the Federal Police? Will there be a Federal Currency?"

"My husband is discussing all these matters right now with many politicians in the other West Indian Islands and on the main land. They must find a solution."

"I know. They have been discussing these problems for years, according to the *Gleaner,* but they have not even agreed on their goal, much less on the details."

"What do you mean: 'They have not even agreed on their goal?!' They want independence from Great Britain, of course!"

I knew that there was a large section of the Jamaican population, especially civil servants and clerks, who wanted independence. They were the educated members of the PNP. On the other hand, almost no one in management wanted the Jamaican currency severed from the British. I believed that most people were satisfied with remaining a crown colony. Then there were people like Amy who had never even given it a thought that there could be a remote possibility that a flag other than the Union Jack with the Jamaican coat of arms in its center could ever fly from Kings House. I thought it wise not to bring that up.

"That is just it. Some want Dominion Status like that of Canada, some a West Indian Republic abolishing all titles of nobility. Others want very loose connections to the other West Indian Colonies, some want to exclude British Guyana, some British Honduras as well, and others want complete independence from Britain and from each other. There has never been a referendum. There cannot possibly be a referendum as long as there is this War going on. So no one knows what would be the most popular form of government here in Jamaica and in all the other potential Federation Members.

"To me a West Indian Federation seems most unnatural. All members have a lot of trade with Great Britain and practically none with each other. They all export more or less the same things. So they are competitors and not supporters of each other. Besides the old Lady of Thread Needle Street (the Bank of England) guarantees that their currencies are on par with that of the British Isles."

Mrs. Manley was furious. This lively argument went on like this for the three, two hour sessions I painted her. I painted her furious. When I later exhibited the painting, lots of letters were written to the *Gleaner* from: "How could anyone dare to do that to Mrs. Manley," to: "Yes, that is the real fighting Mrs. Manley not the sweet smiling timid looking lady, we usually see in the paper!"

I, personally, had always admired the lady. She was a most prominent politician, and she argued with me, a nobody in politics compared to her, and she remained my friend just the same. I was the only one for whom she sat. So she must have thought a lot of me as an artist. She could have told me not to mention politics to her, but she was gracious enough not to take advantage of her superior position in society. I do not believe that I influenced her thinking. I wonder if she remembered me, when history proved my predictions correct and hers wrong. I have a book of flags of all nations. The flag of the still-born West Indian Federation is shown in it.

The painting now hangs in my house. When Jamaicans visit who knew her, I usually get favorable comments. To others it is just another one of Arnold's paintings.

# THE WAR ENDS WITH A CRESCENDO!

By 1944, it became increasingly clear that the Allies would win. The reports of 1,000 bombers' raids on "military targets only" dominated the news. The town of my birth, Hamburg, alone suffered 48,000 dead in three night raids. Most people were amazed that Germany, which absorbed the brunt of the raids, would not surrender. To me that was no surprise at all. I had seen with my own eyes, how the *Gestapo (Geheime Staats-Polizei* = Secret State Police) had controlled the Germans in the internment camp in Jamaica so far away, and completely cut off, from their home base in Berlin. So long as the *Gestapo* existed, the unfortunate people would take their chances of surviving a bombing raid, rather than complain, thus exposing themselves to torture and a horrible death in a Nazi concentration camp.

There was fierce fighting in Italy. The Italian Marshal Badoglio and the King of Italy suddenly changed sides. Benito Mussolini was captured by Badoglio's troops. German paratroopers freed Mussolini in a daring airborne raid.

Under the command of the American General Dwight D. Eisenhower, American, Canadian, British, and a few Free French under General de Gaulle landed in Normandy on June 6, 1944. It was the very beach from which William the Conqueror set out to subdue England in 1066. Especially the British, under General Montgomery, on the left flank met severe resistance.

On the right wing, under General Patton, the Americans made surprisingly swift progress, first heading south and then swerving east through Paris and toward the German border. The Germans launched a counter offensive trying to retake the important Belgian supply port of Antwerp. Patton turned his victorious soldiers north and ended the "Battle of the Bulge."

General Omar Bradley, one of the most brilliant generals of the War, landed practically unopposed at the French Riviera and marched swiftly toward the Rhine. Mussolini and his mistress were captured by Communist partisans in northern Italy. They were shot and hung upside down in a village square for all to see.

At about that time, the Russians entered Poland. The Nazis had made it a policy of treating the Slavic prisoners and general population terribly. Now the Russians and their Slavic Allies paid the Germans back with interest. Almost all males 15 to 65 disappeared somewhere in Siberia and were never heard from again. Millions of girls and women were raped and killed. The winter of 1944/45 must have been horrible all over Europe. In Jamaica everybody looked happy, expecting peace in Europe any time.

On April 12, 1945, President Franklin D. Roosevelt suddenly died from a stroke. The transition to President Harry S Truman was very smooth. Just about that time the Russians entered Berlin. Hitler and his wife of one day, Eva Braun Hitler, had himself and her shot by his trusted bodyguard on April 30. To avoid Mussolini's fate, their bodies were doused with gasoline, burnt and the ashes were dispersed. He had taken office ten days after his major antagonist, on Roosevelt's 51st birthday and survived him by 18 days but as a defeated dictator.

Hitler had designated Admiral Dönitz, not one of his inner circle, as his successor to surrender the German forces unconditionally. Europe lay devastated, but at least there was no more shooting.

There was no love lost between the Russians and the Americans. At several places where they met, Russians shot at the Americans inflicting casualties. General Patton, who had taken most of Czechoslovakia and German States between the Czech border and Berlin which had been designated East Germany at Tehran, retreated grudgingly despite the vehement begging of the local population. He had to hand over those Germans to the Communists. The previously much touted principle of self-determination went by the board. I felt very sad over the division of Germany. It was certainly going to cause severe international tensions. It might even cause another War!

There was some celebrating in Jamaica, but the continuation of the very bitter and cruel War in the Pacific cast gloom over all attempts of merriment. It was obvious that Japan would never again mount a powerful attack, but the Emperor's forces vowed to fight to the last man in the defense of their Island Empire. Their government and military forces were under the command of General Tojo.

Their still formidable navy was under the command of Admiral Yamamoto. The Americans broke the Japanese naval code and picked up the Admiral's agenda. When the Admiral got within the range of American planes, he was shot down.

The American General Doolittle had his B-25 land-planes loaded on an aircraft carrier. They bombed Tokyo for the first time. His planes landed in China. The raid did great psychological damage to the Japanese, though not too much physical destruction. After the Americans captured Iwo Jima and Okinawa, Tokyo was bombed every day. There no longer was any pretense of going after military targets only. Tokyo and Yokohama were burning from one end to the other.

The first atomic bomb was released and destroyed Hiroshima completely with the loss of hundreds of thousands of lives on August 6, 1945. At the time, I believed that the reports were typical war time exaggeration. I could not imagine that any bomb could be that powerful. Before the Japanese had a chance to evaluate their options or even decide on the wording of a petition for an armistice, a second atomic bomb totally annihilated the town and population of Nagasaki on August 9.

The Japanese petitioned for peace. The *Missouri*, the largest American battleship sailed into Yokohama Bay. The Japanese delegation went on board and surrendered their country unconditionally. General McArthur became the Governor of Japan.

I believed then, and I still believe, that the bombing of Nagasaki was quite unnecessary. The bomb on Hiroshima, I believe, would have been quite enough to induce the Japanese to surrender if they would have been given sufficient time to evaluate the damage done to that city.

At any rate, the atomic bomb made it unnecessary to take Japan with amphibian forces. Such an assault would have cost an enormous amount of American, as well as more Japanese lives than the atomic bombs extinguished.

# STALIN'S WAY TO DIVIDE THE WORLD OR ELSE!

The War was over! There were celebrations everywhere. I did not feel like celebrating. So many young people my age, several of whom I knew, had died due to this long series of errors, ignorance, miscalculations, and wishful thinking by so many arrogant fools called politicians in high places in all of the warring nations. Europe from the Volga to the Atlantic, from Spitzbergen to Sicily lay devastated. The Far East from Burma to Midway Island and from New Guinea to Manchuria were in no better shape. All because a bunch of narrow minded politicians could not agree on some strictly economic matters.

More than anything I wanted to know what happened to my Jewish relatives in Hamburg and to Eckart and his family. Eckart had written me a letter after he had marched into Czechoslovakia as a sergeant in the German Army.

He wrote: "We marched unopposed right by the powerful defense lines high in the Sudeten Mountains. If the Czechs would have decided to defend their mountain forts instead of giving in to Hitler and Chamberlain, we Germans would have had a very difficult time to overwhelm those defenses." That letter was now seven years old.

Stalin's troops had stalled long enough in Poland before invading Germany, to kill out all Polish troops and politicians who adhered to the Polish Government which had been formed in London with the blessing of the Western Allies. East Germany, Poland, Romania, and Bulgaria all were designated: "Soviet Sphere of Interest."

Winston Churchill lost the election to Attlee. Churchill got up in Parliament and said: "During the recent campaign Mr. Attlee billed himself as a very modest man. And I must say: Mr. Attlee has a lot to be modest about!"

Churchill was right, of course. The conferences in Potsdam, where Stalin, Truman, and Churchill conferred and later in Tehran, where Stalin, Truman, and Attlee divided up the world, were disasters for the West!

435

The world press reported that they all agreed that democratic governments should be empowered in all countries. The media led the populations of the world to believe that there would be a just peace where people would be allowed to vote as to who was to govern them. Their euphoria was to be shattered soon. The Russians did not bother to define the word: "Democracy." It became very obvious that Stalin meant by "Democracy" murderous Communist dictatorships absolutely subservient to himself.

The whole world was divided into "Spheres of Influence." In Asia Russia annexed the Japanese southern half of the Sakhalin Island, a severe blow to Japan. Though the island itself is cold and sparsely inhabited, the fishing in its waters was of great importance to the population of Japan which normally gets its protein from fish.

China was lumped into the "Soviet Sphere of Influence" and Chiang Kai-shek was abandoned by the West to fight a losing battle against Mao Tse-tung whom the Russians supplied with the latest captured Japanese weapons. Those arms had been turned over to the Russians when the Japanese surrendered their forces in Manchuria. The Communist Chinese certainly knew how to use those guns!

Korea was liberated from Japan, but it was immediately divided into North and South Korea arbitrarily at the 38th parallel. The Koreans were never consulted. North Korea was at once made into a Soviet Republic. The Russians established an important naval and air base there. I saw in 1945 that dividing countries like Korea, Viet Nam, Palestine, Israel, and Germany could bring no peace, but would be the cause for unrest and even war! Of course, Stalin liked it that way. The communists always fished in troubled waters and benefited.

Truman and Attlee had the choice either to agree to Stalin's demands or to fight his huge victorious army. Incidentally, the Soviet Army walked on British boots and carried American made ammunition and enjoyed its popularity thanks to the Western press, radio, and *News Reel*. Despite its huge size, however, the Soviets were no match for the West if Truman had decided to call Stalin's bluff. The Soviet Air Force was nowhere near a match to the British or the American and its industrial capacity was dwarfed by that of the U.S. The Americans at that time also had the monopoly on the atomic bomb. The Soviets had to back down or be defeated. Truman and the press gauged the feeling of the American people correctly: They were tired of war and the Russians were popular.

The Soviet Union annexed eastern and northern sections of Finland, cutting that nation off from its access to the Arctic Ocean. It annexed Estonia, Latvia, Lithuania, the eastern half of Poland, the easternmost province of Germany: East Prussia, and Moldovia, a province of Romania east of the Prutul and Prut rivers. The Prut is a tributary of the Danube.

Stalin proceeded to establish Communist dictatorships in North Korea, Poland, East Germany, Romania, Bulgaria, Yugoslavia, and Albania. The latter two, though Communist dictatorships, proved to be mavericks and refused to take orders from Moscow. It seemed ironic to me that the Western Powers went to war to restore democratic governments in Poland and Czechoslovakia and ended up being satisfied that almost all of central Europe, including Poland and Czechoslovakia fell to a dictatorship every bit as horrible as that of Hitler's! Yes, just about half of the world's population was now under absolute communist dictatorships, forced upon them with murderous *"Gulags"*, forced labor camps.

Just as after World War I, there was no plebiscite as to whom the people wanted as their rulers. Now, in 1945, Moldovia was severed from Romania and given to Russia. East Prussia, which had 1.3 million German and no Russian inhabitants was given to Russia. All Germans were forcefully removed from that province and replaced by four million Russians. Some Germans made it to the West. What happened to the rest of them, no one in the West knows. The southern parts of Poland were given to the Ukraine and Poland was compensated with all of the German provinces east of the Oder-Neisse Line. Some 20 million Germans lived there. Some made it to the West. Most disappeared in Siberia. Germany itself was split into East Germany and West Germany. Wilhelm Piek was made the dictator of East Germany by Stalin and Ulbricht his Prime Minister.

Ulbricht had been the chief torturer in the Spanish Civil War for the Communists who had been sent by Stalin to help the Loyalists. When Ulbricht saw that the cause was lost, he supervised the shipment of all Spanish gold to the Soviet Union. Now this man was Prime Minister of East Germany. Later when Piek died, Ulbricht succeeded him as President.

I saw as an untenable situation that Germany was divided into six very unequal parts: The western third, with some 65 million people, was occupied by American, British, and French troops. Austria, including Vienna, (which had been the German capital until 1866) was occupied by Russian and American soldiers. All of East Germany, except for Berlin, was occupied by Soviet troops. Berlin itself was occupied by Russian, American, British, and French forces. They were supposed to administer the city jointly. As mentioned above, all of the third of Germany east of the Oder-Neisse Line except East Prussia became Polish. East Prussia itself became Russian. Königsberg, the birthplace of the State of Prussia, where the Kings of Prussia were crowned not too long ago, became Kaliningrad, a Soviet naval base. The millions of Germans east of the Oder-Neisse line were deported. Many fled to the West, but an enormous number disappeared in Siberia. I was glad that the mad Morgentau Plan was abandoned shortly after the first few factories and shipyards were destroyed as the first steps of its implementation.

To summarize the six entities which were once a united Germany:

1) West Germany, needed a new capital. Bonn on the Rhine was chosen.

2) Austria, its capital, Vienna, was the German capital until 1866. Some claim, till 1871.

3) East Germany, a Soviet vassal state.

4) West Berlin, a small Western enclave, half of the city cut off from the rest of the free world.

5) The huge sector the Poles took over, where all Germans lost their homes and were chased out.

6) East Prussia, now a Russian Province, all Germans were deported and replaced by Russians.

Not satisfied, in a very bold move, defying Stalin's agreement with Truman and Attlee, the Soviet Army overran two independent countries, Hungary and Czechoslovakia, which were not part of the "Soviet Zone of Influence" as defined in the agreement at Tehran. The Soviets knew that Great Britain was exhausted by the War and it had exasperating economic problems due to its introduction of Socialism, and the United States of America had disarmed and was not likely to go to war over two totally landlocked republics in Central Europe.

When the Soviets massed troups at the Greek border, and the Communists in Greece started very provocative riots, it was eventually too much, even for the docile American Government. Truman sent American soldiers into Greece upon the request by the Greek Government and issued the Truman Doctrine: Any Soviet soldier crossing the border of any other country will be met by fully armed American G.I.s.

When I was a little school boy, before Hitler was even a threat, my Geography teacher told the class: "Rivers make the worst possible borders. Water is, after air, the most important material to sustain life. Rivers are the centers of communities. They are the drinking water supply and the main ingredient in much of manufacturing. It keeps us, our products, and our streets clean. We need it for waste disposal. Rivers supply us with fish, and they provide the possibility of transportation of large amounts of goods. In short, they are the life blood of a community and bind it together. That is one reason why big cities occupy both banks of rivers. It is the reason why Germans occupy both banks of the Rhine and why Strassburg on the West bank and Kehl on the East bank of the Rhine are naturally one community and Alsace, though under a French flag remains a German speaking province up to the Vosges Mountains. The ridge of those mountains are a natural border, because the ridge is a water divide and a natural divide of cultures. The people east of it speak German and those west of it speak French. Making the Rhine a political border is a very artificial act and will always cause trouble between Germany and France."

This seemed to me then, and it still seems to me now, to be an elementary truth. The conferees in Tehran, however, did not know that truth or simply ignored it, as it was so easy to describe river frontiers. The Danube became the border between Austria and Slovakia. Slovakia's capital, Bratislava, is right on that river. They made the Oder and the Neisse the new borders between Germany and Poland.

When President Truman was later asked why he chose those

rivers as borders and allowed Berlin to be completely isolated from the West, he answered that he did not know where those rivers were exactly, and that he thought Berlin was bordering the Western Zone. I was stunned! Here was the American President, whose country had just fought a most bitter war for four years, and he did not even look up the proposed borders on a map! He signed a document of enormous importance and possibly a cause of a future war without even trying to understand what it involved, chasing thousands of families out of their homes, just because some advisers told him to sign. It was beyond my comprehension that anybody, let alone the President of the United States, could be so callous and irresponsible!

# IMMEDIATELY AFTER THE WAR

I feared that the Allies were making the same mistakes of 1919 all over again, taking huge chunks of Germany away, loading its economy with enormous reparation payments, causing unemployment, inflation, poverty, and hunger, the grist for the mills of which the radical parties, like the Communists and right wing chauvinists feed on.

Fortunately, I was wrong. The animosity of the Soviets toward their former Western Allies caused the Americans, the British, and even the French to seek friendship with the defeated Germans. The press kept reminding the world of Karl Marx's words: "Socialism and Capitalism cannot long endure together on this planet. Therefore, it is the obligation of any country which will be governed by Socialists to overthrow all other forms of government." This slogan had given the Comintern the impetus to develop the Communist parties in all the Free World Countries and to subject them to Stalin's power.

The four Allied powers, the Soviet Union, the Americans, the British, and the French held together long enough to prosecute and hang Nazi war criminals. But a significant rift was widening over the interpretation of the meaning of "Democracy" and human rights abuses in the countries which were in the "Russian Sphere of Influence."

I saw the peace settlement as extremely shortsighted and impractical. Since the Americans got into the War the Allies had four long years to come to an agreement! Was this the best they could come up with?! Their leaders should be ashamed of themselves! What had become of Winston Churchill's plan to unite all of Europe into one federated state with a strong central government similar to that of the United States of America?

Before the War, in his propaganda speeches, Hitler had criticized the Kaiser for having fought a war on three fronts and thereby he had stretched the army too thin. The Germans in World War I under the Generals v.Ludendorff and v.Hindenburg had at least won on the eastern front against the Russians. The western

441

front held against the combined attacks by the French, British, Canadians, and Americans.

It was the southern front, held primarily by Bulgarians and Austro-Hungarian troops of Slavic descent, which collapsed as the troops rebelled against, and in many cases killed, their German speaking leadership. Thus, they opened the way for French, British, and Greek troops to force the central powers to give up. Most of the Slavic and Hungarian soldiers wanted a Communist government allied to Lenin, or just simply peace. Then, there was the revolution which started in Kiel, the German naval base. These were the events which ended World War I.

Kaiser Wilhelm II had fought on three fronts. Adolf Hitler, on the other hand, in the end fought on four fronts: First and foremost was the Russian, which stretched from the Arctic Circle in Finland, to the Crimea on the Black Sea. Second was the front in France. Then there was the third front in Yugoslavia against Marshal Tito and his communist partisans. He managed to be forced to fight on a fourth front in Italy. Unlike the Kaiser and his Generals, Hitler succeeded to lose on all four fronts.

What probably saved the West Germans from the same fate as that suffered by their parents, where Germany had been condemned to pay unrealistically high reparation costs, was the belligerent attitude of the Russians toward the Western Nations.

Years later, I met a former German bomber pilot who told me that the Americans would not release him and his fellow air crew members in 1945, but told them to keep in shape to possibly make combat flights again. There had been no doubt in any German airman's mind, that they should be prepared to fight the Russians. They were by no means happy to take orders from American officers with good reason: The Western Nations treated the defeated Germans as equals in only the western third of the former Germany. The eastern two thirds were under Stalin's thumb with the Americans' approval. If there were to be a war against the Soviets, the Western Allies wanted to battle it out on German soil rather than fight in Poland or Russia.

Immediately after the War, the Western Allies disarmed. The Russians on the other hand used their huge army to take Hungary and Czechoslovakia, two countries which were supposed to be outside of their "Sphere of Influence." Right after the armistice, especially Czechoslovakia had experienced a tremendous boom. The Communists crushed it, and replaced it with grinding poverty.

The Western Nations did nothing to stop the Soviets. The American Secretary of State, Stettinius; and Vyshinsky, his Russian counterpart, were too busy creating the United Nations in San Francisco to let a little thing like the overrunning of two European Democracies dampen their euphoria. Nikita Khrushchev, who had succeeded Stalin and Malenkov, tried to absorb Communist Yugoslavia as well. However, Marshal Tito warned him that he had better not try! How could Soviet Russia have justified attacking another Soviet state?

In China the war raged on. I felt sorry for Chiang Kai-shek and especially for his brave wife who tried so hard to persuade the West to help the anti-Communist forces in China. The West gave lip service and token help. Mao Tse-tung seemed to be winning with Russia's strong support.

# THE QUAKER MISSION IN HIGHGATE

At least the War was over. It was as if a great load had been lifted off my chest. I had been allowed to move about within five miles of my home for the past four years now, but I had not felt really free until the threat of internment had been removed at last.

The Quakers had been very helpful to our group in the internment camp, especially Clifford Meredith, a plant pathologist, and Mrs. Dorothea Simmons, the main financial and active supporter of the Quaker Mission in Jamaica. She came from a very rich Boston, Massachusetts, family and spent her money freely on Friends' causes. She invited Willy and me to stay at her house on the North Coast for two weeks. She usually rented it out to wealthy Americans in peace time.

It was quite a job to get there. I had to get to Highgate first, where the Friends' College was, where Willy taught Handicraft. Reverend Lewis Davidson, a convinced Pacifist and Presbyterian Minister, was the Headmaster and Manager of the Friends' College, really a high school, a part of the Quaker Mission. Mrs. Davidson was teaching English and was a tremendous help in running the school.

Lewis Davidson had wanted to start college level courses when he was the Headmaster of the Wolmer's Boys' School. He interviewed me then, about three years earlier. I had hoped that I might continue my formal education there. However, his ambitious plans and my hopes were dashed when he refused to allow a cadet corps to be started in his school. His Board of Directors dismissed the stubborn Scotsman and hired someone who did allow military training of the boys. I wonder how many men would have stood by their principles and have themselves fired from the position of Headmaster of one of the most prestigious schools in Jamaica rather than bend a little and allow those who wanted to do military exercises, to train voluntarily. I admired the man.

I thought about the Quakers while I rode my bicycle before sunup from Arlington Ave. to Spanish Town, uphill along the beautiful Rio Cobre, onward to Linstead which is a few hundred feet above sea level; quite a ride of about 25 miles. From there, I had to push my bicycle up Mount Diablo, a steep five miles or so and about 1,000 ft. higher to Highgate. Thirty miles may not seem very much to people used to riding in cars, but it is quite a hike in the tropical sun in the beautiful Island of Jamaica.

I met Helen and Paul Abrikian. He was a surveyor. He was born in the Armenian part of Turkey. The Armenians are Christians. Right after World War I, the Turks went on a religious frenzy, killing all Christians whom they could find. Paul's parents were killed. As a little orphaned child, he fled to a port. He managed to smuggle himself onto a Greek ship, claiming that he belonged to one of the passengers. The passenger did not give him away, so he landed in Piraeus, the port of Athens. He was taken in at an orphanage.

A young American nurse spotted him there. She took the little boy in. She had volunteered as a Quaker woman to look after the wounded during the recent World War I and stayed on in Athens to look after a seriously wounded British Major Simmons. The Major never quite recovered. They got married and took little Paul with them to England. Paul studied engineering in London. The Simmons bought a fairly large estate in St. Anns in Jamaica because Mr. Simmons could no longer take the cold, damp climate of England. He did very well in the hills of Jamaica. Dorothea Simmons made the Quaker Mission her life's work.

A young, idealistic, Quaker girl, Helen, came from Worcester (pronounced: Woostr), Massachusetts, as an English teacher to the Highgate Mission. She and Paul got married. Paul earned a fairly good living as a highly respected surveyor. At the time I met them, they had two very lively, sweet, little girls: Dorothy and Margaret.

The Mission comprised an orphanage for little boys to age 16, a girls' middle to high boarding school, a high school with a strong accent on handicraft, a Meeting House, retirement residences for old missionaries, offices, and residences for all who worked at the mission.

Harry Wellons and his wife were in charge of the overall mission. The couple came from Virginia. They were not much older than I was. They were a very energetic, idealistic, and cheerful couple. I liked them right from the start.

Phulie Brown was the Matron of the Lindale Girls' School.

She had visited us several times in the internment camp. She started to gray at the temples. She was a chocolate-brown very good looking woman of East Indian descent. She had been adopted and raised by two American Quaker Missionaries who had retired. They still lived nearby in a nice little cottage.

Clifford Meredith and his wife had a little house and laboratory near the mission. He had been called from the University of Iowa to find a cure for the "Panama Disease" which was killing out the bananas, Jamaica's number one cash crop. He was studying the new wonder drug, which had not yet been released for use: Penicillin. They called it by a new word which just then entered the English language: Antibiotic.

Willy had big plans. He wanted to build a large work shop, build more looms like the one he had brought with him from the internment camp, make spinning wheels like the one we had repaired and start spinning and weaving classes. He also started to make molds for sun dried bricks, made from local clay and straw, to make interior walls for a new residence building which he planned to build. He was teaching several classes on how to treat native vines so that they would make good basket weaving materials, and he taught how to make all kinds of baskets.

I was received at the mission like a long lost friend. Helen and Paul Abrikian invited me to stay with them overnight. We went to the Meeting House and I saw an American Square dance for the first time in my life. Harry Wellons proved to be an excellent caller. I had to take part, though I did not know what I was doing. The whole bunch of people was so kind and friendly towards me, it warmed my heart. I had never been used to that much kindness since I was a child.

# AT DOROTHEA SIMMONS'S HOUSE IN OCHO RIOS

Willy and I took a "bus" to the North Coast. The bus was a one ton truck with slats on its sides. These slats were supporting planks which served as seats, laid flat across the truck. Under these seats were market baskets. People were squeezed in tightly on the seats. Those, who could not find room to sit, hung on the outside. We were among those. The drive led through Fern Gully, a very beautiful road through a mountain pass covered with lush vegetation, mostly tree ferns and bamboo.

The coastal road led right past our destination. It was a lovely house. We had two servants to wait on us and two riding horses which we rode bareback into the sea to give them a bath once a day. We needed the relaxation. Willy had been interned six years, from Sept. 4, 1939, to V-J-day on August 29, 1945. It had made him very nervous person, and he had become a chain smoker. On his return to Highgate, he could not relax. There were too many things he had started, and projects he wanted to start, as well as people who asked him to help them, to give him one free waking minute.

Even though I had been free all but one year and nine months of the War, it had not been exactly an easy time for me either. We sent the servants home. We were both good cooks and really did not need any help, but one of the women insisted to make our dinners in the evenings. After all that interaction with other people where we had to watch each word carefully before we brought it out over our lips, we did not want anyone to ask us questions, tell us that breakfast or lunch was ready, or offer to help us. We needed no-one, period, but we accepted the offer of dinner in the evenings.

Swimming on the North Coast is just beautiful. There is a barrier coral reef some half mile out, so that the water near the shore is normally quite calm. The water is very warm, in the 30° Celsius range. I decided to swim to the estate owned by the very rich Henriques family. It was about two miles west of the house. Willy donned a broad straw hat and wore a shirt and shorts and followed me in a small rowboat.

It must have taken me about two hours to swim those two

miles, as I swim a relaxed breaststroke. Finally we reached our destination. The elderly caretaker was very cordial. He told us that none of the Henriqueses was there. We admired the aquarium which was built out into the sea with large loose stones. The dominant inhabitants were a four foot long shark and a large sea turtle. They did not harm each other nor the smaller fish which scooted in and out of the crevasses between the stones.

"Where did you catch the shark," I asked.

"Right out ya so." He pointed to where I had just swum.

"You are joking! I just swam there, and since I have no clothes with me to protect me against the sun, I'll have to swim back same way."

"Yes Sah, better you na me, Sah." He laughed. On my swim back I hugged the shore more than on my way out. It was nice to come back to our well-laid table with all the refinements of civilization, just as the sun was setting.

The two weeks went far too quickly. We took the same drive back to Highgate in the packed, colorful truck. I would have loved to stay at the mission in Highgate for a while, but I felt a strong urge to get my business started again, and Amy, too, merited some consideration.

# SOCIALISM AND RED TAPE IN THE U.K.
# AND JAMAICA

Because of the War, all factories had been converted to war production. The papers and radio had announced over and over again that all German factories were destroyed. *News Reel* photographs by Allied planes certainly seemed to confirm the total destruction of German cities. But how did those reports square with this *News Reel* report: "The first truck in the world, built for civilian use since the beginning of the War has just rolled off the Ford assembly line in Cologne, Germany." Since the factory was owned by an American Company, the bombers had apparently been instructed not to destroy that German-run armament factory. The nearby, world famous, and beautiful Gothic Cathedral of Cologne which took over 1,000 years to build from carved sandstone, was not so carefully spared. It received a direct hit from a 500 pound bomb through the center of its roof. Fortunately, the bomb did not explode.

For me, the important fact was that for the foreseeable future I could not buy any electrical material. We still had to cope with that antediluvian 40 Hertz current in Kingston. It was impossible to get any neon transformers. In America and Canada, they used 60 Hertz. In Europe, they used 50 Hertz. There were no other sources for neon transformers. This problem concerned me more than all the events in the rest of the world.

I was surprised how prices for neon material had increased. I found myself in a totally new economic environment. The terribly misnamed Competent Authority still doled out permits for the importation of material. Neon had the absolute lowest ranking priority. I could forget about getting any permit to import anything from countries with, what was then considered "hard currency" such as America or Canada. I was told to buy my glass from Czechoslovakia, a Communist Country. Their glass was excellent and cheap, but they would not coat it with fluorescent powder for me. I tried to do it myself, but my experiments did not produce a marketable product. I could use the Czech glass for red and blue signs only.

449

England was run by a socialist government. Everything was controlled and one needed permits to buy just about anything. Since the prices were controlled, the manufacturers saved by making very inferior products. They were getting the same amount of money for good products as for shoddy ones. So, shoddy ones they made. Whereas, before the War, one could rely that any product from Great Britain was of the most exquisite quality, now one could almost be sure that any U.K. goods were not worth their money.

Mr. Attlee sent Sir John Foote to be the new Governor of Jamaica. Sir John was the brother of the leader of the radical left wing of the Labour Party, Michael Foote. Sir John appointed Norman Manley to be the first minister of his new executive government. Universal suffrage was to be used in the next election. That would freeze out the Jamaica Democratic Party, whose members comprised mostly the Jamaican business people and the majority of the taxpayers. Under Manley's and the Governor's directions one needed to obtain permits for just about anything from clerks who did not know what you were talking about, nor did they care to know. Of course, those who had pull, I hesitate to use the words: could bribe, got all the permits for hard currency items.

Eventually, I was able to buy some 50 Hertz transformers from England. I hoped that by not loading them to their rated capacity, they would work. They did, but their quality and capacity did not compare with those I had imported before the War from the U.S.A., besides, their lead time for future orders would be one year! I bought wire to wind my own transformers from a firm in the town of Ramsbottom, England. It was very hard to make a living. The cost of the material had gone up so very much. I had to compete with painted signs and newspaper advertising, which were two very cheap ways to advertise in comparison to neon.

Henter built me a winding machine. I used No. 38 gauge Brown & Sharpe wire, which is as fine as a human hair and tore very easily. Transformers have up to 15,000 Volts and it needed 4 turns per Volt so that a transformer had up to 60,000 turns in its secondary! Insulating the windings against the core at such a high voltage was another problem. I imported Trinidad asphalt which had been refined in England. It was the best insulation I could find.

For the cores I bought burnt out power transformers from the Jamaica Public Service Co., cleaned their silicon steel core sheets and had some of my help cut them to size. It all cost a great deal of time and experimentation. 15,000 Volt transformers were too hard to wind and insulate. I made transformers of no higher voltage than 10,000 V.

Finally I let Suarez, a man from British Guyana, wind my transformers. I supplied the material. He was winding ballasts for Stanley Motta who had started a fluorescent lamp factory. That was a new form of lighting, which had just been invented. Since they used argon and mercury in the tubes, all people looked very sick if those lamps alone were used without a blend of incandescent lamps to give some red into the illumination. Neither argon nor mercury vapor produce any red or yellow light when they are ionized by an electric ark. Today the lamp manufacturers use argon, neon, and mercury in the lamps. The neon in the mix gives the white light more than sufficient red in its spectrum to make the people look healthy. I had that idea long before the lamp manufacturers had it. I had used neon in my "Mirrorlites" practically since I had been released from the internment camp on October 28, 1941. I felt really good. I thanked the experiments we did in Father Blatchford's lab in St. George's College.

I took work besides neon. Nathans gave me some commercial art work to do. Mr. Ashwell, an architect from South Africa, gave me some wiring to do.

# GERHARD AND I HIKE TO THE BLUE MOUNTAIN PEAK

After "V-J day," the day the Japanese surrendered, all blood letting stopped at last. Gasoline became available and Gerhard bought himself a very large, black, 1933, Ford V-8 car with folding seats behind the front seats in front of the back seats. The trouble was tires were rationed and we were not eligible to get any. I bolted the treads of blown tires to worn out tires with good side walls. I lined them with shaved down parts of tires, so that the bolt heads would not puncture the inner tubes. In those days, when artificial rubber was still a new invention, all tires required inner tubes. They had to be pumped up almost every day.

Dorrie and Gerhard loved Farm Hill, an old coffee estate 4,000 ft. above sea level in the Blue Mountains. Gerhard told me that by hiking up the Blue Mountains frequently, he and Dorrie were in excellent shape. He doubted very much that I, as a mere swimmer, could climb the mountain as well as he could. We decided to go to the Blue Mountain Peak, seven miles from Mavis Bank and 7,640 ft. above sea level. He always wanted to go down the densely forested north slope. We carried dehydrated supplies to last us for three days and a very sharp machete.

Gerhard drove his newly acquired pride, the 22 year old V8 up the winding road to Gordon Town. As we crossed the bridge there, the steep, winding, gravel road led up to Cumberland Gap, a good 2,000 ft. above sea level, and then down the other side of the pass to Mavis Bank about 1,000 ft. above sea level. The road became so narrow that in many places two cars could not pass each other. The car could not negotiate two of the hair pin curves without stopping, reversing to the edge of the cliff, and then going forward again, before we reached Cumberland Gap. Going down to Mavis Bank, there were also two such curves. During the entire drive, Gerhard alternately leaned on the horn and then listened for a possible horn from another car or even a truck.

We left the car on a meadow belonging to a man whom Gerhard knew and walked down to the Green River. The Blue Mountain Range is the only granite part of the Island. The rest is porous limestone. We took off our shoes and socks, rolled up our pant legs, and waded across the river. The stones are large and round. Small stones would have been washed away during rainstorms when the river becomes a raging torrent. The stones were green from their copper ore contents, hence the name of the river.

Now, the climb up to Farm Hill began in earnest. Gerhard set the speed. We marched at a pretty good clip. I had no trouble keeping up with him. I knew that as a champion swimmer, I was in superb shape for any kind of physical test. We even passed an elderly woman walking barefoot very slowly while carrying an almost empty market basket. Her shoes were in the basket to be worn and shown off only in the market as a status symbol. She had probably already been walking since sunrise from the Papine market via Gordon Town and Cumberland Gap. She said a very friendly: "Good afternoon, Sah," as we passed her very quickly.

After a while, Gerhard needed a rest. We sat down for a while, and the elderly woman passed us. She had a big smile on her face, as if she were saying: "I knew all the time that you could not keep climbing at that pace." We never caught up with her again.

We now came to the world famous Blue Mountain Coffee country. Mrs. Steadman's beautiful house, Torre Garda, loomed over us, but we did not stop. Gerhard told me that she had come from England long ago, and that she was venerated and feared by the local people, who ascribed the power of witchcraft to her.

At 4,000 ft. altitude, we passed Farm Hill. It was a very well-built stone house, possibly 150 years old. It had a hand split cedar roof. There were a few fruit trees around, even apples besides the, to be expected, tangerine, orange and grapefruit trees. The many coffee trees were overgrown with Wynne grass. Everything looked very run down. Gerhard told me that a Scotsman, by the name of Stoddard, had once made his money off this property but was now too old and arthritic to climb the mountains.

We hurried on as we did not want darkness to overtake us. After Farm Hill, the area is fairly level for a while. We passed Whitfield Hall, another old coffee estate. Extremely tall eucalyptus and pine trees surrounded the stately house of 80 x 40 ft. There had once been a beautiful flower garden. There were especially fuchsia and many other garden escapee's growing wild all around the estate. Here too everything looked pitifully neglected.

As we walked along the relatively level area from Whitfield Hall to Abbey Green, we heard water rushing very near below us. There was a cave. Gerhard told me that it was an abandoned Spanish copper mine. It was half filled with crystal clear water. Its overflow rushed down the mountain as a brook. We filled our water bottles. I resisted the temptation to take a bath.

Not far from there we came upon Abbey Green. This coffee estate had a large concrete coffee drying area, which is called a barbecue in Jamaica with low sheds at its edge. When Mr. Stoddard was still active, the red coffee fruits, each containing two green coffee beans, were spread out on the concrete to dry in the day time, so that they would not rot or contract mildew. At sun down they were swept up and stored in the low sheds. This drying was repeated daily, until the pulpy outside had withered and opened. Then the coffee would be washed, the dried shells would float away, and the green beans would then be dried once more, bagged and shipped. The taste and quality of the beans depended greatly on the proper drying at cool, high altitudes.

I asked Gerhard: "How did they get the cement up here, a good four miles from, and 3,000 ft. above, the nearest road which a dray could possibly have used?"

"Mule or head loads. For each cubic foot of cement, they needed three of sand. Women carry the sand on their heads up that steep path to this day, eighty pounds at a time, roughly four gallons, if the sand is really dry, from that brook 2,000 ft. below us. They bring up two loads per day per woman." That seemed an awfully slow and tedious process!

I looked down where one could barely make out a stream bed through the crowns of the trees. I knew Jamaican women worked hard, especially when they had a child to support. They usually did not get much help from their men, but this seemed extreme! I doubted that I could have walked up and down that steep track twice per day even without any weight to carry.

Shortly after Abbey Green the path became very steep. There were a few scallion patches on the side of the mountain. The people burn some land, and plant scallion. They do not have to bend down as the mountain side is almost vertical. That method of agriculture is very harmful to the land as the many eroded areas demonstrated. Nobody seemed to care. Nobody represented the owner.

We reached the peak at sundown. We had hiked only four and a half hours. I had never heard of anybody doing it in less than that. Most hikers take eight hours to go to the peak.

There is a concrete hut with a fireplace and bunk beds on the very peak. There are lots of fuchsias and hydrangeas planted all around the hut. A ranger must have visited the area regularly. The sunset was beautiful. We were high above the clouds. We could see the North Coast. Turning, looking past Sugar Loaf in the east, the second highest peak in Jamaica, we could discern the East Coast and then the South Coast. In the west was the "Cockpit Country" at the horizon. We made a fire in the fireplace to get the place warmed up and boil some soup. We used up all of our water.

The West side and the high parts of the Sugar Loaf were catching the last red rays of the sun. The Cockpit Country far to the West was in darkness already. We could not help but marvel at those hardy Maroons who played such a significant role in the history of this Island.

When the British landed in 1655, they quickly took what is now Port Royal and crossed the bay, now Kingston Harbour, to the limestone hill at the present Port Henderson. General Venable, the uncompromising, fanatic Puritan, then made the devastating mistake and approached San Juago de la Vega from the south through an enormous swamp. The British beleaguered the capital of the third generation of the Catholic Spanish settlers. Not only were the opponents of different nationalities, but they also considered their enemies heretics, who had to be killed in a most cruel fashion to save their souls, of course!

For the time being, the British had no time to think of killing. They contracted yellow fever and 3,000 of the 5,000 who had landed, died of the horrible malady. The Spanish and their slaves retreated across the few paths across the limestone mountains to the North Coast.

Many of the African and Arawak slaves of the Spanish had run away. They ruled the mountains. The Spanish called them the "Marones" (the Brown Ones). They became known to the English as the Maroons. Since the invaders were as cruel as the Spanish, the Maroons sided with the known evil, the Spanish. Not until the British bribed the Maroons, did they have a chance of killing out the Spanish.

Only nine Spaniards escaped alive in an open canoe to Cuba in 1660. The Maroons kept ruling the mountains from the Sugar Loaf in the east, where they had their practically inaccessible capital, Nannytown, to the west end of the Island. Occasionally they raided the estates. The plantation owners feared them and requested that the military get rid of them. The army lost a lot of men in numerous expeditions trying to capture Nannytown and other Maroon settlements. They had no success. Finally, the British were able to cut a road across the mountains and make it relatively safe to cross the Island.

Not till after the emancipation of the slaves by the order of Queen Victoria on August 1, 1838, did the British succeed to make a peace agreement with the Colonel of the Maroons. The Maroons gave up the eastern part of their domain including Nannytown and the Blue Mountains, and the British promised not to interfere with them in the western mountain ranges. A British flag never ever flew over the "Cockpit" mountains. No road led through those limestone hills. There never was a government school nor hospital. I wondered if that was such a good agreement for the Maroons.

A full moon rose and it was getting chilly. We put on all of our clothes and admired the landscape and the top of the clouds bathed in the most gorgeous moonlight. We laid some more sticks on the fire and went to sleep soundly.

In the morning we woke up, freezing! We started down the north slope as we had intended. We had to find water to make coffee and boil rice and warm up our "Bully Beef," as the Jamaicans called tinned corn beef. The going was very rough from the start. The moist prevailing trade winds from the Northeast allowed a very dense forest to grow down the north slope.

We took turns cutting a path through the dense underbrush of ferns and all kinds of climbing plants. We never knew what we were stepping on, as the plants under our feet gave as we trod on them. The most tenacious resistance to our advance was the "Chinese Bamboo". I do not know why it was called that. It was no thicker than a quarter inch. It grew and twisted itself around trees, bushes, and ferns. I hit it as hard as I could with my sharp machete. As I raised my arm, so the climber would rise up again unharmed. We could not get through. We soon learned to go around those thickets. We blazed trees with the machete so that we could find our way back. Finally at about ten, we found water.

There was a clear little brook flowing down the mountain. We had no view at all. There was dense underbrush, trees, and tree ferns all around us. We cleared enough around the edge of the brook to start a good fire. Our clothes were wet on the outside from the mist and the dripping trees. The coffee we brewed was the best we ever tasted and so was the soup. Hunger makes the best cook.

We had planned to go further down the mountainside after our breakfast, but Gerhard told me that he felt terrible. I looked at him and was frightened. He was as pale as a ghost. We were very far from civilization. I was forcefully reminded that parties climbing mountains should never be less than three. In case one should get incapacitated, one could stay with the disabled person, while the third would go for help. The path we had hacked was of no use. Dense fog enveloped us, and I could not see the marks we had blazed. I chopped a new path upward and Gerhard followed me until we reached the peak. We rested a while and slowly went down towards Abbey Green. As we reached lower altitudes, Gerhard felt much better. He insisted on driving and we reached home in good spirits.

Gerhard proved to be right in one respect. Swimming does not develop all the muscles needed for mountaineering. From walking down hill, not up hill, the muscles in the front of my shin bones hurt for quite a few days! From then on, I noticed that the women from the mountains had thick muscles in the front of their shins. The men wore long pants so I could not see their lower legs, besides, their legs did not really interest me enough to bother to look at them anyhow.

# GOING ON A PICNIC TO THE YALLAHS RIVER

Amy told me the news that a group of us were going by bicycle on a moonlight picnic in the Yallahs River. Gasoline was still rationed and hard to get. After sundown about six young couples, some recently married, some just friends, rode east along the coastal road past the entrance of the Palisadoes, across the bridge of the Dry River, all the way to the Yallahs River, some ten miles east of Kingston.

In those days, there was no bridge across the Yallahs River. It flows through the driest part of the Island. Rain clouds usually come from the northeast. They seldom rise over the Blue Mountains which loomed high and majestically to the left of us bathed in beautiful, blue moonlight.

The Yallahs is a very broad, mostly dry river of sand with many islands with bright green plants between lazily running water. When it had rained heavily in the Blue Mountains, a half mile wide, but shallow, wild, foaming brown torrent will change the riverbed around these green islands, washing away all ants and other crawling insects. That is why we sat on the islands in the middle of the river while we sang popular songs and had a very friendly good time.

From the bicycle ride we had gotten hot. The typical cool night breeze down the mountain to the sea made it very comfortable. It was getting late, and we decided to ride home again. The full moon is very bright in Jamaica. Fortunately, the sky was cloudless. Everything looks so much cleaner in moonlight than in the harsh glare of the tropical sun. That made for a beautiful trip back.

# GERHARD WANTS A HOUSE IN THE BLUE MOUNTAINS

My shop was not very busy. Gerhard said to me: "I have bought eight acres of land in the Blue Mountains near Farm Hill. Go up and build me a house on it. Twelve feet by eight feet would be a good size for a weekend house. There is a little village nearby where you can find lots of workers. They know where to buy lumber and shingles."

Gerhard drove me to Mavis Bank. Eddie, a powerful 20 year old, carried my tools up the four miles climb. I lodged in a small building belonging to Farm Hill, and started to buy some lumber. A few men came to help me. They proved to be very incompetent in every way. They could not saw very well, and when they promised to come: "Soon, soon ah marnin'," they trudged in about noon and wanted a full day's pay when the sun got red. The people there had no idea of time. They did not know the hour, the day, in most cases not even in which month they were. They dug the holes for me to sink in the six bullet wood supports on which the house stood.

The cool air of this coffee region was wonderful and invigorating. It was beautiful up there. In the evenings, when I watched the sun set, the loudest sound I could hear was my own heartbeat. It gave me lots of time to think. I am a worrier. I wrote a poem up there on January 27, 1945. I did not translate it until August, 1998.

# ERINNERUNGEN UND BESORGNIS

*Freund weilst du in der Ferne,*
*Hüte Dich vor Einsamkeit,*
*Denn du siehst sie alle vor dir*
*Trotz Distanz in Raum and Ziet.*

*Was ist wohl aus ihnen worden,*
*Die als Kind du gut gekannt,*
*Die im einst vertrauten Norden*
*Sind noch in dem alten Land?*

*Nicht nur tausende von Meilen*
*Sind sie alle dir entzogen,*
*Sondern durch des Krieges Grausen,*
*Durch des Schicksals wilde Wogen.*

*Ihre Stadt ist jetzt zertümmert.*
*Ihre Wurzel ist zerschlagen.*
*Und statt Stolz, den sie einst zeigten,*
*Müssen sie jetzt Trauer tragen?*

*Ich sitz' hoch auf kaltem Berge*
*Über tropenheißem Tal.*
*Da ruft mir der Kiefern Rauschen*
*Meine Kindheit noch einmal.*

*Arnold P. Von der Porten*
*27. Januar, 1945*

# MEMORIES AND APPREHENSION

Friend, if abroad you make your home,
Despite distance in time and space
When you stay too long alone
The haunting past stares in your face.

What has become of those you knew
When you were a child at play?
They waved good-bye with tears for you
In gathering clouds where they would stay.

Hamburg, on the warring continent,
Thousands of miles are you from here
Where relatives and friends have spent
Six years of horror, death, and fear.

Bombed City, who's alive and who has died?
Burnt are the houses.  Is there food?
Where is your swagger and your pride?
Is mourning the prevailing mood?

In the high mountain's chilly breeze
Above the tropical valley's floor
The rustling of dark fir trees
Brings my childhood back once more.

> Arnold P. Von der Porten
> January 27, 1945
> Translation from German: August 31, 1997

What would become of the Glasslite Company. I had written letters to many companies in the U.S., England, France, Germany, and even to Czechoslovakia, a Communist Country. None of the electrical equipment manufacturers would make 40 Hertz neon transformers for me. All electrical material was in short supply due to the need of replacing all the electrical installations which were destroyed in the War. They would not even dream of making anything which was not standard. And 40 Hz. was certainly a freak!

Would it ever make enough money to support myself and perhaps a wife? I was well over 27 now in the summer of 1945. Should I ever get married? Where would I find a wife? Amy and all the rest of the Jamaican girls thought a man who worked with his hands below their dignity. A few of my fellow swimmers from good families worked with their hands, so that prejudice was slowly starting to break down. V.G. Crawford was a motor car mechanic and Bewick, one of the fullbacks on my water polo team, was a car electrician. Both were working for the Dodge agency.

Gerhard had warned me that getting married was easy. Staying married, even with a wife of the same cultural background, was not always easy, even if one loved one another. He told me that marrying someone with a totally different set of values, and one who never experienced similar hardships to the ones we went through, would never understand us, and a marriage would never work. Therefore, he advised me not to marry a Jamaican girl, regardless how decent and loving she might be. Other women would look down on her for having married a person who works with his hands, and that would eventually get to her and make a happy marriage impossible. I sat up there in the stillness of the progressing darkness near Farm Hill in the high Wynne grass which was killing the coffee trees and pondered nights on end.

But Dorrie was forever homesick for Offenbach on Main. I knew from tales of others, that going back to the home of one's childhood would be terribly disappointing, as one was really looking for one's youth. Such a search would be futile. I also remembered how I did not fit in at my parents' home in Brooklyn,

462

though my parents were the same, Mama's love most certainly was the same, their language was the same, even the furniture was the same, but I was not!

I was sure that I would never go back to Hamburg. Germany had kicked me out! I had the bitter taste of resentment in my mouth every time I thought about it. I once had wanted to be a doctor, just like my father. Now, I certainly did not want to be like my father. He seemed far too selfish and belonged to a long past time. He never even tried to understand me when I was in Brooklyn. He sent us neckties for Christmas when we were interned. The ultimate proof of a total lack of understanding! So my thoughts meandered evening after evening. In the meantime, the house grew very nicely during the day. I did most of the work myself.

I was coming to the conclusion in the evenings that I was now a Jamaican. All my interests were in this Island. I was fully accepted in every phase of my surroundings: Amy, the swimming clubs, the artists, the contacts at work, the Quakers, and the workers. I had joined the Jamaica Manufacturers Association and had been voted to be one of the Directors.

I did not want to marry a girl who would feel homesick for another country. I would never leave the Island. Why should I ever want to? I wanted an intelligent, well-educated Jamaican girl. Amy would be ideal. But would she and her parents consent? She told me that her parents would soon be coming home. What would they think of me? Why should Amy want to leave her happy, sheltered home to live with a poverty stricken guy, who could not even find a vendor who made a fireproof neon transformer? I never before nor ever since have had the opportunity to sort things out in my mind, as I had on that lonely mountain.

I went back to town. Gerhard and Dorrie loved the house which I had built. When they did not visit it for a few months, and they arrived at the spot, the house had vanished. It had been stolen for the price of the lumber. No one in the village, about a mile away, admitted knowing what happened to the house.

463

# NO HONEST WORK IS DEGRADING

My neon shop, proudly called the Glasslite Co., was now in the two-car garage and its storeroom-office was a small, easily-locked room between the garage and the Jamaica Macaroni Factory. As the weather was usually good in Kingston, most of the sign work was done in the backyard. My shop was responsible to keep the shared facilities clean.

It was the rule in my neon shop that the newest apprentice had to clean the shop and the toilet for the employees. One day as I walked by the rest room, it was immediately obvious to my nose that it had not been cleaned recently. I opened the door and was shocked! It was putrid! Even the floor and the wall were filthy. I called the new fellow. I knew that it was "common knowledge": "White people make Black people do all the degrading work for them."

I had taught every one of my employees their work. I was very popular with them. This new apprentice really represented an unexpected problem when he said: "I am not going to touch such a filthy place. I use my hands afterwards to eat my sandwich. This is not a craftsman's chore." It would have been an extremely bad management principle if I had excused the boy and had told another to do the cleaning which had been so terribly neglected.

I got myself a bucket of water, some rags, cleanser, and gathered all of my employees around me and made them watch me clean the toilet. For effect, I specially did not use a toilet brush but merely a rag and my bare hands. I had cleaned toilets before in the internment camp but never one as filthy as that! Then I washed the walls, the inside of the door and the floor with a stiff broom with soap and water. When the place was spotless, I got a bucket of whitewash and gave the walls and inside of the door a new coat.

I washed my hands and ate my sandwich before an absolutely silent semicircle of my five employees and the day shift of the Jamaica Macaroni Factory who also used the facility. I reached into my pocket and paid off the new apprentice with his week's pay plus two weeks' severance pay as required by Jamaican law and calmly sent him home. I never again had the least bit of trouble concerning disobedience of an order.

# I JOIN THE QUAKERS

I decided, now that the War was over, that I should join the Quakers. Despite my urge to do just that ever since I was released from the internment camp, I had waited this long, as I did not want anyone to think that I joined only for political reasons. People might have thought that I joined in the hope that the Friends would feel obligated to me in case of any more arrests.

Clifford Meredith soon informed me that I was accepted. The Highgate Monthly Meeting was a programmed Meeting in accordance with the Indiana (U.S.A.) Five Yearly Meeting, one of the main financial supporters of the mission in Jamaica.

Dorothea Simmons bought a very big house, 11 Caledonia Avenue near Cross Roads, opposite the Nuttal Hospital. Clifford Meredith came every weekend from Highgate, and we went to meditate at the new Meeting Room. We founded the Kingston Monthly Meeting of Friends, the first unprogrammed Quaker Meeting in Jamaica in modern times. The Meeting is called "unprogammed," because there is no paid clergy nor any other one particular person to lead the worship. Members sit quietly, meditate and when they feel a great urge to say something, they can do so, and they will do so. It is the usual form of Quaker worship in England and east of Indiana in the United States.

I have to say "modern times" as George Fox himself, the founder of the Religious Society of the Friends of Jesus, the Quaker Movement, first came to Barbados and then to Jamaica in the 17th century and established Meetings there. In Barbados, George Fox took a special interest in the Roman Catholic Irishmen whom the Puritans had sold into slavery.

This attempt to introduce friendship and tolerance to the harsh political climate of the 17th century in Jamaica took place shortly after the most intolerant British Puritans had finally killed out the last of the equally intolerant Roman Catholic Spaniards in a disgustingly cruel war of attrition from 1655 to 1660. Before the arrival of the British, the Spaniards had had a flourishing agricultural colony on the island for three generations. They had also augmented their work force of native Arawak slaves with

466

imported African slaves. George Fox, his party, his teaching, and his condemnation of the institution of slavery, must have been a real thorn in the sides of the leading Puritans. Unfortunately, nothing of the original mission remains.

# DORRIE, GERHARD AND FARM HILL

Dorrie and Gerhard just loved Farm Hill at 4,000 ft. altitude in the Blue Mountains. There was a lot to be said for it. Both had longed for privacy during their long internment. Farm Hill certainly was remote, four miles from the car road at Mavis Bank and 3,000 ft. higher, in a four mile, steep climb. The house was built from local granite stones and had survived well over a hundred years and did not look any the worse for wear. The property had supplied the coffee for Buckingham Palace not too many years ago.

Mr. Stoddard had died. Two ladies had inherited the property. They told Gerhard that it was a lovely estate of 900 acres and included Whitfield Hall. It had made Mr. Stoddard a very rich man. They felt very sorry that they were too old and weak ever to climb to Farm Hill again and that they certainly could not manage it.

To my great surprise, one day Gerhard told me: "I have just bought Farm Hill for a pound an acre." His face lit up with a big smile. I was shocked! £900.=.= ! I was drawing £2.=.= per week from my Glasslite Co. for my personal use. £900.=.= would mean 450 weeks' take home money for me! Almost nine years' pay!

"Where are you going to get all that money from?! You told me that you still owed Judah & Randall (his lawyers) a lot of money for helping you and Dorrie to get out of the internment camp. Besides, the macaroni factory is not doing too well since the Competent Authority allows pasta to come in from America and Canada. Your fledgling agency business is hardly bringing in anything so far."

"I am going up there and sell to the people in the neighborhood land from the fringes at £5.=.= per acre. The Government has promised them to finance land purchase for penniless country people. I hope to sell enough to have the down payment by closing time. Ask Mrs. Simmons if she will buy Whitfield Hall with 20 acres. You know that it is a most beautiful place."

I went to Dorothea Simmons and she got in contact with Gerhard and bought Whitfield Hall. She went up there and entertained a niece from Boston at the house. Willy and I went with the party. We did the cooking. It was a most delicious meal. The niece did not seem impressed. My feelings were a little hurt. I thought that we were at one of the most beautiful spots on earth with the most perfect climate in an 80 ft x 40 ft mansion, had a sumptuous meal, and this young girl was not even impressed. Dorothea Simmons was as charming and friendly a hostess as could be, which more than made up for the snooty girl.

I really thought that Gerhard had gone mad when he bought Farm Hill. To my great surprise, he managed to sell enough land to make the down payment as promised and all was well. I had restored a painting which he found at Farm Hill. It had been painted by the long since deceased father of one of the ladies. Gerhard told me: "When they saw that painting, they were so happy, that I felt sure that they would have given me Farm Hill even if I did not have the money for the down payment."

Dorrie and Gerhard moved to Farm Hill. Gerhard stayed in Kingston four nights a week. His office was on the second floor of the Macaroni Factory. The climb up and down the mountain kept Gerhard in very good physical shape.

# THE WORLD'S BEST DRIVER IS GERHARD

One day when Dorrie and Gerhard were up in Farm Hill, Dorrie fell deathly ill. She had to get to the hospital as soon as possible. Gerhard and Eddie, who always seemed to be around when one needed him, made a stretcher out of two sticks and some blankets. Dorrie only weighed about 100 lbs. They got another strong man and they carried Dorrie to Mavis Bank, where Gerhard's 1933 Ford V-8 was waiting. It was now 1945 and the car had seen better days.

Gerhard drove up to Cumberland Gap, the 2,000 ft. high pass through the mountains. Soon after the pass, there is a hairpin bend. Gerhard drove to the precipice, stepped on the brake, and the brake rod snapped! No brake at all, neither foot brake nor hand brake! He quickly rammed the gear into first speed and turned off the engine. The car stopped inches from the precipice! He put the car into reverse, switched on the engine, reversed, went back into first gear and thus negotiated the dangerous curve.

It was lucky for Dorrie and Gerhard, that the auto industry had not yet thought of fluid drives, he would never have been able to stop that car, if it should have had a fluid drive.

He kept the engine in first speed all the way to the very sharp hairpin curve near Gordon Town. Whenever the speed became too great, he switched off the engine. He resisted the temptation to go into second speed to go a little faster, as he knew, that his car could never go around that hairpin curve without driving right to the precipice, reversing, and then going forward. The river was a good 30 ft. vertically below that curve.

The government (I do not know, if they had anticipated Gerhard's plight or not,) had wisely built a retaining wall at that curve. The old Ford had an excellent chrome steel bumper. Though Gerhard tried, he could not bring the car to a total stop in front of the retaining wall. He bumped it gently. Neither the wall nor the bumper were damaged. The wall certainly helped. He reversed and got around the most dangerous curve, and was able to take Dorrie to the Hospital to save her life.

The brake rod was welded and the car functioned fine, just as well as before. I never heard Gerhard mention this drive again. To me that was the ultimate presence of mind.   It was a most extraordinary feat!

# THE WORLD'S LUCKIEST DRIVER AM I

One Monday morning at sunrise I climbed down from Farm Hill. I got into Gerhard's 1933 Ford V-8 at Mavis Bank. The car was climbing up to Cumberland Gap, when the weld on the brake rod failed. I remembered Gerhard's fantastic drive with dangerously ill Dorrie in the back of the car.

I had plenty of time to think. The car was still climbing and I did not need any brakes. I reached the top of the Gap. From there on it would be all downhill. There were three hairpin bends. The second one I knew I could make it in one, but the other two were really miserable. One had to drive right up to the precipice, reverse, and then make it. How could I do that without any brake? When Gerhard drove, the brake rod had broken at the very first hairpin bend. Should I go or not? What were the alternatives?

I could pull the car off the road and walk 5 miles to Papine 1,200 ft below me. What then? How could I get tools up here to take out the defective brake parts, take them and my tools to Kingston, get the brake rod welded properly this time, hike with them and my tools back up to Cumberland Gap. I would need the help of a mountain man. A man from Kingston could never walk up these mountains with tools on his head. For the repair work a mountain man would be no help at all. Should I finally succeed in getting the brake working reliably, then I could drive down to Kingston. It would take all of three days! Too exhausting, too impractical. Besides, if I should leave the car there, would it still have a battery, tires, yes, wheels when I came back? This was a bad time. The car was essential. Gerhard was hard pressed for money, and I had none at all. No one could tow the car to Kingston down this mountain road. So, that alternative was not available either. Driving was the only way. Gerhard had done it, I could do it, too.

I started the car. In first speed, the gears were whining at an uncomfortably high pitch. I was afraid I would brake the transmission. I changed to second. I switched off the car, and it stopped. I pressed the clutch and it rolled again. I left the engine switched off with the gear in second. I released the clutch pedal to slow it down and pressed the clutch to roll faster. All went according to expectations.

Imperceptibly, the angle of decline became steeper. I could no longer stop the car. It was speeding up! One could no longer call the noise the gears made: "whining." They were howling! I did not dare to depress the clutch to try to change to first. If I even got it into first the gearbox would most certainly explode. I was going far too fast to ever hope to get the gear into first. Besides I needed both hands to steer now!

The first hairpin bend was just a short distance away. I knew this road like the back of my hand. There was no level stretch between where I was and that frightening curve! There it was!

I crossed my arms over the steering wheel, spun the wheel all the way around to the right and back to its original position. If there had been hard pavement, the car would surely have rolled over, but here on the loose gravel it skidded and turned 180° in a cloud of dust. The left back wheel was stopped by the low bank on the side of the road. I was around the curve! This was probably the only time anyone had made this curve in one without reversing.

Gerhard had almost gone over its edge when his brake rod snapped the first time. It was really crazy to build a car, where both brakes rely on one weld! Making the emergency brake completely independent from the foot brake would cost a little bit more money, and Ford might sell less cars.

I had no time to muse. I had missed the only opportunity to slam the transmission into first as it slowed down in the skid. The road got steeper all the time and the second hairpin bend was near. I had gone around this one without reversing once, but I was going at perhaps two miles per hour. Now I was racing toward it at, who knows at what speed! I again crossed my arms over the steering wheel. This time it was a left hand curve. I spun the wheel around and back again as fast as I could. When the dust cleared I was around the curve, still on the road and the car was still racing.

The third and final curve came up. It was by far the tightest one. For a minute I toyed with the idea of letting the car scrape the mountainside and wreck it. But the wall on my left was hollowed out and partly curved over the road. It was an American car and the driver's seat was on the left. The very first thing that would have touched the mountain would be the windshield on my side. It would have torn off my head. No chance! I had to cross my arms over the steering wheel, spin it to the right and immediately to the left as far and fast as I could. The car skidded around, the bumper hit the retaining wall. It had been made of uncut granite stones weakly cemented together. Again I was enveloped in dust. The car had been bounced back onto the road by the demolished retaining wall. As I now drove on in the hardly declining road, I heard the stones roll down into the river. They had saved my life! What is more they had saved Gerhard's car.

I felt good as the car crossed the bridge into Gordon Town. The nicely paved road, though curving as the mountain wall curved, was easy to descend to Papine. I could use the high speed gear with my right hand on the switch key, turning it off and on, to regulate the speed. From Hope Gardens on, the road was almost straight all the way into Kingston. I had wanted to take the car to Henriques Garage, the Ford Agent, in Church Street. They were known to do reliable work.

It seemed like forever since I had left Farm Hill at sunrise. It was rush time in Kingston, but traffic was light. Most pre-war cars had rusted into oblivion, and only very big shots could get dollar permits to get new American cars. Europe had not yet resumed exporting cars.

Just at 8 o'clock, as I drove through the lovely park which interrupts King Street, there was a brand new 1946 Ford V-8 in front of me. It had aluminum bumpers. The policeman on point duty stopped this pretty shining vehicle and I pressed the brake and promptly smashed in the rear end of that brand new sedan. Its bumper turned into a pretzel and did nothing to protect that beautiful car. How could I have forgotten so quickly that I had no brakes?

I had never even heard of car or liability insurance. All the money which Gerhard and I had could not possibly pay for the damage I had caused to that car!

Four very pretty girls clambered out of the car in front. They looked really angry. The tall policeman came rushing up to me, note book and pencil in hand. He officiously licked his pencil and cleared his throat ominously. The young gentleman, who had been driving all those pretty girls, stepped between the policeman and me. His brows were knit. But suddenly he gave me a big smile.

"Mr. Von der Porten, I saw you play last week against Kingston [Swimming Club]. You were fabulous! I always go to see the water polo games. The way you stopped the shot right after half-time! I was sure it was going to be a goal!" The policeman kept clearing his throat.

The young gentleman turned towards the policeman: "Why don't you go back to do your duty!"

"But, Sir, it is..."

"Mr. Von der Porten and I can look after everything. Go back to your point duty."

"Yes, Sir, Mr. Henriques." He saluted snappily and was gone. That was a great relief for me.

The girls looked puzzled. The lovely new V-8 looked totaled!

"I am Fabian Henriques, my uncle owns the Ford agency. What is wrong with your car?" He looked. He did not see any damage.

"The brake rod snapped."

"Good thing you were not going fast." He looked very sympathetic. "It is a Ford. Bring it to our garage. We'll fix it. Here, give them my card as you leave the car." He scribbled a name on the card and the words: "See me."

They did not weld the brake rod. They installed a brand new one. It is nice to run into a fan of yours. This run-in was literal. Since they were at it, they even gave the car a tune-up, and they never charged a penny. All's well that ends well. Water polo! What a sport!

# GERHARD, FARM HILL AND AGRICULTURE

Gerhard had heard so much about the excellence of the Jamaican Agricultural College at Hope Gardens. It was run by the Government to improve the level of farming and ranching in the Island. He went there many times and discussed the possibilities of what to do with Farm Hill. Most of the coffee trees had been killed by Wynne grass which had been imported as a good feed for live stock.

As so often with introduced plants, that grass changed the ecology of the area. Its tight root system choked the coffee plants to death. Gerhard had tried to reap the coffee. When he paid his men by the hour, they lazed around gathering very little, and when he paid them by the pound, the bag contained unripe berries, leaves, twigs, clumps of moss and the sorting took forever. He had to give up.

Gerhard decided to try cattle. He bought cows in Old Harbour from Mr. Perry who had one of the best herds in all of Jamaica. The animals were trucked to Hardware Gap and driven from there to Farm Hill. He had hired an overseer (busha) who had graduated from the agricultural college and who specialized in cattle raising. Unfortunately, the man turned out to be a lazy, drunken bum. The cows were not used to the high altitude. They had been raised on thinly sliced sugar cane and not Wynne grass. The busha neglected them when they got sick, so they died one after the other. Farm Hill cost Gerhard far more than he could afford. Gerhard had bought fruit trees: coffee, grapefruit, oranges, tangerines, nutmeg, etc. The climate there was most excellent for those trees, but the busha never had them planted and the seedlings dried up.

It was obvious that Gerhard either had to go to Farm Hill and run it full-time, or sell and cut his losses. Fruit trees, including coffee, took seven years before one could hope to earn a penny from them. In the meantime, one had to keep the local goats and the Wynne grass from them. They had to be watered until they were strong enough to withstand a drought.

Water itself was quite a problem. Drinking water was collected by running gutters from the roofs to cisterns. Springs were far away. With the lazy people up there, watering seedlings regularly seemed an impossible task. Besides, Gerhard did not have any capital and certainly could not hold out for seven years before that farm might show a profit. He decided to sell.

He and Dorrie had become more and more gloomy ever since bad reports came down from Farm Hill. Fortunately, Gerhard's agency business, the Antilles Trading Co., started to pick up and he was fairly well off. It was still very difficult to obtain permits to import goods which had to be paid for in dollars. Gerhard represented mostly West European exporters and did quite well.

# 167 PRINCESS STREET

One day, Gerhard told me that he had sold Farm Hill for twice as much as he had paid for it and for his losses combined. He was going to buy 167 Princess Street with the Farm Hill money as a down payment.

I rode my bicycle to Princess Street. 167 was on the west side of the street, half a block down from North Street. It had 150 ft frontage and was a whole block deep all the way to the lane in the back, more than 250 ft. That was huge for a lot in the business district of Kingston! Unfortunately, the land was a good three to four feet above the level of the street which made it useless as a building lot for a commercial building. There were quite a few run-down buildings on the lot. They were built from excellent local, termite-proof hard wood and very good, red brick which were better than anyone could buy at that time. A few shingles on the roofs were missing, but the rest seemed of good quality cedar.

The sanitation seemed to be awful, as black soapy water ran down into the street, and lots of miserable looking squatters crowded around one faucet in the yard. There were also swarms of little children. They had the distended bellies caused by protein malnutrition. Some were completely naked, some had on nothing but a dirty "marino" (sleeveless white undershirt.) I felt sure that it would be practically impossible to collect any rent from that crew. How could Gerhard have bought such a run-down place? Nobody else would have given a red penny for it! That place could be nothing but trouble! Removing squatters was practically impossible under the present socialist political climate.

Gerhard did not have to wait long for trouble to arrive: A powerful looking Black man in a very shabby army uniform with lots of officer's insignia arrived with a miserable looking, limping elderly woman. "I 's fram the Bustamante Labour Union, Sah. I represents the renters at 167 Princess Street. Dis laidy fall dong an she hurt she self. What you gwain do about it, Sah?"

"Nothing. If she is a tenant, she is responsible for what happens in her own home."

"I tries to be nice, Sah, but iffen uno na gwain compensate dis

478

laidy, I'm gwain to go to the sanitary inspector at the KSAC (Kingston's governing body.) Him is gwain make uno fix up the plaiace afore uno can collec any more rent."

"I don't take kindly to threats. Do what you like after you get off my property. Good-bye!"

Sure enough, a tall, young Black man in a navy blue business suit, nicely polished black shoes, wearing a starched white shirt with a black tie and a white sun helmet on his head, arrived in Gerhard's office. "I am the Sanitary Inspector, Sir. You have a property at 167 Princess Street?"

"Yes."

"I have a list of sanitary violations on said property. You are required by law to bring all dwellings on your rental property into conformity with the latest revisions of the Jamaican Sanitary Code, Sir."

"I just bought that property. I used all my money for the down payment. I have to collect a lot of rent first, before I can afford any of the repairs you suggest."

"No, Sir, not: suggest, Sir, demand! You have no choice, Sir. You are not going to collect another penny of rent until you bring the property up to standard."

"How are you going to stop me from collecting rent? You tell me!"

"I am going to condemn the property! I am going to drive everybody off the property!"

"You can't do that! That is cruel!"

"Not so cruel as letting the people get sick because they live in unsanitary conditions. Are you going to fix the sewage and water supply system, Sir?"

"You are bluffing. You don't have the power to drive the people off that property after they have lived there so long."

I had to admire Gerhard. I had escorted the inspector into Gerhard's office and was listening. Now the inspector's pride was obviously hurt. His authority was questioned by this damned German.

"Oh yes?! Bluffing?! Good-bye, Sir." He turned around and left in a huff.

Gerhard got in contact with some men who could take down

479

buildings. The inspector was as good as his word. He drove off all of the squatters in a couple of hours. Gerhard could never have done that in a year, even with the best lawyers' help! Before night fall all the miserable huts had been torn down and the water faucet had been replaced with a pipe plug. The next day the building material was sorted into neat piles. Material of such quality was almost impossible to get right after the War. Gerhard advertised it and sold it in a day. He advertised: "Clean fill dirt free, if you dig it yourself." Trucks arrived and lots of pick axes and shovels dug down the property to street level in a week.

Now he really had a wonderful property. The Bank of Nova Scotia would be only too happy to lend him the money to build a huge steel building to cover the whole property. But first, a dangerous condition had to be remedied. The houses on the neighboring property were right on the line and three to four feet above Gerhard's newly dug down land. There was nothing but soil underneath them. A foundation had to be built under them to prevent them from sliding down in the next hurricane season. That could cost Gerhard all he had and more in law suits.

Dorrie and Gerhard decided that they had to see Dorrie's sisters after the many years of war and separation. Gerhard told me that he had hired a contractor to put underpinnings under the neighboring housing. All I had to do was to pay him in proportion of the work he had done. He expected it to be completed in four weeks at the latest. He transferred the money into the Glasslite account and I wished them a happy trip to Germany.

The contractor had never worked for us before. He took me for stupid and suffered from the common belief that White people had unlimited funds. He did next to no work in the first week. I wished that I could have fired him and could have done the work myself with my Glasslite crew, but the contractor had a firm contract. When I saw that his men were idling and next to nothing had been done the first day, I told him that I was going to pay him in proportion of the completed work and no more, and if he did not do a lot better the next day, I would not pay him at all. He just laughed and told me that Mr. Porten had told him that he would get a quarter of the pay every week.

"That is right," I told him, "if a quarter of the work is done every week." He did not take me seriously. He should have!

At the end of the week I did not pay him as he came to 4 Arlington Avenue to collect his money to pay himself and his workers. He had done nothing the entire week. He obviously believed that he could get a lot of money out of me by dragging the work on for many months.

We quarreled and he threatened to have me killed if I did not pay him. This time it was I, who did not believe. Maybe I should have. Finally, at sundown he took off in his two ton truck without getting a penny from me.

It was near midnight when his truck arrived at Arlington Avenue. All his men were there with sticks and even some machetes. I did not want them to break down the door. I put my pants on over my pajama pants and went outside in my slippers. The men immediately surrounded me.

"What do you want?" I asked them.

"We want our money!"

"I did not hire you, Mr. Bennett hired you. Ask him for your money."

"Him tell we, uno na pay him, so him cian't pay we! We gwain kill uno, yah!" The circle around me grew very small indeed. They were excited. I knew, because they were sweating though the night was fairly cool. I could smell it more than I could see it. My ear tips burned and my heart was beating very fast.

"You see, I am in my pajamas. I have no money on me, and I have no money in the house. The money is in the bank. I have to sign a check. Iffen uno is gwain kill me, who is gwain sign the check? All ah you, the whole ah you, is gwain hang in Spanish Town, but uno is nah gwain get any money. Make I talk to Mr. Bennett, and you go back inah yo truck, yah."

I used the Jamaican dialect. It was general knowledge that foreigners are too stupid to understand the Jamaican way. Besides, White people were fair game to be robbed in every which way possible. I wanted to be as Jamaican as possible.

Mr. Bennett stepped forward to glare at me in the bright moonlight. His men were still all around me. I felt my pulse racing. The situation was very hairy. Murders are fairly frequent in Jamaica. I had to preserve my composure.

I said: "I told uno, I want to talk to Mr. Bennett one. Uno want to get paid, uno go back inah yo truck." Mr. Bennett motioned with his head, and the men left the premises and stood in front of the truck.

"I shall withdraw money from the bank early on Monday morning, and I'll pay you some money so that you can give your men something, but neither you nor your men deserve it, as you have done next to no work. Remember, if there is not a lot of work done by next Saturday, I shall not pay you at all! You understand me?! The sum agreed upon is final, if you finish faster, you get all the money faster. If you fool around like this week and take forever, you will get no more money, and YOU will have to face your men. They now know that I am serious and don't frighten easy. I am not going to pay for nothing!"

He argued that Mr. Porten had promised to pay him so much a week. I told him that he was wrong. Mr. Porten promised him to pay him so much and expected the work to last about four weeks. "Besides," I told him, "he is out of the country and what I say now, goes. You can complain to Mr. Porten all you want, when he comes back in three months' time." Finally he and his men got back on the truck and drove off. It was a nice feeling to see that gang go! My heartbeat gradually returned to normal.

I went to the bank as it opened on Monday morning at 10 a.m. and drew some money out and went to 167 Princess Street. The men had already done more than they had done the entire week before. I paid the contractor, and he paid his men, there was next to nothing left for himself. That latter fact caused another short argument. I did not see any reason for me to back down. I paid so little in order to put the emphasis on my statement that the amount agreed upon was final.

I had seen that his men had been paid. Surely, they would not be keen to confront me again. The upshot was that the work was finished and paid for ahead of schedule. I was glad. I had feared that a severe rain would have come and would have washed one of the houses from the next door property unto the newly dug level of 167 Princess Street.

# DOROTHEA MARIA VON DER PORTEN

The Jesuit Priests had fought successfully to get Gerhard transferred out of the internment camp to St. Joseph's Hospital. There caring nuns had nursed him back to health. Dorrie and especially Gerhard had a lot of reasons to be thankful to the Roman Catholic Church. They embraced that faith wholeheartedly. They had themselves baptized and had a Catholic Church marriage to supplement their secular one. They both remained ardent Catholics to the end of their lives.

Dorrie and Gerhard wanted a child for the longest time. They saw Dr. Rose Parboosingh. She was a well-known general practitioner and her husband was a well-known surgeon in Kingston. He was a Jamaican of East Indian descent. Incidentally, they were also very active in the Quaker Meeting. Finally, under Rose's guidance, Dorrie had a baby, Dorothea Maria. She arrived on this earth on September 23, 1945. She was a very pretty baby and not only the family, but also all the workers at the macaroni factory loved her.

Earlier, Dorrie and Gerhard had moved to a house half-way between Papine and Gordon Town. It was a very large older two story house with attached servants quarters just above the high water mark of the Hope River. The gorge at that point is very narrow and granite walls tower high above that damp, shaded valley. Moss and lichens covered the trees and bushes which grew out of every crack in the steep walls of the canyon. Its water supply was provided by a ram (a hydraulically operated pump) a little upstream. Just above the house a very beautiful granite bridge arches over the river. The faithful Ruby moved into the servant's quarters of the house and took good care of mother and child.

At first they had no electricity. Kerosene and gasoline lamps lit the house. After a while though, before the baby was born, they got electric wiring installed in the house, and their refrigerator was moved there. They had to buy a pole and line to the main road before the Jamaica Public Service Co. would connect them to their net.

# REPAIRS AT WHITFIELD HALL

Major Simmons, Dorothea's husband, never took any interest in the Quaker Movement. He loved his estate in St. Anns. He never quite recovered from the wounds he received in World War I. He slept with a hand gun under his pillow. Unfortunately, that was known to his employees on the farm.

One night, his trusted foreman tried to kill him. I do not know why. He found the weapon under the pillow and shot and severely wounded poor Mr. Simmons in the head. The bullet was lodged in the inner ear. The bullet was removed. It cost the Major his hearing on one side.

Dorothea nursed him for a long time, but the wound kept draining and failed to heal. Eventually, they saw that an operation was absolutely necessary. They decided that they wanted it done in the United States.

Dorothea phoned to tell me that she had engaged a contractor to renovate Whitfield Hall. She asked me to check on the contractor from time to time. She told me that the main beam over the hall needed replacing. For that she had instructed the man to cut down one of the huge eucalyptus trees and to fashion a beam from it. There were lots of minor items such as sealing the cedar bath tubs in the two bathrooms. There was a cistern which caught rain water for drinking, cooking, and washing. That might need sterilizing, etc.

She gave me her address in the States. I promised to report to her regularly. I wondered if she would bother to read the reports as she would probably be totally absorbed with the health problems of the Major. He might not even survive! I hoped that I would be up to the task. I had had some pretty bad experiences with labor in the Blue Mountains and contractors which I did not hire. I was sorry for the Simmonses but I was glad that I could repay Dorothea for some of the kindness she had shown me while I was interned and afterwards.

Every Saturday, after I closed my shop at 1:00 p.m., I climbed up the Blue Mountains. Sometimes Gerhard lent me his car. I left it at Mavis Bank. But most of the time I took a tram car (trolley) to Papine and rode on a truck which carried market women home from the Papine Market to Mavis Bank. Dorothea Simmons had picked a very good contractor. I never met him, but his work progressed very nicely.

One weekend, Willy came along. He had traveled all the way from Highgate, and we climbed the mountain together. I told him: "I do not like the cistern. I have discovered a little stream a little distance above the house. We could dam it and run a pipe directly into the house, bypassing the sad looking vat." I had started to build a little dam of stones. The water ran through the spaces between the stones, but the dam raised the water table behind it, so that the water level would be above the intake of the pipe at all times.

I brought a few tools with me. Both of us carried them up the mountain. The contractor had transported new galvanized iron water pipes to the building. We screwed them together leading from the dam to the house. We cut them to length, threaded them and connected them directly to the piping in the house. We built up the dam, and had the water intake halfway up the dam, so that no silt would get into the pipe.

We went into the house and filled a bath tub. The pressure was pretty good and the tub filled with beautifully clear water. The contractor had put in modern toilets, no more out houses. We had added an unlimited water supply. It made us feel good that we were able to add a little something, which Dorothea Simmons had not expected nor bargained for.

# THE NEED TO EAT AND RUM WIN OVER CONSCIENCE

In Kingston, life was difficult. The neon material was so terribly expensive and difficult to obtain. It was most frustrating. My customers balked. I could not get any orders. At last the Swiss Consul called me. He was the manager of the Jamaican branch of the Swiss Rum Co. I liked his rum very much and on the rare occasions when I had a drink, I would mix a planters' punch with Coruba Rum, aged and bottled by the Swiss Rum Co. Jamaica rum is the best tasting rum and popular the world over and Coruba Rum tasted the best of the best, as far as I was concerned. Since I had joined the Quakers I had given up even having a social drink at a special occasion.

J. Wray & Nephew and Myers were by far the dominant distillers in Jamaica. Their rums were so well introduced that there was hardly any demand for Coruba Rum. The Consul wanted me to make ten outdoor signs reading: *Coruba Jamaica Rum.* And he wanted them flashing. He wanted all Jamaica to know that his brand was there, and the public should try it.

Ordinarily, this would have been a dream order. But now, should I promote the drinking of alcohol which I would not want my friends to touch, and with which I had had such a bad experience only eleven years earlier? I promised to submit a sketch of the proposed signs.

That night I hardly slept. That was not like me. Usually I fall asleep a few minutes after my head touches the pillow. But that night I wrestled with my conscience. I had seen a lot of unhappiness come out of bottles. I certainly needed the money. But alcohol! I had almost died from it! But then it was a very good rum and the streets of Kingston, on which I walked, were paved with the revenue derived from the tax on rum. I had no other order. My helper and I had to eat.

By morning, I had made up my mind to try to get the order. I made a beautiful sketch, copying the trade mark exactly on transparent paper. I used white carbon paper, transferred the sketch to black construction paper and used tempera paints to draw in the lettering. The customer liked it and bought ten signs. I had found a supplier in England who made 50 Hertz neon transformers. When I loaded them to about 80% capacity, they worked, though they were getting hot. At least they did not burst into flames as some of Suarez's transformers had done.

Now there arose the problem of ten flashers. Ready made imported flashers did not work. I knew that from very unpleasant experience. The springs kept breaking in the tropical heat and the air saturated with moisture. I devised my own flashers without springs. I used the gear motors of broken flashers and made a cam of insulating material mounted on the output shaft. I lined the cam with zinc sheet for contacts and had pieces of copper tubing for brushes rubbing on the zinc sheet for the "on" time of the sign and on the insulation for the "off" time alternately. To make sure that the copper would make good contact, I used the lead stripped from the ends of lead cable as weights. That worked fine. Now I had to get ten small gear motors. I found them advertised in a trade magazine in England. There were twenty of them sold as war surplus. I bought them all. That was a lucky break.

I had no sooner installed the flashers when the Jamaica Public Service Co. called me up: "We have any amount of complaints about radio interference from the flashers you installed! Silence them or take them down or we'll disconnect the power to your signs!" I am not an electrical engineer. I had to find out by trial and error what size capacitor I would need to suppress the spark. A radio repair man gave me a rough idea of the size range. I eventually found the right capacitors. It was an unexpected expense. Tuition, I called it.

# REPAIRS AFTER HOURS

Once in a while, Amy and I drove to the Carib Theater to see a movie. One evening as we approached the theater, I noticed that the *Coruba Rum* sign was flickering. I dropped Amy off at the movies and told her that I would only be a minute, but I had to fix the sign first. Amy objected to my climbing the building in my good clothes without a ladder, and to my letting her go alone to see the show. She always objected every time I dropped her off and fixed a sign. There had been several similar situations.

After I had climbed to the roof, I noticed that an insect had bridged an electrode wire to the metal sign. I had to remove it. Unfortunately, it was on the face of the sign that was directly over the street, and I could not reach the spot. I had to climb down again and get a rope. I had no rope in the truck, but found a long piece of No. 12 gauge iron wire. That would do just as well. I climbed up again, twisted the wire around the uprights of the sign, leaning against the wire, hanging over the street, I removed the suicidal insect with an insulated pliers, and went to untwist the wire. As I touched the end of the wire, it broke and hung over the street from the far support of the sign. Earlier, wanting to fasten it really well I had twisted the wire to the verge of breaking. Now, barely touching it, it broke!

When I got to the theater, the show was over. I did not mind. I did not mind Amy's mild reproach for leaving her alone in the Carib. I was just glad to be alive.

# A PAINFUL HEALTH PROBLEM

For some time it hurt a little to urinate. I thought that the trouble would go away. I had not gone to a doctor since the trouble with my heel. I did not want to go now. One day while servicing a sign, I had to put my left lower leg over a rope, so that I had both hands free while leaning over the street. Suddenly, I felt an extremely sharp pain as if someone were slicing my insides with a knife just below the kidney.

I got off the sign as fast as I could and sat in my truck, hoping that the pain would go away. After I got home, I had the painful experience of passing a kidney stone. When I washed it, I noticed that it had very sharp edges and points. I took it to Dr. Rudi Aub. He and his wife, Ruth, a trained nurse, examined it carefully.

Rudi told me that stones were either acid or alkaline, and that mine was alkaline. He told me that I did not drink enough water which often happened with swimmers. Though they exercise very strenuously, they do not feel any thirst, because they do not get hot. Still they should drink water. He prescribed a diet, but mainly admonished me to drink a lot of water. He also warned me that I probably had a similar stone in the other kidney, and that I might, therefore have a similar attack again. He did not give me any medicine. He promised that the bleeding would soon stop and all would heal by itself.

All healed as he had predicted. I soon forgot about the possible other stone, and even about drinking a lot of water.

# THE FATE OF SOME WATER POLO
# PLAYERS

I had originally become the goalie of the Jamaica All Star Water Polo Team because my predecessor had gone back to his native Cuba in 1938. I had the honor to remain in that position until I left Jamaica in 1953.

My club was the Jamaica Amateur Swimming Club. Immediately after the declaration of war by Prime Minister Chamberlain on September 3, 1939, Malcolm Finleyson our best player, fastest swimmer, center half, and captain of our team took a ship to his native England. The ship never arrived. He was one of the very first casualties of the War. It hurt me particularly hard, as he was the one who had lured me away from the Kingston Swimming Club to offer me the position of goalkeeper for the "A" team of his club. I had a great admiration for the capable leader. It struck me as an irony that this young man, one of the very best long distance swimmer whom I shall ever meet, probably drowned.

Our left forward, Robin Hunter, also of English descent had not been heard from for a long time. He had joined the Royal Air Force and was the tail gunner in a large bomber. His plane had received anti-air craft fire in a night raid near Munich, Germany. After they were out of the range of the anti-air craft shells, he was said to have walked from the rear of the pitch dark plane towards the front, when he fell right through the weakened floor of the plane. Now, that the War was over, he wrote home that he had parachuted and had been interned under terrible conditions near Munich for the rest of the War. I never met him again. I heard that he had become a complete recluse.

Ronny Henriques, the captain of a new opposing club, also a member of the Jamaica All Star Team, had also gone to England. He joined the paratroopers. He was dropped over Arndheim in the Netherlands behind the German lines. He received a shot through his thigh and was captured. The War was almost over at that time. His wound healed very well, and he returned to Jamaica with an English wife. He resumed a very normal life.

It might be a good place to note here, that little by little, I found

490

out that every German boy whom I mentioned by name in this narrative, was killed during the War.

# THE RAMSEYS

Iris Alexander was Mr. Chen's secretary. She and her fiancé, Noel Ramsey, visited me a few times in the internment camp. Their cheerful dispositions made me feel really good every time they came. I was very grateful that they had the courage of their friendship. It was not the most popular thing to do, to visit "a damned German" in the camp.

Shortly before I was released, they had gotten married and lived in a very nice neighborhood at No. 2 Skibu Avenue, near Half-Way Tree Rd. It was a pretty large house. Iris's father was in poor health, and Noel became the man of the house. Noel was an accountant at the Government Printing office. Iris's mother was a well known dressmaker with a delightful sense of humor, and Iris's sister, Daphne, was a floorwalker at the Times Store in King Street. So there were five living in that house. You could not possibly find nicer people. For families to live together even after the children grow up and get married is not at all unusual in Jamaica.

Mr. Alexander was a retired merchant. He loved roses and could talk about them at great length. He knew all their names and countries of origin. Some of the roses were of great value because of their fragrance, particular coloring, or country from which they had originally been imported. His rose garden was extensive and immaculate.

They had laid out a very professional looking badminton court and installed flood lights. Noel had several siblings. Especially Carol, a successful lawyer, and Eric, an accountant, and his sisters, Kitty, a secretary, and May Locke, who had married a medical technician in the British Army, John Locke, were there every Friday night along with many other guests. I was always welcome. We often played till midnight. Incidentally, John Locke was an accomplished painter. He sold quite a few of his canvasses to augment his army pay.

The weekly badminton at the Ramseys became a delightful social event. Lots of young couples and singles came to play and chat. I became quite a proficient player. Only Carol and Eric could beat me. However, most games were played doubles, because we were so many, and all of us wanted to play. When it became known that I had become friendly with Miss Barry, they asked me to bring her along.

Amy was not active in any sport except hiking. She often walked along remote trails to collect plant and insect specimens for the Science Museum of the Institute of Jamaica and the Jamaica Natural History Society. She was the secretary of that very prestigious group of scientists and school teachers. Finally, she joined me one evening to play at the Ramseys. She played only one game of doubles. Never having played before, she played poorly, as was expected and considered only natural by all. Amy sat on the side lines, and everybody wanted to talk to her, probably to check her out to find out what I saw in her and vice versa.

When playing doubles, Eric and Carol were the most popular partners as their teams usually won. The very evening Amy came with me for the first time, we decided to have a little singles tournament. Eric and Carol beat all their opponents, including me, and finally the great match, the match we had all waited for, started.

It was a most exciting game. The brothers played all out. They both wanted to be the best. We all watched tensely in admiration of the agility of the two contestants. It was an amazing show. The shuttle cock remained air borne in long volley after long volley. Each player had great endurance. Neither could wear out the other. It was 12 all. 15 was the winning score, unless there was only one point difference, then the game had to continue until there was a difference of two points.

Suddenly Amy yelled: "Stop! **Stop!**" All were alarmed. There, the girl with the hardly audible soft voice suddenly proved that she did have a very powerful yell, and that she could use it in a dire emergency.

Carol caught the shuttle in his hand in the middle of a volley. "What's the matter?"

"Are you hurt?" Anxious questions came from all around.

"That beetle! The Institute has not got a specimen of it!" Amy got up and rushed toward the net in the middle of the court. Finally we all discovered that there was a big black beetle slowly crossing the badminton court.

493

"We have lots of those in the rose garden," Noel said. "They are a real pest, and we kill them every time we see them."

"Oh, but they are rare, please give me a container." Someone emptied a match box and handed it to Amy. "No, that won't do. This is a wood eating beetle and it will easily eat through the match box. It has to be a metal container."

After some searching, Iris at last found a metal container holding some medicine tablets. She transferred its contents into the match box and Amy happily pushed the ugly black insect into the medicine container, oblivious of the stares of disbelief from the spectators and contestants. Amy's great night of triumph for science!

By this time it was almost midnight. It had become too late to restart the contest. We never did find out who was the better player, Carol or Eric, but the museum had a new specimen which Amy's great friend, Miss Audrey Shaw, in the entomological section and also the museum artist, mounted with great care and labeled it with its Latin and common name, location, date and time, and by whom found, and its range on this globe.

Audrey married Alan Wiles. She has become quite famous throughout the Island as an accomplished artist. Her painstaking illustrations of plants and animals on the land and in the surrounding sea are of the most exquisite quality. Along with Amy, she has become an authority on the plants and fauna of Jamaica.

Badminton anyone?

# THE DOUBLE DATE

Mary came from Morant Bay to visit Amy for a few days, and Willy came to visit me for the weekend, great for a double date. We could go to the Carib (movie theater). It was not too far from Amy's house.

Unfortunately, Willy and I had only one bicycle between us. We had to walk the three miles up to Lady Musgrave Road. We had left in good time and we were brisk walkers. On the Old Hope Road, not far above the Nuttall Hospital, we came across Dr. McFarlane, Jamaica's most renowned surgeon. He was staring at his flat tire. He looked pretty desperate. "I am already late for an emergency operation at the Nuttall and now this!"

Of course, Willy and I got busy and changed the tire for the doctor. Who knows, we may have saved someone's life.

Naturally, we were arriving a bit late at the Barry residence. The girls had even finished dressing. Usually, when I arrived on time, I had to wait until Amy had finished dressing. But this time Amy was all dressed and had to wait until the time the movie started. Unheard of! Most annoying!

Without waiting for an explanation, Amy let us know in quite precise terms, that we were late. Neither Willy nor I could get a word in edgewise. That was not too bad. I could deal with that but now Kathleen chimed in, and she could be most insulting. When I told Kathleen to stay out of it, she became quite abusive and worse, Amy took her side, saying that I had no right to tell Kathleen to shut up.

I had told Willy what a nice girl Amy was, and now this reception! I wanted to wash my hands after that tire change before we got into the car. I could not even excuse myself to do so. I was really annoyed by now. There was Willy, a stranger to them. I was late for the movies, dirty and a little sweaty, and on top of it all, this scolding from somebody who usually lets me wait to the last minute when we were going out! It was too much!

I walked right off the verandah. "Come Willy, let's go!" He did not budge.

Always the peacemaker, he tried to calm the roiling waters. "Arnold, come back here."

I had had it with the Barrys and that little brat especially! And Amy taking her side against me when she was definitely most insulting! I kept on going with a very quick pace. I could not care less if Willy stayed. Enough is enough!

Willy, being much taller than I and living in the country where everybody walks to wherever they go, finally caught up with me. He had been running. He was almost out of breath. "Turn around, Arnold, Amy looked so upset. Don't make a mountain out of a mole hill." I kept right on walking, and he kept right on talking.

Finally I said to Willy: "It is better we break up now. We are far too different in every way. Suppose we should ever get married, it would be a disaster! You see, Amy takes the side of that little brat even though she insulted me. I did not come to see that insolent kid. How could I trust Amy ever to come down on my side?"

"If you want to break up, do it in a decent way. Not when you are annoyed and in a senseless quarrel." Willy was ten years my senior. I never minded his counseling me. I usually followed his advice and never regretted it, but this time, I decided against his admonitions. Very definitely so! We made excellent time the three miles back to Arlington Avenue. It is easier to walk downhill anyway.

When we arrived, there was the big old Dodge parked in front of the gate. Amy was at the wheel and Mary sat besides her. I marched straight past them upstairs to my room. It was over! I was not going to be used by that girl any more. As far as I was concerned, she could jump in a lake!

"Come on, Arnold. Just a few ill considered words. You should not have taken it to heart." Willy kept on and on. "It must have hurt Amy badly to have swallowed her pride and come here. You could not have wished for a more profound apology. Go and make up and don't do anything hastily." Willy the Quaker, the peacemaker at all times under all circumstances.

I looked out of the window. The girls were still there. We washed our faces and hands, especially the latter and went down. Mary opened the car door and went into the back seat. Willy sat beside her, and I sat next to Amy. We drove back to Lady

Musgrave Road, sat on the verandah and chatted most amicably as if there had never been a harsh word, let alone a quarrel, till very late at night. Eventually, Willy and I walked the long way home again through the deserted streets. It was the third time that we walked that distance that night. Oh, the power of that slim woman!

The sound of our shoes caused all the dogs to bark and cocks to crow. In Jamaica, if a dog barks at night, another will soon start to bark until dozens are barking. A cock will not be outdone by a mere dog, so he crows. Other cocks hearing that, will want to prove that they can do better. So, when one walks late at nights, one will not go unnoticed.

# TAKING AMY TO THE MOVIES AND THE TURTLE

At the corner of South Camp Road and East Queen Street, there was the Palace Theater. One sat under the stars and that enhanced the ambiance. Gerhard lent me his car and I took Amy to the show.

On the way there and before the movie started, Amy told me about a soft shell turtle. A specimen can weigh 200 lbs (90 kg). Some fishermen had caught a female when she had come to shore and was about to lay her eggs. They had brought it to the Institute. Mr. C. Bernard Lewis, the Curator, wanted to buy it, as there was none in the museum, dead or alive. No agreement could be reached, however, as the men wanted far too much money. They walked away angrily, taking the turtle with them. Mr. Lewis felt sad. He told Amy that he did not think that the poor animal would survive the rough handling by those men.

After the movie, Amy told me that the men would probably dump the unfortunate creature just beyond the Palisadoes where the road is very close to the sea. Amy decided that we should drive there and have a look. I told her that the battery of the car was in a pretty poor condition, and that it might die on us with all that night driving. Never mind the excuses. She did not mind taking that chance.

In those days, the generators were not strong enough to replenish the batteries when the headlights were on, unless you drove very fast. Jamaican roads were not built to drive fast enough to replenish the drain on the battery when the headlights were on. (Alternating current generators were not yet used in cars at that time.) We drove along the Windward Road past Rock Fort, past the Palisadoes to where the road almost touches the sea. Some fishing boats lay on the beach.

"Stop here! This is probably where it is. They must have dumped the turtle near here. If it has died, one has to act quickly to preserve it, as it has a soft shell, and it will rot very soon after death if it is not treated." I turned the car around and stopped where we had passed the fishing boats.

Fortunately, I always carried a flashlight in the car. We

searched for trails leading into the bush. We found one. We could also smell decaying meat. We followed the stench until we stood by the turtle. Only about 50 to 100 ft. of dense bush separated us from the road. The very large carcass was crawling with maggots, ants, beetles, and many other despicable insects. All kinds of flies were buzzing all around it and us. We had to be careful that ants would not crawl up on us. There were thousands of them.

At nights, the wind blows down from the cool Blue Mountains toward the much warmer sea. Even though we stood on the wind side, the stench was overpowering!

"It is too far gone to be salvaged," was Amy's judgment.

"It certainly stinks!" was my comment. I was sick to vomit! but I successfully fought the urge. We got back to the car. It was past midnight.

I tried to start the huge, heavy, ancient car with the ancient tires and the ancient, moribund battery but the starter only groaned dishearteningly.

"All right, Amy, you sit at the wheel, press the clutch all the way to the floor. I'll push, and when I yell: 'Now,' you let up the clutch pedal slowly. When it starts, pull up the hand brake and press the clutch all the way down, hold it down and put the gear into neutral. If it threatens to die, pull out the hand choke a little bit till you hear it idle nicely, though I don't think that that will be necessary as the car is still hot."

The car was certainly heavy. So close to the sea there was no decline to help me either. I had to push it past the dead turtle, and this time we were on the lee side and therefore the recipients of its full aroma. The stench was vile! I had to get up enough speed so that the car would start in the second gear. The reeking dead meat was quite an incentive to do my utmost! I was doing all right! "Now!" I yelled.

Amy let go the clutch. The car started. She depressed the clutch and pulled up the hand brake. I ran next to her and opened the car door. She moved over and took her foot off the clutch. The car made one surprising and frightening leap forward and then died.

"Why didn't you put it into neutral?!"

"Oh, I'm sorry." The stench was putrid to the maximum degree! Amy took out a handkerchief with some perfume on it and held it over her nose. I was furious and Amy was "sorry". It was sufficient ground to break up even the best of friendships.

The builders of the road had put in depressions at intervals, so that storm water would drain off across the road. Murphy's law would have it that our back wheels were in the center of one such depression. I rocked and rocked the car back and forth. I could not get it out, especially with Amy's almost 100 lbs added to the already heavy car. She had to come out to help. She did. We rocked in rhythm. Amy certainly had that, rhythm. Finally, the back wheels were on level ground. I did not take a deep breath of relief! The air was totally saturated with the stench of death.

Amy apologized again, but that did not fix anything. I was vexed (mad in Americanese). "Get back into the car. And this time don't forget to shift the gear into neutral once it starts!" I forgot my manners. I did not say "please" once.

My clothes were glued to my body from perspiration. I pushed and pushed. The odor of decay was still overpowering, but it became less with every step I took. I had to get us away from there! The car was rolling. "Now," I yelled. It started. "Put it into neutral!"

"I did already."

"Fine!" I jumped in. In a few minutes, the cool air from the mountains filled our lungs. All was forgiven. Life was just beautiful!

# NEW YEARS 1945-1946

New Years Eve was approaching and I was practically broke, a dilemma I had become quite used to by then. Every penny I could get hold of went into neon material. Its price had inflated terribly during the War. Nevertheless, I asked Amy to go to the Glass Bucket with me on New Years Eve.

The Glass Bucket was the swankiest night club in Jamaica. It had a most excellent band in the style of Tommy Dorsey's and a singer who could rival Bing Crosby. I had made an estimate: I had just enough money to pay for the cover charge. I knew that Amy would be satisfied with one drink, and I would certainly not have more than one rum punch. I also had to put black market gasoline into Gerhard's car, which I had to borrow again. That would leave me with only a few shillings until I could collect for the next neon sign.

Just as I was about to leave to pick her up, Amy phoned me: "Arnold, Mary has come in from Morant Bay with her cousin and her brother, Dave. I told them that we would pick them up at Greenwood Avenue where they are staying for the holidays."

I was embarrassed. Dave was a lawyer and a prominent PNP man, (the socialist independence party). He could spend lots of money. I could not even afford a round of drinks! "Why did you do that? I don't even know Mary's cousin. Dave has a nice sense of humor, but I cannot keep up with his or Mary's drinking. It's going to be most humiliating for me."

"They have no transportation, so I thought that it would be nice if we picked them up."

"All right, if you absolutely want that."

I had only one good suit. It was light brown. The two Moyston men wore black tuxedos with black ties, gold cuff links, and black, jeweled buttons on their stiff, starched shirts. Mary and Amy wore beautiful, new, evening dresses glittering with sequins down to their toes.

I had recently made a three dimensional Glass Bucket neon sign. It consisted of a large eight cornered angle iron bucket. Yellow crinkled glass were its sides. There were several irregularly shaped white neon tubes inside the bucket to give the impression of ice cubes. Out of the bucket reared a champagne bottle, painted Cordon Rouge, the most popular brand of champagne at that time in Jamaica. A large green neon tube in the shape of a handle seemed to suspend the bucket. Actually, steel chains allowed the entire sign to swing freely. The bottom of the sign was made from steel sheeting and supported the transformer.

Proudly, I showed my passengers my very unique sign as we drove into the parking lot. They barely acknowledged my statement. They hardly uttered a word. We got a pretty nice table. Dave suggested that we order a fifth of rum (one fifth of an imperial gallon) and split the cost.

I did not have enough money for that, so I said: "No, but you go ahead, I don't drink. I'll order a lemonade." Amy did not like rum on the rocks or just diluted with water. I ordered a drink for her. So Amy sipped her drink, and the three Moystons just sat there and drank their rum and water. Somehow, I could not get a conversation going.

I was disgusted. I had looked forward to this evening. It was totally spoilt! I decided to pretend to be drunk. I jumped over a chair at a neighboring table and knocked it down in the process. I walked around bouncing into people and deliberately bounced into one conceited guy who had been particularly antagonistic toward me during the War. At that time, he had already a few drinks, and he wanted to fight me. I pretended that I was quite willing. About half a dozen men jumped up and held us back, so no blows were exchanged.

I spotted the Ramseys. Noel's pretty sister, Kitty, wore a full-length, bright-yellow, evening dress with a short train. It was beautifully embroidered and sparkled with sequins. Its train in the back was, if fashionable, also very impractical. I asked her to dance. She, seeing me so intoxicated, refused. I was rudely persistent.

Iris persuaded Kitty to go ahead. Kitty got up and we tried to dance. I never was a good dancer and Kitty could not follow me. I did not plan this, but I stepped on the train of her dress as we turned, she fell, holding onto me. I had not expected that and fell right on top of her in the middle of the packed dance floor. That caused a

502

huge commotion. She was furious! I apologized and offered her a hand to guide her back to her table. She most emphatically refused any assistance from me! She was obviously hurt, not only figuratively but also most certainly physically. She limped very badly. I must have nearly smashed her hip bone. This was a really messed up night!

People were murmuring and I could hear it: "Look at Von der Porten, so drunk, and it is still so early in the evening!"

"I never knew he drank." There were many other similar remarks.

Amy very desperately wanted me to sit down beside her. Every time I came back to the table the two Moyston men sat there like dressed up statues with a half empty glass of rum and water before them. I had hardly taken a sip from my lemonade. Mr. Abner, the very popular owner and manager of the place, kept watching me. He was obviously trying to make up his mind as to whether or not to throw me out.

I wanted to go home, but there was still quite a lot of rum left in that bottle. I proved to be right when I assumed that the Moystons were not ready to leave, until the last drop of "sugar water" in that bottle had dried up.

The crowd cheered when at last it was midnight and a new year had started. I have often wondered why people do that. The beginning of a new year is not a particular achievement by anyone. It is good for nightclubs and the rum industry though.

It was past 4:oo a.m. when the rum bottle was dry at last. I drove the Moystons to their relatives' house and then took Amy home. She did not say one word to me. She got out of the car with a very chilly: "Good night," turned her back on me and went into her room.

The sky was turning light, as I reached Arlington Avenue. I knew that Amy would soon phone and lecture me. That meant that I would not get much sleep if I went to bed now. I picked up my swimsuit and drove to the Springfield Club. After I had swum a few laps, I noticed that the Campbells were starting up their motorboat. They had a house with a pier just about 2,000 ft. west of the club. A. C. Campbell, the owner of Rapid Vulcanizing, my favorite hardware store in Jamaica, and his son, Douglas, the captain of the All Star Water Polo Team, were getting fishing gear ready. I swam over to join them. We did not catch any fish, but it was a most beautiful sunrise over the glass smooth water of the Kingston Harbour.

Douglas was wondering, of course, why I had gone swimming so early on New Year's Morning. He invited me to the living room and brought out a fifth of rum. I told him my troubles of the night before. He pointed out that I needed a stiff drink to console me, and that he would help me. We polished off the quart of rum and ginger together. I was feeling much better. As a matter of fact, nothing could have bothered me at that point.

At around 11:oo, his cousin arrived with her two little daughters of about eleven. They turned on Jamaican folk music. I showed them how to do belly dancing. I was still in my swimming trunks which had dried in the meantime. Everybody was delighted with my dancing. They had quite a collection of records so that the dancing obviously had to continue for a long time.

After a while, I was getting very hungry and sleepy. All I had in my stomach since the year before, was a pint of rum with some ginger ale. Excellent though it was, it was not generally recommended in place of food.

I thanked Douglas for consoling me and for providing me with the proper where-with-all to drown all of my troubles. I went to the pier, took a dive and swam back to the Springfield Club to put on my clothes, then drove back to Arlington Avenue, made myself a sandwich and slept till nightfall.

The telephone woke me. As expected, it was Amy. "Where were you? I phoned all morning." (I had anticipated just such phone calls and had judiciously side stepped them.) "Where have you been?" Also as expected, her anger had cooled and had been replaced by curiosity. She even sounded quite worried. "Please come up to see me." I gave the car back to Gerhard and obediently rode my bike to Lady Musgrave Road. All is well that ends well.

# GERHARD, SOCIALISM, SUGAR AND SUCCESS

Mr. Attlee had beaten Winston Churchill in the election after the War. Mr. Churchill and his Conservative Party had campaigned on a platform that they would not allow the British Empire to break up. He also passionately advocated a cohesive West European Union under one strong central government. He pointed out correctly that countries of the world are not independent, but interdependent, as the War had shown. Sadly, he was ahead of his time. The British voters were too chauvinistic, too narrow minded. They lacked his vision. They booted him out.

Disappointed, he said: "The British People have given me a decoration for winning the War: The Order of the Boot!" He was bitterly hurt. When his successful rival took his seat in Parliament, he had regained his old sense of sarcastic humor. He got up and told the Honorable Members: "During the election Mr. Attlee had billed himself as a 'modest man,' I can assure you, Honorable Gentlemen, and this entire Nation that he has a lot to be modest about."

Years proved Mr. Churchill right in all respects: Socialism, thanks to Mr. Attlee's brain (or the lack of it), sent Britain's economy into an abysmal fall. The separation of the British Colonies bathed India, Pakistan, Kenya, and Nigeria in blood and ruined the economies of all the Colonies and just about destroyed that of the British Isles, as well. It took Mrs. Margaret Thatcher, a Conservative, a quarter century later to restore Great Britain as a major world trading nation.

Sir John Foote, the brother of the leader of the radical left wing of the British Labour Party, Michael Foote, was sent to Jamaica. He steered the Crown Colony to more and more Government control. He appointed the Socialist, Norman Manley, "Chief Minister", a new title. Mr. Norman Manley took over a lot of the economic decision making from the Colonial Secretary. One had to get permits for all imports.

It was easy to obtain permits for buying goods from Great Britain and even the Communist Countries, but only the politically very influential could buy goods from the United States and Canada, the "hard currency" countries which had the goods to sell, especially the neon supplies.

Fortunately, Australia was considered a "soft currency" country, so that Gerhard could buy all the flour he needed from there. All the European and Asian countries were fully occupied making goods for their own devastated cities and did not want to bother with little, out-of-the-way Jamaica.

The criterion for import permits in Great Britain and Jamaica was a percentage of goods your firm imported in 1938, the last full year before the War broke out. If your firm did not exist seven years earlier, then you were plain out of luck: No permits of any kind. You could buy permits at exorbitant prices, of course, from the few established pre-war firms. That was not what "Socialism" intended to accomplish, but that is what it did in actuality.

Fortunately, Bill Masterton was a very reasonable gentleman. He had been a ships' engineer. He had been stranded in Jamaica many, many years earlier when he had gotten drunk on shore, and his ship had left him. He knew hard times. He knew what we had gone through during the War. We had always paid him cash for all repairs we could not handle. He allowed Gerhard to buy a steel building to cover the entire lot at Princess Street and charged only the usual commission to the seller. The new manager of the new Princess Street Branch of the Bank of Nova Scotia, was happy to take Gerhard's mortgage. Gerhard's Antilles Trading Co. now had a huge warehouse and office. I got a nice part for my neon shop in the northeast corner of the building for a reasonable rent.

We were very active in the Jamaica Manufacturers Association. Gerhard was the Director of the Food Processing Group. His old friend Mr. Farquharson, the Marmalade and Guava Jelly Manufacturer and exporter, came to Gerhard:

"Mr. Von der Porten, the legislature now wants to make it a law that all sugar mills must sell all their sugar to the Jamaica Sugar Association, (a government control board) at world market price, and that the Association will then sell all Jamaican sugar to the Food Control Board in London 'to cut out the middle man.' What will happen to my business?! Where would I buy sugar?" He looked very unhappy.

506

"Mr. Vendreyes and I shall see Mr. Manley at once, Mr. Farquharson. We shall insist that local demand must be satisfied first at the same price the British Board buys sugar ex factory. After all, the local demand is only a drop in the bucket in comparison to the entire sugar crop. I am sure that the legislature will find our request reasonable."

"I certainly wish you luck!"

Vendreyes, the President of the Jamaica Manufacturers Association and Vice President of the Jamaica Chamber of Commerce, and Gerhard were successful. Mr. Farquharson and all the Chinese-Jamaican wholesalers were happy.

The British Parliament and the Jamaican Legislature apparently did not realize what far reaching consequences government control of sugar would have on the industries which used sugar in their products. Nor did they seem to be aware of the important role middlemen played in the orderly, just and equalizing distribution of products.

One nice sunny morning, a little, not particularly significant looking, well dressed gentleman walked into Gerhard's office:

"Mr. Von der Porten?"

"Yes, Sir."

"The Bank Manager at the Bank of Nova Scotia has recommended you as a very reliable and enterprising businessman starting up in the post-war period. I think that we can do business together. My name is Magnus Friedmann.

"This is my position: I manufacture quality chocolate products. Since I fled to England from Poland in 1939 when the War broke out, I cannot get any quota for sugar of my own. The established sugar barons, Cadbury, Fry, and Rountree don't like me, but they are willing to sell me part of their sugar quota for more money than they could possibly make if they used it for their own manufacture. I cannot make money. I'll go broke that way. You, Mr. Von der Porten, are going to buy the entire sugar crop of Jamaica for me, manufacture Fudge and ship it to me at 1½% above your cost."

"What is Fudge?"

"It is pure sugar mixed with 1%, by weight, with gelatin. I shall send you the gelatin in one pound packages. You get yourself a cement mixer, turn a bag of sugar inside out, add 1 lb. of gelatin, empty the contents into the same bag, sew it up, put your mark on it, get yourself a government chemist's report that the contents of the bag is not pure sugar according to the parameters of the law. You ship the bags to the La Selles, DeMercado Wharf and the bank will pay you against presentation of the wharf receipt. I have established an irrevocable letter of credit with the Bank of Nova Scotia. La Selles promised me to do the rest. There is no law against making, selling, buying, nor shipping fudge."

He gave Gerhard a purchase order and a copy of the letter of credit. Gerhard bought the entire sugar crop of the Island. The cement mixer was working all day for days on end. Drays took the fudge and the Government Chemist's certificates to La Selles Wharf in the afternoons. Gerhard took the wharf receipts to the bank as it opened in the mornings before the mill could present Gerhard's checks which had been mailed the day before.

For the first time since Gerhard and his, long since disappeared, partners had opened the Continental Club in 1934, Gerhard was out of debt and was making a lot of money. The British Food Control Board in London did not receive a bag of Jamaican Sugar for a whole year until the stupid laws were rescinded in Jamaica and in Great Britain. The Jamaican Sugar Association was furious but helpless until it was dissolved by law. Oh, if Karl Marx could only see his Socialism now!

# SOCIALISM PLUS COCOA BEANS EQUAL MONEY FOR GERHARD

One bright morning, Mr. Magnus Friedmann strolled again into Gerhard's office. The two men greeted each other warmly. "The Jamaican Government has done it again, Mr. Von der Porten. The Jamaica Food Control Board has offered to buy all cocoa beans from the Jamaican produce buyers. The price which the produce buyers should pay will be advertised daily in the *Jamaica Daily Gleaner*. The Jamaican Government has guaranteed to pay the buyers five pence per pound over their cost.

"They plan, mind you plan, to ship the entire crop to the British Food Control Board in England. The British Board would ration the cocoa in proportion to the users' 1938 consumption. Since I was not in business in 1938, I would be left out in the cold. Cocoa is in extremely short supply in Britain right now as there is a lot of rioting by the independence movement in Nigeria, the world's main cocoa supplier. Many of the planters have fled for their lives and may never return to that colony.

"The Jamaican Legislature passed a law that no cocoa beans may be exported except by the Jamaica Food Control Board. You, Mr. Von der Porten, are going to buy out the entire Jamaican cocoa crop for me. This is what you will do:

"You put an ad into the *Gleaner*, stating your address and that you will pay a penny a pound more than the price advertised by the Food Control Board. Turn each bag of cocoa inside out into your cement mixer to check that what you buy is really free of impurities. Re-use the bag, put your mark on it, and ship it to La Selles Wharf. You will be paid by the bank against wharf receipt for your cost plus 1½%. Here is your copy of my irrevocable letter of credit which I established with the Bank of Nova Scotia and my open purchase order for all the cocoa you can buy."

"But Mr. Friedmann, you just said that the Jamaican Government will not allow the export of any cocoa except through the Jamaica Food Control Board. It would not suit you to sell to them. You would not get any for your own use. What are you going to do with the cocoa lying in La Selles warehouse? What use is it to you there? What use is it to anybody?"

Mr. Friedmann just smiled. He was putting out a great deal of money. The smile told that he knew exactly what he was going to do. It also told that now was not the time to tell anyone of his plans. "Don't worry, Mr. Von der Porten, I am not going to lose any money or have sleepless nights." With that he got up, left, and I never saw him again.

Gerhard did exactly as Mr. Friedmann had told him. Trucks rolled in all day, every day. Gerhard's warehouse was busy. Drays took the cocoa to the wharf all day. Every day the Government's offer for cocoa went up. It doubled and quadrupled. It went sky high! Gerhard still bought at one penny above the government advertised price. It suited him, as he still got his 1½% above his cost. The bank told Gerhard that Mr. Friedmann's letter of credit would not run dry. It was an amazing deal. It filled up the warehouse on the wharf, and still more was coming.

The Director of the Food Control Board was desperate! He told Mr. Randall, Gerhard's lawyer, that he would have Gerhard arrested! Mr. Randall told him: "That's a great idea. Do that, and we'll sue the Government for more money than it collects in a year in taxes! Remember, Mr. Von der Porten is trading within the law which you, yourselves, recommended to the Legislature." Since Mr. Randall was one of the most prominent and respected men in all of the Island, nothing more was heard about arresting or suing.

A year passed by. Gerhard told me that Mr. Friedmann had come back to Kingston and demanded from the Government to pay him for the cost of the cocoa plus five pence per pound as their law required them to pay the buyers. After all they themselves had made that the law! The Government did not have any money in the budget for that kind of a loss. The new cocoa crop was about to come in. Nigerian cocoa was projected at half the price of the Jamaican. Obviously, the Jamaican Government was in a bind.

Mr. Friedmann was magnanimous. He let the Government off the hook. He was willing to keep the cocoa, if the Jamaican Government would allow him to import all his candy making machinery to Jamaica duty free, and if the Jamaican Government would not charge him any income or other taxes for ten years.

Furthermore, the Jamaican Government would not license any other candy manufacturing company for ten years.

The Government was glad to oblige. It had a new employer at a time when unemployment was most severe. Mr. Friedmann liked the climate in the beautiful, high elevation town of Mandeville. That is where he established his factory. No taxes for ten years and low labor cost in the country where his raw material grew. Besides, the good knowledge of his English market should have given him a good advantage over his competitors.

# GERHARD SAVES THE JAMAICA SOFT DRINK INDUSTRY

The socialist governments in Jamaica and Great Britain favored the long established companies by basing all their raw material purchase quotas and the permission to import from "hard currency countries" on their consumption in 1938. This system was a very unfair one. Many new companies had sprung up in the past seven years and many old ones had changed their requirements drastically.

In Jamaica, the soft drink industry was particularly hard hit by this lopsided system. Coca Cola, Pepsi Cola, 7-up and Canada Dry franchise holders got almost as much syrup, as many bottles and crown corks as they could sell, but all the small bottlers, mostly Chinese, who were without clout in the Chamber of Commerce, got permission to buy only one tenth of their required syrup, bottles, or crown corks from their usual suppliers from the States or Canada. As was their standard practice, the Chinese suffered in silence and looked for ways to beat the system.

Gerhard had always maintained good business relationships with the Chinese since he had worked for Mr. Tie Ten Quee. Ernest Lee, a second generation Chinese-Jamaican, was one of Gerhard's salesmen. Lee gathered information as to how much syrup was required to satisfy the demand.

Gerhard went to New York to the Greenwood Laboratories in Long Island, N.Y. They cooked up a plan to help the Chinese bottlers. While there, all syrup imports to Jamaica were reduced to 10% of that of the previous year. Now even the big bottlers were out of luck. Coca Cola, Pepsi, 7-up, and Canada Dry went off the market. They could only be had in expensive bars and restaurants. Great Britain struggling under socialist rule and suffering from a chronic sugar shortage could not supply the flavored syrups to replace those from America.

Fortunately, the law did not specify the percentages of essential oil and sugar in a syrup. The Greenwood Laboratories Chief Chemist and partner sent us a stainless steel homogenizer. I rigged it up in Princess Street. Then he came in person and showed us how to mix the right quantities of Jamaican sugar, American

512

caramel (for the brown color), water and essential oil; homogenize and handle it.

The barrels which came from America and which were labeled "Syrup," contained pure essential oils, the concentrated flavor for soft drinks. The ratio to make the syrup was about 10% essential oil. The rest was local sugar and tap water and a little caramel. Thus, Gerhard could supply his customer with ten times more syrup for his bottling plant than his import permit allowed him to import. That was also good for local sugar sales.

Gerhard found a vendor in France to supply his customers with all the bottles they needed. A vendor in England supplied all the necessary crown corks. The soft drink industry was saved. Gerhard, Lee and their local Chinese bottlers did very well. Franchised bottlers who were required to buy all of their supplies from their franchiser, were very badly hurt by the restrictive law.

Zimba Cola was Gerhard's biggest seller. Greenwood Laboratories supplied Egypt, then a British Protectorate, with Zimba Cola. They now told Gerhard to supply that country with all of their Cola needs as Egypt too was a "soft currency country." The Egyptian market dwarfed the Jamaican. Fortunately, the Jamaican cooper industry is very well developed because of the rum export. So, Gerhard could buy enough barrels.

All the business was done in British Pounds. Greenwood Laboratories was paid in Jamaica. The owners often came to Jamaica to have luxurious vacations. I suppose that is how they used up some of their British money. They might also have bought Jamaican sugar paid for in Jamaica and shipped to Long Island. I really do not know. I do know that Gerhard did very well and was now a well established businessman.

# AMY'S PARENTS COME HOME

I spent many pleasant evenings at the Barry residence. When I could afford it, I took Amy to see a movie. One evening Amy told me that her parents were expected home from America. I received the news with mixed feelings. I would no longer be needed anywhere nearly as much as "the man of the house." On the other hand I was curious as to what Amy's parents were like.

I made a neon sign in red and blue reading: *"Welcome home!"* and hung it in the living room. Amy baked a cake. I had not worked in a bakery for nothing. I had learnt how to make a pointed paper bag, fill it with colored icing sugar, and write: *"Welcome home"* and design all kinds of frills on Amy's cake. Amy appreciated that very much. That took the edge off my worries a little bit as I wondered how Mr. and Mrs. Barry would take me. They must have read quite a bit about me in Amy's letters to them.

I was in the living room when they walked in. There was that man with the pipe again! The horrible Sunday morning, now almost six years ago, on September 3rd, 1939, he had taken all of my possessions which I had in my pockets from me. He had put them in an envelope in that miserable office of the Criminal Investigation Department the day World War II broke out, and I was interned. He had puzzled me then, as to where I had seen him before.

Now the mystery was cleared up. It was in January of that same year when he appeared with his pipe clenched firmly between his teeth at Elise's "Sweet Sixteen Party". He had whisked Amy away from me before I even had a chance to ask her name or introduce myself. He did not seem to recognize me, and I had no intention to bring up the subject. Amy's mother gave me a big smile, and we were friends until the day she died. She had a way of quarreling with the rest of the family and the servants but she was always nice to me.

Life went on pretty much the same. I kept visiting Amy often, and we went out once in a while, money permitting. I had fixed everything in the house before her parents arrived. So, there no longer was much for me to repair.

514

# THE MAJESTIC THEATER

The Majestic Theater was built on Windward Road. I got the job to make the marquee sign and neon decorations all around the screen. All the contractors, their spouses or girlfriends were invited for a buffet with champagne and a show afterwards, the night before the theater was to open to the public. It was a chance for me to shine and demonstrate to all the contractors what my little shop was capable of.

Even though we had not yet been able to obtain a permit from the Competent Authority to buy new tires for Gerhard's car, I borrowed it for this grand occasion. On my way to pick up Amy, I had a flat tire. I changed it to the pitiful looking spare, so I arrived late at Lady Musgrave Road. I could not even give Amy a kiss, as my hands were black from the tire change, and she wore a fabulous long white evening dress with lots and lots of glittering sequins.

I rushed to wash my hands, and we got into the poor, old, beaten up car. We did not want to miss too much of the party. Amy did not want a kiss anyway. She was afraid I might squeeze her and rub off some of the precious sequins. So, no kiss. That annoyed me a little. I had no intention to be that rough in the first place.

We got as far as "Duppy Gate" (Ghost Gate), the no longer used entrance of the Up Park Camp, the southern end of the military reservation at the western entrance of Vineyard Road when the, just installed, spare tire died.

Right at that gate stands a very old cotton tree. That is what they call kapok trees in Jamaica. By far the vast majority of the people in the Island believe that cotton trees are haunted by duppies, the vengeful ghosts of evil, dead people. When such a tree has to be cut down, an animal, such as a goat or a rooster, has to be sacrificed first, and its blood must be sprinkled at the root of the tree.

This particular tree, at the edge of the military camp and Vineyard Pen (the name of the housing development), was supposed to be all the more haunted, as it was said that a British soldier had been robbed and murdered right under this very tree, and that his body had been hanged from its limbs. Several people claimed that they had seen his ghost wandering about right here under this giant cotton tree at nights. Street lighting at that spot was very poor.

Amy and I had changed tires at just about every time I had taken her out. She held the flash light while I got the tools and the spare out of the trunk. I put the jack under the car. She turned the handle while I loosened the lugs. I replaced the tire and she released the jack as soon as three lugs were tight. She held the flash light again while I put the tools and the tire in the trunk of the car. We had the routine pat. It took us "no time flat" as they say in Jamaica, to change tires. But this time I had no spare!

"Don't worry, Amy, there is a gas station down Elleston Road at the corner of Windward Road, just half a mile downhill from here."

"You are not going to leave me here alone. I'm coming with you."

"What, on high heels? You can't help me. Don't worry I'll be right back."

It never occurred to me that Amy, being raised by a series of black superstitious nannies, was frightened out of her wits of duppies! I realized that she would be quite safe under that tree. No Jamaican would go near that tree at nights, especially not if he saw a person clothed in a long white gown.

I trundled the wheel downhill. It was easy. At Windward Road the gas station was closed. Very disappointing! I rolled the tire down Elleston Road to the prison, along Tower Street, down Gold Street to the Public Service Power Station, along Harbour Street to Church Street. The Campbells at Rapid Vulcanizing were just about to go home. I was in luck. My buddies from the swimming club stopped to help me out. I had walked a good three miles rolling that tire in front of me.

Sidney Campbell was an expert at vulcanizing and he did a superb job. He never charged me anything. Time flew. Now I had to trundle the tire all the way back uphill. I was glad that I had left Amy at such a safe place! She was right under the duppy tree. It was almost midnight when I arrived at the car.

Amy was actually happy to see me, but she was also very vexed (mad, in American) that I had abandoned her there under the scary cotton tree for three hours! She let me know in no uncertain terms. She was very quick when she helped me to change the wheel. She wanted to get out of there as fast as at all possible! I had no idea how scared she had been. She never told me till years later.

This was certainly one evening where so much went wrong that even Murphy in his most pessimistic mood and his most infamously pessimistic law could not have believed himself. Surely this was the worst that could ever come! I had missed my opportunity to talk to all those contractors, not even a kiss from Amy, two flat tires, trundling a tire for six miles through half of Kingston in my best clothes. It had been hard work to roll that old wheel uphill, too. And now my girl vexed with me! And all along I had tried hard to do my best in all the miserable situations confronting me! I did not imagine that things could get any worse!

Amy kept an ice cold silence. We finally arrived at Amy's home. Her father was waiting for us on the verandah.

"What is the idea of keeping my daughter out so late?!"

It was the icing on the cake! I had not even had a chance all evening to give her nor to receive from her the slightest peck of a kiss on the cheek, let alone go to the party and film show. Besides my hands were far too dirty from all that tire rolling and changing to even shake her hand if she would have wanted me to do that! On top of that, she was most annoyed with me. Now this: **"What is the idea, etc.!"** <u>**Totally disgusting!**</u> I drove home a most unhappy man.

# AMY'S IDEAS DIFFER GREATLY FROM MINE

In Jamaica, people who work with their hands are generally looked down upon. Gentlemen were supposed to order people to work, and those people received very little pay. A clerk was an educated person and was entitled to much more pay than a plumber, carpenter, electrician, or mason for instance.

Working with my hands everyday, I considered this prejudice very detrimental to the economy, as the people who have a good education could not instruct the workers properly, as they themselves had never done any manual work. Amy, of course, was brought up "properly", very conscious of her upper-class position in this stratified colonial culture.

One evening, we decided to walk to the movies when I saw a big stone in the middle of the street. I picked it up and carried it to the side of the road where it could do no harm to any cars. Amy was shocked! That was work for Quashie! That is what Jamaicans call those on the lowest rung of the ladder of human society. I told her that I did not agree with that part of the Jamaican culture. She was very quiet for a while. I realized that she was thinking about how very different our concepts of proper conduct were. It showed me that we were of two totally different backgrounds, and that it would require an enormous amount of compromise on both parts if we should ever get married.

We had very little in common. She had the highest academic degrees with honors which anyone could ever hope to attain in Jamaica. I had only nine and a half years of formal schooling. She had no interest in sports. I was a swimming champion and the goalkeeper of the All Star Water Polo Team of Jamaica. She hardly ever came to the games when I played. I liked badminton and table tennis. She did not and never learnt to play either. I enjoyed to play bridge. She did not like to play any card games. I liked to play chess, she halfheartedly agreed to learn the game but she never considered any time the proper time to learn.

In the Victoria League, she had become an excellent dancer, especially the "jitterbug". I only knew how to dance the waltz properly, the dance my mother had showed me the last day I was in Hamburg.

Politically, I was very active as a Director of the Jamaica Manufacturers Association. She was politically naïve and did not show any interest, as London knew best what was good for the Empire. I was one of the ten best known painters in Jamaica. Amy did not paint.

There was, however, one undeniable fact that we needed each other, and that we confided in, and trusted each other. Amy had an admirable sense of duty, integrity, and loyalty to the family and the British Throne. Those were qualities which I admired and understood very well. We both liked hiking and biology. She, of course, was considered the No. 1 authority on the Jamaican flora and marine life, excluding fishes, not only in the Colony, but also by the Smithsonian Institute in Washington D.C., Kew Gardens in England and many other institutions of higher learning and museums in the British Empire. She had started a very respectable science library and the very comprehensive herbarium with hundreds of specimens at the Science Museum, a Division of the Institute of Jamaica.

Amy was also the Secretary of the Natural History Society of Jamaica. She organized excursions into the remote areas of the Island. Visitors came from all over the English speaking world to take part in the two week trips to study animals or plants of their particular interests. She proved to be an excellent organizer, getting shelter, mules for transportation, food, and whatever else was needed for those events.

Most importantly, she seemed to like me a lot. She did not seem to care if relatives and friends deplored that she went out with a **German**. She was too much of her own person to let anyone tell her who was, or was not proper company for her. Nevertheless, there were other considerations bothering her. Her idea and that of her father's of earning a living in a gentlemanly way, was to sit in an office, dressed in a neat white shirt and tie, wearing a suit for eight hours a day, do the paper work, get paid for it, and hope for a promotion. But there I was, designing, selling, making, and installing neon signs in dirty khaki work clothes. Often when we were going to see a movie, I would see a sign flickering. I dropped

Amy off at the show and climb the building and fix the sign. At times the show would be over by the time I got through and pick her up in front of the theater. She did not like that. I considered it essential for the reputation of my barely paying Glasslite Company.

# VISIT TO MORANT BAY

To both of us, the differences between Amy and me seemed to be insurmountable. In order to take stock of all the pros and cons concerning our friendship rationally, with a minimum of emotion interfering, she decided to visit her best friend and confidante, Mary Moyston, in Morant Bay. I suspected that she would be contemplating as to whether or not to break off our relationship. I welcomed the idea, as I, too, could contemplate the same problem from my point of view without her telephoning me and thereby destroying all hope of being totally objective in my thoughts.

She was gone only a few days, and I missed her already. I could not take time off from my struggling business. The weekend came and Willy Gertig arrived on Sunday morning at about 4:oo a.m. from Highgate. He had to see some people in Kingston. He was dead tired. He had traveled by "bus" all night. Those "buses" are two ton trucks with planks stretched from side to side. Market women sit on these seats and their baskets are underneath and between their legs. Most other passengers hung on the outside of the truck clutching its side rails for dear life.

He had gotten off at Victoria Market where King Street ends at the harbor. It was still night and the tram cars did not run during the night. He had walked the two miles from there to Arlington Avenue. He was surprised to see me all dressed and having breakfast. We ate together and I told him: "You can sleep in my bed instead of making up another one, as I am about to take a bicycle ride to Morant Bay some 30 miles east of here."

It was a very dark night. The moon had set, and the only light came from the stars. When I rode near the sea, I saw the waves phosphorescing as they broke. It was quite a sight. There is a beautiful area on the way, called Roselle, where a waterfall is close to the left side of the road among coconut palms. They grow all around that area, all the way to the sea on the right side of the pavement.

The sky was just starting to show a little color. I could see a man sitting on a tree stump to the right of the road. His face was turned away from the beach. I wondered what he was up to, so early in the morning. I rode on past a few high bushes and looked for the man. He was not there. That was strange. I do not believe in ghosts, yet I got goose bumps. I turned around to where I had first seen the man. There he was as clear as the faint light allowed me to see. I rode toward him once more, and as I passed the bushes he had disappeared as before.

The sun sets and rises quickly in Jamaica which is only 18° north of the equator. Eventually, dawn lit up the landscape, and the sun rose when I was high on the second of the White Horses, as these two steep hills with the sheer white cliffs by the sea are called. I had to walk my cycle up the steep inclines, but I had fun racing down the equally steep declines. Bicycles with several speeds were not yet invented.

When I finally reached Morant Bay and found the Moystons' home, I was told that all had walked to the church. I rode to meet them. When the three Moyston girls and their mother saw me, they were obviously most delighted and greeted me cheerfully. Amy looked at me and said: "You are crazy!"

As we reached the Moyston's house, Mrs. Moyston asked me to put my bicycle in the back. She forgot that her dog was loose, and that it did not know me. The beast promptly bit my leg with several bites. There were lots of apologies, and the wounds were washed out with rum, the Jamaica, all purpose medicine. I spent a very pleasant day there. I liked being the center of attention.

In the evening they invited me to stay overnight. I declined, as I had to be at work the very next morning. Not long after sunset, I rode the 30 miles home. This time, the early moonrise gave me all the light I needed. It had been a very nice, but an exhausting, very long day. I had been up 22 hours by the time I got to bed, but it was worth it! Amy had been all smiles, and that had made it a most beautiful day!

# THE ALL IMPORTANT QUESTION

My business was building up agonizingly slowly. The overpowering problem was the 40 Hertz frequency of the Public Service power net. I was wondering if I should ever be able to support a wife.

I had a very loyal apprentice, George Minott. I told him that I was thinking of getting married, but that I could not even afford to buy an engagement ring. He knew where to get engagement rings at a much more reasonable price than the jewelers charged. He brought me the catalog, and I bought a ring.. The diamond was so big, one could discern it without a lens. It did not matter. It was just as committing as a great big rock.

We often went to the Carib movie theater by bicycle. They could be checked there. On August 9, 1946, I suggested to Amy right after the show: "Let's ride to the Rainbow and have an ice cream before I take you home."

It had rained and the vines between the tables glistened from the light of the colored bulbs. The chairs and the tables had been wiped dry. The waiter brought us the ice cream. I asked Amy: "Will you marry me?" I took out the tiny box with the ring. Amy said: "No", but not very loudly. I had been used to her saying: "No". She hardly ever meant it. She did not offer the least bit of resistance when I picked up her left hand. She lifted the ring finger above the others so as to make it easy for me to slip on the ring. We rode the bicycles to her home. I gave her a great big hug. It did not seem much for such a momentous commitment.

524

# AMY DECIDES TO CORRECT MY SHORTCOMINGS

Amy worked in a very well run government supported institution, and her father had been a civil servant all his life. Working a 40 hour week in an office was the proper way for a gentleman to earn a living as far as Amy was concerned. It saddened her that I could not see it that way.

Now that we were engaged, she considered it her duty to make me over in her father's image. It was a foregone conclusion that I had no intention to be like her father. It became a very stormy engagement often on the verge of being terminated. One evening, we had borrowed Gerhard's car and we drove to the sea. We quarreled over nothing worth quarreling about. She took off her ring and was giving it to me. I said: "If I take that ring now, I'll throw it as far as I can into the sea, I'll drive you home, and that will be the end of it!" She quickly put back the ring on her finger where it belonged, and no such scene was ever repeated.

She noticed that I knew practically nothing about a woman's body though I was well over 28 years old. Being a librarian, she got me a book which described in very delicate language the differences between a woman's and a man's body. It explained why the Bible forbade to "know" one's spouse periodically. I was amazed! So that is why she so adamantly refused to go swimming with me at times, when I saw no possible reason to do so. Now I could understand.

My book learning was not that extensive though I had taken the London Matric, the university entrance exam. I had easily passed part A, English, Mathematics, and German. I flunked part B, Chemistry and Physics, as, due to the War, I was unable to buy the required books.

Amy learnt everything from books. I learnt most things from practice. If I became puzzled, then I would read up on the problem. In that way, my knowledge became fixed in my mind.

Now I was glad to read up on the functions of the female body. It dawned on me: "The wrong time of the month" had nothing to do with astrology. To me it seemed very likely that Amy had read all about the male and the female body, its functions, reactions, interactions, dangers, and cautions before she ever had any practical experience to test the veracity of what she had read in a book.

# PETER GERHARD VON DER PORTEN

Dorrie had become pregnant at a time of great anxiety. Dorothea, her daughter was dangerously ill and the medicines Dr. Rose Parboosingh prescribed did not seem to help at all. The baby was in agony when she had to urinate and Dr. Parboosingh told Dorrie not to give her so much to drink. So Dorrie reduced the baby's water intake. It got worse! In desperation, Gerhard asked Papa's advice. He told Gerhard to stop the medicines, give the child as much as possible to drink and move the family from the damp area by the Hope River to a dryer area. Hesitant because of the 180° opposite direction of the two doctors Parboosingh, Dorrie and Gerhard moved and gave Dorothea lots to drink. The baby recovered very quickly. Papa had saved her life. I always considered him to be a superb diagnostician.

Shortly after that, their second child, Peter Gerhard, was born on November 6, 1946. He was a lovely child. Dorrie and Gerhard were very happy. They took the children to play in the big yard at 4 Arlington Ave. where all the girls of the Jamaica Macaroni Factory spoiled them with lots of attention. They were two sunny little babies. I and everybody else loved them.

When Dorothea was three and Peter two, I drove up to Arlington Avenue. The two little ones were riding their brand new tricycles.

"Look, Uncle Arnold!" Peter yelled. "I have a new bisticle!"

His big sister, more than an entire year older, could not let such a grave mistake stand. "It's a disticle!" she most authoritatively corrected her little brother. They just were two darling little children. Amy and I loved them dearly.

# TONI IN JAMAICA

One day, Gerhard walked into my shop: "Who is Tom? I have a telegram here from New York signed Tom. I don't know any Tom. He expects me to pick him up at the airport. Have you got any idea who he might be? I wish that these Americans would use their last names or at least mention the name of the firm they represent!"

"Tom? I don't know any Tom either. Are you sure that it is addressed to you?"

"Yes, of course, I'm sure. The messenger from the telegraph office was here and I questioned him before I signed for the telegram. It's for me all right."

Suddenly, a light switched on in my brother's cranium: "Toni always wanted to come to Jamaica. Toni looks like Tom if you do not dot the i very clearly. Someone in the telegraph office, either in Brooklyn or here, must have read Tom for Toni. Her wanting to see her little niece and nephew and maybe, incidentally, her brothers, too, finally overcame all of her procrastination. Yes, it can only be Toni. She'll arrive by plane from New York in a couple of hours."

Shortly after she arrived, Amy and I took her to the Ramseys to play badminton. Toni bragged that some time ago, in England, she had been quite good at tennis, "which, as every one knows, is a much more strenuous sport than badminton". She did play some social tennis at Uncle Walter's home as a teenager.

Of course, everyone wanted to please the visitor and let her play doubles just about every other game. Toni loved that. She had not been active in any sport since she went sailing on the Alster in Hamburg from before she got married in 1929 and now it was 1946. This badminton was fun! though she could not smoke during the game. The next day, however, she could hardly move. She had never expected that muscles could hurt sooo much! Maybe she should have stuck to tennis.

Gerhard, the lover of the Blue Mountains, just had to show her Farm Hill after she had recovered somewhat from the racquet sport. We assured her that she would not need the same muscles as those she used in badminton. A mule ride up and down the mountain would not require any effort at all.

The weekend came. We drove to Mavis Bank. The mule was saddled. Toni put out her cigarette. It took quite a bit of man power to get Toni finally in the saddle. I admired the mule for its patience. She slumped forward in the saddle. We could not get her to sit upright. The mountain air is just beautiful with the aroma of many different plants, but Toni had a cigarette clamped between her lips practically all of her waking hours.

I did not go with them to Farm Hill but drove their car back to town. Amy and I picked them up at Mavis Bank the next weekend. Toni had loved it in the mountains. After she slid off the mule, she grabbed a very soft cushion in one hand and her cigarette in the other. She could not sit down without that cushion.

We took her to many places. She always carried a cushion in her left, hand a cup of coffee on a saucer in her right, a cigarette between her lips on the left side of her mouth and her left eye closed, to prevent the smoke from burning it. She carefully arranged the cushion before she sat on it wherever she sat down. Saddles can feel very hard after a while. Riding mules never did become one of her passions.

She stayed with Gerhard and Dorrie and their two lovely children while she was in Jamaica. Amy and I did not see too much of Toni. I believe that she never went swimming even though the blue Caribbean was so near and looked so inviting, at least to me. I told her that swimming does not use the same muscles as either badminton or mule rides. Still she did not go swimming. That was difficult for me to understand. She went home to Brooklyn. No more badminton, no more mules.

# "DON'T GET MARRIED TO AMY !"

Now, that we were engaged, Amy and I had to visit the various uncles and aunts, cousins, and good friends of the Barry family. That to me was an odious obligation. It was usually subtly, and sometimes more directly made clear that none of them liked Germans, and that Amy could do better than that. After all, the British and Americans had spent billions of pounds and dollars to make people hate all Germans. The Nazi government in Germany had been most successful in supplying the Allied propaganda mills with lots of grist.

At any rate, none of those whom we visited seemed to believe that the marriage would last very long if it even should take place. They all advised not to rush into it, I suspected, in the hope that delay would mean cancellation.

Dorrie and Gerhard felt that Amy and I were too different from each other for the marriage to work. Besides, I was too poor and Amy would find it impossible to adjust to such poverty. They advised that I should at least wait until my business became a little more sound. I told Gerhard that I was now 29 and Amy 23 and we were very much adult enough to understand all the consequences of marriage.

I also told Gerhard that I loved Jamaica, and that I had no intention of living anywhere else. I did not want to marry any German girl from Brooklyn or Germany itself who would be homesick for any other country. Where would I find such a girl anyway? My feelings for her would never replace what I felt for Amy. And if I found her, her background, too, would be quite different to mine. The whole idea sounded quite preposterous, most unrealistic!

He and Dorrie often talked of returning to Germany or to emigrate to the States. I told Gerhard that he, himself, had told me that an emigrant will never feel quite at home wherever he should go, as emigrants lose the feeling of identifying completely with any one particular group. I very much experienced that when I went "home" to the parents in Brooklyn. I felt that I was merely a guest all the time I was in my parents' home. He and Dorrie, too, would want to return to the "Small Island" once they actually tried to settle overseas. I, for my part, did not want to marry anyone who would ever want to emigrate from this Island just as I would never want to leave. Never!

Even though I told Gerhard so adamantly that nothing could change my mind from wanting to go through with the marriage, the poverty issue bothered me and made me wonder if I should really do that to Amy. She, of course, knew fully well that I had no money but knowing about it and living it, were two different things.

Willy Gertig, the confirmed bachelor, warned me that Amy was used to a life with servants, surrounded by lots of family, and that many of her family would turn against her if she should marry a German and a poor one at that.

I went to see Hans Stamm who had opened a practice in Kingston. He was very polite and told me that he did not see any medical reason which should prevent our marriage. He pointedly left it at that, avoiding advice on any other aspect.

Reverend Crabbe of the Presbyterian Church on Duke Street, where Amy had once sung in the children's choir, was obviously against tying the knot without articulating it. He never called me to see him. The Barry family did not want a Quaker wedding.

I asked Reverend Lewis Davidson, an ordained minister of the Presbyterian Church. When I had first met him, he had been Head Master of the Wolmer's Boys' School. He had signed me up as a student for the university courses which he had hoped to teach there in the evenings. His and my hopes had been dashed when he was fired for not starting a cadet corps at his school. Implementation of university level courses in Jamaica had to wait several more years because of that.

Now, in December of 1946, he was the HeadMaster of the Friends' College in Highgate. I had gotten to know him and his wife pretty well and considered him my personal friend. He was most enthusiastic. Unfortunately, he did not have the official Government license to issue marriage certificates. It was therefore necessary to involve Rev. Crabbe in the ceremony.

So, it would take two Scots Presbyterian Pastors to marry us. Fortunately they were both Ministers of the same denomination.

The date was set for Saturday, January 4, 1947 at the St. Paul's Presbyterian Church at Locket Ave., Kingston.

# "FOR BETTER, FOR WORSE,
# TILL DEATH DO US PART."

The much thought about day, the wedding, which logically should not even take place which just about everybody had advised against except Amy's parents, Lewis Davidson and, of course, Amy herself and I, was fast approaching.

Williy Gertig, the freedom loving, confirmed bachelor arrived on Friday, January 3rd to spend "the last night of independence" at my place, at 4 Arlington Avenue. He was to be my best man.

In the morning, we had a leisurely breakfast together. I had borrowed Gerhard's car. As we turned right from Arlington Avenue onto Waterloo Road, Willy mentioned: "If you turn left on Windward Road now, there is the Pan-American Clipper (a plane which lands on water) leaving for the States and freedom in half an hour. If you turn right, it will be the road to bondage for the rest of your life." I turned right.

We arrived at the church at 10 a.m., just on time. It was packed. People stood all around the church as well. After all, Amy's father had been promoted to be the Acting Administrator General, a very high fiduciary government post. It was natural for a lot of civil servants to want to see Mr. Barry's daughter's wedding.

Then, of course, Amy was a prominent person in her own right as the leading authority on Jamaica's flora and sea fauna, except fishes. She was also the Secretary of the Natural History Society. That brought out a lot of science school teachers and amateur biologists. Most importantly, there were many of her own age group who liked her and wanted to wish her all the best on this, her most decisive day of her life.

I may claim here that I, too, was well-known, and many came out to see me. I was the goalkeeper of the All Star Water Polo Team and lots of swimmers and some fans were there to see the wedding. At that time, I was also recognized in the art circles as one of the ten best known painters. As the Director of the Miscellaneous Group of the Jamaica Manufacturers Association, I was fairly well-known in politics and my neon sign business, my

Glasslite Co., was starting to light up Cross Roads and Half-Way Tree. Still, I had never expected such a huge crowd.

The church itself was one of the largest in Kingston. It was obviously designed in Scotland for Scotland. It was a Gothic brick building with a black roof.

In Jamaica they design ovens that way. Even though all of the windows were wide open, it was stifling hot inside.

Willy and I sat down on the pew in the front row. Rev. Davidson asked us to join him in the vestry, a room next to the altar region. A large fan provided a pleasant draft through the open doors on both sides of the room.

Amy was obviously late. I did not have time to feel sorry for all those people melting in the church as the good pastor had lots and lots of jokes to tell. No wonder I did not know any of them. They were all clean!

We were rudely interrupted by: "Here comes the bride..." I looked at my watch. Amy was 20 minutes late. When we had gone out on a date she never had been ready when I came to pick her up. So, 20 minutes was really not in the least bit surprising. Only the fancy, lightly starched clothes of all those people in the church must have wilted by then. All clothes had to be ironed in those days as wrinkle free materials with artificial fiber threads were not yet used in clothes.

Willy and I were deprived of the punch line of the last joke as we had to hurry into the church. Amy looked absolutely stunning on the arm of her father. All of her 98 pounds were sheathed in a long, tight fitting, shiny, white, eyelet-over-satin dress draped with a delicate white, orange blossom veil from the tiara to her feet. She held a large bouquet of beautiful, large, white chrysanthemums and carnations. She looked quite calm walking down the aisle, but that bouquet betrayed her. It kept nervously jumping up and down, completely out of control and would not keep still one second. I hardly noticed the bridesmaids, Kathleen, her sister, and Mary Moyston, her maid of honor. Judy Davidson, her cousin, was the little flower girl. I did not notice how her father, escorting her down that interminable aisle, looked without his pipe in his mouth. It was all a big blur.

The good ministers said a lot of words alternately.

Finally Amy said: "...to love, honor and obey, in sickness and in health, for better, for worse, till death do us part."

"I now pronounce you man and wife. You may kiss the bride," said Rev. Crabbe. I did, and I led her out of that church closely followed by Mary and Willie. The Barry's big Dodge drove us to 22 Lady Musgrave Road.

The house was beautifully decorated. The wedding cake stood in the middle of the dining room table which was laden with every imaginable food and delicacy. There were dozens of speeches during which Amy and I held glasses of dark-red port wine in front of ourselves.

Amy kept whispering to me: "I'm so hungry, I haven't had any breakfast this morning."

Finally someone nudged me and whispered: "You are supposed to give a 'thank you' speech."

I was totally unprepared. I looked around the room. There were Dorrie and Gerhard, the Reverends Crabbe and Davidson, the Barrys and all of their relatives, the Ramseys, and a wide range of other guests all staring at me wondering as to what great wisdom was about to flow from my mouth.

I started with: "Reverend Crabbe, Reverend Davidson, family and friends, this is truly the ...."

I looked at Amy's glass full of dark-red wine. Amy held it closely to that beautiful white dress with that beautiful white orange blossom veil. The glass was dancing up and down just as the flowers had done in church as she had walked down the aisle! I thought. "Impending catastrophe! Another word from me and that wine is going to spill all over that exquisite dress!"

Everybody else's eyes must have followed mine. It had not been difficult to read my mind. An absolute silence had come over the great crowd. You could have heard a pin drop.

In desperation I said: "Thank you." The roar of good-natured laughter and applause was deafening. It was my most successful speech ever.

We had to cut the cake and take a bite each. It was a very heavy fruit cake with lots of icing, the standard wedding cake in Jamaica. "This is the first bite I had since last night. It is too sweet. I want something light and salt and a glass of plain water," Amy sounded desperate. One after the other, people kept coming up to us and we had to say something nice. We had to dance the first dance and still no time to grab a bite, as all those wonderful people wanted to congratulate us in person.

"We'll have to go now," said Gerhard. "If you want to reach Whitfield Hall before dark, you'll have to hurry up!" Amy changed to a beautiful, red dress. A servant packed her something to eat. She took it with her. Gerhard, Amy and I got into Gerhard's car. It was decorated with shaving cream, toothpaste spelt: "Just Married." Old shoes and tin cans dangled from its end. Almost immediately after we drove off, it stank!

At the first gas station, corner Old Hope Road and Oxford Road, we stopped. We found out that the stench had been caused by a piece of salt fish tied to the exhaust manifold. It and the rest of the "decorations" were quickly removed. We stopped at 4 Arlington Avenue. Amy changed into proper riding gear, and I into a khaki shirt and pants. We put some clothes into the car and the parcel of food which the servant had packed. Gerhard was a bit impatient. He told us: "Don't stop to eat anything now, if you want to reach Whitfield Hall tonight."

We drove along Windward Road towards the oil companies' tank farms when the car gave out. It was hot. The asphalt on the road had melted and stuck to my feet. The trouble turned out to be the flexible hose between the gas line and the carburetor had sprung a leak and the engine sucked air instead of gasoline.

I walked to the Trinidad Leasehold Tank Installation.

"Sarry, Sah, nobady allowed inside dis gate 'pon a Saturday, Sah," the guard at the gate informed me.

A mechanic, passing by in the distance, recognized me and waved to me.

"I'm in trouble," I shouted at him. "Can you lend me a pair of pliers, a screw driver, and some friction tape?"

"Yes, Sah." He was a lifesaver. At least he saved the day.

I took off the flexible hose, wrapped several layers of tape around it, and it no longer sucked air. I thanked the mechanic profusely as I returned the tools. Near Yallahs River, we turned north off the paved road. Soon, on one side of the road the mountains rose steeply. On the other were tree tops of tall trees, and

536

we could hear the river rushing far below us. We had to climb 2,000 ft. from sea level.

The road was so steep that Gerhard had to shift gears constantly from second to first and back to second. On the few declines, he usually ran in second with the engine switched off so that he would not burn out the brake lining. We had to stop a few times to remove some boulders which the last rain had deposited on the road We had quite different opinions of the drive. Amy and I thought that it was just absolutely gorgeous! Gerhard gave vent that he considered the road horrible!

At last, we reached Hagley Gap, the end of the car road. Gerhard turned around the car and was gone. He did not want darkness to overtake him on this almost unfamiliar, steep mountain road. We were 2,000 ft. above sea level. It was only four miles from here to Whitfield Hall and only 2,000 more feet to climb.

The road from Kingston to Mavis Bank, which we usually took, was a little shorter and better maintained gravel. It was about four and a half miles from Mavis Bank to Whitfield Hall. One had to wade through the Green River though and climb 3,000 ft. It would take longer and time was very limited. Mrs. Simmons had bought the ancient coffee estate from Gerhard, and I had supervised its restoration. Now Dorothea Simmons graciously lent it to us for our honeymoon. The next problem was to find Eddie who was supposed to have met us here with two mules.

# OUR WEDDING NIGHT

After some asking around, we eventually found Eddie in a bar.

"Where are the mules, Eddie?"

"Oh, is today, Sah?" He trotted off. After a while he came back with two mules, Queeny and Dick. I knew them both. Dick was the one we had had at Arlington Avenue during the War to transport the macaronis to Mr. Chen's warehouse and to fetch the white limestone from the quarry to make cleanser, etc. It was a male, very tall, powerful, but also slow mule. Gerhard had given him to the drunken overseer when he had tried to make Farm Hill an agricultural enterprise. Queeny was a smaller, younger female and a quick-walking animal. Eddie had saddled them expertly and they looked fine, ready to go.

Amy mounted Queeny and I Dick. Amy was an experienced rider and managed her mule very well. As we came to the first little house on the way up the mountain, Dick insisted on going into the yard and stopping by a hitching post. The mule obviously expected me to get off and go into the house. It dawned on me that the overseer probably stopped here to get a drink. It was customary around here, where the huts were spaced good distances apart, to offer visitors a shot of rum when they arrived.

I yanked at the bit, trying to turn the mule around, but eventually I had to get off and lead the beast to the exit of the small yard before mounting again. By this time, Amy was far ahead of me. At the next little home, the same thing happened. I could not break the mule out of his long established routine.

It reminded me of the first time Gerhard had sent me to Farm Hill for some job he had wanted me to do. It was still war time then.

I had told him: "I don't know where Farm Hill is."

"Don't worry. Just mount Dick. Past Gordon Town he knows exactly how to get there."

It was an all day mule ride from Arlington Avenue to Farm Hill via Papine, Gordon Town and Mavis Bank. The mule went its slow walk, hardly faster than a person would walk. I had to rely on its memory 100%, as after Gordon Town, I had no idea of the way to

Farm Hill. The night that mule foraged on the tall Wynne grass and the next day I rode the animal all the way back. The day after that, I had muscle pain in my back. I never knew that those muscles existed and could hurt so much!

On that trip, I had learned several things about mules. One, they knew their way unerringly; two, they liked to walk on the very edge of a precipice; and three, they richly deserved their name of being stubborn! At the time of that long ride, it was mango time. When the mule spotted a mango by its smell, it went to eat it, even if it was at the very edge of the precipice. It would suddenly walk off the path, bend over the edge and eat the mango. I, the rider, had to fight hard not to slide over the neck of the beast and down the mountainside as Dick bent down for this delicacy! Fortunately, I was quite athletic and could stay on the mule, but my heart missed a few beats every time the mule delighted to eat a mango at the rim of a very steep decline.

While musing, we had arrived at one more hut. Dick had stopped and reminded me of the situation at hand. This time, after I noticed that Amy was at least a mile ahead of me beyond a bend and out of sight, I pulled my pocket knife and cut myself a strong stick. I did not mount the mule again but went behind it and chased it up the mountain in a trot, using my stick liberally on its backside. As I realized that Amy was just around the next bend, I mounted the animal and appeared right behind my bride as I, too, rounded the bend.

Amy was indignant: "Where were you?"

"Right behind you."

"No, you were not!" I was too badly out of breath to argue. Besides, she was right. So, I let her have the last word. She usually had that anyway. With the help of my stick, Dick decided to keep up with Queeny, and we had a wonderful ride through the unsurpassed beauty of the Blue Mountains.

We passed Farm Hill and a mere half a mile later we arrived at Whitfield Hall at sundown. The sky was painted red. The wind was whistling through the mighty and tall fir and eucalyptus trees at the entrance path to the ancient manor. We dismounted, and I carried my beautiful bride in her red riding suit over the threshold into the hall of the house.

We found the housekeeper in the back. "Did you prepare a dinner for us?"

"Oh, is today, Sah?" These people in the Blue Mountains never know the day of the week, the month of the year, and sometimes not even the year they are in. We gave her a few shillings and she trudged off to the nearest village about a mile away past Farm Hill and Torre Garda to buy a chicken.

Amy had not eaten nor drunk anything, except a nibble at the wedding cake, for some 20 hours. She was ravenously hungry! I, too, was famished. Fortunately, I had had a good breakfast with Willy which now seemed eons ago with all the many things that had happened since. Amy unwrapped the food the servant had packed for her at Lady Musgrave Road. It turned out to be a tiny piece of the wedding cake! Amy was disappointed, to the brink of tears but she insisted that I should have a nibble too.

At last, Ida came back with a chicken. She wrung its neck, plucked and cleaned it. It was late when we had a very good dinner of chicken, rice, local scallion, and other local vegetables. The old woman looked after the mules, washed the dishes, and then went home. As it was getting very cold, I started a cozy fire in the fireplace. We sat around the glowing logs a while and listened to the wind roaring through those tall trees outside. As we got warm, we decided to turn in.

Starting to undress, I opened the second and third top buttons of my shirt, when I suddenly had a terrible nosebleed out of my left nostril. The excitement of the day, the high altitude, the very dry air, and chasing the mule up the mountain were catching up with me.

As I lay on the bed, Amy brought me some cold wet towels. She really hurried but by the time she came back the other nostril was bleeding, too! This time she got really frightened. There was no chance of getting any help from anybody at all up here. I calmed her down as best I could and told her that I often had nosebleeds. This was true but I did not remember having one so fierce and prolonged. The cold compresses did not seem to help. I pressed my finger above the top lip. That had usually helped but it did not this time.

I felt more sorry for Amy than for myself. She looked so

beautiful in her red riding outfit but distraught by the low light of the kerosene lamp as she stood there helplessly by my bedside. She most likely wondered if her brand new husband was going to bleed to death on her wedding night while she just stood there and could not do a thing about it.

I was glad that Willy and I had dammed up the little brook a short distance above Whitfield Hall and had run a pipe from there to the house when the building was renovated. So, at least we had some cold running water.

The next thing I knew there was the bright daylight of Sunday morning. I found myself lying on my bed, fully dressed, only the three top buttons of my shirt were open. Amy was in the kitchen with Ida looking after breakfast. So, that was our wedding night!

# THE BLUE MOUNTAIN PEAK

We had timed our wedding so that we would have a full moon on our honeymoon. We decided to go to the Blue Mountain Peak, almost another 4,000 ft. above us. We packed a large basket of food and rented Queeny for Amy and another mule for me.

Right after breakfast on Wednesday morning, we rode past "Monkey Hill," an absolutely vertical, bare, granite protrusion rising about 200 ft. straight up behind Whitfield Hall to our left. We passed the great house, Abbey Green, with its large barbecue, as they call the large, cement coffee-bean drying area in Jamaica. It seemed a shame that no one cultivated the wonderful Blue Mountain coffee anymore. It was the best tasting coffee I ever drank. It was still gathered and sold by a few but not in commercially viable quantities.

We had very good mules. We reached the Peak before noon. Fuchsia and hydrangeas were blooming all around us. We had brought warm clothes and did not mind the wind. We let the mules graze. We had a very sufficient lunch and enjoyed the view on an exceptionally clear day. In the far distance, the sea glistened on three sides, north, east, and south of us. In the west were the Cockpit Mountains. Their sharp, shoe destroying, white limestone surface was hidden by dense forest. We could identify several peaks.

It was so beautiful and peaceful up there that I proposed to have supper and watch the sunset over the Cockpit Mountains. In the afterglow of the sunset, we put the bits back into the mouths of the mules. On my suggestion, we did not mount them right away but wait till we got to the path leading down the mountain. The moon rose and bathed the landscape in its silvery, bluish light.

Amy mounted her mule gracefully and with ease. As I approached mine, it bolted and ran down the mountain. The opposite mountainside across the valley was gloriously and clearly illuminated in the most delightful moonlight but the path which led down, where I heard the hooves of my mule clip-clopping, was on the shadow side of the mountain. It was so dark, I could not see my hand in front of my face.

Every time I caught up to the beast and was about to grab its rein, it bolted. Since a mule can see in pitch darkness and I cannot, it had the advantage. The path becomes very uneven in places. On the right side, the mountain rises quite steeply, on the other, it goes down unstoppably if one should make a misstep. I had to give up following the sound of the hooves. I could not see my feet nor the path. It became too dangerous to walk without anything to guide me and warn me if I approached the edge of a precipice.

"I'll have to hold on to the tail of Queeny." That good lady of a mule did not mind at all. It was used to that. The rough going was too much for my shoes. I lost the sole of my right shoe. My feet were too soft for the gravel and soon my right foot sole started to bleed and hurt. I clenched my teeth hard for the rest of this interminable walk. As we finally came to Abbey Green, there is an expanse of grass and bushes on an almost level area. I heard the mule grazing. I followed the sound and this time I could approach the recalcitrant beast from the front and cut off its progress down hill! I almost had it when it turned around and raced back up in the direction of the peak. I gave up.

We reached Whitfield Hall. I made a fire in the Franklin stove in the kitchen and put on some water to heat. Then I got a good fire going in the great hall to warm up the place before washing my abused feet in the beautiful cedar bathtub.

The next day, early in the morning, the owner of the mule banged on the door.

"Where is my mule?" Amy and I put on housecoats and the three of us together went out to look. There, high on Monkey Hill, right at the very edge of the vertical cliff stood the mule fully harnessed, head high as if to mock me. I paid the man and he went for the mule.

I repaired my shoe the best I could without proper tools. It held until we were back in Kingston. We refrained from any more distant excursions. We went for walks right around Whitfield Hall. We were careful not to be caught on foot after dark without a flashlight. I had cleaned my foot with rum so that it did not get infected. I could walk on it, as long as it was bandaged. Amy watched it even more carefully than I did.

Sunday we rode down the path to Hagley Gap and Gerhard drove us back to the real world.

# OUR FIRST HOME

With my shattered finances it was difficult to find a house with a rent which we could afford. Fritz Lackenbach from Vienna, my former fellow internee, had a little house on the place which he had bought in Gordon Town. We did not like each other but I did not have to move in with him. And if he was willing to let bygones be bygones so was I. It suited both of us to make peace. I rented the little cottage on a ledge of a hill overlooking Gordon Town for £2.=.= ($8.oo American in those days) per month. The house was about two miles uphill and north of Papine, the nearest tram car (trolley) terminal. We had no car, so that we either had to make pick-up arrangements, or walk. At that time, Gerhard and family lived in a large isolated house by the Hope River, halfway between Papine and Gordon Town.

The hut we rented had two rooms, 8 ft. x 8 ft. with 7 ft. high ceilings. In the front, running the entire length, was a 2 ft. wide verandah with a balustrade. In the back was a 5 ft. wide bathroom 12 ft. long. The bathroom had a dark green concrete bathtub. It, the hand basin, and the toilet emptied into a cesspool. Not far from the bathroom was an unattached shed, 7 ft. x 7 ft. without any water. It served as a kitchen.

There were sockets with a bulb each in the living room and in the bedroom, none in the bathroom. Those were the only electrical facilities in the house. The wiring looked frayed. It had to be replaced soon. The view over the little town, the valley, and the mountains surrounding us was very nice.

We used Gerhard's car to move Amy's brass double bed which she had inherited from her grandmother, a wardrobe, and a chair into the bedroom. That filled up that room completely. In the living room, we had my bed from Arlington Avenue, camouflaged as a couch, two chairs, and two little end tables. To the kitchen we brought a 3'-6" high x 4'-0" x 3'-0" packing case. That was the kitchen table. A coal pot served to make the meals and heat the irons to press our clothes.

545

A young woman from the neighborhood presented herself. We hired her for six shillings ($1.50 American) per week as a servant to cook for us and watch the house when we were at work.

Expanding his agency business, Gerhard was getting in a lot of samples. One was a very beautiful porcelain wall lamp. I bought it and fastened it over the hand basin in the bathroom so that we had light in that room now. I bought a 250 ft. roll of outdoor No.12 rubber-covered wire and ran it from Lackenbach's house up the cliff to our "palace" and throughout the house and into the kitchen shed. Now we had safe wiring and light in every room. I bought 20 ft. of ½" galvanized water pipe and the necessary fittings and connected it to the bathroom inlet pipe, and ran it into the kitchen, bent it so that we could put a sink under it. We bought a sink. Its discharge fed the plants down the cliff.

A two foot wide verandah was of no use, so I widened it to four feet and put a couple of deck chairs on it. I was lucky, a friend of mine had bought a new refrigerator. He wanted to get rid of his old one. I bought it for next to nothing. It was the best model which Frigidaire had ever made. It had white porcelain enamel on the inside and two tone gray porcelain enamel on the outside. It used Freon as the refrigerant, and a pressure switch to control its temperature. In all the time I serviced refrigerators, I had never seen one of these early models of Frigidaire give any trouble at all. It was a real gem and would outlast any new refrigerator and outlast me, too.

I had done Dr. Ernst Lobbenberg a lot of favors in the camp and also later, when he had moved to Barbican, a very posh neighborhood. He bought himself a new gas stove as his old one was broken. I looked at the old one. It was a very luxurious unit. One pipe had been broken off in handling. That was all that was wrong with it. I told him but he said that he had already bought a much better one and begged me to get the old "scrap" out of the house. I changed the burners to use propane and installed it in Gordon Town. If we had not emigrated from Jamaica, we would probably still have that gas stove and the Frigidaire. They were both better than any subsequent models ever built.

To get to work we had to rise very early in the morning and walk a mile down the road to Gerhard's house. It was a bad arrangement to become so dependent on Gerhard's schedule.

Fritz Lackenbach had a car but neither he nor Lotte could drive. He suggested that Amy should drive him to and from work. I walked down to Gerhard's place and drove in and home with him. Dorrie had two babies, Dorothea and Peter, and did not go to work for a while. Faithful, old Ruby served as a nursemaid. She was a good, reliable woman.

The predictions of Dorrie and Gerhard, the relatives of the Barrys, and many other well-meaning friends seemed to come true. Amy and I disagreed bitterly over really very petty matters. Before our marriage Amy had given me the impression that my perfection was unmatched by any other human being. Now that I was married, she noticed that I did have some shortcomings. It seemed that marriage made sure that I would not go to my grave without being aware of all my faults.

Once we quarreled over how to squeeze a toothpaste tube. Those tubes were made from pure tin in those days. If they were not squeezed from the bottom, they tended to burst and get one's hands and basin smeary, worse, waste toothpaste! I showed Amy how to squeeze the tube the one and only, the absolutely correct way. She pointed out to me that she had always squeezed it from the top, and that is the way it is done in Jamaica. Compromise could not be reached on this vital issue. We have separate toothpaste tubes to this day, though with the new much stronger plastic tubes, it no longer matters whether you squeeze from the top, bottom or compromise and do it from the middle.

Much more serious was Amy's concept of money. She could not understand that only a tiny part of the money I took in for my work could be used for our expenses. I explained that the money had to pay wages and had to buy new stock for my shop, and that money in a bank account would inflate very quickly. She countered: "A pound is always a pound." I tried to explain the fallacy of that argument. We were having the most glaring example right before our eyes, as the value of the pound had decreased terribly during the War and it was still decreasing. It sounded weird to her that the purchasing power of the pound decreased. Despite some angry disputes neither Amy nor I ever stooped to name calling or using profane language. We both were too proud for that.

One night, to escape Amy's maddening criticism, I walked down to Gerhard's place and took his car, drove into the mountains, and slept in the open car. The next morning, when I drove to pick up Gerhard, he was very angry with me for taking his car without letting him know. When he saw that I was unshaven and upset, he calmed down. We drove to Princess Street. I told him that our marriage was over. He wanted to know what we had quarreled about.

"It was trivial not even worth remembering but it had been fierce, incessant, and she keeps on and on for hours! I am never going back! <u>Never!</u>"

I worked in the shop for a while.

By lunch time, Gerhard called me. "You made a solemn vow. Your trustworthiness, your honor is at stake. You'll have to go back."

I never argued with Gerhard. He was always right. Besides, I reasoned that life without Amy would be very empty. He had warned me against the marriage and had predicted that we would find it difficult to adjust to one another. He had also said that once we were married there would be no turning back. Divorce was no solution. It would bring regrets but never happiness. Evening came. We drove to his house. I got out of the car and walked the mile uphill to Gordon Town. I was wondering what Amy would say. I still very much loved that woman! When I arrived we kissed and made up.

We had a dog which Amy had wanted and a cat, I had wanted. The servant must have ill-treated the dog. It would not let anyone touch it, not even Amy nor me. Several times in the first few months, our marriage was truly symbolized by those animals. We fought like cats and dogs spoiling all of an evening. To any outsider though, we presented a united front. That was not difficult as we loved one another dearly.

We suspected that the servant was throwing parties for her boyfriend and others while we were at work. We fired her and found a gem: Lena. She was young and very hard working. She told us that she had several children for a boy named Rudolf. I had noticed in the macaroni factory that women with small children work very hard in Jamaica because usually they are the ones who support the results of their mistakes. Lena's pleasant disposition, her tidiness, and getting us our breakfast and dinner on time, made life easier for us.

Eventually we hardly had a disagreement anymore. We got used to each other and decided to do all in our power to make the marriage work. It was difficult and required my making allowances for Amy's faults, even for squeezing toothpaste tubes the wrong way. I myself had no faults, of course. Amy just imagined that I did. The cat and the dog came to a détente, too.

Lena had been an orphan, raised by American nuns in a nearby convent. When she was 14, a boy, about her age, entered the chapel from the back entrance where Lena was cleaning right behind the pulpit. She said that he raped her right there behind the altar. At any rate, she became pregnant and was chased out of the nunnery.

Unfortunately, her boyfriend proved to be a hopeless and violent drunk. He made her several more children. Lena, herself, had the burden of providing for those children. On top of that Rudolf would beat her if he thought that she had money on her, take away the money and drink or gamble it away.

Rudolf worked in the bakery in Gordon Town not far from our little hut. When he did not show up for a few nights in a row (bread is baked at nights,) the young Chinese baker fired him. He begged to get his job back. He failed. Lena went to the baker and begged for her boyfriend. The baker made Lena stay the night with him as a condition for her man to get back his job. So, Lena also had a half Chinese son. She loved that baby more than all the others.

Gradually, over several months, we got to know the whole story. Amy and I felt sorry for the woman who proved to be an excellent worker and was very loyal to us. She came early in the mornings and got our breakfast ready. We felt comfortable to leave the house in her care while we went to work. In the evenings, dinner was always ready when we came home. This improved our home life very considerably.

# HIBISCUS ESCULENTES

At about sunrise every Saturday morning we would see some women carrying their vegetables to the market in Papine two hundred feet lower and a good two miles down the road from where we lived in Gordon Town. Some of these women must have walked half the night down the Blue Mountains with their wicker baskets on their heads. Those baskets weighed about 100 lbs! Besides the vegetables they often had a chicken resting on top and the mandatory pair of shoes.

Those shoes were a status symbol. Every self respecting market woman possessed a pair of shoes. She would walk through the night over the roughest terrain and carry her precious footware on top of her vegetables. Just before coming into view of the market she would stop, have someone help her lift the basket from her head and put on her shoes. Then she would ask someone to help her put back the basket on her head, and she would proudly march into the Papine market with her shoes on.

We had no car in those days. There was no market in Gordon Town. It was difficult for us to buy our vegetables. There were all these women walking by us with all those vegetables for sale. So, Amy stopped one once. We offered to buy all of her basket full at the regular price she would get in Papine. That would save her the long walk back and forth and a full day of hawking.

The woman thought it over for almost a whole minute and then turned us down. We were amazed! We had made her a lucrative offer. Slowly it started to dawn on us that going to market was her great social event, possibly for months! If she would have nothing to sell she would not have a right to sit down at the market among her friends and she would miss all of their chit-chat.

Since we could not interfere with the market women's social life we had to go to the market to buy our food. The women squatted on the ground and had little heaps of vegetables spread out on burlap bags. Each pile cost quatty and gill. [1½ pence and 3 farthings (4 farthings equaled 1 penny), so the cost was 2¼ pence].

Amy, the head of the Botany Section at the Institute of Jamaica, went up to a woman and pointed to one little pile. The woman wanted to give Amy another pile. Amy said: "No, no, not that." She turned to me in desperation: "Arnold, what is that again, *Hibiscus Esculentes, Hibiscus Esculentes, Hibiscus Esculentes?"* I had no idea what she was talking about, and all the dear market women in the vicinity stared at her as if they thought that they were dealing with a crazy person. Finally, a light switched on in my dear wife's cranium. "Okra!" she shouted. Never before nor ever since have I seen so many happy market women. They sold us quatty and gill worth (7¢ U.S.) of okra with pleasure. By the way, I was happy, too.

# OUR FIRST CAR

Unfortunately, Lackenbach proved to be a very demanding and ungrateful man. When Amy drove him, he ordered her around as if she were his paid chauffeur. When she had to stay a little late at work, he became very indignant. Naturally, Amy resented that very much. I never did like the man but I did not want a real fight.

In the spring of 1947 we scraped our pennies together, and I bought our first car. It was a real beauty. It was a straight six cylinder 1932 Studebaker Dictator. Amy and I had our nastiest fight over that purchase. She was angry that I did not choose it with her. I did not see any reason to have her present as she did not know anything about cars. We had agreed that a car must be bought. So, I went ahead and got one that looked very strong and reliable. I had her very much in mind when I bought it, as it was very similar to her Dad's. Why should two people do the job, one could very nicely accomplish alone?

I have since come to realize that I was most insensitive. It was our biggest purchase in our young marriage. I should have at least asked her if she wanted to buy the car with me. She was absolutely right but I did not see it that way then. I was 29 now and so used to doing everything by myself that asking anyone to do something with me never occurred to me. That Studebaker hardly ever gave any trouble. We both loved that car. After all, neither of us had ever owned a car before. It was a status symbol. We had arrived! Above all, we loved the independence it gave us from miserable Lackenbach and extremely busy Gerhard.

I could resume my art classes at the Institute with Mrs. Edna Manley. I painted a lot those days. Early in 1948, I painted a portrait of Amy and a self portrait using the bathroom mirror. As a back ground I painted the mountains as we saw them from our front verandah. Amy came to the classes with me one night and modeled. Topper painted the best likeness. He gave me that picture as a present. I appreciated that very much. That painting now hangs in our living room.

# "DELIVER JUST ONE DRUM OF CARBIDE"

One day Gerhard had a very important appointment right after work.

"Arnold, please deliver this drum of carbide for me."

"I can't get that into my car. It is too big for the door."

"Use my car. I'll drive yours. Drive to Arlington Avenue when you are finished, and we'll swap cars again."

"All right."

At 5 p.m. my crew went home, and I was alone on the almost deserted Princess Street with Gerhard's abused, but faithful touring car and a 224 lbs. drum of calcium carbide. It is used for acetylene welding as it makes acetylene and lime when water is added. I opened the back door of the ancient touring car and rolled the drum to it. It proved too wide for the door. I had to shut the door and lift it over the side of the car. I weighed all of 135 lbs. myself. I could lift 224 lbs. plus the weight of the iron drum itself but this drum had nowhere to grab it properly. It was an ungainly thing. I opened my shop and got out some long beams and rolled the drum to the top of the door and over it. The drum went into the car and crashed right through the floor boards onto the pavement!

This was a real dilemma! I could not move the car with that drum right on the pavement. There was no way to get help. I should have phoned Amy and let her know but she was far from my mind. She was waiting for me at her parents' home. Her father picked her up after work, and I picked her up at Lady Musgrave Road as I usually worked later than she did. I had to get that drum off the pavement into the car, by hook or by crook! I spent hours repairing the floor boards, and finally got the drum well enough supported and could deliver it. It was a nasty job to get it out of the car again.

"Where have you been all this time?! What took you so long to deliver just one miserable drum?" Gerhard wanted to know. He kept quiet after I told him about the floor boards.

Amy's reaction was somewhat different when I arrived at Lady Musgrave Road well after dark. She was predictably furious! I did not mind. In comparison to what that miserable carbide had done to me, her scolding was nothing. What a day! My explanation eventually calmed her down and peace was restored. I never again volunteered to deliver drums of calcium carbide. No, not even one!

# MAMA AND PAPA IN JAMAICA

One day Mama and Papa arrived on a Pan-American Air Ways plane. Imagine, Mama had been terribly scared to sail on an ocean liner from Hamburg to New York, expressing her fear by saying: "Water has no beams." Now, this same woman's curiosity as to what Jamaica was like, and the imperious orders from Papa overcame her fear of flying.

Gerhard had a couple of sedan chairs built to carry over parents up to Farm Hill. They did a little bit of walking in the vicinity. Amy and I came to visit, too. I had forgotten to buy the meat as I had promised. So, I had to walk all the way down the mountain right after I had arrived, drive to Kingston and then back again all in one day. Even for a well trained swimmer that was a lot.

I felt very neglected and a little angry because our parents only took notice of Dorrie and Gerhard. They paid very little attention to me which I did not mind so much but they practically ignored Amy. That I did mind! Amy was their brand new daughter-in-law. They could have made a little bit more of a fuss about her.

Papa had always had heart trouble ever since I remember. He always carried pills in two vest pockets, one pocket full of pills to speed up the heart rate, the other pocket contained medicine to slow down the heart. Early in the morning, two days later, Papa got very sick. He looked as pale as a ghost and was very listless. Mama looked terribly worried. Papa said that he needed a special medicine right away.

Amy and I walked down the mountain and went to Dr. Aub, my former fellow internee. He gave me the needed prescription. We went to Kinkeads Drug Store on King Street and made the arduous journey back up the mountain. Amy was not only a very good hiker but also a very good sport. If she was hurt by the little attention my parents, Dorrie, and Gerhard paid to her, she never let on, and she climbed the mountain back up with me. Whatever the medicine was, it did the trick. Papa was soon his old self again.

Because of my parents, Amy and I had driven the car up the long, bad road to Hagley Gap instead of the shorter and somewhat better road to Mavis Bank. That way my parents had a shorter walk from Farm Hill, and there was no river to ford. My parents refused the sedan chairs and its bearers. Faithful Eddie and a mule carried down the luggage. My parents walked all the way to Hagley Gap. We stopped often and rested. I was worried all the way that either Mama or Papa would suffer a heart attack but nothing happened.

In Kingston my parents stayed at the Myrtle Bank Hotel, by far the best in Kingston. Dr. Aub came to visit them when I was there. The two doctors chatted so intensely, and Mama listened so attentively that they never felt the earthquake which shook the pier where we sat by the harbor. They were so used to big trucks passing and rattling their apartment in Brooklyn, that they were not even aware of the little bit of rumbling and shaking of a very minor earthquake.

It seems that Mama never had Physics at school, obviously a flaw in the Royal Saxon School System. As the day of departure drew nearer she said:

"Arnold, when we took that big ship from Hamburg to New York, I was so scared. The ship is built from iron. When you put iron into water, it sinks. How could that huge ocean liner float?"

"Suppose, Mama, that ship weighs 20,000 tons but it encloses an enormous volume of air, many more than 20,000 cubic meters, maybe five times as much, 100,000 cubic meters, then the average cubic meter of the ship weighs only one fifth of a ton. Water weighs one ton per cubic meter. The ship displaces as much water as it weighs, namely 20,000 tons, that is 20,000 cubic meters of water which will be the same amount of ship which will be below the water line. Then 80,000 cubic meter of ship will be above the water level."

Mama did not look satisfied. I think that she did not quite follow me. It did not matter. The worry of the voyage on the passenger liner was in the past. She was much more concerned over the impending flight back to New York.

"Arnold, did you see that big plane we arrived in from New York? How can such a huge plane, all of it made from metal, fly?"

"Mama, the engines push air away from the front of the plane to the back. Because the wings are higher in front than in the back, high pressure is created under the wing, and a low pressure above the wing. That lifts up the plane. That is the principle of aerodynamics."

"Yes, yes I understand what you say, but how does it fly?"

On the whole, I was disappointed with my parents' visit. I never got a chance to show them anything that I would have liked to show them. I was still the little teenage boy to them, just to be sent on errands but not to be treated as an adult. I was almost 30 in the summer of 1947. The joyful anticipation of seeing them again had probably raised my hopes unrealistically high.

# CHRISTMAS, 1947

With the few transformers I owned, I had the idea to rent out signs reading: Merry Christmas, Season's Greetings, or Happy New Year. It kept me very busy for November and December. I could not make much money that way but I could store the signs and then rent them out the next season when they would cost me nothing. It was going to be a very lean Christmas. Amy took home £ 3.-.- (U.S.$ 12.oo) and I drew £ 2.-.- (U.S.$ 8.oo) per week.

Gerhard was busy lining up manufacturers whom he could represent. They sent him samples and he tried to sell their products. Among the samples there were French watches and toffees from England. The toffees were in beautiful metal tins sealed hermetically with a strong tape. After a while, those samples were useless. I bought two identical tins of the best toffees and a French gold lady's watch, the best one Gerhard had among his samples. Its band did look a little like electric lamp cord but it had real golden clasps. I cut the tape of one of the tins, opened it, carefully unwrapped the top toffee, tied the watch and its band with fine tie wire to make it as small an item as possible and wrapped it into the toffee wrapper. I sealed the tin so that it did not show that the tin had ever been opened. I was quite ready for the first Christmas of our marriage. Lena had made us a very tasty dinner for Christmas Eve.

I had gotten a large branch of a juniper tree, and we had hung all sorts of decorations from it. That was our Christmas tree. After dinner I gave Amy and Lena two identical looking tins of toffees. I expected Amy to become most indignant for giving her and her servant identical presents, but Amy, knowing how broke we were, smiled cheerfully and accepted her candy with a big smile and a hug.

I urged Amy to open her tin but she just smiled happily. I finally opened it for her, pretending to cut the tape. I passed her the open tin. She took the top candy.

As she started to unwrap it, she said angrily: "Just some electrical wire! This is not the first of April!"

I just managed to stop her from throwing the little package at me. "Please, unwrap it a little further." She did and was very delighted with that watch as she had no other. This was turning out to become a really wonderful Christmas.

Lena, too, was happy with her present. We let her help herself to the abundant Christmas dinner and take some home for her children. We were about to pay her but she begged us to keep the money for her. Rudolf had been drinking and was sure to beat her and take away her money if she carried any. She needed the money for her children. She left the house right after washing the dishes.

She had hardly gone a few steps when we heard her scream piercingly. It raised goose bumps! I jumped up. Amy begged me not to go out. I was out of her reach to hold me back. It was a pitch dark night. At first, coming from a lighted room, I could not make out anything. Then, I saw a long knife reflecting the light from our doorway.

"Put down that knife!" I yelled as loudly as I could. He let Lena go and faced me. I could only see the blade and the white of his eyes as he wore dark clothes. I heard Lena's footsteps as she ran away. I told Rudolf that we would not pay Lena until after the new year. "This is Christmas, Rudolf, go home peacefully." He did.

I went back into the house. Amy was trembling, or did I just get that feeling from my own shaking.

"Suppose he would have killed you!"

"What else could I have done? He was about to knife Lena."

Amy hugged me like never before.

# NEW YEAR, 1947/1948

Right after Christmas, 1947, Willy came to visit us from Highgate. He had a most beautiful girlfriend in Kingston. She was obviously from a very good family, charming and well educated. The four of us piled into our Studebaker Dictator and drove to a new nightclub corner Hagley Park Road and Spanish Town Road: The Captain Morgan. The place was pretty well patronized but not overcrowded. We danced a lot and drank very moderately. It was a most pleasant evening. We had our photograph taken by a professional photographer.

It was early morning by the time we dropped Anita off and took Willy home with us.

I asked him: "Why don't you marry her? She obviously loves you and she is certainly beautiful and vivacious."

"She is also 12½ years younger than I am. It would not at all be fair to her. I do not want to get too emotionally involved with her. She will certainly make a good wife for somebody, but not for me. I am almost 40. That's too old for such a beautiful, young girl. Besides, I love my freedom as a bachelor. I do not intend ever to get married." Famous last words.

# MEET DR. SAM NEVINS

One nice afternoon, while my shop was working busily, a middle-aged White gentleman walked in, all dressed in white from his expensive looking white Panama hat down to his white leather shoes.

"You must be Arnold," he loudly proclaimed as he walked in. "I'm Dr. Sam Nevins. You can call me Sam. I bring you greetings from your sister, Toni. She and I run a medical laboratory in Brooklyn, see? Where's Jerry?"

His voice was very loud for a mere conversation. He spoke with a most definite Brooklyn accent. Besides, he used the word: "Jerry." It was too recently after World War II when that word was used in a derogatory way, meaning Nazi Forces! Nobody would have dared call Gerhard, or even refer to him, as: "Jerry!" He was usually referred to as Mr. Porten. In a social gathering like the chess club where people drop the Mr., he might be addressed as Porten. Very few select friends might be familiar enough to call him or refer to him as Gerhard. People in Jamaica are just very formal by American standards.

All of my men stopped working and looked at this phenomenon. In Jamaica, where people do not have to compete with loud traffic noises or booming radios as in Brooklyn, people speak softly unless they are vexed, of course. Here was this man coming into our shop for the first time, talking with a voice that could be heard from the doorway to the lane 250 ft. away!

I had just hired a boy from the Blue Mountains who had never before seen "the moon in ah de street," as he called the street lights or "a house 'pon wheels" (trolley car). The first thing I had to do for this teenager, was to buy him his first pair of shoes. I would not have my employees run around barefoot. He just stood there, his mouth wide open, and stared at that apparition from Brooklyn.

I told Nevins: "I have just received a telegram from Gerhard. He is stuck at Mavis Bank because his car won't start." A man would have had to carry that telegram over the Cumberland Gap to Gordon Town, the nearest telegraph office, that would have taken four hours. "Gerhard needs help right away. I am going to drive there now to help him. Do you want to come along and see a bit of the countryside? The Blue Mountains are beautiful but the drive might be a bit rough."

"How far is that?"

"15 miles, an hour's drive."

"Oh, that's nothin'! We, in America, drive that to and from work every day! Sure."

While he went out to pay off his taxi, my new apprentice from the Blue Mountains came over to me: "Koo-yah, (Gee whiz) Mr. Arnold, what ah way 'merica man dem tahk funny doah (though), eeh?"

I had gathered my tools and loaded them into my trusted, powerful 1932 Studebaker Dictator, probably one of the heaviest cars ever made. Sam was waiting for me.

"You said that you will take a whole hour to drive 15 miles? You should see our Brooklyn taxi drivers! They drive that in less than a quarter of that time through the heaviest traffic!" He certainly knew how to make a man feel good!

Princess Street was crowded in the early afternoon. I leaned on the horn and the people waited until the last moment to get out of the way, inches from my bumper.

Sam clutched the dashboard and looked worried: "Suppose you hit them?"

"I won't. If I slow down for them, they'll think that I'm a tourist, they'll block my way, make me stop, and then beg me for money."

We went the short way to the top of Princess St., turned right on North St., left on Slipe Rd. to Cross Roads, up the Old Hope Road and through the beautiful Hope Gardens. Even sophisticated Sam was very much impressed by the gorgeous botanical garden. We got out on the Gordon Town Rd. That is a very well paved road but the sharp hairpin bends made my passenger nervous.

"Don't worry, Sam, I live at the end of this road. I drive it twice every day."

He saw the bridge at the end of Gordon Town. "You are not going to drive over that! It is too narrow!"

I just drove on. The bridge was wide enough for a two ton truck. Now the road was all gravel and usually not wide enough for two cars to pass each other. There were many hairpin bends where I had to drive to the wall of the mountain, reverse to the precipice and then go forward to negotiate the bend.

I kept blowing my horn intermittently and then listened. At one time I heard a horn in answer to mine. I quickly climbed the left bank to the very edge of the precipice and stopped with my hand on the horn. In a cloud of dust, a two ton truck rounded the corner in front of me and skidded to a halt. Its cab was next to Sam's window. He could have shaken hands with the driver if he had not crawled underneath the dashboard.

I had left-hand steering. The truck had been built for British exports and had right-hand steering. The driver grinned. He seemed to be glad that we both had stopped in time to avoid a collision, or was he grinning at my poor shaking passenger? I backed the car for a distance until I found a spot where the road was wide enough for the truck to get by.

After the Cumberland Gap we coasted downhill in second gear as Mavis Bank is 1,000 feet lower than the Gap. Eventually, we reached our destination. It had taken about an hour. I heard no complaints about slow driving.

Gerhard gave me a big smile. I introduced Sam. Gerhard practically ignored him. He had been waiting for many hours after walking down the mountain, starting at sunrise. He was now too concerned with his car and wanted to know why it would not start.

I checked the electrical system. It worked fine. I checked the carburetor. It was empty. I sucked gas out of the tank, filled the carburetor. Gerhard started the car. Sam and I got into the Studebaker and took off. We had gone about a mile when I noticed that Gerhard was not following us. I parked so that a car could pass us in the unlikely event that one should drive along this lonely road. We sat by the roadside high above a river and waited.

A man with a shining machete came moseying along the road toward us.

I said to Sam: "Don't open your mouth. If he hears your American accent,"

Sam interrupted me. I had meant to complete my sentence by saying: "he is going to beg us for money."

Sam looked scared and whispered: "He can have all the money I have on me, as long as he does not hurt me."

"Don't be ridiculous! All people here walk around with a machete. It is their all purpose tool. He is just a peasant tilling his soil. Probably going home for lunch." The man was near enough now.

I said: "Good afternoon."

"Good afternoon, Sah."

"How is de missus?"

"She fine, Sah."

"And de picney dem?"

"Dem fine, Sah," he said with a smile.

"And yo girlfriend?"

"She fine, too, Sah," he answered with a guffaw, and he walked past us. Poor Sam, he looked frightened to death. A good thing, he did not live in Jamaica. If he would be scared of every worker who walked past him with a machete in his hand, he would be a nervous wreck in no time at all.

"We'll have to drive back for Gerhard. There must be something more wrong with his car than gas evaporated out of the carburetor."

Gerhard was glad to see me. I told him that we had stopped just about a mile down the road. When he did not come, we went back.

The carburetor was empty. I checked the fuel filter. It was clean. I took the fuel pump apart. It had a big tear in it. That was the trouble. The gas was leaking into the crank case instead of going into the carburetor. I checked the oil in the crank case. The gas which had leaked in there was not noticeable. So that was not going to be a problem. The fuel pump needed a diaphragm. We did not have any. So, we decided that I should push Gerhard up to the Cumberland Gap in his heavy, old 1933 Ford V-8, and from there we could let the car roll down to the hairpin bends where we would have to push the car manually around the bends.

We had gone about a mile steeply uphill when the old Studebaker boiled out. We had to stop. The back wheels of the Ford were in a brook. That put its rear bumper below my front bumper. "What are you going to do now?" asked Sam.

After some thought, I suggested that I take the tube out of the

Ford's spare tire. It had been patched many times and was of no great value any more. Gerhard readily agreed. I let the air out of the tube, took it out of the tire, and cut a diaphragm out of it, and put that into the fuel pump. We knew, of course, that gasoline would dissolve the rubber, but we also knew that it would take the car back to Kingston, where we could buy a new diaphragm and a tube for the spare tire.

Tubeless tires had not yet been invented. Those old tubes had to be pumped up about twice a week. I primed the carburetor. The car started. Its bumper was hitched underneath that of the Studebaker. I stood on the Ford bumper and Gerhard took off very carefully and headed for Kingston.

My poor radiator was still steaming angrily. With the help of a large rag I gingerly took off the radiator cap.

Sam asked: "How are you going to fill it? You have no container."

"That's what the good people at the Studebaker plant made hubcaps for. They knew this would happen to me." I started the engine and filled the radiator with a good many hub caps full of water.

The drive back was pretty uneventful. Even Sam eventually stopped clutching the dashboard as if that would have given him an extra measure of safety. It was too late to go back to the shop, so I picked up Amy and drove Sam to our little cottage in Gordon Town. When Amy was out of earshot, he marveled that I should have given up the comfortable apartment of my parents and the "American way" for this little hut which was so poorly furnished. I told him that I just loved Jamaica, the freedom of having my own shop, and that I did not ever want to go back to Brooklyn. That seemed incomprehensible to him.

Lena served us a good dinner. I made him a very proper Jamaican rum punch. Even though Amy and I did not drink, a bottle of rum is surely to be found in every Jamaican house. Our very congenial conversation lasted till late at night. We promised to show him more of Jamaica. I drove him back to the Myrtle Bank Hotel and said: "Good Night." He wore a smile from ear to ear and said: "Those Brooklyn taxi drivers are sissies compared to you!"

# BRILLIANT JOHN BARRY

John graduated from Woolmer's with a London Matric first of his class and second of all the high school graduates in all of Jamaica. He was also the youngest to ever hold a British Lieutenant's Commission. He shared the title of School Boxing Champion with another graduate of another school. He was the Champion Breaststroke Swimmer of his school. I had something to do with that. He was well loved by all the girls because he had a sunny disposition.

John became a teacher at Knox College in Spalding for a semester. He received an agricultural scholarship which entitled him to study veterinary medicine in England. It was not exactly what he had hoped for. He had always wanted to study human medicine. Still, he was very happy to study any medicine at all and then go to England! Great!

Amy was very proud of her younger brother. We decided to give him a farewell dinner at our little house in Gordon Town. I found a six feet by four feet cover of a packing case, supported each end with our two little tables, put a table cloth on it, and there, we had a dining table. We all crowded around it. In my toast I mentioned that it would probably be the last time that all of the family would be together. I proved to be right.

The great day came. The ship left from Port Antonio. I wrote a little poem of the event which describes the day better than I can now relate it in 1998 almost 50 years later.

# John goes to England

Johnny off to England goes.
The house shakes to its eves
As temper and excitement grows
And the Barry family leaves.

The car is packed with odds and ends
"Let's hurry to the boat!"
His ears John now to each one lends
And all give him a note.

Traveling all its comfort lacks
Too many 're in the car,
Besides there are soft drinks and sacks.
The distance is so far.

The time is creeping slowly by.
Photos are taken long since.
Talk has worn thin and dry.
Oh, shippers, this is nonsense.

But finally the whistle blows.
And loudly goes the gong.
And Mama wipes her running nose
And says: "Dear John, so long."

Oh, could you hold one minute more,
Jamaica is so nice.
Just touch its so beloved shore
I would give any price!

A film now makes the eyes so blind.
The boat has up its steam.
Now, turn about, and you will find
The future, hope, in eyes new gleam.

By: Arnold P. Von der Porten
September 29, 1948.

567

# IN THE NEON SHOP

Gradually, the little neon shop picked up.  I delivered two signs to the movie theaters in Montego Bay.  On my way there, I had a flat tire.  I found it difficult to change the tire with the old Studebaker fully laden with a large neon sign on its roof.  The jack would not lift the heavy car plus the weight of the sign.  Ozzy and I found a sturdy tree trunk, used it as a lever, and lifted the back wheel off the road.  My workman held the tree trunk down while I changed the tire.

I thought it imperative to trade the car in for a pickup truck.  I had received an order from the *Industrial Garage,* the Ford Agency, to make them signs for their new building on Church Street.  They had had a disastrous, fatal fire and their new building was almost finished.  I made them neon signs reading:  Lincoln, Ford, Mercury.  They traded in my old Studebaker for an English Ford pickup truck.  I agreed to pay them the difference in equal monthly payments.  I liked that little truck very much, though its springs proved to be of very poor quality and had to be replaced often.

My big customers were the Chinese groceries, the movie theaters, and the gasoline stations.  There were three oil companies doing business in Jamaica: Esso, Shell, and Trinidad Leasehold.  I would drop my men off at the sites with the signs, tell them how to install what they had made in the shop and go about my business, selling, buying or going back to the shop.

One day I left George, my main metal man, with a new apprentice at the Trinidad Leasehold gas station at Half-Way Tree to put a sign on the roof.  Unfortunately, my twelve foot ladder just barely reached the roof.  The macadam pavement was soft so that the ladder sank in a bit as George stepped on it.  It was a really hot day.  I told the apprentice to make absolutely sure that he held the ladder really tightly as it was practically vertical.  George and I got the sign into position.  I climbed down again and left George to fasten and connect the sign.  I promised to be back in an hour.

When I came back, George was sitting on a step holding his head.

"What happened?"

"There was a sudden downpour, and I rushed to the ladder. John had let go and had run for shelter. The ladder went over with me, and the back of my head hit the pavement."

I looked where the top of the ladder lay. There was a dimple in the pavement. I was sure that it was a perfect negative of the back of George's head.

"Are you all right? Do you want me to take you to the doctor?"

"I'm all-right, Sah. You hold the ladder, Sah, and I'll connect up the sign."

"No, no George. You hold the ladder and I'll connect the sign."

We drove back to the shop and I fired the apprentice. George never mentioned the accident again. All of my crew were very loyal to me. I felt especially fatherly toward Teresa whom I had trained as a neon glassblower, Ozzie, my electrician, who married her after I left Jamaica, George and his brother Reggie, my chief metal workers.

Teresa had been brought to me shortly after I was released from the internment camp by the Catholic Priest in charge of the Holy Rosary Church. He told me that she could sweep out my shop after school. He told me that she came from a desperately poor family with lots of children, and that she was a wonderful student. He hoped that I would pay her some money so that she could buy some shoes, as it was a requirement for all students in the Catholic School to wear shoes. I bought her a pair of shoes. How else could she sweep out the neon shop with all those glass splinters on the floor?

One has the best chance of becoming a good glassblower when one learns the trade while one is still young. Teresa came every afternoon punctually and eventually took over more than half the glassblowing. She had a surprising power over the men I hired, and when I was out of the shop she took charge quite naturally.

One of the nice parts of my shop was that there was never any theft of any of my material, tools, or loss of stock in the stores by any of my customers. I never had to lock my storeroom. I would forget my watch on the work bench all day, yet I would find it just where I left it. It was a nice feeling to have such an honest set of people working for me.

One day a customer came into my shop: "Mr. Von der Porten, I am the Agent for an American insurance company. They sent me

569

some money which I was to use for advertising. Now they are going to send out a representative to check up on me. He will want to know what I did with the advertising money. Can you make me a sign for £150.=.=? I want to rent a spot at the Red Gal Ring, you know the sharp curve on the Stony Hill Road. It has to be built and lit in two weeks."

"All right I can do that. Fifty percent with the order, balance on completion."

I just made it by the time limit. I had another electrician, McFarlane. I sent him, Reggie and Joe, a youngster whom I had hired from the Quaker orphanage in Highgate, to install the sign. I made an appointment with the electrical inspector to inspect the sign at 4:30 p.m. and for the Jamaica Public Service to connect it at 5:00 p.m.

I drove the three of them and the sign to the spot. I personally marked the posts how deep they had to go into the ground. I dug a few spades full at the exact spots where the posts had to go into the ground. They should have had no trouble to get that sign ready by 4:00 p.m.

"I'll pick you up at four o' clock sharp." I drove away. I felt sure that I had everything under control.

At 4:00 p.m. I came back. The sign was in the exact same position as I had left it. I looked for my three men. Bad luck! There was a mango tree not a hundred yards from the site. It was mango season! It is almost impossible to get anybody to work in the mango season. I should have spotted the tree in the morning when my men did! There they lay, the three of them, soundly asleep under the mango tree with lots of mango pits all around them. I was furious! I informed them of this fact in clear, unmistakable terms. They said that they were sorry. What was I to tell the customer? I drove the three mango stuffing, irresponsible good-for-nothings back to the shop and after giving them a piece of my mind, I fired the three of them. I phoned the customer who was forgiving as long as I got it up the next day.

Teresa had opened the shop the next morning. As I got to work a few minutes later, there were McFarlane, Reggie, and Joe working away as if nothing had ever happened. I walked right up to McFarlane. He was the eldest man in the shop.

I said as sternly as I could: "Mac, I fired you yesterday!"

"Yes Sah. Me cum back, Sah," he answered with a big grin all over his face, as if he were doing me a favor and forgiving me for throwing him out. All the men burst out laughing. I could not help laughing myself. It had taken a long time to train each man in my crew. Where would I get better skilled and honest men? Besides, the loss of their jobs would mean a major disaster in their lives. It would seriously hurt them. I certainly did not want to do that. On the other hand it would make little difference to me if I had to get new men. They would not be better than the ones they would replace.

Finally I said: "Did you eat enough mangos yesterday, and can you spare me the time to put up the sign today?"

"Yes, Sah!" I took the same crew up, and they did a very good job. They all stayed with me until I left the Island.

# VACATION AT SILVER HILL WITH HELEN AND KATHLEEN

During her school holidays in 1950, Helen Fitton, Toni's daughter, came to visit us from Brooklyn. Amy and I took off a week from work and rented a building on an old, no longer functioning coffee estate, called Silver Hill north of Hardware Gap below Cinchona Peak. We took Kathleen, Amy's sister, along with us. The girls, both 16, got on very well together. They sat in the back of my little pickup truck as it climbed up the mountain, then through Hardware Gap at about 3,000 ft. altitude and down northward beyond the pass a few miles to where we had to leave the truck and carry our supplies a mile uphill on foot.

The old coffee estate was still magnificent. It was built from large cut stone. A ten foot diameter cedar water wheel looked as if it were waiting to be put to use again. A large square basin, built of field stone, which had once served to wash coffee could hold about three to four feet of fresh water. We could quickly fill it from a clear brook to overflowing and actually swim in it. The great house itself stood empty. It was supposed to be haunted. No one lived in it though its hand split, possibly 100 years old, shingled roof seemed quite good.

We had a modern little bungalow, two bedrooms, a bathroom and a large kitchen with a dining table and enough chairs. The water came from the brook which had once driven the mighty waterwheel. Now a modern pipe led directly into our modern plumbing. We had brought kerosene lamps, kerosene, food, drinks, and flashlights from Kingston.

Not far above us, the brook widened into a pool. It was a lovely spot for the four of us to go swimming. That area was so thinly populated that mosquitoes could not live there. (There just were not enough people to supply them with blood.) We went there practically every day. We took long walks up and down the mountain paths.

Toward the end of our stay we rented a mule and set out right after sunrise. All of us wore khaki slacks. That was sensible wear as we were walking past thorny bushes, and the girls wanted to ride the mule. Amy and the two girls took turns riding, 20 minutes each and 40 minutes walking. We had to climb over a ridge, down again, and finally up. Just before noon, we reached the Cinchona Peak, about 5,000 ft. above sea level, only about 2,500 ft. above our cabin. It is very beautiful, wild country. We had excellent weather. It was a most enjoyable hike.

There is an old overgrown botanical garden at the peak. A farsighted governor, in the 1800s imported valuable and useful plants from all over the tropical world and planted them there. Cinchona bark is used to extract quinine to combat malaria. Because those trees were planted there, the peak is named after them. Here grow many varieties of tea, many spices, and good crop plants. If only someone had shown enough initiative, it could have made Jamaica a rich country. No one followed through. It is sad.

We could not stay too long. We wanted to get back to Silver Hill before dark. Helen was fascinated by the steep, practically vertical mountainsides. She decided to climb a few. I was worried and followed her, staying just a little bit below her, so that I could catch her if she should fall. My worries were unwarranted. She was quite surefooted.

Where the path forks, one side going to Silver Hill, and the other to where the mule is stabled, the mule absolutely wanted to go home. Helen, who was riding the beast at the time, had to use all of her considerable riding skills to head the mule to Silver Hill. Saturday came and my little English Ford pickup truck carried us back to Kingston.

# HECTORS RIVER WITH AMY, HER MOTHER, HELEN, KATHLEEN, AND ALAN

Helen stayed with the Ho-Sangs, a wealthy Chinese family. Early one Sunday morning we picked her up again. We had rented an empty house by the sea, surrounded by a coconut plantation, from the Jones family of Hectors River. Mr. Jones was a very prominent and wealthy planter on the North Coast. Mrs. Jones, originally from Philadelphia, Pennsylvania, was the clerk of the Jamaica Yearly Meeting of the Friends. They were extremely nice people.

My truck was laden to its limit with household items, such as beds, chairs, food, clothes, etc. Dad drove his big Dodge. It had four passengers: Mom, Amy, Helen, and Kathleen. Alan drove with me in the truck. It was quite a drive around Point Morant, the eastern extreme of Jamaica. We finally arrived and Alan, 15, showed his much appreciated skill of opening water coconuts with a machete. He opened green coconuts which have not yet developed much of their solids inside. The drink from a freshly opened coconut is cool and most refreshing. There were coconuts all around us.

We got the truck unloaded and the beds assembled. Amy and her mother busied themselves getting dinner ready. There was still time to take a swim in the blue and warm Caribbean Sea before sundown. It was a most beautiful spot. Dad and I had to go back to Kingston as we had to go to work the next morning. We left the Dodge with Amy and rode back in my little truck. The four ladies and Alan had a most wonderful two weeks. Dad and I spent the weekends there as well. The last Saturday, early in the morning, I picked up Dad. We stayed most of the day at the beach.

Sunday morning, after a refreshing swim, we packed up. On our way home, we visited the Joneses. I played some Ping-Pong with Keith and Arnold Jones. They had a stunningly, beautiful sister, Mary. Years later, Arnold Jones became Minister of Labour under the Bustamante Government after Jamaica became independent. He died under mysterious circumstances. Some say he fell from a balcony when the balustrade gave way, others claim that he had been killed.

We also visited the Quaker boarding school at Hectors River, the site where the Quakers held their Yearly Meetings. That school was on high ground, a very beautiful spot overlooking the sea. It was a great vacation for all of us, even though Dad and I could only stay there on the three weekends.

We dropped Helen off at the Ho-Sangs, where there were quite a few girls of about Helen's age. They all had a wonderful time together until it was time for Helen to go back to Brooklyn.

# PREGNANCY, WRONG DIAGNOSIS, TROUBLE

We had been married for about two years when we decided to start a family. Peggie George, Amy's cousin on her mother's side, recommended a "marvelous" young doctor, Dr. Narcise. From the start, Amy had problems. Unfortunately, the physician did not notice that Amy had lost the fetus. He claimed that she was pregnant in the fallopian tube. Four doctors decided that an operation was necessary. Dr. Parboosingh cut Amy open from the chest right down and never found a fetus.

Amy did not heal readily and was in the Seventh Day Adventist's Hospital for two months. All feared that we might lose her. Dr. Narcise had given her an overdose of a medicine and she was dying. Good fortune had it that Dr. Stamm was in the hospital. He rushed in, and treated her, and stayed with her for several hours and saved her life. I spent my evenings in the hospital. It was a terrible time for both of us.

We had been to the Quaker Meeting just about every Sunday. The Parboosingh family were very active members. The Quakers came often and encouraged Amy when she was awake enough and not under too much medication to ease her pain. Antibiotics, such as penicillin, were not yet in use. Dr. Rose Butler-Parboosingh told me that Amy's abdomen would always protrude. Her beautiful figure would be ruined forever, but she would still be able to have children.

I asked for the hospital bill. The office told me that there was none.

"How about the doctors' bills?"

"There is none."

No one ever told me who took care of those bills. I assume Dorothea Simmons and the Quakers settled them. No one from the Presbyterian Church ever came to see Amy nor inquire about her. Rev. Lewis Davidson had gone to Mandeville to become the head master of Knox College, a boys' high school.

After this experience, Amy and I were really close. Never before had I realized what a treasure I had in that lovely woman.

Amy officially joined the Quakers. She felt that the Presbyterians had abandoned her, whereas the Friends had welcomed her with open arms.

# MARIGOLD, A NEW DIMENSION

One good Sunday morning, a stranger from America came to the Quaker Meeting at 11 Caledonia Avenue. After the meeting, he told us that he was a Quaker from New York and that he wanted to meet growers of ginger, sarsaparilla roots, nutmeg, pimento, and other spices. He wanted to import them to America. He felt that the prices were artificially high because of too many middle men. Members of the Meeting told him that he would have to go to the Mandeville area. They might as well have told him to go to the moon. He had no idea where Mandeville was nor how to get there. I told him that I would be willing to take the day off from work and drive him there. I figured I shall drive to Spaldings and ask my dear friend Rev. Lewis Davidson. I had not seen him since he had married us. I knew that the Millers grew ginger in that area. Mrs. Miller was the daughter of the very old Mrs. White, a very active Quaker. Lewis Davidson would certainly know how to find them.

Early the next morning we left Kingston, drove through Spanish Town and on through beautiful Mandeville to Knox College in Spaldings. We were led into a large classroom full of adults. They had all come for a seminar led by Lewis Davidson. I was told that Rev. Davidson had someone in his office and that he would see us as soon as that person would come out.

Suddenly Willy Gertig came up to me followed by a young lady: "What are you doing here?"

"I was just about to ask you that same question."

"I came here to take a seminar. I want to introduce you to Marigold. I just met her here. We are engaged."

That news hit me like a bomb. Willy had never been one for many words. I shook hands with that tall blond. She had a winning smile. At that time Lewis Davidson came out of his office and asked us in. That is how I met Marigold. Boy! That sure was sudden!

Lewis Davidson gave us directions, and the New Yorker pressed on. I had no time to see the elated couple again that day. We drove to the houses of several growers. My guest seemed very disappointed with the prices. The growers had formed an

578

association. They pooled their crops and sold them together so that they could not be played one against the other by buyers. The Friend from America promised to write them from New York. We drove back to Kingston.

A few weeks later, Amy and I got a printed invitation from Marigold's mother. It turned out that Marigold was the niece of the wife of Amy's Uncle Earl, the brother of Amy's mother, so that Amy and Marigold were cousins by marriage. At any rate we were invited to Highgate for the wedding of her daughter, Marigold, to Mr. Wilhelm Gertig. Willy (the absolutely confirmed bachelor) asked me to be his best man.

On our way there, I wrote a little ditty to the tune of the popular and easy to learn South German *Schnadelhupfer*.

Lewis Davidson and his charming wife had come from Spaldings to the Friends College and just about everybody of the Highgate Quaker Mission was at the wedding. After the ceremony, we all had dinner at the Abrikians. I noticed that the affair needed livening up, so I sang my *Schnadelhupfer:*

Summer school in Spaldings is quick touch and go.
And Willy and Marigold sure found it so!

(Refrain by all:)
> Holla dree hee hah ho,
> Holla dree hah ho,
> Holdree hah hopsassa
> Holla dree ho!

> To flirt with a woman is sure lots of fun
> But our friend Willy forgot how to run.

(By all:)
> Holla dree hee hah ho, etc.

> Variety is still the real spice of life
> So bachelor Willy has now taken a wife.

(By all)
> Holla dree hee hah ho, etc.

That loosened up the party quite a bit and it was real fun. Of course, no alcohol was served at a Quaker wedding, a fact which I heartily endorsed.

We drove home that same evening. Marigold was a nurse, and the mission in Highgate could certainly use a nurse. We did not see Marigold and Willy very often. When they came to Kingston he no longer stayed with us. The couple usually came together and stayed with her mother.

# WE MOVE

Amy was expecting again. I asked Fritz Lackenbach to have a proper stairway built, as the steep path would become too difficult for Amy to manage in a short while. He was unwilling to spend the money, and since he could terminate our stay there at any time I did not want to spend any more money on his house.

We looked for another residence. Amy's parents' house seemed the most practical since her Dad drove her there every evening until I came after work to pick her up. On my suggestion, we moved in and paid rent for the part of the house which we occupied. That sort of arrangement is not at all unusual in Jamaica. We saw almost at once that we had to find another solution.

I found a little house at Red Hills Road. It was in a rural neighborhood. Goats roamed the street and the yards. It would be difficult to maintain a garden, especially a vegetable garden.

The house was brand new and quite roomy in comparison to the one we had in Gordon Town. All rooms were considerably larger than the ones we had lived in before. In the front there was a bedroom. To the right of it was a covered verandah. Behind the bedroom was another bedroom with a door to the bathroom to the back and one to the dining room. The dining room doubled as living room. It had two other doors, one to the front verandah and one to the covered back porch. The back porch was broad. It ran almost the length of the house to the bathroom. Behind the bathroom and part of the back porch was the kitchen. Behind it was the maid's room and a bathroom for her.

Looking at the house from the street which was north of us, there was a lime tree to the right of the drive near the gate. About 15 feet to the right of the dining room was an ackee tree and way in the back were two breadfruit trees. A poor-looking wire fence marked the outline of our domain as far as humans were concerned. Goats had no respect for wire fences.

Lena did not want to relocate at first, so we hired another woman for a while. After a month or so, Lena begged us to let her come back to work for us again. The other woman did not like to be so far from her friends and quit. Lena took up her rightful place with us. It worked out fine.

We were the only White people for miles around. We got on very well with our landlord who lived two houses to the west and our neighbors despite their goats. With the men of my shop we built a gate of termite proof Bullet wood, wide enough for our pickup truck and too difficult for goats to try to climb over. After a few weeks, we also built a car port of termite proof Jamaican hardwood between the dining room and the ackee tree.

Amy with her great knowledge of the local flora, planted a hedge of three poisonous plants, one behind the other, around the entire property, as goats will not go though poisonous plants. On the outside there were very quick, but not very high growing Jerusalem Candle Sticks. Their stems are filled with a milky fluid and they bear a small red flower at their tips, hence their name: Jerusalem Candle Sticks. Behind them we grew a row of red Poinsettia. They looked really beautiful at Christmas time. On the inside there was a thick, four foot high row of dark, prickly leafed and white flowering Jamaica Holly, (no relation to the real Holly Trees.) This hedge was most successful esthetically and functionally as well, as we had no more trouble with goats.

We planted a very nice flower garden in the front and a very helpful vegetable garden in the back. Sugar cane grew behind the kitchen and bathroom as the wash basins and the bathtub emptied into a shallow ditch in the back. Just the right thing for sugar cane. We also planted bananas and plantains. They, too, did very well. We were very happy in that house.

# ACTIVE IN THE MANUFACTURERS ASSOCIATION

## ICE CREAM CONES.

In the late 1940s and early 1950s I became quite involved with the Jamaica Manufacturers Association. As the Director of the Miscellaneous Group I was asked if I could help an ice cream cone manufacturer. He had bought a machine that baked the cones with gas burners. Unfortunately, the flames blew out when the Kingston city gas was lit. The poor manufacturer was frantic. Here he had sunk all of his little bit of capital into this expensive machine and now it did not work!

I got myself a book on flame speeds with various gases. There is a very definite relationship between the throat of the burners to the diameters of the orifices of the burners to achieve a successful flame. I had the orifices of the burners drilled to the correct dimensions, the flames burnt beautifully and the manufacturer was happy.

## ARBITRATING A STRIKE.

Another time, the clay brick factory fired a thief. The factory was a member of my group. The Bustamante Labour Union wanted the man reinstated and threatened a strike. Both sides accepted me as the arbitrator. The management was four of a Jamaican family of East Indian descent. The union team of four, and the dismissed worker were all Black Jamaicans. As usual, I was the only White.

Though race was never mentioned, racial tensions between East Indians and Blacks were clearly there. For eight hours the two sides yelled at each other, sometimes several at the same time. It was difficult to keep a semblance of order. Fortunately, the table at which we were sitting, was wide enough to prevent them from actually hitting each other. Both sides lied incessantly and kept contradicting themselves.

It became obvious to me that the laborer had been employed there for a long time and had at one time been a good worker. In recent months he had stolen and was absent from his work very often, so that management could not rely on him. Management had a good case. Unfortunately, they quite obviously kept lying and contradicting each other and even themselves. Their figures were very vague and changed constantly. I asked to see attendance and payment records. None were produced.

Eventually, after a very long, steaming hot day, I recommended that the Union Business Agent, all by himself, with no one accompanying him, should see the Company Accountant the next day, and if the wage record showed that the man had been absent frequently without a reasonable excuse, the Company should pay him two weeks' wages and dismiss him or give him two weeks' notice in accordance to the labor law of Jamaica. The man had never been proven a thief in court, and the company had not produced two witnesses to claim that the man was a thief, therefore the company could not discharge him on the grounds that he had stolen. By that time I had a splitting headache from the shouting, the tension, the heat and the total unpleasantness of the situation. Headaches were most unusual for me.

The company felt that if they followed my advice, the union would have control of their factory, and they would no longer get any work done. The union insisted that the man be reinstated without any further debate. So since neither side wanted to follow my suggestions, I was frustrated and felt that the entire, most unhappy day was a depressing waste of time. I had failed. A very bitter strike ensued, and the factory, the only factory making bricks from clay in Jamaica, went bankrupt. The Jamaica Manufacturers Association, in particular the Miscellaneous Group, had lost a member. No clay bricks were manufactured in the Island any more. All that because of a miserable thief.

## THE JAMAICAN TARIFF LAW.*

The Jamaican Book of Tariffs provided different import duties on various categories of goods: Dry Goods, Hardware, Lumber, Electrical Goods, Oils, etc.

"Hard" currency, i. e. U.S. dollars or any other currency readily convertible to U.S. dollars was in very short supply. Jamaican

---

* See the chapter: *The Birth of the Jamaica Manufacturers Association*

exports, mainly bananas and sugar went to England, a "soft" currency country.

One needed a hard to get Government permit to use Jamaican or British pounds to import any goods from "hard" currency countries like the U.S. or Canada. Usually, the annual amounts on those permits were 10% of one's annual imports in 1938. Emergency "hard currency" import permits were sometimes granted for spare parts for "essential" American machinery.

We, in the Jamaica Manufacturers Association, believed that the Jamaican consumers would be much better served with the limited "hard" currency available if we would change the tariff code into totally different categories:

1) Absolute raw materials, duty free.

2) Slightly manufactured, a low duty.

3) Finished goods, high duty.

Luxury goods, a very high import duty.

Cheap raw materials and high duty on finished goods would boost Jamaican manufacture and that in turn would reduce unemployment and make more finished goods available for the consumers.

Four of us, Harry Vendreys, our President, who was also the Vice-President of the Jamaica Chamber of Commerce; the Director of the Perfumery Group, I have forgotten his name; Gerhard the Director of the Food Group; and I, the Director of the Miscellaneous Group spent many evenings together to write a draft for a new Tariff Law Proposal. When we had finished we had included every item that was in the current tariff but the categories had changed dramatically.

With high hopes we submitted our work to the Colonial Secretary. The latter's office asked the exceedingly powerful Chamber of Commerce for their opinion. That group was most certainly not interested in having things manufactured in Jamaica. They held the lucrative, monopolistic import quotas for all foreign manufactured items including extravagant luxury goods. Naturally, they squashed our work. It was a bad blow for Jamaican Industry. Without those proposed duties on finished goods, the fledgling factories just could not compete with the huge concerns of Europe, the U.S. and Canada.

# DRINKING WATER.*

Kingston was fast running out of drinking water. A group of British engineers were called in from England. They saw the large and deep clay bed on top of the limestone in the Mona region, just south of the Long Mountain. That clay would certainly hold water. Almost all of the Island, including the Long Mountain, is limestone except the Blue Mountain range which starts immediately north of Papine and ends just south of Port Antonio. That range is solid granite.

The British Engineers recommended building a reservoir on top of that clay bed on top of that limestone with a canal from the Hope River to feed the reservoir. Since the British Governor and the British Colonial Secretary knew that all British experts in London were always right, the reservoir was built according to plans drawn in London, England. The reservoir was named after the Governor who approved its construction and, incidentally, was governing during my internment, Richard's Reservoir. The designers must have had data on the annual rainfall in Kingston and built the canal leading to the reservoir accordingly. In England they certainly knew about rainfall! After all, it rained there almost every other day.

Most of the year the Hope River is a mere trickle. When the canal was opened, nothing much happened. Then the rains came! Unlike in London, almost all of the annual rainfall can come in one week! And it did! Boulders, washed down the river, blocked the pretty little entrance to the canal and torrents flowed all over the Hope Gardens and Papine. No water obliged to drip into the reservoir.

Back to the drawing board! A wider canal was built. The first rainfall after its completion, water actually flowed into the reservoir. Unfortunately, it did not stay. The construction crew had bulldozed away all of the clay down to the bare limestone to make the dike around the reservoir. The result was that the area around the reservoir sported a new greenery which had never been there in this very dry region, as the rain clouds do not usually climb over the Blue Mountains. There were new salty and evil tasting wells

* See the chapter: *The Birth of the Jamaica Manufacturers Association*

coming out of the Long Mountain on its south slopes. That water ran over the coastal road into the sea. I wish I could have brought the experts back from London to look at their fantastic work.

I do not know what the Jamaican Government has done since, but the reservoir holds some water now. However, the water shortage for Kingston has become very acute, as predicted by all of the Directors of the Jamaica Manufacturers Association before 1950.

Around 1950 I wrote a memorandum to the Board of Directors of our Association, that it were most urgent to dam off the Hope River Valley north of Papine where a stone bridge leads across that river. The valley is very narrow there. Steep granite walls rise high on both sides. No water would seep away there as granite is absolutely impervious. That would be the spot to build a large reservoir to provide Kingston with all the water it could possibly use.

The memorandum was approved by the Board, and we sent it to the Colonial Secretary. That was the end of that. In 1986, Amy and I visited Kingston as Amy had been invited to a conference of the International Association of Independent School Librarians. We stayed at a small hotel in Barbican. Its almost empty swimming pool was covered with green slime. There was no water to clean it nor to fill it up. There was a very good looking young American woman parading around in her swimsuit. I cannot fault her for that. It was very hot and because of an acute power shortage the air conditioners could not be turned on. Besides, next to a swimming pool, even a useless one, her attire was perfectly correct.

On our last day, as we were about to enter the taxi to take us to the airport, she passed near me.

I said: "A pity that there has been no rain to fill up the reservoir so that you could use the pool. It is spoiling your vacation."

"Oh, I'm not here on vacation. I have a PhD in Geology. I'm sent here by the American Government to explore the possibility of getting water to Kingston. I'm here three weeks now, and I'll have to fly home tomorrow. I guess Kingston is a nice place to build a city, but there is no way to get water there."

"You are 100% wrong. There is a site which I recommended some 36 years ago just a mile east and then a mile north of here,

587

where a dam could be built on granite rock, creating a most successful reservoir. There is my memo to that effect gathering dust in some government office. Sorry, I have to catch a plane. Good-bye."

I entered the taxi, and Kingston is still without water thanks to a series of inert governments.

## HOW TO SAVE THE AIRPORT.

One day Ozzy, my electrician, and I were installing white neon tubing inside of some show cases in a little store at the airport on the Palisadoes. The Palisadoes are a seven mile long strip of land separating the Kingston Harbour from the open Caribbean Sea. On the east side it connects to land and on the west side is Port Royal, a shadow of its historic past. There is a deep inlet west of Port Royal. During World War II, the Americans built the airport halfway down that strip into a swampy area on the bay side. They drove huge steel retaining walls into the swamp on three sides of the airport and filled in the area with sand. They killed all the mangroves. They paved over the area, built hangars and administrative buildings, and when the War was over they gave it to the Jamaican Government.

Now, as Ozzy and I were working, Mr. Saunders, the manager of the airport came over to me:

"Mr. Von der Porten, can I see you in my office for a few minutes?"

"Certainly, Sir." We sat down on comfortable chairs. He looked worried.

"I have a problem, Mr. Von der Porten. You are a technical man. Maybe you can help me. I am a member of the Natural History Society. That's how I know about your wife and you. I have heard about you at the Manufacturers Association."

"What's your problem, Sir?"

"The airport is sinking and the American airlines want to send much bigger planes here in the future. I doubt that the tarmac can take the load. I asked England for help. They sent four engineers here who examined the airport and especially the runways carefully. Then they wrote two 'white papers'. Two of the engineers recommended to improve the present airport. The other two want it condemned, and a new airport built between Kingston and Spanish Town."

"But that land is swampy too and is the best banana and sugar land. It would be bad to cut down on our exports, when you have land for an airport right here."

"Very true, and it would be terribly expensive, too!"

"Now look at the road to the airport, Mr. Saunders. You notice how, in many places, the side of road which is nearest to the harbor has sagged, and the pavement has broken up, even though concrete retaining walls are supposed to protect the shore line? The concrete has cracked and has been patched many times, and still the road sags. The more concrete you put, the worse it gets, as the weight of the cement presses on the silt below and lets the waves wash the fine sand away.

"Did you notice how nice and without any cracks the road is where the mangroves were left standing at the edge of the water? The mangroves look healthy, and the shore line is creeping toward the water. That is the benefit of a mangrove swamp. Now, if you would break up all the concrete retaining walls around the airport and plant mangroves instead, your airport would never sink, regardless of how waterlogged the sand under the tarmac might be, as water cannot be compressed. It will not change its volume under pressure not even under the weight of the heaviest plane. That is a fact of physics. So, if you follow my advice, break up the concrete and plant mangroves, the airport will stop sinking."

He gave me a big smile, shook my hand happily and followed my advice. Now almost 50 years later the airport is still there and accommodates huge jets of a size that Mr. Saunders and I never even dreamed about at that time.

# APPLYING TO BECOME A BRITISH SUBJECT

Jamaica was my home. I loved the Island. Germany had once kicked me out, and I did not fit in, in New York. It seemed only logical that I should become a British Subject like Dorrie and Gerhard. I hired Mr. Lake of the prestigious law firm of Lake and Nunez to look after my application. I regretted that choice, as it turned out that Mr. Lake was very lazy. Since my German passport had expired in 1938 I was stateless.

Since the Nazi government in Germany had been deposed, I could reclaim German citizenship. But I had no sense of loyalty to Germany at that time nor did I want to return to that country. The narrow chauvinism of practically all of those Europeans who had never lived outside of their nation-state went against my grain. It was the underlying cause of the frequent wars throughout the European history. The wars caused bad blood, and that in turn caused more wars. I knew that I would never again fit in anywhere in Europe. I had married a Jamaican wife who would never feel homesick for another country as so many foreign born women professed to feel. My wish to become a British-Jamaican was very sincere. Besides, we were going to be parents of a child. It was important to us that the child be born of British parents.

Though still very, very poor I was a well-known and respected person in Jamaica. I had my own business since March 1, 1939. Since I had joined the Jamaica Manufacturers Association, I had been elected as one of their Directors heading the "Miscellaneous Group". I had been elected to be one of the Directors of the Electrical Contractors Association. I was a Member of the Jamaica Chamber of Commerce. I had helped to introduce the manufacture of pasta. I had the only neon shop in the entire British West Indies. During the War, I manufactured cleanser, calcium additive for chicken and cattle, ran trucks and small factories on charcoal when gasoline and electric power was in short supply. That was as far as the business world was concerned. I still held the record for the 200 m breaststroke Junior Swimming Championship of Jamaica. I was the goal keeper of the Jamaican All Star Water Polo Team, one of the ten best known painters of that time and cofounder with Clifford Meredith of the Kingston Monthly Meeting of Friends.

I felt that I had made a very positive contribution to the Island, and I saw no reason why the application should be turned down.

# THE JONESES FROM INDIANA

Amy and Mack Jones arrived in Kingston. They had been sent by the Richmond, Indiana, Five Yearly Meeting. They were to run the Kingston Monthly Meeting and were to live upstairs at the 11 Caledonia Avenue Quaker Meeting Building. They had great plans to set the world on fire and expressed great sympathy for the Jamaica Independence Movement. They knew all about it from the American press. They lived upstairs in the Meeting House opposite the Nuttall Hospital and just a bit north of Up Park Camp. The sight of British soldiers who often passed their home revolted them. They told me that those men were the symbol of oppression of the noble aspirations of the Jamaican people to be free.

I pointed out that most Jamaicans were quite happy with the crown colony status. They told me that they would like to meet some influential Jamaican people to explain the American way to them. Amy's classmate, Avis Ingram, had married Lesley Henriques. Avis had a master's degree in French from the MacGill University in Montreal, Canada, and was considered one of the brightest young Jamaicans in many fields. Lesley and his father owned the most prestigious jewelry store in Kingston. Both had brown skin colors. Lesley was a bit darker than Avis. Because Lesley was a member of the Kingston Swimming Club I knew him well. Amy and I considered the Henriqueses' good friends.

We and the Joneses visited them. No sooner had we arrived when Amy Jones broke the unspoken, but most sacred taboo, and brought up race! She lashed out against the White soldiers "swaggering" past her windows, being a gross provocation to the Negroes who justifiably craved for freedom. Mack would not be outdone. He loudly praised the late President Roosevelt for having influenced the colored peoples in the Americas to strike against the United Fruit Company which was owned by "exploiting" White people, until it had to go out of business.

My better half and I wished that the floor would open and swallow us and deposit us at some other place. Those newcomers to the Island, in this so class conscious society, put the very much upper class Henriqueses on the same social level as the rabble in the street which hung around the Up Park Camp. Then they as much as condescended that even though they themselves were White, they most graciously did not consider the brown Henriqueses inferior. Who were they to talk that way! The Henriqueses were top Jamaican Society!

Then the Joneses went on to explain the American election system, being second to none, without apparently having any knowledge as to how a crown colony is governed. I tried to change the subject but the ardent Quakers did not take the hint.

Finally Lesley very politely told Mack: "Mr. Jones, you come here from a foreign country to a British Country, to a British home, as guests to a British couple. Without any provocation you insult our British ways. Do you realize that my wife and I can vote here in Jamaica, and that we can vote in England if we take up residence there even though Englishmen cannot vote in Jamaica? Do you know that the Jamaican Government runs a huge deficit every year, and that the British Government pays that debt and keeps the Jamaican pound on par with the British pound? The London University pays half the cost of the University of the West Indies, not only here, but also in other West Indian Islands. England pays half of the cost of our hospitals. I cannot think of any reason why we should ever want to sever the ties to the Mother Country.

"As far as the United Fruit Company is concerned, it was the best and most employee oriented employer Jamaica ever had. The precedent set by the extensive sabotage is viewed by us employers with great apprehension. President Roosevelt and his vicious American press and Sir Stafford Cripps, the English Socialist leader, and his Labour Party controlled papers, greatly disturbed the peace and the economy of Jamaica even though they could not benefit from their malevolent actions. To their excuse, one may say that they were ignorant of the situations in the colonies, and they may have sincerely believed that they were doing some good. It was a sad day when the United Fruit Co. sold out and left this Island forever."

Trying to get a light conversation started again was obviously contrived. We took the Joneses home as soon as it seemed polite to leave.

# THREE COUSINS ARE BORN WITHIN TWO MONTHS

Late in March, we received the news that Irma had a baby girl, Martha Anne Sandage, in Elmhurst, Illinois, on March 21, 1951. It was her third child, her second daughter. Irma's two sisters-in-law, Amy and Dorrie were expecting also.

Since Amy had lost a child earlier, the doctor had warned me that Amy would most likely not have much time between the first contraction and the actual birth. So, when Amy alarmed me that it was time to go to the hospital we phoned the doctor and the hospital. We rushed to get our clothes on and drove as fast as we could to the St. Joseph's Hospital on Deanery Rd. It was a horrible drive! Amy kept moaning and told me to rush. I was scared that the baby would come during the drive right in the tiny, little cab of our pickup truck. Besides, the drive was long, as we had to drive diagonally through all of Kingston from Spanish Town Road.

As we arrived, the doctor was there and the nuns were ready. One nun and a secular nurse rushed Amy on a wheelchair into the hospital while I parked my truck. I ran into the foyer and up the stairs three risers at a time. I raced into Amy's room and saw her standing in the bathroom. White foam was coming out of her mouth. It was a most frightening sight!

"Amy! What is happening to you?!"

"Nothing, why?"

"That foam coming out of your mouth!"

"I'm cleaning my teeth. I did not have time when we got up this morning."

I gave a sigh of relief. How could she have thought of something so unimportant at a crucial moment like this! But then she moaned. The two nurses put her back into the wheelchair and hustled her away. A few minutes later, the sister told me that I was the father of a healthy-looking boy! What an elated feeling! Father of a son! It was April 28, 1951.

We took our Michael Paul Von der Porten home three days later. We had prepared everything. He slept in the very cast iron crib Amy had slept in after her birth. Everything had been scrubbed, his baby clothes and diapers had been boiled to make sure that they were sterile. We had a dozen baby bottles, a special sterilized container for them and the nipples. That boy had everything a baby could possibly need. Plastics had been invented during the War in the quest to substitute silk for parachutes and natural rubber mainly for tires and insulation for wires. Plastic bottle inserts, to make burping unnecessary, had not yet been thought of.

Dorrie was not one to be outdone. She had her third child, her second son, Robert Gerhard von der Porten, on May 20, 1951. Meis came from Germany for the occasion to be by the side of her elder sister. She was a great help. For one she was a very cheerful person. Someone we needed after that miserable War.

It was happiness all around. A good thing that we cannot see into the future. It would destroy the joy of the moment and would certainly make life very gloomy.

# MEIS IN JAMAICA

Meis certainly helped Dorrie and Gerhard a lot. Even though her husband, Willie Müller, was missing at the Eastern Front she still managed to keep a cheerful disposition. She told me that she still hoped that her Willie would soon turn up, released from a Russian prisoners' of war camp. I knew, and she probably also knew that the chances were practically zero. Yet, almost daily there were reports in the German papers that a former prisoner of war, who had been presumed dead, arrived in Germany. The returnees were so few in comparison to the enormous amount of the "missing at the Russian front," that one could still say of the trickle of home coming soldiers: next to zero. I kept my mouth shut and Meis never talked about the subject anymore.

Dorrie and Gerhard really appreciated her visit. It was a happy time for them. They had three lovely children now. Meis, Dorrie's favorite sister, was there, Gerhard's business was doing quite well, and, most happily, the threat of internment had disappeared almost six years ago. Though Dorrie and Gerhard's future looked rosy, they were still very bitter. This bitterness gnawed at them, and poisoned their dispositions for the rest of their lives. It seems a paradox that they became the closest couple I ever met. They loved and trusted each other absolutely.

Though Meis had suffered a great deal more from the War than we three, Dorrie, Gerhard, and I, she had kept her happy nature. Meis told me that during a bombing raid on Frankfurt and Offenbach the hospital caught fire, and women were sent down an evacuation chute. Some gave birth and their infants died for lack of help during that horrible experience. I never asked if she was one of those women. I just suspect that she was. I did not want to prolong that conversation, as I saw that she became very emotional. We never mentioned the War again.

Meis liked to go paddling. The owner of the Springfield Club, Murray Jacobs, had a Klepper folding kayak. He lent it to us. We paddled in the moonlight. It was too hot to do that during the day. We took Alan, Amy's little brother along. He was 15 and a pretty good swimmer by then. As it was fairly cool, Alan and I kept our sleeveless undershirts on, tucked into our swimsuits. We decided to paddle across the harbor, about ¾ of a mile to the Palisadoes. The water was very calm as we started out. Since the stiffeners in the boat were very hard, we took a narrow air mattress along for Meis to lie on in the middle of the boat. It, of course, raised the center of gravity but the water spread out before us as smooth as a mirror. Alan sat in the bow and I did the steering in the stern.

We were a little beyond halfway across, when clouds started to play hide and seek with the moon. A strong land wind sprang up and the water became correspondingly rough. I decided to abandon the direct course straight across for one, so that the wind would be directly at our stern. It would be safest if the waves came directly from behind. It would be the least likely chance that the waves would swamp our little craft. Unfortunately, Alan worked hard to counter my efforts to change course. He manfully tried to head the boat in the previously agreed direction.

I called out to him: "Let me do the steering!"

He turned around: "What?"

His turning around upset the balance. Our little boat turned turtle. We were all good swimmers. We tried to push the thought of sharks out of our minds. We had to right the kayak as soon as at all possible. I realized that we must under no circumstances lose the paddles! So, I told Alan that he must hold on to those vital paddles and leave the rest to Meis and me.

It was easy to right the boat but it was full of water. We had a tough time bailing it. We had nothing but our hands doing it. Meis climbed into the boat, while I counter balanced it in the opposite side. Alan handed her the paddles, and he, too, climbed in. With all that water in the boat plus the two people, the sea was up to the gunwales. There was no possibility for me to hold also.

My mind could not get rid of the thought of sharks. I wished that I had a cup or something to bail out some of the water! They paddled and I pushed. My undershirt ballooned out and impeded my swimming. It was not long before a huge Portuguese Man O' War, a fiercely stinging jelly fish, got caught inside of my undershirt. It stung so terribly that for a moment I feared becoming paralyzed but I kept swimming holding on to the boat until we reached the Palisadoes.

The three of us felt a bit chilly. The two paddlers had sat with wet clothes in the wind, and I had swum a good distance. I was probably warmer than the other two. We ran up and down the beach till we felt warm again. Then we decided to paddle back across the harbor straight into the wind and then along the coast until we reached the Springfield Club. We were in good spirits and were happy that we had this adventure.

# MICHAEL AND SERIOUS WORRIES

The joy of having a child was tremendous! Things were all going our way for a while. Unfortunately, Amy did not have sufficient milk to nurse the infant. He proved to be allergic to cows milk. We changed to glucose solutions, thin oats porridge and whatever the doctors and nurses recommended. Nothing helped the little fellow. He was wasting away. We changed doctors from Dr. Rose Parboosingh to my former fellow internee, Dr. Rudolph Aub. Dr. Aub corresponded with my father in Brooklyn, but the baby did not improve.

Finally, we took him to Brooklyn. Papa did not want to treat him himself. He asked Dr. Moses, a former classmate of his, who had been a pediatrician in Germany and was now a general practitioner in New York. He came to visit us and examined our little Michael very carefully, and we went to his office several times. We tried all kinds of different formulas, goats milk, soybean milk substitute, and lots of other nutrients on the doctor's advice. He did a little better on goats milk plus vitamin B for a while.

Toni checked his blood.

She told me: "The child has no T-cells." Not until more than a quarter century later, when "severe combined immune deficiency syndrome" (S.C.I.D.S.) was explained to me, did I understand the significance of the lack of T-cells.

Papa told me to take the baby back to Jamaica. The warm climate would be better for him. He consulted with Dr. Moses and would write Dr. Aub. I am pretty sure he knew what the outcome would be but he did not have the nerve to tell Amy and me. We took our little bundle of sorrow back to Kingston as it was getting cool in New York in 1951.

I had to work. I had to earn money more than ever before but my heart was not in it. I could not wait until I could close the shop in the evenings and rush home to see how my little boy was doing.

Many of my best customers had fixed annual advertising budgets. I gave them the option of renting the signs. That way I would not make anything the first year I put up the sign, but I was free to use second hand material as the sign remained my property.

That helped, as it was still very difficult to get new transformers. Many of my signs were over a year old, and my one year's free service guarantee had run out. I had a lawyer, Carol Ramsey, my Badminton friend, who had drawn up my rental contract forms, draw me up a service contract form. For an annual fee I would maintain the signs. That paid quite well, giving me an income from those contracts.

Amy and I had full confidence in our doctors who tried very hard to help our precious little boy. We did not see how poorly he looked. We did not feel unduly worried that he could not stand up by himself. He could stand only a few seconds holding on to his crib. After a while he could not even do that. We did not even know that he was fatally ill.

# THE HURRICANE IN 1952

Early in the hurricane season in 1952, there had been many warnings. When I arrived in Jamaica in 1933, I experienced the aftermath of a hurricane which had hit Kingston. And again, one hit us in 1946 but they almost always hit the North Coast, and left us here at the South Coast in peace, thanks to the mighty barrier of the Blue Mountains. I did not take the warnings seriously, when Meis wanted to paddle just once more across the harbor in full moonlight before returning to Germany.

Alan had gone to England to study. So, Meis and I went alone. We paddled across the harbor in beautiful moonlight. On the way back, it got quite windy and cloudy. We were both experienced paddlers and made it back without incident. I had hardly gotten home when heavy rain and strong winds started. It was the last time I ever paddled in Jamaica.

It rained all of the next day. In the evening, we heard on the radio that the hurricane was headed straight for Kingston. Many ships which happened to be in the Caribbean had sought refuge in the harbor. We closed all doors filled the bathtub, pots, glasses, cups and whatever would hold liquid with drinking water.

Around 10 p.m., the wind howled so loudly that we had to shout at the top of our lungs, standing almost next to each other, to be able to communicate. Amy had to get a bottle of formula for the baby.

I yelled: "Make sure that you close the door to the kitchen when you leave!"

"Of course!"

She got back into the house without mishap. Minutes later the lights went out. We had to rely on our flashlights. We remained fully dressed. The house was made out of concrete but the rain hit the east side of the house, where the bedrooms were, so hard that the water penetrated the concrete like a filter and water ran down the walls and covered the tiled floor.

We moved into the dining room on the west side of the house as I was afraid that the east wall or at least a window would cave in.

Over the noise of the storm we heard a frightening sound like thunder emanating from the kitchen.

"There goes the roof of the kitchen!" I yelled.

"Oh! I forgot to close the kitchen door!" Amy yelled back.

I stared at her in disbelief. How could anyone ever forget such an elementary thing in a brewing storm! Amy held our little bundle, poor little Michael, in her arms. She looked so pathetic and unhappy by the glow of the flashlight. I could not say another word. Rivulets of water had come from under the closed door of the baby's bedroom but there were still plenty of dry spots for us to sit and worry.

It was still dark when the fury of the storm, wind, and rain abated. We fell asleep. Michael was no worse off for the hurricane. He had slept through most of it. At daybreak it was calm. It still rained a little bit. We went into the kitchen. The roof was in tact. A tree had been blown through the kitchen window which was on the wind side. Its branches and foliage had been pressed together so tightly that no wind could have gotten through to blow off the roof. Except for the glass and the splintered remnants of the window frame the kitchen looked pretty much intact.

We looked outside. We would not have recognized the landscape! Our neighbors were sloshing about in the rain in rain coats. Their house had lost its roof and a wall had caved in. They were looking for their goats, their livelihood.

We had a tall ackee tree next to the carport. One of the two main branches had broken off just above the trunk and had disappeared. All our plants were flat and covered with mud. The two breadfruit trees had bent over at the roots and were flat on the ground and covered with a gray mud. They looked like a total loss. The most amazing sight was our lime tree. All the green parts of the leaves had disappeared, only the ribs of the leaves shone white as hair-fine lace work with water dripping from this absolutely silvery white. It looked unbelievably beautiful!

There was no running water. All electric and telephone wires were down as most of the poles had broken and lay across the streets. There was no radio. We were cut off from the world. The storm had washed deep gullies across the street in front of our house. We were lucky that we had bought lots of bread and rice and

602

that we had drinking water in every container. We were especially lucky that the house we had rented was practically new and had withstood the onslaught. To say nothing of the kitchen, where the tree's foliage had been squeezed into the window so tightly that it had so effectively blocked the wind so that the roof stayed on! We had no idea when electricity, telephone, water, gas, and sewer lines would be restored, or even when the streets would be passable again.

Our neighbors put an emergency thatch roof over the part of their house which was still standing. There were plenty of big branches lying all about to make the frame and lots of coconut bows to make the actual thatch. Their goats had an abundance of fallen foliage to browse on.

For two days, I could not leave the house. I noticed that the breadfruit trees were not broken. They had just bent to the ground right above the roots. Mud covered the entire trees, trunks and foliage, completely. That made me think that they would never recover. I cleaned up our garden the best I could, and wondered what had become of the rest of Kingston.

On the third day, I took my bicycle to town. The first few miles I had to push my bike more than I could ride it. I went to Princess Street to look at my neon shop and Gerhard's warehouse and office. The area around had been pretty much cleaned up. There was no power nor telephone but water had been restored.

I had just used the last money we had to buy new transformers. What I needed now was glass and electrodes. Almost all the neon signs I had passed were broken. Some had disappeared completely along with the roofs they were mounted on. Most were under guarantee by me and many belonged to me. They had been rented out. It was a sad situation. But at least the steel building had survived the hurricane unscathed.

I rode down to King Street. Almost all stores were closed. Crews cleaned out debris from stores where the roofs had been blown away. People were actively putting Kingston back together. I chained my bike to a fence in front to the Bank of Nova Scotia and went in. It was packed. Mr. Brown, the assistant manager, a Canadian, stood behind the counter along with all of his other employees. Kerosene lamps stood on every desk and several stood on the counter. I figured that it would take all day for him to get to me. I was pleasantly surprised when Mr. Brown spotted me in all of that crowd and beckoned to me to see him.

"How do you do, Mr. Von der Porten?"

"That all depends on how you have breakfasted this morning and feel as a consequence, Sir."

He smiled: "How much do you need?"

"Five hundred pounds," I said boldly.

That was equal to all the money I dared draw annually for ourselves out of the company in those days.

He told a girl near him: "Bring me the Glasslite card."

He scribbled something on the card. "You can overdraw up to £ 500.=.=, (U.S.$ 2000.oo in those days) Sir."

"Thank you very much, Sir." We shook hands and I rode my bike back to Princess St. and wrote an order for glass and electrodes. I rode my bike back home to see if they, too, had running water as yet.

There were neither a newspaper nor radio. I stopped at some stores to find out what other damage the storm had done. A yacht with two wealthy American families on board had sought shelter in the harbor. The skipper had assumed that the safest place would be at the Palisadoes as the waves would have no time to form right in the lee of the land. He tied his ship firmly to the radio mast. The storm toppled the mast. It fell on top of the yacht and killed all on board. Several freighters had been tied to each other at Webster's Wharf. The hurricane had squeezed them together like an accordion. They were nothing but scrap.

All the squatters who had stayed in their shacks near the Hope River at Papine had been washed away as the river came down like a huge wall of water. There were many more stories of death and destruction from all over the town.

It was too late in the day to try to reach Arlington Avenue to find out how Gerhard and his family had survived the hurricane. I knew that the factory building was very strong. I was not too worried. I just had to get home before nightfall. There were still lots of fallen poles, loose wire, tree trunks, and parts of roofs on the road, therefore it was essential that I reached home before dark.

604

The moon would rise late and there would be no illumination of any kind until it did.

The hurricane just about bankrupted me. Good service was my only advertisement. Most of my signs were under guarantee, and I rented out many others. I would not be able to collect any money until the signs were working. Since my shop was only a few blocks away from the Kingston General Hospital, I got back power after three more days. Our block was about the first to have all the utilities restored. That, at least, was fortunate.

As soon as the roads became passable, I drove my crews around to salvage as much material as possible and remove signs which were a total loss. To my surprise, many signs which had been mounted against concrete walls had withstood the wind and rain. The block-out paint which separated the letters from one another had been washed away on the wind side, but otherwise the signs were intact.

My being a pack rat now paid off. I had saved all the paper patterns of all signs which I had made. They were most useful now! I could reproduce all signs which had been destroyed. As power was restored, the neon signs on the roofs which had withstood the hurricane lit up. My customers were very pleased. I had won their confidence and I got many orders for new signs. I most certainly needed the money.

Great Britain sent a lot of relief money to help the Jamaican Government to rebuild Kingston. The politicians of the independence movement grumbled that it was not enough. I felt that they should have been glad that they received all of that help. If their senseless independence had been achieved, England would certainly no longer feel motivated to send any help at all! Nevertheless, when anything went wrong, England was always blamed by the P.N.P., so, why not blame her for the hurricane aftermath, too. As a matter of fact, why not blame her for the hurricane itself? It would make just as much sense.

Gerhard and family had survived the storm very well. The mighty lignum vitae trees in the back of 4 Arlington Avenue and the tall house just east of their home had proven a very effective wind break. Their macaroni factory started producing again as soon as power had been restored.

# A MOST UNHAPPY ENDING

As Amy and I both had to work, we had a nurse staying with the baby during the day. One day, she phoned Amy that she did not like the way the baby was breathing. Amy phoned me and we rushed home.

It was early in August, 1952. We took the baby to the Nuttall Hospital. We had often taken the boy there in our little pickup truck to get blood transfusions. This time I noticed a subtle difference as we got into the truck: Vultures were circling over our house. They always know when death is near. I refused to admit to myself that I knew that this was going to be Michael's last trip on earth.

Amy was allowed to sleep in the room next to the boy's. The Joneses let me sleep in the Meeting House. They were very helpful, let me bathe and gave me suppers when I came from work.

My worried Amy had told me that her mother had lost two little sons with similar symptoms. That told me that she, too, feared the worst. I still hoped that medicine had advanced so far that our little one could be saved.

Dr. Aub told me: *„Arnold, es sind nicht alle Babies lebensfähig."* ("Arnold, not all babies have everything to keep on living.") I did not know what he meant.

He knew that there was an unmistakable symptom. It showed up in the blood. The body did not generate any T cells. Toni, Papa, and all the doctors had known for a year that our struggle to keep our precious boy alive was doomed to failure but no one had the nerve to tell us. They had told us that it was an allergy, and that he might outgrow it.

One morning, I noticed that the fever was going down. They took his temperature every half hour. If the curve continued like that, his temperature would be normal in the late afternoon. As it became normal, the little fellow looked at me and motioned that he wanted me to pick him up. I did. He snuggled against my face. He died in my arms as his temperature kept dropping and as the sun turned red on August 11th, 1952.

The Quaker Meeting Room served as the funeral chapel. His closed little white coffin rested on the table by the window. A few weeks later I painted the view in water colors without the coffin. The picture hangs in our little office right by the computer.

Amy was expecting another child. She had become very sick when our boy died. The doctors feared that she might have a miscarriage and advised her against going to the interment. I buried him under a lignum vitae tree in the graveyard of the Anglican Church at Half-Way Tree. I cried uncontrollably while Mack Jones read the 23rd psalm over the open grave. I did not care that all of my employees were watching. Most of the people from the Institute, where Amy worked, were there, so were Dorrie and Gerhard, the Barry family, and many from the Quaker Meeting. I was too despondent to pay much attention to them. It was horrible! There was nothing in the world Amy and I wanted as much as that little Michael. No words could possibly describe our sorrow.

THE OMEN

# ALL IS CHANGING

Though my shop started to pay for more than just bread and butter for the first time, and though I did not need much of the overdraft at the bank my heart was not in my work. Amy was expecting again. That was a great joy mixed with the great fear that the next baby might have the identical "allergies", as the doctors called them, as Michael.

The independence movement, the People's National Party (P.N.P.), was gaining strength and started to become very hostile to Whites. We, of European descent, were only two percent of the population, and a lot of unreasonable hate was directed against us. A lot of people, including most of the Whites, had a strong prejudice against the Germans. That complicated Amy's and my social life for us.

Someone had written something nasty about me to the Colonial Secretary's Office, and my application for naturalization was denied. I asked to be allowed to face my detractor at a hearing in the Colonial Secretary's Office as it is British common law practice that the accused has a right to defend himself in the presence of the accuser. That, too, was denied. I did not really care. I had wanted my son to be born of a British father. It was too late for that anyhow.

I had been stateless since 1938 due to the Nürnberg laws. I could claim German citizenship now that the Nazis had been thrown out but at this time I did not want to have anything to do with Germany. I felt a strong resentment toward the Germans. In the internment camp almost all of them had followed the directives of the top Nazis not to speak to those of us of the "Jew Group". To me that was a sign of cowardly subordination. The Italians had shown a lot more of a sense of personal independence and pride.

My lawyer, Mr. Lake, told me to write my story and my reasons why I so much wanted to become a British Subject and reapply. He more or less admitted that he had fallen asleep at the switch and had not done his utmost to get my application through. I told him that my pride would not allow that. But then I thought that

Amy wanted me to be British. Mr. Lake told me that he was sure that the application would be approved this time. So, I wrote my story which corresponded mostly with the first part of this one I am writing now. He resubmitted my application.

My men in the shop, except for one, were all for the P.N.P. I sensed that they were thinking of joining the P.N.P. union. I was paying much better wages than all other small shops. Besides, I gave them a share of the profit after every job when I got paid.

I called them all together: "I have no intention of paying any union delegate any of my and your hard earned money, money we have worked for with our brains and our hands, and have him abuse me on top of it. If you join any union, I'll drop everyone's pay down to minimum wages. You can then strike all you want. I shall rather close the shop down, than give in to any union demands. I can always find work. I do not need a neon shop."

It was very quiet. No one said a word.

Teresa later told me: "Don' worry, Mr. Arnold. No one gwine join any union. You treat us right, Sah."

Besides politics, religion too was discussed with a passion in the shop. Teresa had always been a fervent Catholic. George, my main all-around man, had joined the Seventh-Day Adventists. Rubin, my part-time artist and sign painter, was a passionate Jehovah's Witness. The one follower of Bustamante was hard pressed to defend his views against the vast P.N.P. majority. Eventually the arguments became so excited and fierce that I had to forbid both subjects, religion and politics, from being mentioned in the shop. I threatened to fire anyone who brought up either of those two topics. I was seriously worried that they were going to fight physically.

# THE BIG MOVE

Mama kept writing me form Brooklyn that she and Papa were getting old and that we should come to New York. She longed to see me. I remembered how miserable I had felt in Brooklyn in 1937/38, and at first did not pay any attention to her pleas. But then, suppose the next baby is allergic? The doctors in Jamaica certainly did not know how to save our little boy. New York was the center for the most advanced medicine. (I did not know then that even the best doctors in the world did not know in 1951, how to help a boy who was born with an immune deficiency.) Then there was the strident anti-white propaganda and its effect on the general population. The uneducated seemed to equate freedom with rudeness, yes, even lawlessness.

I realized that, if my father should die, there would be no one who would give me an affidavit for a visa to emigrate to the States. Time itself was against me. One of the reasons why I was happy to have married a girl who was born in Jamaica, was that she would never be homesick as many foreign-born wives of others were. Now if I took her to America, would she be homesick?

In the past, she had always wanted to go to the U.S., but I did not hear of that desire recently. But then, recently we had not talked about anything except about trying to save Michael. At any rate, I asked my parents for an affidavit. We did not have to use it, but it was nice to have.

Papa wrote how much annoyance the running around to get the affidavit cost him. It finally arrived. After all the complaints by Papa, I was not sure that we should use it. The misery of 1938 returned to my mind's eye. The last few months before Christmas, 1952, my little shop kept me very busy.

The lawyers in Jamaica were also the insurance agents. Carol Ramsey wrote a policy to insure my neon signs so that after a small deductible, I would get back the cost of repairing them even after a hurricane. I added the cost of the insurance to my rent charges and maintenance charges. My financial future never looked better in Jamaica. We procrastinated until my father's affidavit had almost expired.

Now Amy made her feelings clear to me. She did not want to face the same hospitals again when the new baby's time to be born came. She had lost all confidence in the doctors in Jamaica. New York seemed like a great promise for a much better future for her and her coming child. She wanted to go! The sooner the better!

It was too early to hear anything positive or negative about my application to become a British Subject. My being stateless complicated my immigration to the U.S. somewhat. I got a certificate from the Jamaican Government that I would be allowed to enter Jamaica at any time in the future. That satisfied the American Consul.

We took all of our belongings to Amy's parents. I took all cash out of the bank. Because the money represented a very small portion of the total value of my company, I got a permit to convert my money to American dollars. I signed my shop over to Gerhard. There were signs almost complete. Gerhard would be able to collect for them. Glasslite Co. had no debts.

At the last minute I told my crew: "I am leaving Jamaica. Mr. Porten will not have the time to supervise you. You will now run the shop. Do it as if I were still around to supervise. It is your livelihood. Remember that. Good-bye."

If I had tried to say another word I would have burst into tears. All I had worked for ended here and now.

On January 16, 1953, Amy and I said good-bye to our family and Jamaica at the Kingston Airport. Our hearts beat in our throats and my face burned as we entered the big four propeller Avianca Colombian airliner which should take us to the fairly new Idlewild Airport in Queens in eight hours to meet Toni and also: great uncertainty.

Arnold P. Von der Porten was born in Hamburg, Germany, November 30, 1917. He had to leave high school half a year before graduation, as he was an anti-Nazi. In October of 1933, he migrated to Jamaica, British West Indies. He had a very difficult life because of pervasive poverty. Became a very good refrigeration mechanic.

Went to New York to study glass blowing. Was then called back by the Jamaica Public Service Co., to take over commercial refrigeration for that company.

Became Jr. Swimming Champion of Jamaica, in the 200m breaststroke, and was a goalkeeper for a water polo team.

Started the very first neon shop in the British West Indies March 1, 1939. Having arrived with a German passport, he was interned September 3, 1939, with Nazis, Jews, and Italians.

Was a "Guest of his Majesty King George VI" for one year and nine months. Released, he became a Director of the Jamaica Manufacturers Association, a member of the Jamaica Chamber of Commerce, and a Director of the Electrical Contractors Association.

Was one of the ten best known oil painters of Jamaica.

Became goalkeeper for the All Star Jamaican Water Polo Team.

Married Amy Barry January 4, 1947. She was 23 and he was 29. Their first child, Michael, died in 1952.

Migrated to the United States January 17, 1953, and worked as a glassblower, industrial foreman, production manager, and a mechanical designer.

Attended Rutgers University College, New Brunswick, NJ, and graduated with a BS in Business Administration, in 1965.

Sent all four children, Richard, Marguerite, Christopher, and Arlene through private schools and to colleges.

Retired from Johns-Manville as the machinery design-engineer for their factory in Manville, NJ, August, 1980. Retired to Gainesville, Florida, October, 1994, with his wife of over 50 years.

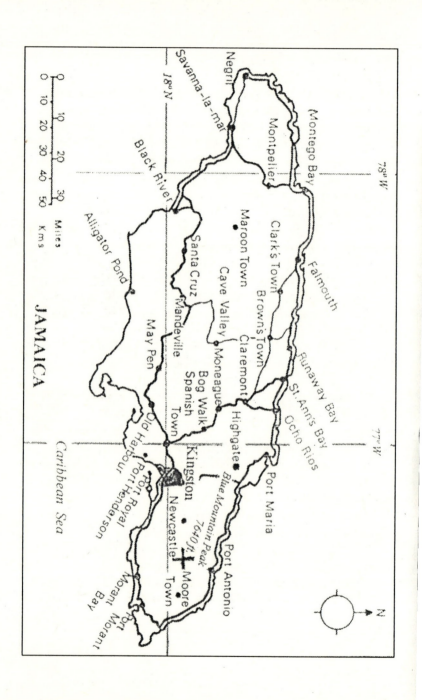